Utilisation of Electric Energy

Utilisation of Electric Energy

E OPENSHAW TAYLOR

Revised in SI Units by V V L Rao

UTILISATION OF ELECTRIC ENERGY IN SI UNITS

UNIVERSITIES PRESS (INDIA) PRIVATE LIMITED

Registered Office
3-6-747/1/A and 3-6-754/1, Himayatnagar, Hyderabad 500 029, Telangana, India
info@universitiespress.com; www.universitiespress.com

Distributed by
Orient Blackswan Private Limited

Reginstered Office
3-6-752, Himayatnagar, Hyderabad 500 029, Telangana, India

Other Offices
Bengaluru, Bhopal, Chennai, Guwahati, Hyderabad, Jaipur, Kolkata, Lucknow, Mumbai, New Delhi, Noida, Patna, Visakhapatnam

First published by Orient Blackswan Private Limited 1971

Original edition 1937
First published in India in 1965 by Orient Blackswan Private Limited in arrangement with English Universities Press Ltd, London

SI Edition 1971
Twenty-second impression 2018

ISBN 978 81 7371 700 0

501530

Cover and book design

Printed in India at
Navya Printers, Hyderabad 500 013

Published by
Universities Press (India) Private Limited
3-6-747/1/A and 3-6-754/1, Himayatnagar
Hyderabad 500 029, Telangana, India

Editors' Introduction

To the Electrical Engineering series

It is perhaps not an exaggeration to say that until comparatively recently books on Electrical Engineering subjects could be divided into well-defined classes, viz, students' textbooks and specialised works for the engineer in practice. Few books were of value to both types of reader, and in the past this state of affairs was perhaps satisfactory enough.

In the opinion of the Editors of this series the situation has now changed considerably. The very rapid increase in both the numbers and magnitudes of the applications of electricity, the greatly extended areas of supply as a partial consequence of the existence of the National Grid, and the far greater complexity of modern life in general have all tended to alter the requirements both of students and of experienced engineers as regards technical literature. It is now necessary that engineers, both on the manufacturing and supply sides of the industry, shall have a knowledge of a very wide range of subjects in addition to their own specialised line. On the other hand, young, technically trained engineers entering industry require something more than a mere knowledge of fundamental principles if they are to become of value to their employers within a reasonable space of time.

Fortunately, as a result of the high standard now reached in colleges and secondary schools, a wider course of reading on the part of the more advanced student is nowadays more feasible, and a smaller proportion of the time in engineering colleges is required for the teaching of purely fundamental principles.

Thus the requirements of advanced students and of experienced engineers appear to be more nearly similar than in the past, and it is the object of this series to fulfil this dual purpose. While it is not intended that the books shall be of sole interest to those engineers working in the particular field with which they deal, purely academic aspects of the subjects will not, in general, be discussed.

It will be the endeavour of the Editors to include in the series books upon essentially practical subjects with which more advanced students should nowadays be familiar, and to choose as the authors of these books engineers with a thorough knowledge of their subjects, whether their activities may be in the academic or in the industrial sphere.

To satisfy the needs of readers who may wish to extend their study of any particular branch, the authors of all the volumes in the series will give references to the more important reference works and original publications.

H. COTTON.

E. W. GOLDING.

University of Nottingham.

Preface to Second Edition

EXPERIENCE gained in the use of the first edition has not indicated the need for any major change in the arrangement; the opportunity has, however, been taken of bringing the subject-matter up to date by the inclusion of various recent developments, such as automatic regulating gear, high-frequency heating, fluorescent lighting, and various other smaller items. Some new worked examples and questions have also been added and the bibliography has been rewritten.

The author is indebted to Mr. J. P. Kelly, B.Sc., for suggestions and for reading the proofs.

E. OPENSHAW TAYLOR.
Edinburgh.

Preface to First Edition

ALTHOUGH a number of books have been written on the utilisation of electrical energy for various particular purposes, such as electric traction, electro-chemistry, or illumination, there have been few, if any, which cover the whole range of the more usual applications in a single volume and in a manner suitable for the student or general engineer who has not had occasion to specialise in any particular branch. An idea of the importance of this aspect of electrical engineering and the scope for further development may be gathered from the facts that in this country alone about 10,000,000 h.p. of industrial drive is still purely mechanical, only about 50 per cent. of the houses are wired for electricity, and only about 3 per cent. of the total length of railways is electrified.

It has been the intention of the author to fill this gap in existing literature and provide a book which will prove of value to students, to general sales engineers connected with the supply industry and manufacturing firms, and also to civil and mechanical engineers who are becoming increasingly large users of electrical energy.

As it is intended, however, to cater largely for students, general principles have been stressed rather than practical details of construction, although the latter have been included where necessary, together with a bibliography giving references for more detailed information. Also, a number of illustrative worked examples have been included in the text. The standard is approximately that of the London University B.Sc. (Eng.) Examination in Electric Power (Utilisation), but it also covers the requirements of other examinations, such as the Installations section of the I.E.E. Graduateship examination in Electric Supply and Installations.

A number of questions, with answers, are included at the end of each chapter; these are arranged to give students practice in dealing with the various quantities concerned and to amplify various points occurring in the text. Copies of examination questions are not included, since students taking any particular examination can easily obtain copies of the examination papers from the appropriate authorities.

The book is based on lectures delivered to final-year students at the City and Guilds College, and the author would like to record his thanks to Professor C. L. Fortescue for help and encouragement, to Mr. A. L. Fielding for suggestions with the manuscript, to Mr. R. H. Taylor for suggestions, reading the proofs, and for checking the answers to the examples, and to Mr. T. McVey for preparing the drawings; thanks are also due to the following firms, who have supplied information and lent photographs or blocks for illustrations: Messrs. ASEA Electric, Ltd., British Insulated Cables, Ltd., B.T.-H. Co., Ltd., Crompton Parkinson, Ltd., Electric Furnace Co., Ltd., English Electric Company, Ltd. Philips Lamps, Ltd.; to Brown Boveri, Ltd., General Electric Co., Ltd., Marryat and Scott, Ltd., Metropolitan-Vickers Electrical, Co., Ltd., and Oerlikon, Ltd., who have supplied information, and, finally, to the Editor of the *Electrician*, for giving permission for the reproduction of certain material written by the author for that journal.

E. OPENSHAW TAYLOR.

South Kensington.

Preface to the SI Edition

THE present edition is the SI version of the fifth edition of this well-known book on 'Utilization of Electrical Energy', a popular text-book for B.E. and A.M.I.E. (Sec. B) students in this subject. While preparing this edition, it is made Indian student-oriented and examination-oriented. SI is the latest form of metric system and absorbs in it the 'Rationalised Metre-Kilogram-Second-Ampere (RMKSA) system', so well-known in the field of electricity for the past quarter of a century in India, U.K. and U.S.A. SI stands for "Systeme International d' Unitès" in French. This abbreviation is now adopted by the International Standardising Organisation as the abbreviated name of this new system of Units in all languages. An introductory chapter, describing the salient features of the SI Units, is given just before Chapter I, so that the reader may have a clear picture of this new system adopted in this book. Indian Parliament had passed the Act No.89 of 1956: 'The Standards of Weights and Measures Act'. By this Act, India went metric 13 years ago. Though the 1956 Act recognizes the six basic units of SI, a Bill is under preparation modifying that Act so as to legally recognise all the SI Units.

The Plan

In preparing the SI edition, the chief points kept in view, are the following:—

(1) As SI is an 'absolute' system, the F.P.S. or other gravitational units used in the previous edition have all been changed. 'W' and 'g' are dropped, wherever possible (while the value of 'g' in FCS = 32 ft/s^2 the value of 'g' in SI is 9.806 55 or nearly 9·81 (m/s^2).

(2) The metric 'tonne' (abbreviated as 't'), is used instead of the British long ton. The British ton = 2240 lbs; the metric ton (t) = 2205 lbs $\therefore$ 1 ton = 1.016 t.

(3) As far as possible, metre, kilometre, millimetre, have been used. In rare cases, centimetre and Angstrom unit

(though not an SI unit) = 10^{-10} m, has been retained for reasons stated in chapter V.

(4) Most of the conversions have been based on 1″ = 2.54 cm or 25.4 mm;
1 mile = 1·6 km; 1 $m^2 \simeq 11$ ft^2; 1 $m^3 \simeq 35$ ft^3
Force of 1 lb = 4·45 newton or 1 newton = 0·225 lb,
1 kg = 9·81 newton or 1 newton = 0·1019 kg,
1 lb mass = 0·4536 kg.
Energy 1 ft lb = 1·358 joules; 1 joule = 0·7374 ft lb
1 kWh = 3·6 M joules;
1 joule = $0 \cdot 2728 \times 10^{-6}$ kWh,
1 Btu = 1055 J or 1·055 kJ,
1 Btu/ft^3 = 37·26 kJ/m^3, 1 cal = 4·187 J.
Power: 1 hp = 746 W, 1 kg cal = 4187 J.

(5) The horsepower has been eliminated throughout the book as it is not a recognized unit in SI (being a gravitational unit).

(6) Wherever force occurred only 'newton', has been used, reserving 'kilogram' only for mass. In the previous edition, there was considerable confusion between the usage of the words "weight", "force", "mass", especially, when the same word 'ton' or 'pound' was used for all these three. That confusion is now completely eliminated.

(7) While applying the conversion factors, liberal or "rational" rounding off of the values, keeping the specific end in view, has been done.

(8) As there are two distinct energy units: joule and kilowatt-hour, both are freely used and a detailed calculation of energy consumption from five different energy sources, one table 'joule-oriented' and the other 'kilowatt hour-oriented' has been given in Tables VI (a) and (b) of Chapter III, while eliminating Btu, Chu, calorie and other FPS or CGS heat units. Of course, kilojoules and megajoules, as well as kilowatt hours, have been freely used.

(9) As for power, the basic unit being a watt, and 1 hp = 746 w ≃ 3/4 kW, for several purposes, kW and MW have been used.

In accordance with the Indian Standards, IS: 325-1961 (Feb. 1962), 2nd Revision, as per the list of preferred output ratings of induction motors upto and including 250 kW, the following kW ratings have been adopted in the present text, eliminating altogether 'hp' for motor, wherever that term occurred.

PREFERRED OUTPUTS

kW	kW	kW	kW
0·06	0·75	11	90
0·09	1·1	15	110
0·12	1·5	18·5	132
0·18	2·2	22	150
0·25	3·7	30	160
0·37	5·5	37	185
0·55	7·5	45	200
	9·3	55	220
		75	250

(10) *Reference and Bibliography*: As this SI edition is meant mainly for Indian readers, and as all the references given in the earlier editions were to British books and journals, most of them being 25 to 40 years old, all these references have been totally omitted, and, instead, a bibliography of (i) important publications of ISI and others in India on 'SI' and (ii) a few foreign publications on SI have now been included. All of them are of very recent origin, only in 1960 - 1969.

(11) In the last Chapter: VI : *Economic Aspects of Utilizing Electrical Energy*, to facilitate easy conversion, £1 has been assumed as Rs. 24. This at once gave 1 penny = 10 paise. This assumption is not unreasonable but realistic, apart from convenience in conversion.

(12) Wherever references to U.K. practice or tariffs or B.S. specifications had been given, they were all deleted.

(13) Wherever necessary the worked-out problems in the text, have been reworked using SI Units. Also, the problems at the end of each chapter, have been reworded in the language of SI Units, using the latest internationally accepted 'Signs, symbols and abbreviations' for SI Units— (see item No 10 in BIBLIOGRAPHY).

(14) In consonance with the rewording of the problems, new graphs or tables have been drawn using SI units and agreed symbols or abbreviations.

(15) Fresh answers to all the questions (reworded in SI) have also been given at the end of the book.

I would be failing in my duty if I do not express my thanks to Prof. K.S.B. Eswaran, Retired Professor of Electrical Engineering, College of Engineering, Guindy, who has been almost my collaborator, especially in the working of the numerical examples and other advice in the conversions. With all our care, checking and rechecking, it is quite possible that a few numerical errors might have escaped our notice. If the readers bring such errors to my notice or that of the publishers, we will gladly rectify them in a future edition.

My thanks are also specially due to M/s. Philips (India) Ltd., Madras, and their Principals, Messrs. PHILIPS GLOELAMPEN FABRIEKEN, EINDHOVEN, HOLLAND, for the very valuable information, Tables and data and pictures and Bibliography supplied on 'Illumination'—(Chapter V).

We fondly hope that the Indian electrical students and engineers who use this book, will find it useful both for their examinations as well as during their service in industry, for constant reference. We would request them to send us useful suggestions from time to time, so as to highlight the value of 'coherence', the main feature of 'SI' units which consequently reduces the labour of calculations considerably to arrive at the correct answer in the SI unit-one and only one.

V. V. L. RAO
Madras,
31st Jan. 1970

Contents

Introductory Chapter on SI Units

1.0. The system of units used throughout in the present, revised edition of this book, is known as SI, an abbreviation for 'Systeme International d' Unites". It is a comprehensive, logical and coherent system, designed for use in all branches of science, technology and engineering. It was formally approved in 1960 by the General Conference of Weights and Measures (CGPM), the international organisation responsible for maintaining standards of Measurement. In 1962, both the International Organisation for Standardization (ISO) and the International Electrotechnical Commission (IEC), endorsed that recommendation. Since then, about 30 countries, including the major industrial ones—(except the USA and Canada), have declared their intention of making SI the only legally acceptable system. It is quite obvious that, since a metric system is at present used by 90% of the world's population, and bids fair to spread to 100% and since the principal metric countries have agreed to adopt SI, then it will, in a matter of years, be the only system used throughout the world.

1.1. Apart from its intrinsic merit, it has the great advantage that only ONE system covers all situations—both (i) theoretical and (ii) practical. So, when once everyone uses this system, considerable mental effort that is now wasted in converting from one system to another, can be saved and that saving can be better devoted to more important things.

1.2. The essential features of SI:

(1) SI is the latest evolved form of the metric system. There are six basic units (see para 2·0 for definitions), the 'metre' and 'kilogram' replacing the 'centimetre' and 'gram' of the old CGS system (see *Table I*).

(2) The derived units are directly related to the base units (*Table II*). This is the meaning of 'coherence'. A system of units is said to be coherent, if the product

or quotient of any two unit quantities in the system, gives the unit of the resultant quantity : e.g.
the unit of area is a square metre : $m^2 = m \times m$,
,, ,, ,, volume is a cubic metre : $m^3 = m \times m \times m$,
,, ,, ,, velocity is a metre/second : $= ms^{-1} = (m/s)$,
,, ,, ,, acceleration is a metre/second$^2 = ms^{-2} = (m/s^2)$,
,, ,, ,, force is a newton : $kg\ ms^{-2} = kg \times (m/s^2)$.

Note : that the coherent unit of velocity is the metre/sec (m/s), and *not* the kilometre per hour (km/h).

Newton, the coherent unit of force, is that force which imparts to unit mass an acceleration of one (metre/second^2). Thus, the unit of force, Newton(N) is the kg m/s^2. This is a most important unit, because it forms the essential component of many of the units which are commonly used in engineering, such as *pressure, stress, energy* and *power*.

The unit of energy is the *joule* (J), which is the work done when a force of one 1N moves a body a distance of 1m = 1N.m (which is named a *joule*).

The use of auxiliary or subsidiary units is discouraged in SI. Thus, the unit of pressure is one 'newton per square metre' (= 1N/m^2) ; the 'atmosphere' and the 'torr' are not used. Similarly, the 'calorie', 'horsepower', are not used. All forms of energy (except light) are measured in joules (J), and power in (joule/sec) or *watt.* Frequently, multiples of '*joule*' and '*watt*' will be needed such as GW, MW, kW (see *Table III*). However, the unit electron volt (eV) remains for the time being.

(3) Electrical units are rationalised and are obtained by giving the value of $4\pi \times 10^{-7}$ H/m to μ_0, the permeability of free space. (Giving that value to μ_0, automatically fixes the value of $(10^{-9}/36\pi)$ or $8{\cdot}854\ 185 \times 10^{-12}$ F m^{-1} to ϵ_0, the permittivity of vacuum or free space).
The value of $\mu_0 = 4\pi \times 10^{-7}$ H/m, leads to the new definition of ampere, which is now the fourth base

unit as the unit of electric current. All the other electrical units are derived directly from the base units and are identical with the practical units.

(4) Multiples and fractions of units are normally restricted to powers of $10^{\pm 3n}$, where 'n' is an integer. That means in *Table III* below deca (10^1), hecto (10^2), deci (10^{-1}) and centi (10^{-2}) are non-preferred. So, the centimetre is prohibited on the strict SI. On the other hand, the step between 1 mm^3 and 1 m^3 is so large that the litre ($=10^{-3}$ m^3) is retained as a convenient unit of volume. Similarly, for areas, between 10^3 and 10^6 m^2, the $dam^2 = 100m^2$ (called the 'are') or the $hm^2 = 10^4m$ (called the 'hectare') will be used, with a preference for the hectare (nearly equal to 2.5 acres). Similarly, the moment of inertia or second moment of area, say, of steel beams would involve astronomical figures, if expressed in mm^4, or microscopic figures if expressed in m^4, so it is probable that cm^4 will be used in that field.

For mass, 1 metric tonne (t) = 1000 kg and 1 quintal (q) = 100 kg, are convenient and hence used in this book as these two units are allowed in SI.

(5) The ISO had laid down the general principle that any unit, which is already internationally recognized and used, shall not be lightly discarded even though the unit in question be a non-SI unit or a non-preferred multiple of an SI unit. Under this rule, the internationally accepted units of time, viz. the minute, hour, day, week, month and year will continue to be in use. The division of the circle into 360 degrees and the subdivisions of the degree, the minute and second will also continue for trignometrical purposes. The supplementary SI Unit, the *radian*, will figure in dynamics and some other problems. The *steradian* will figure in illumination; also the unit angstrom ($=10^{-10}$m) in light (see chapter V).

— —

Tables: SI Units—Names and Symbols

TABLE I

(i) *Base Units :*

Quantity	Unit	Symbol
length ..	metre	m
mass ..	kilogram	kg
time ..	second	s
electric current ..	ampere	A
thermodynamic temperature ..	kelvin	K
luminous intensity ..	candela	cd

(ii) *Supplementary Units :*

Quantity	Unit	Symbol
plane angle ..	radian	rad
supplementary angle ..	steradian	Sr

TABLE II

Derived units with special names :

Quantity	Unit	Symbol	Relation to other Units
force	newton	N	kg ms^{-2}
energy	joule	J	N.m
power	watt	W	J s^{-1}
electric charge	coulomb	C	As
,, potential	volt	V	J c^{-1}
,, resistance	ohm	Ω	VA^{-1}
,, capacitance	farad	F	CV^{-1} = As V^{-1}
magnetic flux	weber	Wb	Vs
flux density	tesla	T	Wb/m^2
inductance	henry	H	Vs A^{-1}
frequency	hertz	Hz	s^{-1}
temperature	degree Celsius	°C	t/°C = T/K-273·15
luminous flux	lumen	lm	cd sr
illumination	lux	lx	lm m^{-2} = cd sr-m^{-2}

TABLE III

Decimal fractions and multiples (preferred)

fraction	prefix	symbol	multiple	prefix	symbol
10^{-3}	milli	m	10^{3}	kilo	k
10^{-6}	micro	μ	10^{6}	mega	M
10^{-9}	nano	n	10^{9}	giga	G
10^{-12}	pico	p	10^{12}	tera	T
10^{-15}	femto	f			
10^{-18}	atto	a			

TABLE IV

Units and their relationships to CGS units

(i) *Electrical units*:

1 A $= 10^{-1}$ emu $=$ C/10 esu
1 V $= 10^{8}$ emu $= 10^{8}$/esu
1 Ω $= 10^{9}$ emu $= 10^{9}/C^{2}$ esu
1 F $= 10^{-9}$ emu $= 10^{-9}C^{2}$ esu
1 H $= 10^{9}$ emu $= (10^{9}/C^{2})$ esu
1 T $= 10^{4}$ emu (gauss).
1 Wb $= 10^{8}$ emu (maxwell)
1 Am^{-1} $= 4\pi \times 10^{-3}$ emu (oersted)
$c = 3 \times 10^{10}$ cm/s in the above CGS equations

(ii) *Other Uuits*:

length:
1 micron $= 10^{-6}$ m
1 ångström $= 10^{-10}$ m
1 X-Unit $= 10^{-13}$ m
1 fermi $= 10^{-15}$ m

area: 1 barn $= 10^{-28}$ m^{2}

force: 1 dyne $= 10^{-5}$ N

energy: 1 erg $= 10^{-7}$ J
1 calorie (15°C) $= 4{\cdot}1855$ J

pressure: 1 bar $= 10^{5}$ N m^{-2}
1 atmosphere $= 1{\cdot}013\,25 \times 10^{5}$ Nm^{-2}
1 torr $=$ 1 mm of Hg $= 133{\cdot}322$ N.m^{-2}

viscosity:

(i) dynamic: 1 poise $= 10^{-1}$ N s m^{-2}
(ii) kinematic: 1 stokes $= 10^{-4}$ m^{2} s^{-1}.

Symbols and Abbreviations

Principal Symbols and Abbreviations used in this Book
Symbols for quantities are in Italic type, and abbreviations for the names of units are in ordinary type.

A	ampere
C	coulomb
C	capacitance specific heat
cd	candela
cm	centimetre
Hz	cycle per second
E	electric stress, electric field strength electromotive force illumination
F	force (mechanical) luminous flux
f	frequency
G	percentage gradient
g	gram
g	acceleration due to gravity
H	henry
H	barometric height heat (energy) tension
h	hour
h	head
I	electric current luminous intensity
J	joule
J	moment of inertia
K	a constant
k	radius of gyration
kg	kilogram
km	kilometre
kVA	kilovolt-ampere
kVAr	kilovar (reactive kilo-volt-ampere)
kW	kilowatt
kWh	kilowatt-hour
kWs	kilowatt-second
L	inductance luminance
lm	lumen
lx	lux
MW	megawatt
m	metre
min	minute
N	newton
N-m	newton-metre
n	rotational speed (rev/min)
P	power
p	number of poles pressure
Q	electric charge reactive power volume rate of flow
R	resistance (electrical)
r	number of revolutions

r	resistance (electrical) per unit length
	specific resistance to motion
rad	radian
rev/min	revolution per minute
r.m.s.	root mean square
S	apparent power; rating of machine
s	second
s.t.p.	standard temperature and pressure
T	absolute temparature
	tension
	time
	torque
t	time
t	tonne (metric)
V	[illegible]
V	voltage
v	speed (linear)
v	volume
W	watt
Wh	watt-hour
W	energy
	mass ratio of flow
	weight
w	density
	weight
X	reactance
Y	admittance
Z	impedance

Greek letters used as symbols for quantities, in this text.

α	acceleration
β	retardation
ϵ	emissivity
	permittivity
η	efficiency
θ	temperature (T = absolute temperature)
λ	rate of heat dissipation
μ	coefficient of adhesion
μ	permeability
μf	microfarad
ρ	resistivity
T	time constant
Φ	magnetic flux
Ω	ohm
	solid angle
ω	angular frequency
	angular speed

CHAPTER I

ELECTRIC DRIVE (EXCLUDING TRACTION)

THE success of an electric drive for any purpose depends on the correct choice of the driving motor for the particular conditions under which it has to operate, and in making this choice attention may have to be devoted to any or all of the following factors.

(1) *Electrical Characteristics :*

Running characteristics.
Starting characteristics.
Speed control.
Braking.

(2) *Mechanical features :*

Type of enclosure.
Bearings.
Transmission of drive to driven machine.
Noise.

(3) *Size of motor :*

Whether for continuous, intermittent, or variable load.
Whether its overload capacity and pull-out torque are adequate.

(4) *Cost :*

Capital cost.
Running cost—losses, power factor, maintenance, and depreciation.

It can thus be seen that the choice of an electric motor for a given drive includes a large number of factors, and although in any particular case some of these may be definitely fixed by existing circumstances, others will probably be conflicting, and a thorough understanding of the various possibilities is therefore essential to the making of the most satisfactory compromise. Although the question of cost has been placed last in the above list, it must be remembered that in any commercial concern it is this factor which ultimately governs all others, since the correct motor to choose is that which will give the required service at the minimum overall cost. This feature applies of course to all applications of electricity and not only to electric

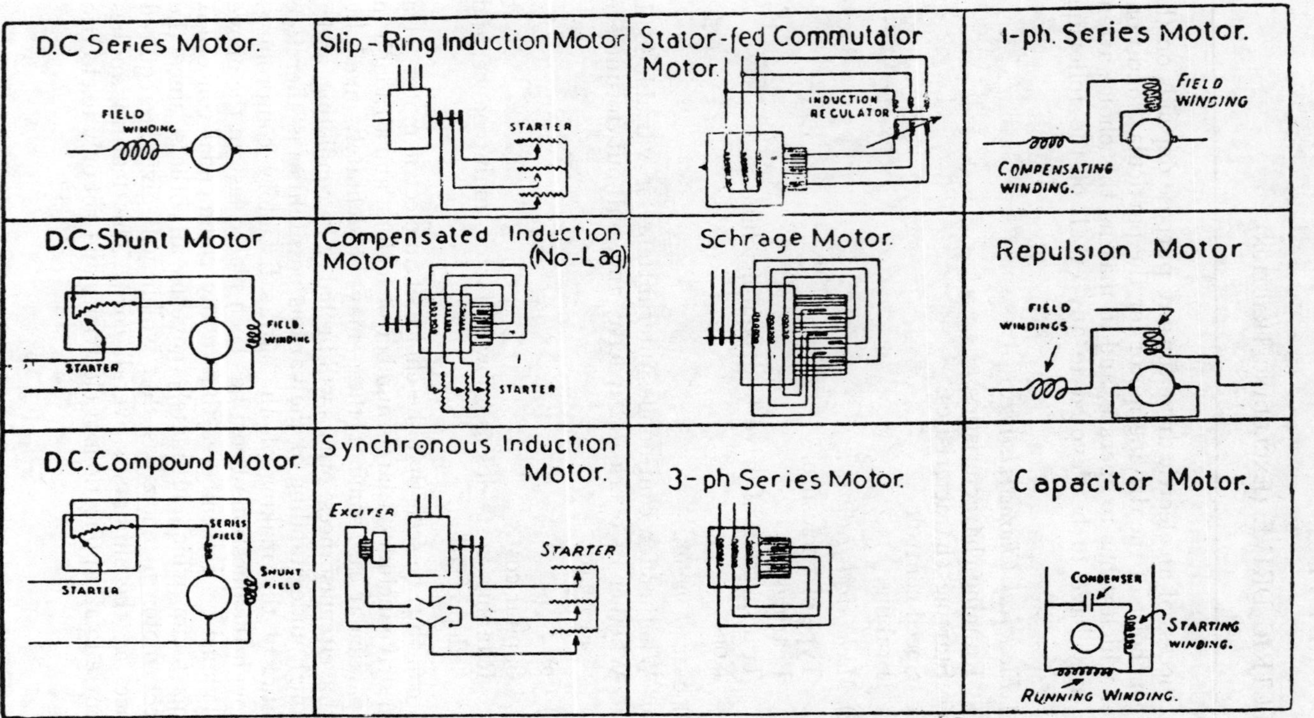

FIG. 1—CONNECTION DIAGRAMS OF COMMON TYPES OF MOTORS.

drive—consideration of it has therefore been considered separately in a general manner in Chapter VI.

1. RUNNING CHARACTERISTICS

A full discussion of the design and behaviour of the various types of electric motor available is beyond the scope of this book. A brief review of the more common types is, however, given below.

So far as the electrical behaviour when running under normal load conditions is concerned, the chief points which must receive attention are :

Nature of the speed-torque characteristic required.
Losses and efficiency.
Magnetising current and power factor (a.c. motors only).

Other features, such as temperature-rise and insulation strength, are taken care of by Indian Standard Specifications,* so that if a user purchases a motor built by a reputable firm in accordance with the appropriate specifications he may rest assured that it will be satisfactory in these respects.

Types of Motor Available

The more important features of the various types of motor in common use are summarised in Table I ; connection diagrams and typical characteristic curves are given in Figs. 1, 2, and 3.

D.C. Motors.—The d.c. shunt and series motors are too well known to warrant further description ; the shunt motor has a speed-torque characteristic giving a speed which drops only a few per cent. between no load and full load and a characteristic of this type, which is also possessed by many a.c. motors, is commonly called a "shunt" characteristic. The speed of a series motor falls as the torque increases, as shown by the curve in Fig. 2, and such a characteristic is commonly called a "series" characteristic. The compound motor, which has both shunt and series windings arranged to assist each other in producing the flux, may be given any characteristic between that of a series and a shunt motor by suitably adjusting the proportions of the series and shunt ampere-turns ; if the former are made to oppose the shunt winding an approximately constant-speed characteristic can be obtained or even one in which the speed rises slightly with the load—such an arrangement is known as differential compounding, and although useful in certain cases, there is the danger that on heavy overloads or at starting, the series

*See Appendix and Bibliography at the end of the book.

field may overcome the shunt field and tend to make the motor run in the wrong direction.

The 3-phase Induction Motor.—Of all the types of motor available, the 3-phase induction motor is by far the most common and can be built in any size from a few watts up to several thousand kW. The type of rotor used, i.e. wound rotor, squirrel-cage rotor, or double squirrel-cage rotor, is governed by the starting characteristics required and is discussed more fully

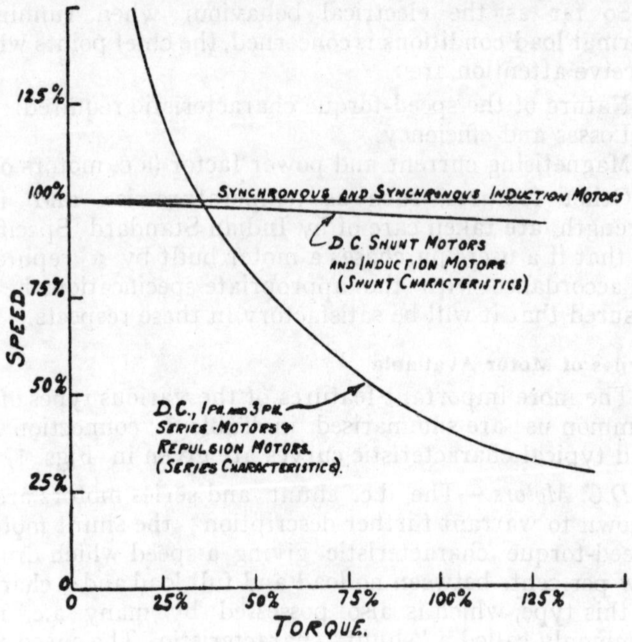

FIG. 2.—TYPICAL SPEED-TORQUE CURVES.

under that heading. As seen from Table I, the induction motor possesses the disadvantage of a power factor less than unity.

The Compensated Induction Motor.—This is a modification of the plain induction motor designed to give approximately unity or a slightly leading power factor over the whole range of loads. In the most common type, the " No-Lag " motor, the primary winding is placed on the rotor and the secondary winding on the stator, as shown in Fig. 1. There is also a commutator winding on the rotor in addition to the primary winding and e.m.f.s. are collected from the commutator and injected into the secondary winding in such a way as to provide the required power factor improvement. A typical power-factor characteristic is shown in Fig. 3.

The Schrage Motor.—This is also a modification of the plain induction motor, designed in this case to give it a variable speed ; there is again a commutator winding on the rotor from which an e.m.f. is collected and injected into the secondary

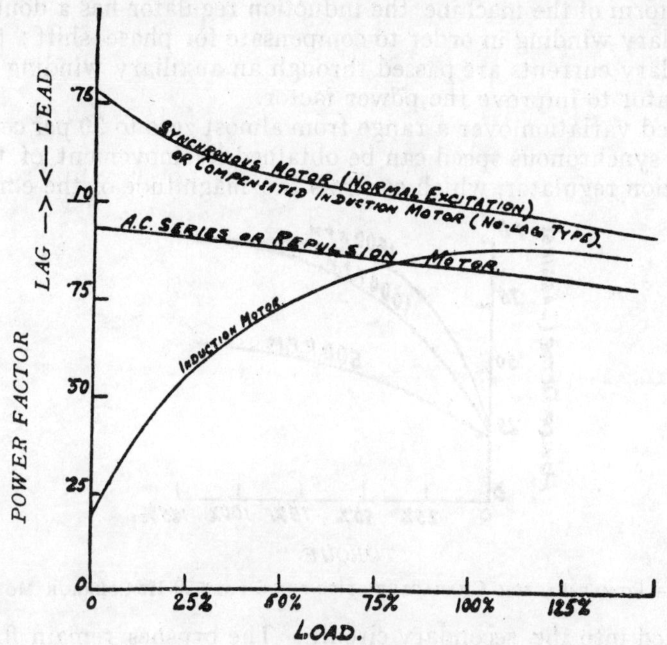

FIG 3.—TYPICAL POWER FACTOR/LOAD CURVES.

circuit (wound on the stator). Two separate sets of brushes are employed as indicated in Fig. 1, and by moving these relatively to one another in opposite directions control of the speed over a 3 to 1 range can easily be obtained ; by moving both sets of brushes together in the same direction some control of power factor can also be effected. The characteristics of this type of motor are shown in Fig. 4, and it can be built in sizes up to 225 kW. to 300 kW. It is a very satisfactory type of a.c. motor for drives requiring a motor with a shunt speed-torque characteristic and a continuously variable speed over a wide range.

The Stator-fed Commutator Motor.—This motor gives characteristics similar to those of the Schrage motor, but has an ordinary 3-phase winding on the stator and a single winding on the rotor, which is connected to a commutator as shown in Fig. 1. In its simplest form there are three brushes per pole pair, and the slip energy in the rotor is converted by the commutator to supply frequency and returned to the supply through an induction regulator or tapped transformer. In the usual form of the machine the induction regulator has a double secondary winding in order to compensate for phase shift; the secondary currents are passed through an auxiliary winding on the stator to improve the power factor.

Speed variation over a range from almost zero to 50 per cent. above synchronous speed can be obtained by movement of the induction regulator, which controls the magnitude of the e.m.f.

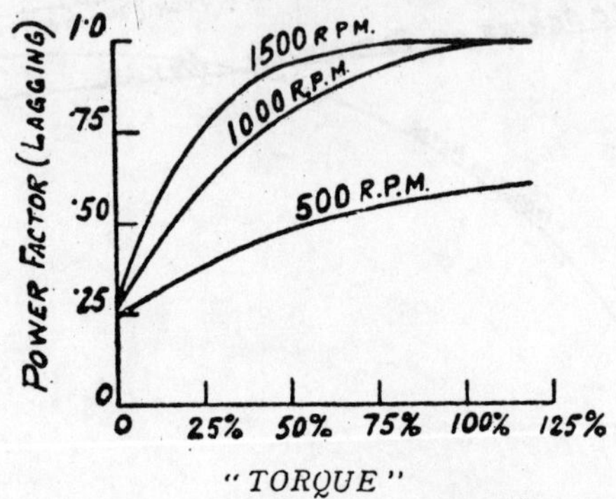

FIG 4.—POWER-FACTOR CHARACTERISTICS FOR 6-POLE 50-Hz SCHRAGE MOTOR.

injected into the secondary circuit. The brushes remain fixed in position and the speed remains approximately constant (shunt characteristic) for any regulator setting. Such motors can be built for the largest sizes that are required and, since the supply is fed to the stator, they can be operated from a high-voltage supply.

The 3-phase Series Motor.—For haulage and hoisting work, where a motor with a series speed-torque characteristic is required, the 3-phase series motor can be used. The stator of such a motor is similar to that of an induction motor except that all six ends of the three windings are brought out, while the rotor has a commutator winding with three sets of brushes per pole pair, these being connected to the supply in series with the stator windings, as shown in Fig. 1.

The Synchronous and Synchronous-induction Motor.—The speed of the synchronous motor is fixed by the frequency and number of poles, and is, therefore, absolutely constant and independent of the load; it has, however, no inherent starting torque, and can only be made self-starting by some special arrangement, such as a squirrel-cage winding embedded in the pole faces, normally used for the plain synchronous motor, or by arranging the field winding in the form of an ordinary induction-motor rotor winding, as in the synchronous-induction motor. In both cases the machine is started as an induction motor—as soon as it reaches nearly synchronous speed the d.c. excitation is switched on and it will then pull into synchronism.

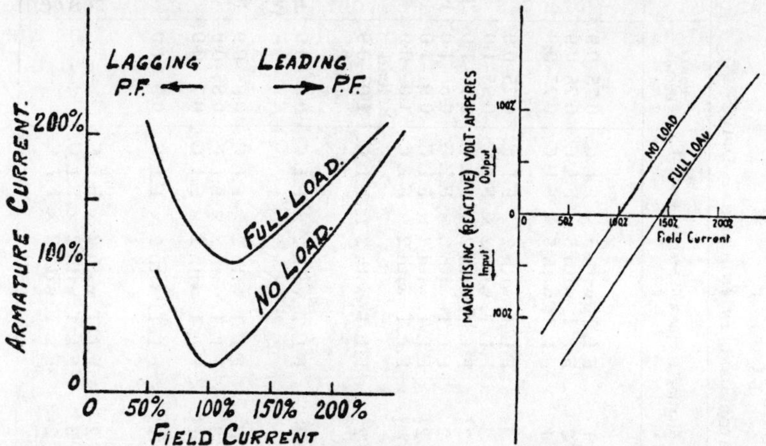

FIG. 5.—VEE CURVES AND REACTIVE VA CURVES OF SYNCHRONOUS MOTOR.

The connections for the synchronous-induction motor are shown in Fig. 1. The d.c. supply for the excitation of either type of motor is almost invariably obtained from a small exciter mounted on the same shaft as the motor. Motors up to any required size can be built, although the cost of the separate exciter usually makes them uneconomical below about 15 kW. Another important feature of the synchronous motor is the fact that it can, by varying the exciting current, be made to take either a leading or a lagging current from the line; if under-excited it will have to draw a part of its magnetising volt-amperes from the supply, and will operate at a lagging power factor like the induction motor; if over-excited it will supply magnetising volt-amperes to the line, and can thus be used to compensate for the lagging power factor of other machines if required (see Chapter VI). These characteristics are shown in Fig. 5.

TABLE I

TYPES OF MOTOR USED IN INDUSTRIAL DRIVE

Type of Motor.	Speed-Torque Characteristic.	Starting Torque and Starting Current.	Power Factor.	Speed Control.	Maintenance.	Relative Cost.
3-phase Motors:						
Plain squirrel-cage induction motor	Shunt	1 × F.L.T. with 5 × F.L.C.	0·75–0·9	None	Very low	1
Double squirrel-cage induction motor	Shunt	2 × F.L.T. with 5 × F.L.C.	0·75–0·9	None	Very low	1·5
Pole-changing squirrel-cage induction motor	Shunt	1 × F.L.T. with 5 × F.L.C.	0·75–0·9	2 or 4 fixed ratios	Very low	1·5–3·0
Slip-ring induction motor	Shunt	2 × F.L.T. with 2 × F.L.C.	0·75–0·9	None	Low	1·5
Compensated induction motor	Shunt	2 × F.L.T. with 2 × F.L.C.	0·95–1·0	None	High	3–4
Schrage motor	Shunt	2½ × F.L.T. with 2 × F.L.C.	0·7 –1·0	3–1 range	High	3–4
Stator-fed commutator motor	Shunt	2 × F.L.T. with 2 × F.L.C.	0·5 –1·0	Full range	Medium	3–4
3-phase series motor	Series	2½ × F.L.T. with 2 × F.L.C.	0·9 –1·0	Full range	High	2–3
Synchronous motor	Constant	¾ × F.L.T. with 2 × F.L.C.	1·0 –0·9 lead	None	Medium	2
Synchronous-induction motor	Constant	2 × F.L.T. with 2 × F.L.C.	1·0 –0·9 lead	None	Medium	2
1-phase motors:						
Series motor	Series	3 × F.L.T. with 2 × F.L.C.	0·8 –0·9	Full range (with transformer)	High	2·5
Repulsion motor	Series	3 × F.L.T. with 2 × F.L.C.	0·8 –0·9	Full range	High	2·5
Repulsion-start induction motor	Shunt	3 × F.L.T. with 2 × F.L.C.	0·85–0·9	None	Medium	2
Capacitor-start induction motor	Shunt	1½ × F.L.T. with 2 × F.L.C.	0·7 –0·9	None	Low	1·5
Capacitor start-and-run induction motor	Shunt	1½ × F.L.T. with 2 × F.L.C.	0·9 –1·0	None	Low	2·0
D.C. motors:						
Shunt motor	Shunt	2 × F.L.T. with 2 × F.L.C.	—	3–1 range	Medium	1·5–3·0
Series motor	Series	3 × F.L.T. with 2 × F.L.C.	—	2 or 3 steps	Medium	1·5
Compound motor	—	2–3 × F.L.T. with 2 × F.L.C.	—	2–1 range	Medium	1·5–3·0

The 1-*phase Series Motor.*—If the field magnets of a d.c. series motor are laminated and a compensating winding is fitted to neutralise the armature reaction, it will operate quite satisfactorily on alternating current, and its speed-torque characteristics will be similar to those of a d.c. series motor. By careful design the a.c. motor can be built in sizes suitable for the heaviest traction service, but the most common application is found in driving small domestic apparatus, such as vacuum cleaners, refrigerators, and the like, in which case a universal motor is employed which can operate either on a.c. or d.c.

The Repulsion Motor.—This motor possesses similar speed-torque characteristics to the series motor, and also is similar in construction, except that the armature is short-circuited on itself instead of being connected in series with the stator. Speed control and starting can be effected by shifting the brushes round the commutator, but commutation is not good except at speeds near synchronism.

The 1-*phase Induction Motor.*—The characteristics of this motor are similar to those of the 3-phase induction motor except that it has no inherent starting torque, and some special arrangement must be added to make it self-starting, as described in Section 2; this adds to the cost of the motor and also takes up space, so that for a given output a 1-phase motor is about 30 per cent. larger than a corresponding 3-phase motor. The repulsion-start and the capacitor motors are the most important types of 1-phase induction motor, the connections of the latter being shown in Fig. 1.

NOTES ON TABLE I

Column 2.—The speed-torque characteristics mentioned are illustrated in Fig. 2.

Column 3.—Discussed more fully in Section 2.

Column 4.—The lower values of power factor given for induction motors refer to low-speed machines.

Column 5.—Discussed more fully in section 3.

Column 6.—Very low maintenance indicates that attention is required only at intervals of several months or even years, for oiling of bearings.

Low maintenance indicates occasional attention to brushes for replacements due to wear.

Medium maintenance involves regular attention to brushes and commutator.

High maintenance arises in machines where commutation is relatively poor and the commutator and brushes must be examined at frequent intervals.

Column 7.—The relative costs given are, of course, only very approximate, owing to the large number of factors which have to be taken into account (see Figs. 34 and 52) and refer to ordinary industrial motors between about 7·5 and 37 kW. Very large or very small motors may differ considerably from the above; for instance, a synchronous motor of several hundred kilowatts will cost about the same as an induction motor of the same size, while one of a few kilowatts would be prohibitively expensive on account of the cost of its exciter.

2. STARTING CHARACTERISTICS

Attention must be given to the starting characteristics of a motor in order to ensure that the available torque will be sufficient to start and accelerate the motor and its load in a reasonably short space of time. This feature is of particular importance in choosing motors which have to start against full-load torque, such as those driving grinding mills, or with motors having to start very frequently, as when operating lifts and hoists. An even acceleration is also important in some cases—e.g. for driving textile machinery, where an uneven torque may result in broken threads.

Some motors are capable of giving considerably more than full-load torque at starting, while others can only produce half full-load torque or even less. Further, to give a large starting torque, some types of motor require a current of several times full-load current, and such large currents are frequently inadmissible on account of the danger of overheating of the supply cables or the motor itself, or on account of the voltage drop caused by them in the supply system, with consequent disturbance of other consumers; to avoid trouble due to the latter some supply authorities issue regulations prohibiting the taking of starting currents above two or three times full-load current.

Starting Characteristics of Load

In order to be able to select a suitable motor and starting equipment, it is necessary to have full information regarding the torque necessary to start the load. Two torques have to be considered, namely, the true starting torque required to overcome the initial static friction and the accelerating torque necessary to run the motor and its load up to speed. The true starting torque is a somewhat indeterminate factor, and in some circumstances, as when starting a line of shafting which has been out of use for some time, it may be considerably greater than full-load torque.

Accelerating Torque.—The torque necessary to run the motor up to speed must be sufficient to overcome the load torque and, in addition, provide the necessary acceleration of both motor and load. Types of load commonly met with may be divided into four categories so far as accelerating-torque requirements are concerned:

(i) Motor started light so that the accelerating torque required is small compared to full-load torque.

(ii) The load torque may increase as the motor runs up to

speed, as with a centrifugal pump or fan, where the torque is proportional to $(\text{speed})^2$.

(iii) Load torque may be constant at all speeds and approximately equal to full-load torque, as with a hoist.

(iv) The motor may be required to start and accelerate against full-load torque and, in addition, to accelerate some heavy moving parts, as with rolling mills or with motors equipped with a fly-wheel.

It is evident that starting a motor in category (i) is quite a different proposition from starting one in category (iv), even though the full-load torque and speed may be the same in each case ; a study of the load characteristic is thus necessary in order to be able to choose the most suitable type of motor and starter.

Another factor of importance is the time taken to run the motor up to speed, since this governs the heating of the motor and control equipment due to the heavy starting currents. Calculations regarding the starting time and torque are discussed in Section 6 of this chapter under the heading of speed-time relations.

Function of the Starting Equipment

If a motor is switched directly on to the supply it will, except in the smallest sizes, take a current much above the allowable limit. The main purpose of the starting equipment is therefore to limit this starting current to a safe value without, at the same time, reducing the starting torque to a value less than that required to start and accelerate the motor and the load. This limitation of current may be done by reducing the voltage applied to the motor by means of a resistance in series with the motor or by some other suitable means.

Starting of D.C. Machines

The torque of a d.c. motor is proportional to the product of flux and armature current and is quite independent of speed. In order to get as high a starting torque as possible for a given current, the flux must therefore be maintained at the highest value obtainable.

The Shunt Motor.—The field winding is connected directly across the supply so that a reduction of the supply voltage would reduce the flux proportionately, and this method is not therefore suitable for starting purposes. If, however, a resistance is connected in series with the armature while full voltage is maintained across the field, the current can be limited to any desired value. Since the flux will be constant the torque will be directly proportional to current, no matter what the speed, as shown in Fig. 6. The magnitude of the starting torque is thus limited only by the allowable current—full-load current will give full-load torque, twice full-load current will give twice full-load torque, and so on. Shunt motors are therefore well suited to heavy-duty starting. As the motor speeds up the resistance is cut out, and the method of calculation of suitable values of resistance for each step is described in various textbooks on electrical technology.

The Series Motor.—With this type of motor the armature current flows through the field winding, so that the flux depends

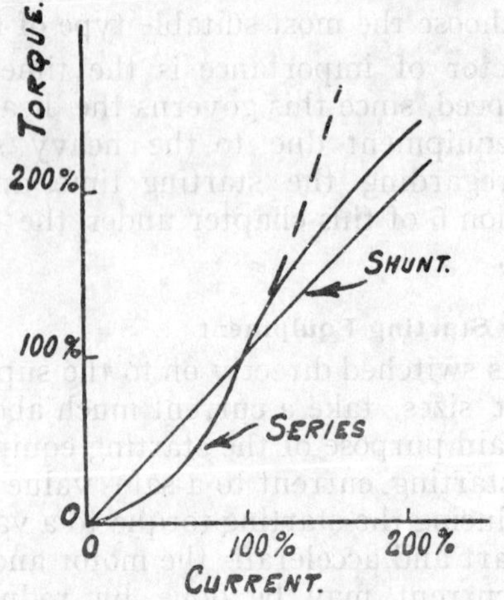

FIG. 6.—TORQUE-CURRENT CURVES OF D.C. MOTORS.

on the armature current and is quite independent of the voltage applied to the motor and its speed. A reduction of the voltage will not, therefore, affect the torque in the same way as in the shunt motor—full-load current will always produce full-load torque whatever the voltage. Variation of voltage is thus a very suitable means of starting a series motor, and resistance connected in series with the motor is generally employed for this purpose. If the flux were proportional to the armature current, the torque would be proportional to $(\text{current})^2$ as shown by the dotted curve in Fig. 6, but in practice, at currents above the full-load value, the field magnets become saturated and the flux tends towards a constant value. Conditions then become similar to those in a shunt motor. It can be seen, however, that twice full-load current will produce slightly more than twice full-load torque ($2\frac{1}{2}$ to 3 times), so that the series motor is even more suited to heavy-duty starting than the shunt motor.

Where two series motors operate normally in parallel the series-parallel method of voltage control can be used, the motors being connected in series at starting, each being therefore supplied with half voltage, and then switched over to parallel for normal running. The applications of this method are, however, almost entirely confined to traction work, and it is fully described in Chapter II.

Starting of 3-phase Induction Motors

The torque and current of an induction motor are approximately given by*:

$$T = K\frac{V^2 \frac{R'_2}{s}}{(R_1 + R'_2/s)^2 + (X_1 + X'_2)^2} \quad . \quad . \quad (1)$$

$$I = \frac{V}{\sqrt{(R_1 + R'_2/s)^2 + (X_1 + X'_2)^2}} \text{ amperes} \quad (2)$$

where V = applied voltage per phase.
R_1 = stator resistance per phase.
R'_2 = rotor resistance per phase (referred to stator).
X_1 = stator reactance per phase.
X'_2 = rotor reactance per phase (referred to stator).
s = fractional slip
K = constant (if made equal to 1, the torque will be in synchronous watts per phase).

It is thus seen that, contrary to conditions with the d.c. motor, the torque depends on the speed, a feature which gives rise to the well-known torque-slip curves of the induction motor. For starting purposes the torque and current at standstill ($s=1$) are of importance, and these are given by:

$$Ts = K\frac{V^2 R'_2}{(R_1 + R'_2)^2 + (X_1 + X'_2)^2} \quad . \quad . \quad . \quad (3)$$

$$Is = \frac{V}{\sqrt{(R_1 + R'_2)^2 + (X_1 + X'_2)^2}} \text{ amperes} \quad . \quad . \quad (4)$$

For given values of reactance, therefore, the starting torque and the starting current vary with rotor resistance in the manner

*Say: *Performance and Design of A.C. Machines* (Pitman).

shown in Fig. 7, the torque reaching a maximum when R'_2 is approximately equal to $X_1 + X'_2$. For normal running the value of R'_2 should not exceed 1 or 2 per cent. of X'_2 or the efficiency will be low, so that, in order to obtain high starting torques, resistance must be added to the secondary circuit and cut out gradually as the motor speeds up. This resistance also keeps the current within allowable limits. The secondary winding of an induction motor is usually mounted on the rotor, and the ends are brought out to slip-rings for connecting to the external starting resistance, thus giving rise to the name *slip-ring* induction motor. On motors which have to start infrequently, a special device is often

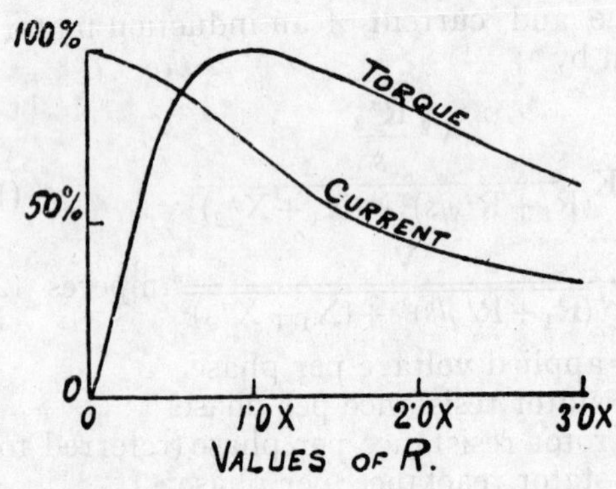

FIG. 7.—STARTING TORQUE AND STARTING CURRENT OF INDUCTION MOTOR WITH VARIOUS VALUES OF ROTOR RESISTANCE.

fitted which short-circuits the slip-rings internally and raises the brushes to eliminate losses due to them when the motor is running.

The squirrel-cage Induction Motor.—The fact that the secondary winding of an induction motor is normally short-circuited on itself enables a very robust type of motor to be built, in which the rotor (secondary) winding consists simply of copper or aluminium bars placed in the slots without insulation and connected at each end to a ring, also of copper or aluminium. Such a motor is known as a squirrel-cage motor, and for ordinary industrial purposes is the simplest and most reliable type available. It is evident, however, that it is not possible to insert resistance in series with the rotor of such a motor at starting, and it will, therefore, have an inherently low starting torque; a motor of normal design will take about five times full-load current and give about full-load torque. Although in special cases it is possible to switch motors of 75 or 150 kW straight on to the supply, this is not usually permissible with motors above 11 to 15 kW.; with motors above this size the voltage must generally be reduced in order to limit the starting current to a safe value, and, as seen from equation (1) above, this reduces the torque in a greater proportion, since torque is proportional to (voltage)^2. The reduction of voltage may be carried out by means of an auto-tranformer, tappings giving 50 per cent., 60 per cent., and 75 per cent. of normal voltage usually being provided, and giving therefore starting torques of 25 per cent., 36 per cent., and 56 per cent. of that obtainable by direct switching.

In textbooks on induction motors* it is shown that:

$$\frac{\text{starting torque}}{\text{full-load torque}} = \left(\frac{I'}{I_{f.l.}}\right)^2 s_{f.l.} \quad . \quad . \quad . \quad . \quad (2)$$

where I' = starting current in motor.
$I_{f.l.}$ = full-load current in motor.
$s_{f.l.}$ = full-load slip.

By making use of this, the starting currents and torques for any particular motor can be calculated as in Example 1 below.

Example 1:—A 400-V, 3-phase, squirrel-cage induction motor has a full-load slip of 4%, a stand-still impedance of 1·54Ω, and a full-load current of 30A. The maximum starting current which may be taken from the line is 75A. What tapping must be provided on an auto-transformer starter to limit the current to this value and what would be the starting torque available in terms of the full-load torque?

Let the transformer have a tapping giving X per cent. of normal voltage,

$$\text{Normal phase voltage} = \frac{400}{\sqrt{3}} = 231 \text{ V}$$

$$\text{Starting current in motor} = \frac{\frac{X}{100} \times 231}{1{\cdot}54} \text{ A.}$$

$$\text{Current on supply side of auto-transformer} = \frac{X}{100} \text{ of current in motor}$$

$$\therefore \text{ Starting current taken from supply} = \left(\frac{X}{100}\right)^2 \times \frac{231}{1{\cdot}54} \text{A.}$$

This is to be limited to 75 A.

* Say: *Performance and Design of A.C. Machines* (Pitman)

$$\therefore X^2 = \frac{75 \times 1{\cdot}54 \times 100^2}{231}$$

$$\therefore X = 70{\cdot}7$$

i.e. a 70·7 per cent. tapping must be provided.

The starting current in the motor will be $75 \times \frac{100}{70{\cdot}7} = 106\text{A}$

Therefore, from equation (5)

$$\frac{\text{starting torque}}{\text{full-load torque}} = \left(\frac{106}{30}\right)^2 \times 0{\cdot}04 = 0{\cdot}5$$

i.e. the starting torque available would be only half full-load torque, and such a motor would be suitable only for very light starting duties.

If a curve is plotted showing the starting torques for various allowable starting currents for the above motor or any other motor with an auto-transformer starter and a 4 per cent. slip, the full curve of Fig. 8 is obtained.

Another very simple and commonly used means of reducing the voltage at starting is the *star-delta switch.* This connects the stator windings in star for starting, and when up to speed the switch is operated and reconnects the windings in delta ; the starting voltage across each winding is thus $1/\sqrt{3}$ of the full line voltage—this reduces the starting torque to $\frac{1}{3}$ of the direct-switching value and is equivalent to an auto-transformer with a tapping at $\frac{100}{\sqrt{3}} = 58\%$; this point has been shown on the curve in Fig. 8. The use of a star-delta switch necessitates the motor being designed for normal operation with the windings delta-connected, and all six ends of the windings must be available.

A resistance in series with the stator can be used to limit the starting current, but the starting torque available with a given current is less than with an auto-transformer—for instance, in the example quoted above, if the current which can be drawn from the supply is limited to 75 A, this is also the maximum current which can flow in the motor winding ; the starting torque is therefore given by :

$$\frac{\text{starting torque}}{\text{full-load torque}} = \left(\frac{I'}{I_{f.l.}}\right)^2 s_{f.l.} = \left(\frac{75}{30}\right)^2 \times 0{\cdot}04$$

$$= 0{\cdot}25$$

This is about half that available with the auto-transformer. The dotted curve on Fig. 8 shows the starting torque available with various starting currents for stator-resistance starting and illustrates clearly the advantage of the former method. The cost of the stator resistance is, however, less than that of

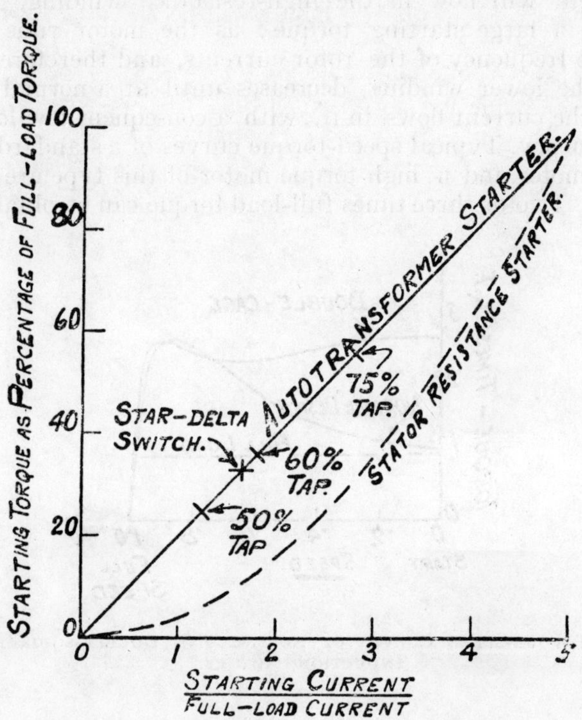

FIG. 8.—STARTING TORQUES AVAILABLE, WITH VARIOUS STARTING CURRENTS AND DIFFERENT TYPES OF STARTER FOR SQUIRREL-CAGE INDUCTION MOTORS HAVING A FULL-LOAD SLIP OF 4 PER CENT.

an auto-transformer, and it finds application in certain cases where only very low starting torques are required.

High-torque Motors.—Attempts have been made to overcome the starting difficulties of the squirrel-cage motor without sacrificing its simplicity by means of what are called "high-torque" motors. One type employs a rotor winding of higher resistance than usual—this, however, only increases the starting torque at the expense of efficiency; a better type is the "Boucherot," or "double-squirrel-cage," motor, which has two squirrel-cage windings on the rotor, one arranged in the tops of the slots and having a high resistance, while the other is arranged in the bottoms of the slots and has a low resistance; owing to its position the winding in the bottom of the slots will have a high inductance, so that at starting, when the frequency of the rotor currents is high, its reactance will be high and the majority of the current will flow in the high-resistance winding, giving therefore a large starting torque; as the motor runs up to speed the frequency of the rotor currents, and therefore reactance of the lower winding, decreases until at a normal speed most of the current flows in it, with a consequent low loss and good efficiency. Typical speed-torque curves of a standard squirrel-cage motor and a high-torque motor of this type are shown in Fig. 9. Two or three times full-load torque can be obtained at

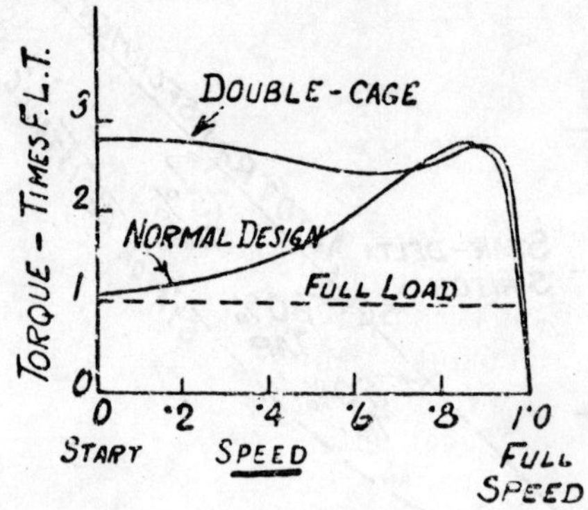

FIG. 9—TORQUE-SPEED CURVES OF NORMAL AND DOUBLE-SQUIRREL-CAGE INDUCTION MOTORS.

starting with about five times full-load current, with, of course, correspondingly smaller torques and currents if the voltage is reduced by an auto-transformer or a star-delta switch.

Limitations of the Squirrel-cage Motor.—In general it may be stated that the starting difficulty limits the application of squirrel-cage motors to drives requiring not more than about 30 kW and where they will have to start against not more than one-quarter to one-half full-load torque. Beyond these limits the slip-ring motor or some other suitable type must be employed. In some cases, if it is not possible to apply the load after the motor has been started and yet a squirrel-cage motor is desirable for other reasons, a clutch is employed so that the load can be applied after the motor has reached full speed.

Starting of Single-phase Induction Motors

A single-phase induction motor has a pulsating and not a rotating field and therefore has no starting torque at all. If it is started by hand or other means in either direction, however, it will run up to speed in that direction. In order to make the motor self-starting, it is necessary to incorporate some device which will produce the necessary starting torque to run it up to speed. Three methods are available, viz.: pole shading, phase splitting, and repulsion-motor starting.

Pole Shading.—A short-circuited copper coil is placed round a portion of each pole, and this coil has currents induced in it by transformer action; these cause the flux in that portion of the pole to lag on the main flux so that a rotating field is produced, enabling the motor to start as a polyphase machine. The starting torque is small and losses occur continuously in the shading coil, so that this method is applicable only to very small motors.

Phase-splitting Devices.—Another method of obtaining a rotating field at starting is to employ a phase-splitting device which produces a two-phase supply so that the motor can be started as a polyphase machine. Motors above about 3·7 kW usually employ an inductor for producing the phase displacement, while smaller motors use a capacitor. The latter are termed capacitor motors and are of two types: the *capacitor-start* motor has the capacitor in circuit only during the starting period—at a certain predetermined speed it and the auxiliary winding are cut out of circuit, either automatically or by hand. In the *capacitor start-and-run* motor the capacitor is connected permanently in circuit and therefore gives a higher power factor when running than is obtainable with an ordinary single-phase induction motor. Capacitor-start motors when switched direct on to the line can produce starting torques of 1 to $1\frac{1}{2}$ times full-load torque with about twice full-load current.

Three-phase motors sometimes employ capacitors permanently connected in parallel with their windings, and are also termed capacitor motors, although the capacitors are used only for power-factor improvement and not for starting.

With the larger single-phase motors starting torques of 30 to 70 per cent. of full-load torque with $1\frac{1}{2}$ to 2 times full-load current can be obtained by the use of phase-splitting devices, so that such motors are suitable only for light starting duties. The starting torque of slip-ring motors can be improved to some extent by the use of rotor resistance, as with the polyphase motor, but the maximum torque is reduced by so doing.

Repulsion-motor Starting.—The repulsion motor has a high starting torque, and in order to be able to combine this with the constant-speed characteristic of the induction motor, two types of repulsion-start induction motor have been developed. One of these employs an ordinary repulsion-motor winding on the rotor with a centrifugally operated device which short-circuits all the commutator segments and raises the brushes when the motor has reached nearly full speed, thus converting it into a squirrel-cage induction motor. The other type employs a squirrel-cage winding in addition to the repulsion-motor winding; the latter is wound in the tops of the slots and therefore has the preponderating effect at starting, while the squirrel-cage winding controls the characteristic when running; the characteristic changes gradually from one to the other as the motor runs up to speed in the same way as the Boucherot motor. Starting torques of two or three times full-load torque can be obtained by either of these methods with only about $1\frac{1}{2}$ to 2 times full-load current. This forms the only practicable method of obtaining a large starting torque with a single-phase induction motor.

Starting of Synchronous Motors

Inherently the synchronous motor has no starting torque, and must be run up to almost synchronous speed by some independent means. In practice, however, in order to make the motor self-starting, it is usually fitted with a squirrel-cage winding embedded in the pole shoes so that it can start as a squirrel-cage induction motor. When it reaches almost synchronous speed the d.c. excitation is switched on and it pulls into synchronism. The squirrel-cage winding can be made to have a high resistance, as it carries no current when the motor is running at synchronous speed, and starting torques of between about half-and full-load torque can be obtained with about twice full-load current. An auto-transformer is usually employed to limit the starting current. Such torques are not, however, suitable for heavy starting duties, and the *synchronous induction motor* has been developed for this purpose. Instead of the usual type of salient-pole d.c. winding a cylindrical rotor with a winding similar to that of a slip-ring induction motor is employed; the motor is started as a slip-ring induction motor, with its good starting characteristics, and when up to speed d.c. is switched on to the rotor and the machine pulls into synchronism and continues to run as a synchronous motor. Although the starting properties of this type of motor are good its running characteristicts, such as efficiency and pull-out torque, are not quite so good as those of the salient-pole synchronous motor.

Starting of A.C. Commutator Motors

Starting of a.c. commutator motors may be carried out by applying a reduced voltage or by shifting the brushes. Both these methods are also used for speed control, and in most cases starting can be satisfactorily effected by adjusting the control equipment to the low-speed position and then switching on full voltage. In some cases it may be necessary to provide in addition special starting tappings on an auto-transformer or a series resistance.

3. SPEED CONTROL

The nature of the speed control required by different industrial drives varies considerably—for instance, some drives require a continuously variable speed over the entire range from zero to full speed or over a portion of this range, while others require two or more fixed speeds only; the former is generally referred to as a variable-speed drive and the latter as a multi-speed drive; sometimes a creeping speed of only a few rev/min is needed for adjusting or setting up the work on the driven machine. In some cases also it is necessary to be able to adjust the speed to some value and then automatically hold it at that figure to within $\frac{1}{2}$ or 1 per cent. under all conditions of load. Another factor which has to be considered in choosing a motor for a variable-speed drive is the relation between the speed and kW of the driven machine. A crane or hoist, for instance, requires the same torque at all speeds, while a fan or centrifugal pump requires a torque proportional to the square of the speed.

Speed Control of D.C. Machines

The speed and the torque of a d.c. motor are given by:

$$n = \frac{V - IR}{\text{constant} \times \Phi} \quad \ldots \quad (6)$$

$$T = I\Phi \times \text{constant.} \quad \ldots \quad (7)$$

where V = terminal voltage.
I = armature current.
R = armature resistance.
Φ = flux per pole.

The speed may be controlled, therefore, by varying the applied voltage, the resistance R in series with the armature, or the flux, and each of these methods is commonly employed.

Field Control.—With a shunt machine, variation of the flux by varying the field current can easily be carried out by inserting a resistance in the field circuit; such a resistance has to carry only a small current, and can be made of the slide-wire type or of the step type with a large number of steps, so that an almost continuously variable speed over the range provided can be obtained. With series motors the variation of flux can be

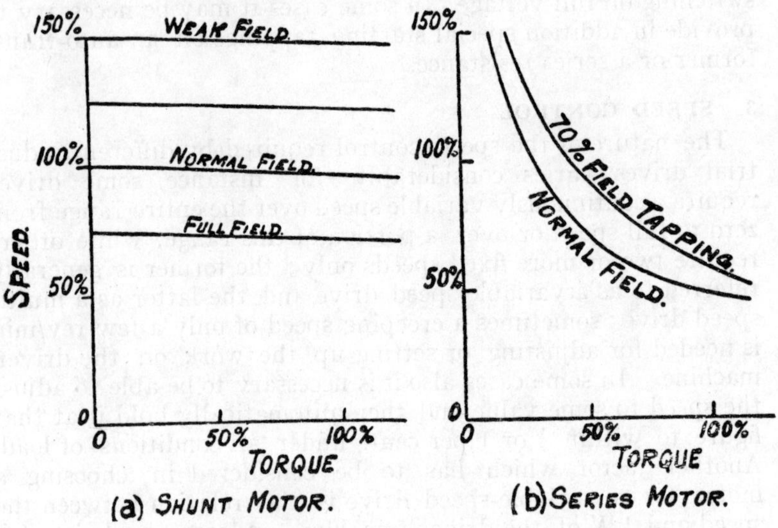

FIG. 10.—FIELD CONTROL OF SPEED WITH D.C. MOTOR.

obtained by diverting a portion of the field current through a resistance (diverter) connected in parallel with the field or by providing tappings on the field so that the current is passed through different numbers of turns. The speed-load characteristics obtainable with field control are shown in Fig, 10. The lowest speed (maximum field) is limited by the heating of the field coils and the saturation of the magnets, while the highest speed is limited by the instability of the motor due to the overwhelming effect of the armature m.m.f. at low fields and also, of course, by the centrifugal forces; with a normally designed shunt machine a speed range of $1\frac{1}{2}$ or 2 to 1 can be obtained, while by special designs it is possible to provide speed ranges of 4 or even 5 to 1. For most drives, however, a variation of $\pm$ 10 per cent of normal speed is all that is required. Creeping speeds cannot be obtained by field control.

Resistance Control.—Resistance added in series with the armature can be employed for speed control, but it is clear from equation (6) (page 21) that with this method of control the speed of a shunt motor will be dependent on the armature current. If used for a drive requiring a constant torque at all speeds, the current will have to be constant and the kilowatt input to the equipment will therefore be the same at all speeds; the output will, of course, drop proportionately to the speed, so that

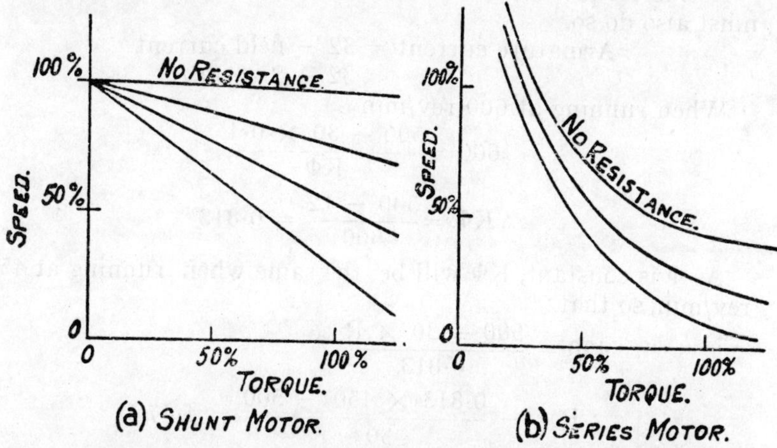

FIG. 11.—RESISTANCE CONTROL OF SPEED OF D.C. MOTOR.

the efficiency at low speeds will be very poor. At half-speed it will thus be about 50 per cent., a little more than half the energy supplied being wasted in the resistance. For drives where the torque decreases with the speed (fans or centrifugal pumps), the losses at low speeds are considerably smaller, and, if the low speed is not required for long periods, the simplicity of this method of control sometimes renders it economical—creeping speeds are commonly obtained in this way. The characteristics of resistance speed control as applied to shunt and series motors are shown in Fig. 11, and Example 2 below illustrates a calculation on this subject.

Example 2 : A d.c., shunt motor runs at 600 rev/min off 500-V mains and takes a current of 32 A when delivering full-load torque. The armature resistance is 0·4 Ω and the field winding resistance is 250 Ω. It is desired to run the motor a (a) 450 rev/min, and

(b) 700 rev/min while still delivering the same torque. How would you arrange for this, and what would be the current and kW-input taken from the supply in each case? Neglect the iron, friction and windage losses.

When running at 600 r.p.m. the kW. input is $\frac{500 \times 32}{1000} = 16$ kW.

(*a*) To reduce the speed we must either increase the flux or insert resistance in the armature circuit. The former is generally impracticable, and we will therefore insert resistance in the armature circuit, leaving the flux the same.

As the torque has to remain the same, the armature current must also do so.

$$\text{Armature current} = 32 - \text{field current} = 32 - 2 = 30 \text{ A}$$

When running at 600 rev/min

$$600 = \frac{500 - 30 \times 0{\cdot}4}{K\Phi}$$

$$\therefore K\Phi = \frac{500 - 12}{600} = 0{\cdot}813$$

As Φ is constant, $K\Phi$ will be the same when running at 450 rev/min, so that:

$$450 = \frac{500 - 30 \times R}{0{\cdot}813}$$

$$\therefore R = -\frac{0{\cdot}813 \times 450 - 500}{30} = 4{\cdot}47\ \Omega$$

The armature resistance is 0·4 Ω, so that 4·07 Ω must be added to the armature circuit to reduce the speed to 450 rev/min.

The input current remains the same at 32 A, so that although the speed, and therefore the output, has been reduced, the input kW. remains the same, the difference between the two being dissipated in the resistance.

(*b*) To increase the speed to 700 rev/min, the flux can be reduced by inserting resistance in the field circuit.

As torque $\propto I\Phi$, if we reduce Φ to a new value Φ_1, the armature current must be increased in the same proportion, i.e. new

$$\text{armature current} = 30 \times \frac{\Phi}{\Phi_1} \text{ A}$$

From (*a*) we have, at 600 rev/min:

$$K\Phi = 0{\cdot}813$$

$$\therefore \Phi = \frac{0{\cdot}813}{K}$$

At 700 rev/min we have :

$$700 = \frac{500 - 30 \times \dfrac{\Phi}{\Phi_1} \times 0{\cdot}4}{K\Phi_1}$$

$$= \frac{500 - \dfrac{12 \times 0.813}{K\Phi_1}}{K\Phi_1}$$

$$\therefore\ 700\,(K\Phi_1)^2 - 500\,(K\Phi_1) + 9{\cdot}76 = 0$$

$$K\Phi_1 = 0{\cdot}698 \text{ (or } 0{\cdot}02)$$

The new flux is thus given by :

$$\frac{K\Phi_1}{K\Phi} = \frac{0{\cdot}698}{0{\cdot}813}$$

$$\therefore \Phi_1 = \Phi \times 0{\cdot}856$$

If the effect of the change in armature current were neglected we should have the fluxes in the same ratio as the speed, i.e. :

$$\frac{\Phi_1}{\Phi} = \frac{600}{700}$$

$$\therefore \Phi_1 = \Phi \times 0{\cdot}857$$

This is almost identical with the more accurate calculation, showing that the change in armature resistance drop can in this case, as in most others, be neglected.

We have thus to reduce the flux to 0·856 of its normal value. If flux were proportional to field current it would only be necessary to increase the resistance of the field circuit in this ratio, i.e. from 250 Ω to $\frac{250}{0{\cdot}856} = 292\ \Omega$. A resistance of 42 Ω would thus have to be added.

In practice, however, the flux is not proportional to field current and the magnetisation curve must be known ; the current corresponding to the new value of flux can be read off the curve as shown in Fig. 12 and the corresponding field-circuit resistance calculated. In this case the resistance will be $\frac{500}{1{\cdot}25} = 400\ \Omega$; 150 ohms will therefore have to be added.

To find the current and kW. input at the new speed :

New armature current $= 30 \times \frac{1}{0{\cdot}856} = 35{\cdot}1$ A

New field current $= 1{\cdot}25$ A

Total current $= 35{\cdot}1 + 1{\cdot}25 = 36{\cdot}35$ A

Wk—input $= 36{\cdot}35 \times 500 = 18{\cdot}17$ kW.

Resistance Control—Shunted-armature Connection.—The series resistance arrangement described above is simple to apply, but for some applications suffers from the serious disadvantage that

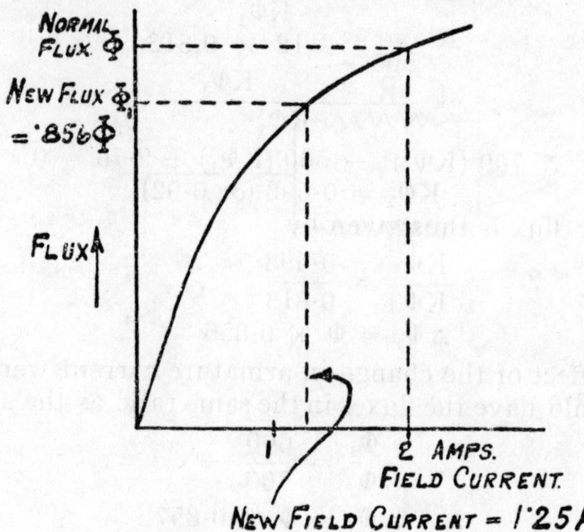

FIG. 12.—MAGNETISATION CURVE FOR EXAMPLE 2.

the speed varies with the load, rising to normal full-speed as the load approaches zero. To overcome this the shunted-armatrue connection can be used in which resistances are connected

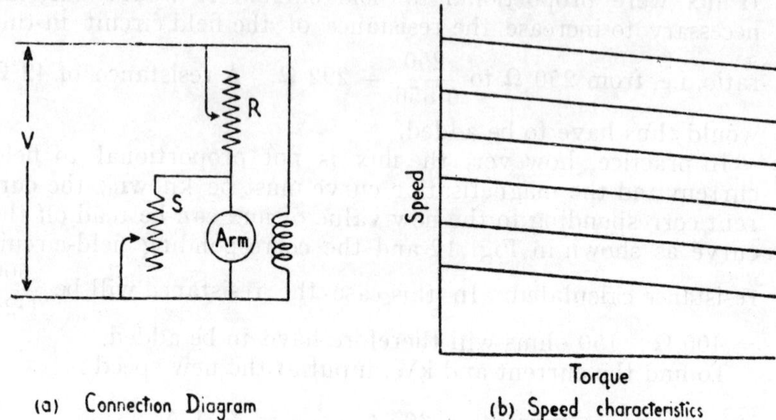

FIG. 13.—SHUNTED ARMATURE CONNECTION.

in series and in parallel with the armature, as shown in Fig. 13(*a*). By a proper variation of the two resistances a range of speed characteristics, as shown in Fig. 13(*b*), can be obtained.

By means of Helmholtz's (Thevenin's) theorem, it can be shown that the motor behaves as though it were running from a constant voltage supply of magnitude $V' = V \frac{R}{R + S}$ in series with the resistances R and S in parallel, as shown in Fig. 14.

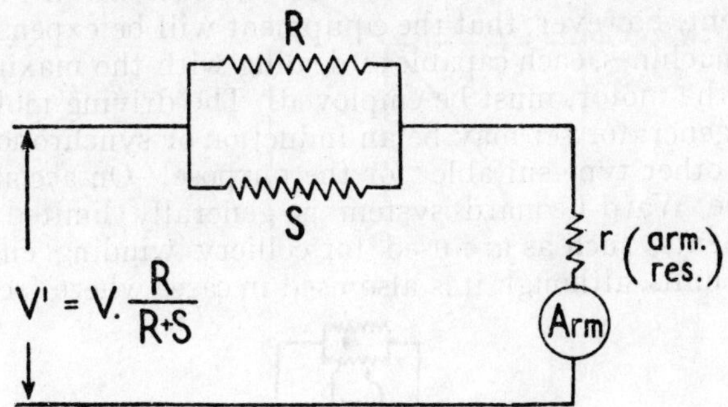

FIG. 14.—EQUIVALENT CIRCUIT FOR SHUNTED ARMATURE CONNECTION.

By using this equivalent circuit, calculations can be made by the usual methods.

The chief disadvantages of this method are its low efficiency and the fact that a heavy current is drawn from the supply at

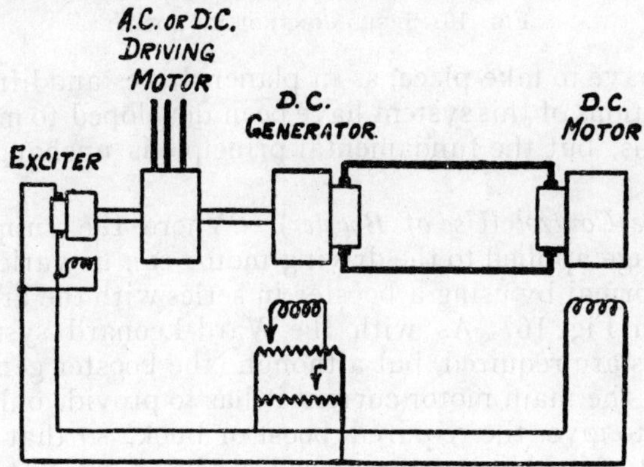

FIG. 15.—WARD-LEONARD SPEED CONTROL.

certain speeds, as is illustrated by Question 5 at the end of the chapter.

Voltage Control (*Ward-Leonard System*).—By providing the motor with a constant separate excitation and supplying it from a special motor-generator set, as shown in Fig. 15, the voltage applied to the armature can be varied from zero to a maximum in either direction, and a corresponding range of speed control obtained, simply by variation of the generator field. When operating at any particular speed the motor will have a shunt characteristic, and gives a series of curves similar to those obtained with shunted armature control, as shown in Fig. 13; it is evident, however, that the equipment will be expensive, since three machines, each capable of dealing with the maximum output of the motor, must be employed. The driving motor of the motor-generator set may be an induction or synchronous motor or any other type suitable for the purpose. On account of the cost the Ward-Leonard system is generally limited to large equipments, such as are used for colliery winding engines and rolling mills, although it is also used in cases where frequent re-

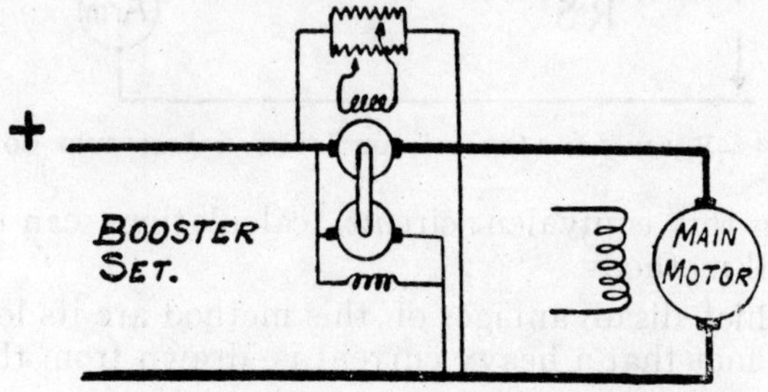

FIG. 16—SPEED CONTROL BY BOOSTER.

versals have to take place, as in planer drives and lifts. Various modifications of this system have been developed to meet special conditions, but the fundamental principle is unchanged in each case.

Voltage Control (*Use of Booster*).—Where the supply is d.c. the voltage applied to the driving motor can be varied above or below normal by using a booster in series with the armature, as shown in Fig. 16. As with the Ward-Leonard system, three machines are required, but although the booster generator has to carry the main motor current it has to provide only sufficient voltage to give the required boost or buck, so that its output and that of its driving motor need not be as great at that of the main motor if only a small range of speed control is required.

Voltage Control (*Series-parallel Connection*).—Where two or more series motors are employed on the same drive, two economical speeds can be obtained by connecting the motors in series or in parallel—in series each motor will have about half-voltage across it and they will therefore run at about half-speed. This method is confined almost entirely to traction work and is described more fully under that heading.

Voltage Control (Use of Grid-controlled Mercury-arc Rectifier).— A modification of the Ward-Leonard equipment employs a mercury-arc rectifier instead of the motor-generator set ; the rectifier may consist of a multi-anode steel-tank or glass-bulb unit or a group of single-anode (thyratron or ignitron) tubes. The rectifier voltage can be varied from zero to a maximum by means of grid control—reversal can only be obtained, however, by reversing the motor armature connections. Such a convertor has the advantages of being a static piece of apparatus, of having a higher efficiency, and of occupying a smaller space than a corresponding motor-generator set. It possesses, however, certain disadvantages, namely, the power factor on the a.c. side

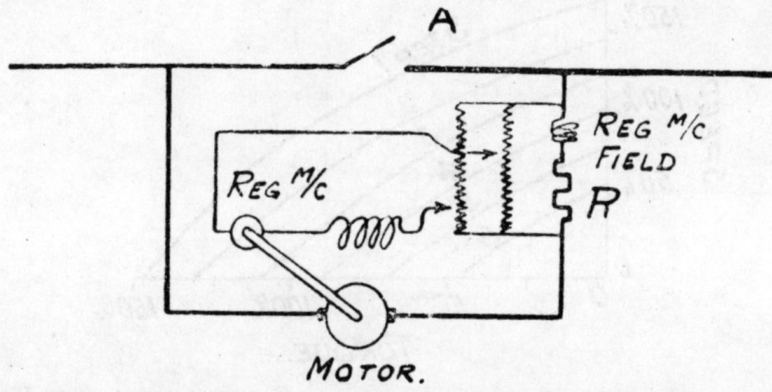

FIG. 17.—CONNECTIONS OF CONSTANT-CURRENT MOTOR.

decreases approximately in proportion to the speed, the control and auxiliary equipment are more complicated than that for the simple Ward-Leonard system, and it has no capacity for energy storage, so that any sudden peak load or other disturbance is transmitted directly to the supply.

The Constant-current System.—For situations where there is a likelihood of the motor being stalled, as with dredgers or excavators, and also with ships' windlasses and capstans, the constant-current system has certain advantages. A constant-current generator must be employed which, by means of a special exciter, delivers a constant current under all conditions of load —any increase or decrease in load results in an increase or decrease of voltage. The connections of the motor are illustrated in Fig. 17. The field of the motor is excited from tappings across the resistance R. A potential divider enables any proportion of this voltage to be applied to the field system in either direction; in addition there is a regulating machine mounted on the motor shaft and connected in series with the field in such a way that its e.m.f. opposes the main field current. Any reduction in speed of the motor thus reduces this opposing e.m.f. and allows the field current to increase so that the torque increases, reaching a maximum when the motor is stalled. Speed-torque characteristics as shown in Fig. 18 are thus obtained, the series of curves corresponding to different positions of the potential divider. A full range of speed control is obtained with the maximum torque when the motor is stalled without any dangerous currents under this condition: these characteristics are similar to those of a steam engine. As the current is independent of the load any number of motors can be connected

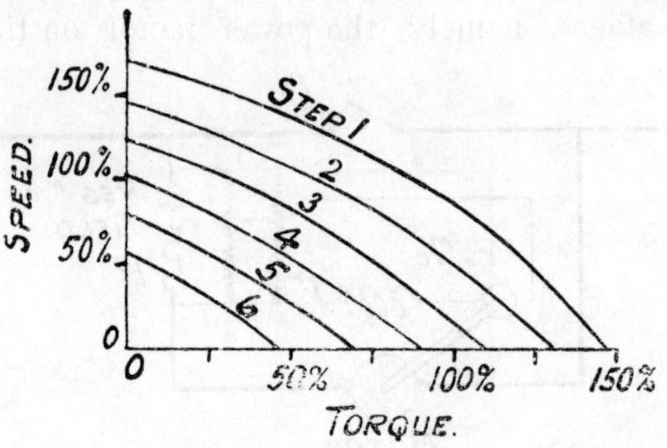

FIG. 18.—SPEED-TORQUE CHARACTERISTICS OF CONSTANT-CURRENT MOTOR.

in series, thus reducing cable costs and compensating to some extent for the additional cost of the equipment compared to that of standard motors and also for the cost of the copper losses, which are constant at all loads. To shut a motor down it is simply short-circuited by closing switch A in Fig. 17.

Metadyne Control.—Another scheme involving the constant-current principle and invented by an Italian engineer named Pestarini was first developed in this country by Messrs. Metropolitan-Vickers. The essential part of the equipment is a metadyne convertor consisting, in its simplest form, of a 2-pole d.c. armature with two pairs of brushes and a 4-pole fieldmagnet, as shown in Fig. 19; one pair of the brushes (a b) are connected to an ordinary constant-voltage d.c. supply, while the other pair, c d, are connected to the load and supply a constant-current output; when used as a speed-control system the load consists of an ordinary d.c. series motor.

Suppose that the metadyne convertor is running at a constant speed. A current (I_1) from the supply will be flowing through the armature winding via the brushes a b, and will set up in the usual way an armature reaction flux (Φ_1) which, as seen from the arrangement of the poles, has a fairly low reluctance path. The rotation of the conductors in this flux causes an e.m.f. ($E_2 = KI_1$) to be set up in them which appears across the brushes c d. The resulting current (I_2) when these are connected to the load, sets up another flux (Φ_2) at right angles to the

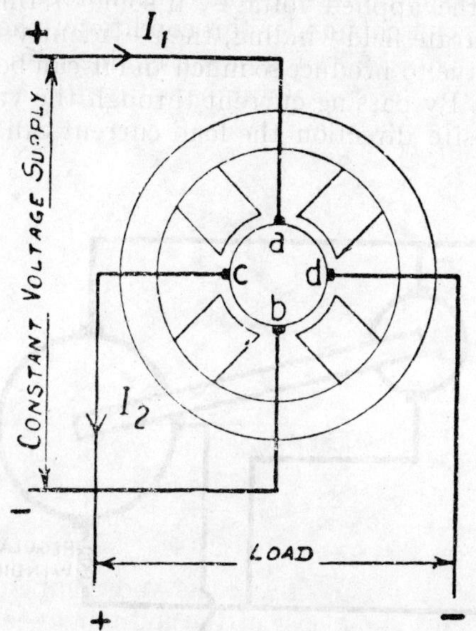

FIG. 19.—SIMPLE METADYNE CONVERTOR.

first, and this causes a back e.m.f. ($E_1 = KI_2$) to be set up between the brushes a b which opposes the applied voltage. As the applied voltage is constant, conditions must adjust themselves so that, neglecting resistance drop, this back e.m.f. (E_1) which is opposing it is also constant ; this e.m.f. is produced by the current (I_2) in the load circuit and this current must therefore be constant. Since $E_1 . I_1 = KI_2 \times E_2/K = E_2 . I_2$, i.e. output = input, no power is required to drive the machine apart from that to supply the losses. This simple metadyne convertor thus transforms the constant-voltage supply into a constant-current variable-voltage supply for feeding the load ; it runs as an ordinary constant-voltage motor so far as the brushes a be are concerned, and acts as a constant-current generator so far as the brushes c d are concerned.

The metadyne described above has no windings on the poles and is capable of delivering only a single value of constant current. To enable the value of this current to be adjusted, the field magnet poles are equipped with a " variator " winding, which sets up a flux in the same direction as that produced by the load current. It has already been explained that the total flux in this axis must be constant in order to produce a back e.m.f. equal to the applied voltage ; if some of this flux is produced by a separate field winding, then evidently the load current will not have to produce so much and it can be of a smaller constant value. By passing current through the variator winding in the opposite direction the load current can similarly be increased.

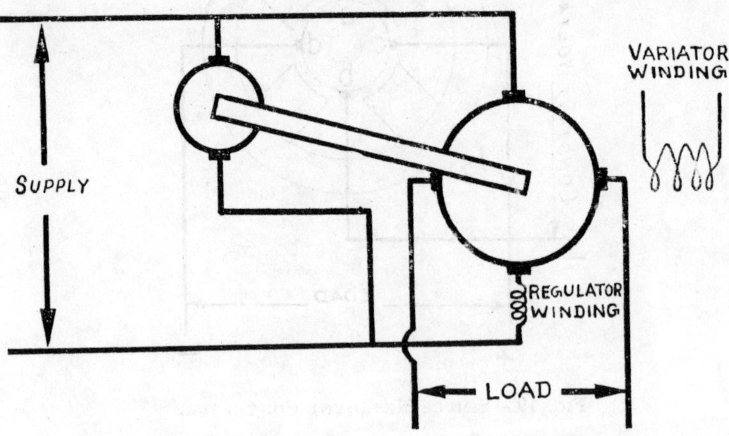

Fig. 20.—Connections of Metadyne System of Control.

If the output current is, say, increased in this way, the voltage remaining the same, the total output will be increased ; a further winding must, therefore, be added, known as the " regulator " winding, which will adjust the fiux in the a b axis, and thereby the back e.m.f. between the brushes a b, so that the current taken from the supply can be increased without a change in speed of the convertor. The correct amount of excitation for the regulator winding is obtained from a small shunt machine mounted on the metadyne shaft as shown in Fig. 20, any tendency towards a change in speed of the metadyne will cause a change in the e.m.f. of this machine, and as it is connected in opposition to the main supply voltage, this will cause a corresponding change in the regulator winding current.

There is, in addition, an exciter for supplying the variator winding, which is also mounted on the main shaft; special cummutating pole windings, which must be provided to secure satisfactory commutation; and for large units a multipolar construction is used. A typical characteristic showing the current and voltage at the output terminals with various values of variator current is shown in Fig. 21.

By connecting a series motor to the output terminals a complete control can be obtained simply by varying the current in the variator winding, thus eliminating all starting resistances. Such a control scheme is well suited for the operation of cranes, hoists, deck winches, etc., and also for traction purposes, this latter application being referred to again later.

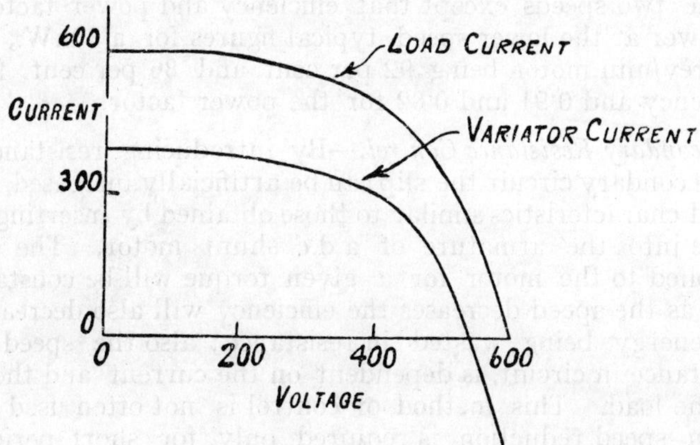

FIG. 21.—OUTPUT CHARACTERISTICS OF METADYNE CONVERTOR.

Speed Control of Induction Motors

The speed of an induction motor is given by:

$$n = \frac{f}{p}(1 - s) \qquad (8)$$

where f = frequency

p = number of *pairs* of poles

s = slip, normally less than 0.03 (per cent.).

Speed may thus be controlled by a variation of frequency, number of poles, or slip. Variation of frequency is not economically practicable except in very special cases, but pole changing is frequently employed for squirrel-cage machines, while artificial variation of slip, by the introduction of a back e.m.f. into the secondary circuit by means of a resistance or an auxiliary machine, is employed for slip-ring motors. It must be remembered, however, that for the great majority of drives the induction motor runs at approximately synchronous speed.

Pole Changing.—Two separate primary windings can be employed wound for different numbers of poles, or, alternatively, a single winding with a switch for reconnecting it to give a different number of poles may be used; in this way two speeds in some simple ratio such as 2 to 1 or 3 to 2 can be obtained. This method of control is more suited to the squirrel-cage than to the slip-ring type of motor, since in the latter case the equipment would be complicated by the necessity for having a pole-changing arrangement on the secondary (rotor) winding as well as on the primary. The running characteristics will be similar at the two speeds except that efficiency and power factor will be lower at the lower speed, typical figures for a 30kW., 1,000/500-rev/min motor being 92 per cent. and 86 per cent. for the efficiency and 0·91 and 0·82 for the power factor.

Secondary Resistance Control.—By introducing resistance into the secondary circuit the slip can be artificially increased, giving speed characteristics similar to those obtained by inserting resistance into the armature of a d.c. shunt motor. The power supplied to the motor for a given torque will be constant, so that as the speed decreases the efficiency will also decrease, the slip energy being wasted in resistance; also the speed, with resistance in circuit, is dependent on the current and therefore on the load. This method of control is not often used except when speed reduction is required only for short periods or where the reduction is only a few per cent. of normal speed.

Use of an Auxiliary Machine.—Instead of absorbing the slip energy in resistances it may be supplied to an auxiliary machine and usefully employed, thus giving an efficient means of speed variation. The use of an auxiliary machine in this way also enables the power factor to be improved, and in many cases such machines are used for this purpose even if no speed control is required.

The various arrangements which are practicable are illustrated in Fig. 22. With each arrangement it may be noted that the slip energy may be either converted to mechanical energy and added to that of the main motor, or it may be converted to

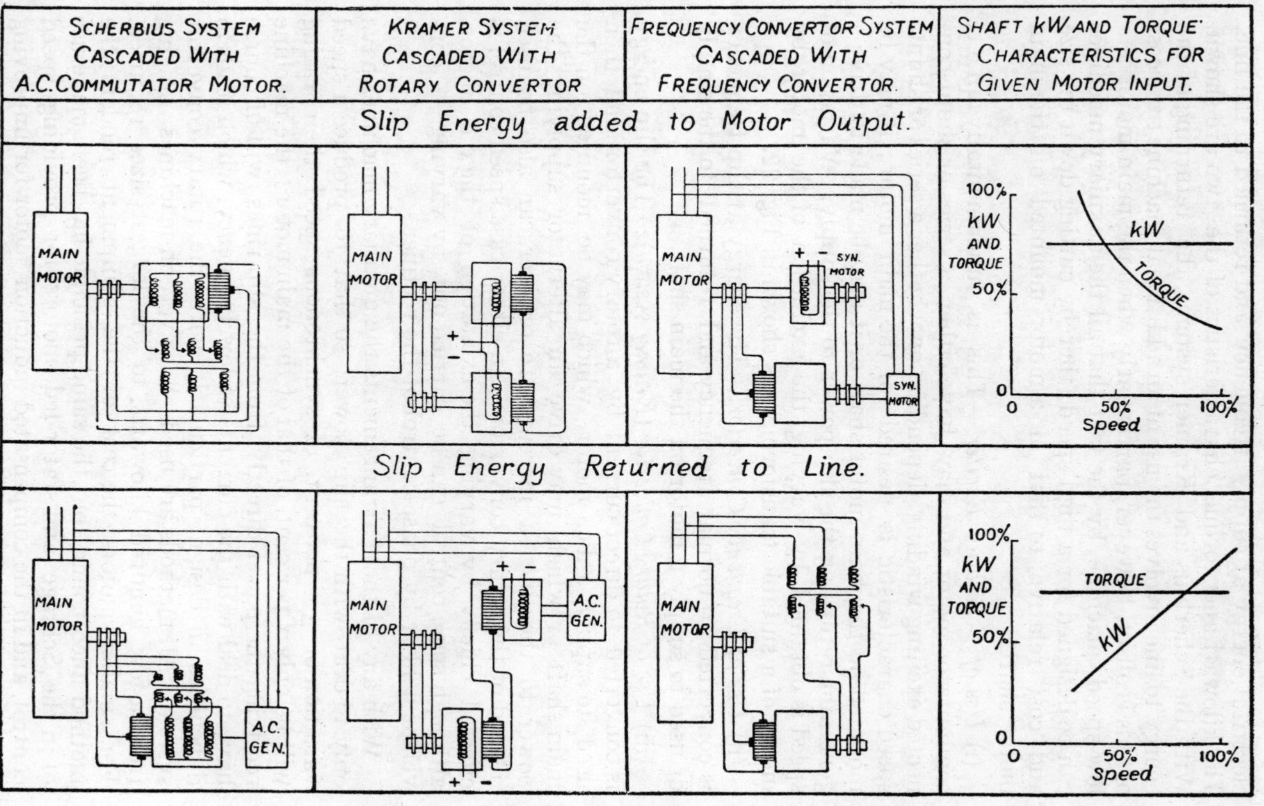

FIG. 22.—VARIABLE-SPEED INDUCTION-MOTOR SETS

electrical energy at supply frequency and returned to the line. The kilowatt and torque characteristics of the two are shown. With the Scherbius and Kramer systems, the returning of the energy to line involves the use of an additional machine ; the cost of this is offset, however, particularly when the main motor is a low-speed machine, by the fact that all the auxiliary machines can be designed for a high speed, thereby cutting down the size and cost relative to that of a motor mounted on the main motor shaft.

(i) *Use of Scherbius Exciter.*—This is fundamentally an a.c. commutator motor and may have either a series or shunt-connected exciting winding, depending on whether a series or shunt-speed characteristic is desired for the main motor ; it may be mounted on the main motor shaft or it may be made to drive a generator returning the slip power to the supply. Variation of speed is obtained by varying the excitation of the motor by means of a suitable transformer, as shown in Fig. 22.

(ii) *Use of Frequency Convertor.*—The energy at slip frequency is converted to normal frequency and returned to the supply or used to supply a motor on the main shaft.

(iii) *Use of Rotary Convertor* (*Kramer system*).—The slip energy is converted to direct current by a rotary convertor and then used to supply a d.c. motor, which may be mounted on the main shaft or which may drive an alternator supplying the power to the line ; a mercury-arc rectifier can also be used instead of the rotary convertor. In either case speed control is effected chiefly by varying the excitation of the d.c. motor, although some control can be carried out by varying the convertor field or by phase-control of the rectifier.

With any of these arrangements the auxiliary machines have only to deal with the slip power, so that to produce a speed variation of $\pm x$ per cent. of synchronous speed their rating will be only x per cent. of that of the main motor ; the machine receiving the power directly from the slip-rings will of course have to deal with the currents of low frequency, which leads to difficulties in design, particularly with the rotary convertor system. All methods are used, however, on machines ranging from a few hundred kilowatts to the largest sizes required. For smaller motors the cost of the equipment renders the method uneconomic, but the same principle has been made use of in the Schrage and stator-fed motors for providing speed control, and in the compensated induction motor for improving the power factor ; the Schrage motor can give control of both speed and power factor, but the compensated induction motor can only give control of power factor. The characteristics of these two types of motors are given in Figs. 3 and 4 and in Table I.

Cascaded Induction Motors.—If two induction motors are mounted on the same shaft or otherwise mechanically coupled, and connected so that the slip energy from the rotor of the first is supplied to the stator of the second, as shown in Fig. 23, the speed of the set, assuming that they are connected so that their torques are in the same direction, will be :

$$n = \frac{f}{p_1 + p_2} \text{ revs/sec} \quad . \quad . \quad . \quad (9)$$

p_1 and p_2 being the numbers of *pairs* of poles on the two machines. If they are connected so that the torques oppose each other, then we have :

$$n = \frac{f}{p_1 - p_2} \text{ revs/sec} \quad . \quad . \quad . \quad (10)$$

By using the motors either singly or together, 2, 3, or 4 different speeds may be obtained, but the power factor is only 0.6

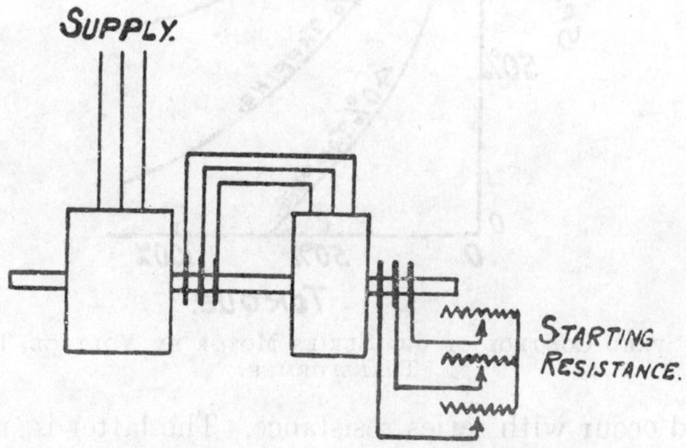

FIG. 23.—CASCADED INDUCTION MOTORS

to 0.8 and the weight of the two motors is high, so that this arrangement, although simple, does not have very wide application ; it is sometimes used, however, for high-power drives for rolling mills or large ventilating fans and the like. In the Hunt cascade motor* an ingenious arrangement of windings is used enabling the two motors to be combined into one, thereby reducing the weight and cost to some extent.

* L.J. Hunt, *J.I.E.E.* vol. 52, p. 406.

A.C. Commutator Motors

Speed control can be obtained with a.c. commutator motors either by varying the applied voltage or by a movement of the brushes round the commutator. The former method employs tappings on a transformer or, occasionally, a series resistance, so that variation in steps is obtained, while brush shifting gives a gradual control throughout the range.

The 1-phase Series Motor.—The a.c. series motor must run with a fixed brush position, so that speed control is obtained, when necessary, by voltage variation. Transformer tappings give variation between zero and maximum speed, as shown by the curves of Fig. 24, without any appreciable additional loss such

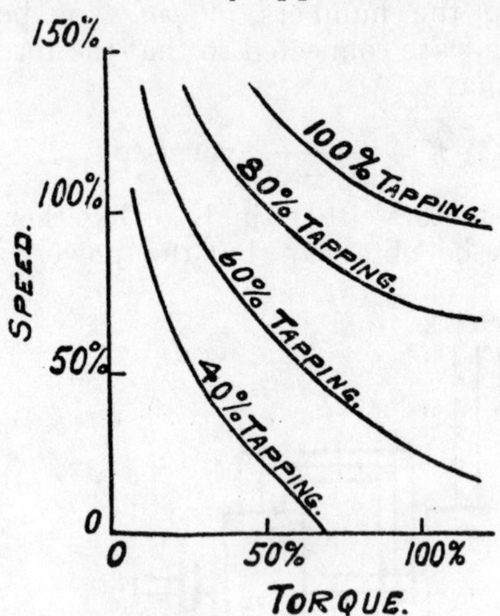

FIG. 24.—SPEED CONTROL OF A.C. SERIES MOTOR BY VOLTAGE TAPPINGS ON TRANSFORMER.

as would occur with series resistance. The latter is used, however, where speed control is only required very infrequently, and where capital cost is of prime importance; it may be noted, however, that the maximum voltage for which a satisfactory design of motor can be obtained is about 300, so that with large motors a transformer is often necessary in any case and the addition of the tappings is only a minor expense.

The Repulsion Motor.—Where the speed range required is between about 0·5 and 1·1 times synchronous speed, brush shifting is the simplest method of speed control, but beyond this range commutation becomes difficult and voltage variation as with the series motor is preferable. Speed-torque characteristics with various brush positions are shown for a typical motor in Fig. 25. It can be seen that at high values of torque the curves tend to become farther apart, i.e. the motor is very sensitive to brush position. This feature is eliminated to some extent in the *Deri Repulsion Motor,* which employs two sets of brushes, one set being fixed and the other movable. The angle of movement to produce a given speed change is in this case twice that of the plain repulsion motor.

The 3-phase Series Motor.—Again brush shifting is the most economical method of speed control and gives a speed range of 3 or 4 to 1 with characteristics similar to those of the repulsion motor.

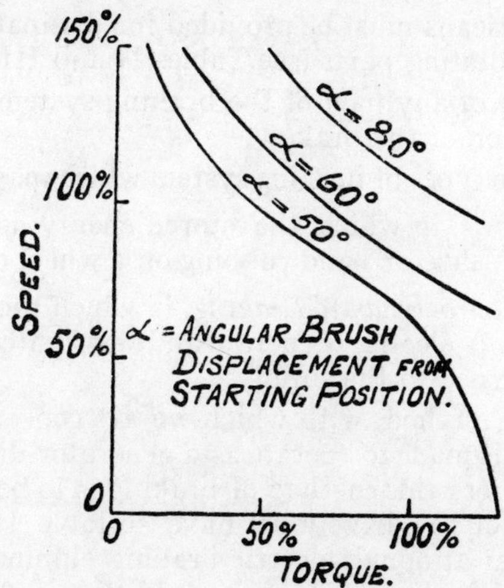

FIG. 25.—SPEED CONTROL OF REPULSION MOTOR BY BRUSH SHIFTING.

Schrage and Stator-fed Motors.—Both these motors, referred to previously give a range of speed characteristics similar to those shown in Fig. 13 for the shunted armature arrangement although there is a tendency for the speed of the stator-fed motor to rise somewhat at no-load.

In the Schrage motor, control is effected by brush shifting which can be done by a handwheel or by a small remotely controlled motor of a few watts rating. The power-factor characteristics are given in Fig. 4.

The stator-fed motor operates with fixed brushes, and the speed is varied by an induction regulator or tapped transformer, which can be situated away from the motor if desired.

4. ELECTRIC BRAKING

In some cases the provision of apparatus for stopping a motor and its driven machine is as important as that for starting it; a planing machine, for instance, must be quickly stopped at the end of its stroke in order to get a high rate of production, while in other cases rapid stops must be possible to prevent danger to operator or damage to the manufactured product. In such cases, and also, of course, for lifts and hoists, effective braking must be provided. The essential features of a satisfactory brake are that:

(i) It should be quick and reliable in action and the braking force should be controllable.

(ii) Suitable means must be provided for dissipating the stored energy of the rotating parts (see Tables II and III).

(iii) A failure of any part of the braking system should result in the application of the brakes.

There are two types of braking system which may be employed.

Friction braking, in which the stored energy is dissipated as heat by a brake shoe or band rubbing on a wheel or brake drum.

Electric or Electro-dynamic Braking, in which the stored energy is converted into electrical energy and dissipated in resistance as heat or returned to the supply.

In the latter method, with which we are concerned here, the driving motor is made to operate as a generator during the braking period. Where this method of braking is to be employed the motor chosen for the drive must have suitable braking characteristics, so that although electric braking eliminates the cost of maintenance of friction brakes, the additional complication and the limitation in the choice of motor which it involves render it unsuitable in many cases. A further point is the fact that the generating action of the motor ceases at standstill, so that although an electric brake can almost stop a machine or load, it cannot hold it stationary, and a friction brake must be provided in addition for this purpose.

Plugging

Plugging is the simplest type of electric braking and involves the reversing of the connections to the armature of the motor so that it tends to run in the reverse direction; in order to stop the machine a special device must be installed to cut off the supply as soon as it comes to rest. This method can be applied to d.c., induction, or synchronous motors, and is particularly suitable where the drive has to be rapidly reversed, as with planing machines and many rolling-mill equipments.

D.C. Motors.—To reverse a d.c. motor it is necessary to reverse the connections to the armature, so that the current in it reverses while that in the field winding remains in the same direction as before. The effect of doing this on series and shunt machines is illustrated in Fig. 26. It can be seen that with both types of motor, when the armature connections are reversed for braking, the e.m.f. of the machine is in the same direction as that of the applied voltage, so that the current which flows round the circuit

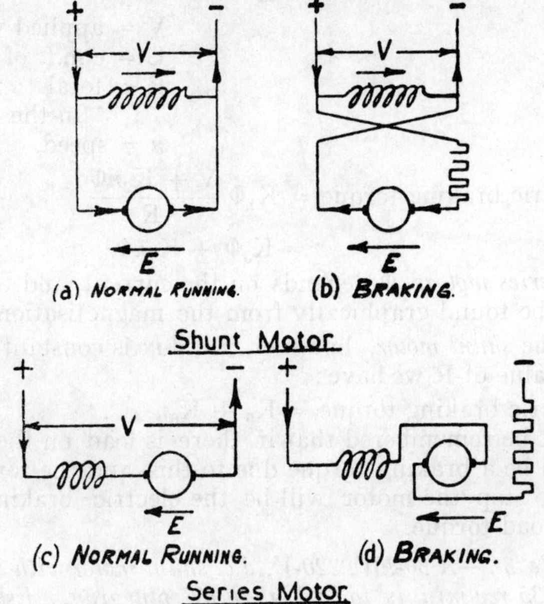

FIG. 26.—PLUGGING WITH D.C. MOTORS.

is produced by a voltage of V + E, which is approximately equal to 2 V. We have, therefore, at the instant of switching to the braking condition, nearly twice normal voltage applied to the circuit, and the current rush will be about twice that which would occur if the motor were started on full voltage with no starting resistance ; to avoid this the switch which performs the plugging operation must reinsert the starting resistance into the circuit and also some additional resistance which will limit the current to a safe value. The kinetic energy of the machine being braked will be dissipated in these resistances, but also, since current is still being drawn from the supply in the same direction as before, this energy, in addition, will have to be dissipated in them ; braking by this method thus requires energy from the supply in addition to wasting the kinetic energy of the machine.

The relation between the braking torque and speed for d.c. motors can be found as follows :

Electric braking torque $= K_1 I\Phi$

$$\text{Current} = \frac{V + E}{R}$$

$$= \frac{V + K_2 n\Phi}{R} \qquad . \quad . \quad . \quad . \quad (11)$$

V = applied voltage.
E = e.m.f. of machine.
R = total resistance in the circuit.
n = speed.

$$\text{Electric braking torque} = K_1\Phi \frac{V + K_2 n\Phi}{R}$$

$$= K_3\Phi + K_4 n\Phi^2 \qquad . \quad . \quad . \quad (12)$$

With *series motors*, Φ depends on the current, and the torque can only be found graphically from the magnetisation curve.

With the *shunt motor*, however, the flux is constant, and for a given value of R we have:

$$\text{Electric braking torque} = K_5 + K_6 n \qquad . \quad . \quad . \quad . \quad (13)$$

It must be remembered that if there is load on the machine there will be a braking torque due to this, and the total torque tending to stop the motor will be the electric braking torque plus the load torque.

Example 3 :—A 30-kW, 220-V, d.c. shunt motor with a full-load speed of 535 rev/min is to be braked by plugging. Estimate the value of resistance, which should be placed in series with it to limit the initial braking current to 200 A. What would be the initial value of the electric braking torque and the value when the speed had fallen to half its full-load value?

Armature resistance of motor = 0·086 Ω
Full-load armature current = 150 A

Solution :

Back e.m.f. of motor = 220 − 150 × 0·086 V
= 220 − 12·9 = 207·1 V

Total voltage when braking = 220 + 207·1 = 427·1 V

Resistance required = 427·1/200 = 2·136 Ω

There is already 0.086 Ω present as armature resistance, so that the resistance to be added is :

$$2{\cdot}136 - 0.086 = 2{\cdot}05\ \Omega$$

$$\text{Torque} \propto I\phi$$
$$\propto I, \text{ since } \phi \text{ is constant for a shunt motor,}$$

$$\text{Initial braking torque} = \text{full load torque} \times \frac{200}{150}\ \text{Nm}$$

$$\text{Full load torque} = \frac{30 \times 1000 \times 60}{2\pi \times 535} = 535\ \text{Nm}$$

$$\text{Initial braking torque} = 535 \times \frac{200}{150} = 714\ \text{Nm}$$

At half-speed, the back-emf falls to half its original value, i.e. to 208/2 = 104 V

$$\text{Current} = \frac{220 + 104}{2{\cdot}136} = 152\ \text{A}$$

$$\text{Electric braking torque at half speed} = 535 \times \frac{152}{150} = \mathbf{542\ Nm}$$

Induction Motors.—The same principle can be applied to the induction motor by reversing two of the stator phases ; this causes a reversal of the direction of the rotating magnetic field,

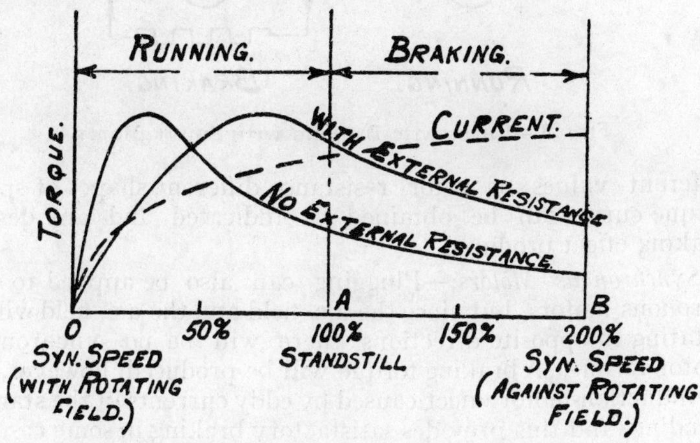

FIG. 27.—PLUGGING WITH INDUCTION MOTOR.

so that at the first instant after plugging, the rotor is running in the opposite direction to that of the field and the relative speed of the two is approximately twice synchronous speed ; the voltage induced in the rotor will thus be twice that normally induced at standstill and the winding must be insulated to withstand this. The conditions during braking can be examined by considering the speed-torque curve of the motor when extended beyond the point of 100 per cent. slip, as show in Fig. 27. Such a curve can be plotted from equation (1). The ordinate at the point B represents the torque at the instant of plugging, and it can be seen that this torque gradually increases as the motor approaches standstill, after which, of course, if it is not switched off it will start up again in the reverse direction in accordance with the ordinary speed-torque curve from A to O. The rotor current can be calculated during the braking period from equation (2) by putting in values of slip between 100 per cent. and 200 per cent. and will be found to be as shown by the dotted curve; it does not increase to any unduly high value relative to the normal starting current at full voltage. By employing

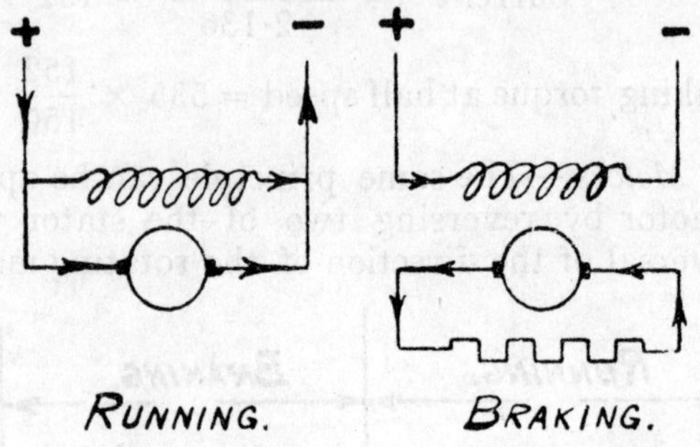

FIG. 28.—RHEOSTATIC BRAKING WITH SHUNT MOTOR.

different values of rotor resistance different shapes of speed-torque curve can be obtained as indicated and any desired braking effect produced.

Synchronous Motors.—Plugging can also be applied to synchronous motors, but since the d.c. field and the a.c. field will be rotating in opposite directions there will be no synchronous-motor torque. A braking torque will be produced, however, due to induction-motor effect caused by eddy currents in the starting winding, and this provides satisfactory braking in some cases.

Rheostatic Braking

With this method of braking the motor is disconnected from the supply and used as a generator driven by the momentum of the equipment to be braked and supplying current to resistances; d.c. or synchronous motors can be braked in this way;

induction motors, however, require a separate source of d.c. excitation during the braking if this method is to be used.

D.C. Shunt Motors.—This type of motor gives rheostatic braking in its simplest form—the armature is simply disconnected from the supply and connected to a resistance, while the field remains on the supply, as shown in Fig. 28. The magnitude of the braking effect can be controlled by varying either the resistance in the armature circuit or the field current. A disadvantage appears however, if the supply fails, since there is then no excitation and therefore no braking effect, but this difficulty can be overcome by fitting a series winding which is only connected during braking.

D.C. Series Motors.—Fig. 29 represents a series motor in the running and braking positions. It will be noticed that the direc-

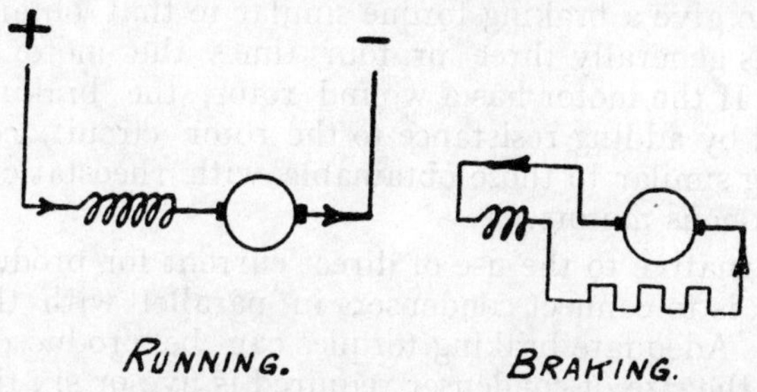

FIG. 29.—RHEOSTATIC BRAKING WITH SERIES MOTOR.

tion of the current in the armature has reversed in the braking condition (assuming that the direction of rotation is the same in each case), so that in order to ensure that the field shall build up it is necessary to reverse the connections of the field winding in addition to disconnecting the motor from the supply. The motor is, of course, acting as a series generator, and it is necessary to remember that if the resistance in the circuit is above a certain critical value equal to the initial slope of the current-voltage characteristic, the machine will not be self-exciting ; in practice, however, the starting resistance is generally employed for braking purposes and its value is usually low enough to avoid this condition.

Synchronous Motors.—So long as the field excitation is maintained, rheostatic braking can easily be applied to synchronous motors by disconnecting the armature from the supply and connecting it to resistances so that the machine acts as an alternator. Tests* taken show that with rheostatic braking on a 750 kW, 1,200 rev/min synchronous motor, the time taken to bring the machine to rest was 0·98 second (9·0 rev) and with a 72 rev/min motor of the same output the time was 1·56 second (0·85 rev.).

Induction Motors.—The induction motor normally draws its magnetising current from the supply, so that if disconnected, as in rheostatic braking of d.c. and synchronous machines, no e.m.f. can be generated and there can be no braking torque produced. If, however, after disconnection, a direct current is passed through the stator winding a steady flux will be set up in the air gap and the rotation of the short-circuited rotor in this flux will cause e.m.f.s to be induced in it which will produce currents giving a braking torque comparable to that obtainable with other methods. The magnitude of the direct current required to give a braking torque similar to that obtainable by plugging is generally three or four times the motor full-load current. If the motor has a wound rotor, the braking can be controlled by adding resistance to the rotor circuit, conditions then being similar to those obtainable with rheostatic braking of synchronous motors.

An alternative to the use of direct current for producing the excitation is to connect condensers in parallel with the stator winding. Adequate braking torques can be produced in this way, but the size of condenser required is five or six times that which would be needed to improve the power factor of the motor to unity under normal operating conditions, so that the method is not usually economic.

Torque-speed Relations with Rheostatic Braking.—These can easily be found in a similar way to those for braking by plugging on page 42.

$$\text{Electric braking torque} = K_1 I\Phi$$

$$\text{Current } I = \frac{E}{R} = \frac{K_2 n\Phi}{R} \qquad (14)$$

$$\therefore \text{Electric braking torque} = K_3 n\Phi^2 \qquad (15)$$

For a series motor the flux depends on the current, and the torque can only be found from the magnetisation curve. For shunt and synchronous motors, where the flux is constant, the above expression reduces to :

$$\text{Electric braking torque} = Kn \qquad (16)$$

* "Dynamic Braking of Synchronous Machines," C. E. Kilbourne and I.A. Terry, *Electrical Engineering*, December 1932.

In the example below, a calculation for a series motor is given ; while Example 8, illustrates the case of a synchronous motor.

Example 4 :—A 15-kW, series motor operating a hoist runs at 450 rev/min on full load and has a total armature and field resistance of 0.3Ω. If the motor is connected for rheostatic braking with (a) 7.5 Ω and (b) 8.7 Ω across its terminals, what would be the speed at which a load giving full-load torque would be lowered? The magnetisation curve of the motor when running at 450 rev/min is given below :

I (*amperes*)	10	20	30	40	50	60
E (*volts*)	108	207	279	320	346	360

Solution:

$$\text{Ful load torque} = \frac{15 \times 1000 \times 60}{2\pi \times 450} = 318 \text{ N.m.}$$

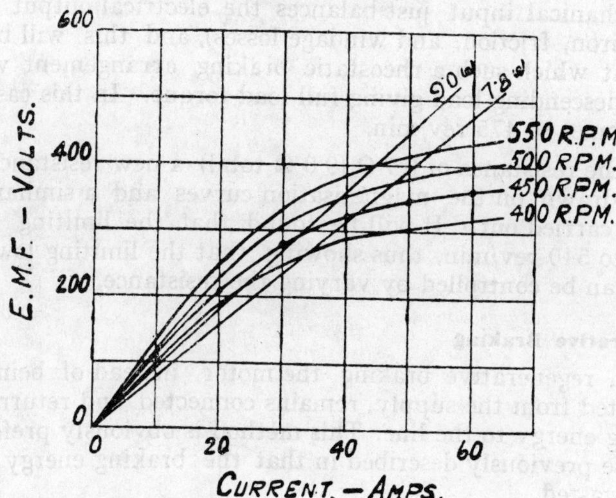

FIG. 30.—MAGNETISATION CURVES FOR EXAMPLE 4.

Output from motor when running as a generator = EI. By drawing the magnetisation curve at 450 rev/min, as in Fig. 30, the current which will flow will be 41.2 A. The output from the machine would therefore be ;

$$E \times I = 322 \times 41{\cdot}2 = 13\text{-}270 \text{ W}$$

The mechanical input to the machine from the load if it were running at 450 rev/min would be:

$$\text{Input} = 2\pi \times \frac{450}{60} \times 318 = 15\text{-}000 \text{ W}$$

The mechanical input is greater than the electrical output, so that the motor will speed up. Suppose it runs up to 500 rev/min.

As the e.m.f., E, is proportional to speed for any given field current, another magnetisation curve for 500 rev/min can be drawn as on Fig. 30.

The electrical output will now be 48·5 A at 380 V, i.e., 18-400 W.

The mechanical input at 500 rev/min will be:

$$\frac{2\pi \times 500 \times 318}{60} = 16\text{-}700 \text{ W}$$

The mechanical input is now less than the electrical output, so that the motor cannot attain a speed of as much as 500 rev/min.

By a process of trial and error a speed can be found at which the mechanical input just balances the electrical output (neglecting iron, friction, and windage losses), and this will be the speed at which such a rheostatic braking arrangement would hold a descending load giving full-load torque. In this case the speed comes to 475 rev/min.

For the resistance of 8·7 Ω (9·0 Ω total) a new resistance line can be drawn on the magnetisation curves and a similar procedure carried out. It will be found that the limiting speed comes to 540 rev/min, thus showing that the limiting lowering speed can be controlled by varying the resistance.

Regenerative Braking

With regenerative braking the motor, instead of being disconnected from the supply, remains connected and returns the braking energy to the line. This method is obviously preferable to those previously described in that the braking energy is not at all wasted.

D. C. Shunt Motor.—With a d.c. machine the question as to whether energy will be taken from or delivered to the line depends on whether the e.m.f. generated by the machine is less or greater than the line voltage, and this depends, of course, on the speed and excitation. Consider a shunt motor running as in Fig. 26(*a*) and suppose that the load causes the speed to be increased above normal, the field current remaining the same. The e.m.f. of the machine would increase, and if it exceeds the line voltage the current will be reversed and power will be supplied to the line, thus tending to prevent any further increase in speed. Alternatively, if the field current had been increased, the same effect would have been obtained and the motor quickly slowed down to the speed corresponding to this new value of field current. Regenerative braking can thus easily be applied with the shunt motor, particularly in cases where it is required to hold a load at a certain speed, as when lowering a hoist; it is not, however, possible to obtain regenerative braking down to very low speeds, since a sufficient increase in field current cannot be obtained.

D.C. Series Motors.—The conditions with a series motor are not so simple, since the reversal of current necessary to produce regeneration would cause a reversal of the field and therefore of the back e.m.f. The complications necessary to obtain satisfactory operation with series motors are not normally warranted for industrial purposes, although for traction purposes regenerative braking with series motors is frequently employed, and the more important practicable methods are described in Chapter II.

Induction Motors.—Regenerative braking with induction motors occurs inherently as soon as the load drives the motor at above synchronous speed, the motor then acting as an induction generator with characteristics obtainable from the circle diagram; a motor having a slip of 5 per cent. at full load will exert a braking torque equal to full-load torque if the speed exceeds synchronous speed by about 5 per cent. Such characteristics are of no use for bringing a motor to rest, but are valuable in the cases of lifts and hoists for holding a descending load at speed only slightly above synchronism. If a two-speed pole-changing motor is employed, a high braking torque is obtained when the motor is switched from full speed to the lower speed, and this is sometimes made use of in high-speed lifts.

5. MECHANICAL FEATURES

The electrical characteristics discussed in the previous sections govern the choice of the type of motor for any particular purpose; of almost equal importance, however, if the motor is to operate satisfactorily over a long period, is the selection of a motor having a suitable mechanical construction for the situation in which it will have to work. Important features which the user of the motor should consider in this connection are the type of enclosure, bearings, transmission of the drive, and the noise emitted.

Types of Enclosure

Some form of protection of live and moving parts is usually desirable to prevent the ingress of dust and dirt or larger foreign

FIG. 31.—SCREEN-PROTECTED MOTOR WITH BELT DRIVE ON TO PAINT COMPRESSOR.
(*ASEA Electric, Ltd.*)

bodies, such as spanners, vermin, and even inquisitive human beings; if, however, some type of enclosure is adopted to give this protection it will also prevent the free ingress of cooling air,

FIG 32—DRIP-PROOF MOTOR WITH DIRECT DRIVE ON TO PUMP
(*Crompton Parkison*)

so that an enclosed motor will not be able to give such a large output for a given temperature rise as an unprotected motor of the same dimensions. The various types of flame proof enclosure are defined by ISS. eg. IS : 2148—1968, and fall into the following classes :

Open Type.—The bearings are supported on simple pedestals or end brackets so that there is no restriction to ventilation and also no protection. Many old types of motor were of this type, but modern practice confines its use chiefly to large d.c. motors which are installed in a room separate from the machine shop. An open-type machine, in this case a d.c. generator, is shown in Fig. 158.

Protected Type.—Some protection is afforded, but large openings are left for ventilation. Such motors are suitable for most industrial purposes.

Screen-protected Type.—A better protection is afforded if the openings of the protected type are covered with wire-mesh screens, as in Fig. 31 : although dust and dirt are not excluded, larger bodies and vermin cannot enter. The degree to which ventilation is impeded depends on the fineness of the screen and the possibility of its becoming clogged with dirt. The motors in Fig. 38 are partially protected in this way in that the larger openings are covered by a perforated screen.

Drip-proof Type.—Where motors are to be installed in very damp situations, such as that illustrated in Fig. 32, a drip-proof enclosure can be used, in which the openings are protected by overhanging cowls to prevent falling moisture from entering the machine.

Totally Enclosed Type.—For very dusty atmospheres, such as occur when driving coal-handling plant, sawmills, etc., the motor must be totally enclosed, so that no dirt or foreign matter can enter and clog the air passages. Since this will also exclude cooling air, all the heat which is generated in the motor must be dissipated from its outside surface, and this surface is frequently fitted with fins to facilitate this; even so, the output obtainable from a totally enclosed motor without exceeding the safe temperature limit is only about 50 to 75 per cent. of that obtainable from a protected motor of the same dimensions, and about 37 kW is the economical upper limit of output of motors with this type of enclosure. To assist in the heat dissipation, and therefore to enable a smaller motor to be used for a given output, most makers have developed a totally enclosed motor in which an outer casing is built round the motor proper and air is blown, by means of a fan mounted on the shaft, between this casing and the external motor surface. Fig. 33 illustrates such a motor driving a fan in a coal hydrogenation plant, where, as can be seen from the illustration, there is a large amount of coal-dust present, which would very quickly clog the air passages of an ordinary protected or screenprotected motor. Another motor of similar type is shown in Fig. 44.

Pipe-ventilated Type.—Another method of overcoming the heating difficulty of the totally enclosed motor, particularly with the larger sizes, employs a duct or pipe through which clean air

FIG. 33.—TOTALLY ENCLOSED MOTOR (WITH OUTER CASING AND FAN) DRIVING A FAN IN A COAL-HYDROGENATION PLANT.
(*Crompton Parkinson*)

is led to the motor from outside the dust-laden building or area. Such an arrangement is shown in Fig. 34. The cost of the piping will, in many cases, be outweighed by the saving in cost due to the smaller size of motor which can be used.

Flame-proof Type.—For use in fiery coal mines or other situations where an explosive atmosphere may arise, a special form of totally enclosed motor must be used which is capable of withstanding any explosion of gas inside the motor without trans-

FIG. 34 —PIPE-VENTILATED MOTOR WITH BELT DRIVE ON TO CHAFF-CUTTER. (*B T -H Co*)

mitting the flame to the outside. Such motors must be capable of withstanding the force of any internal explosion and must have metal-to-metal flanged joints at least 25. mm. wide—even though

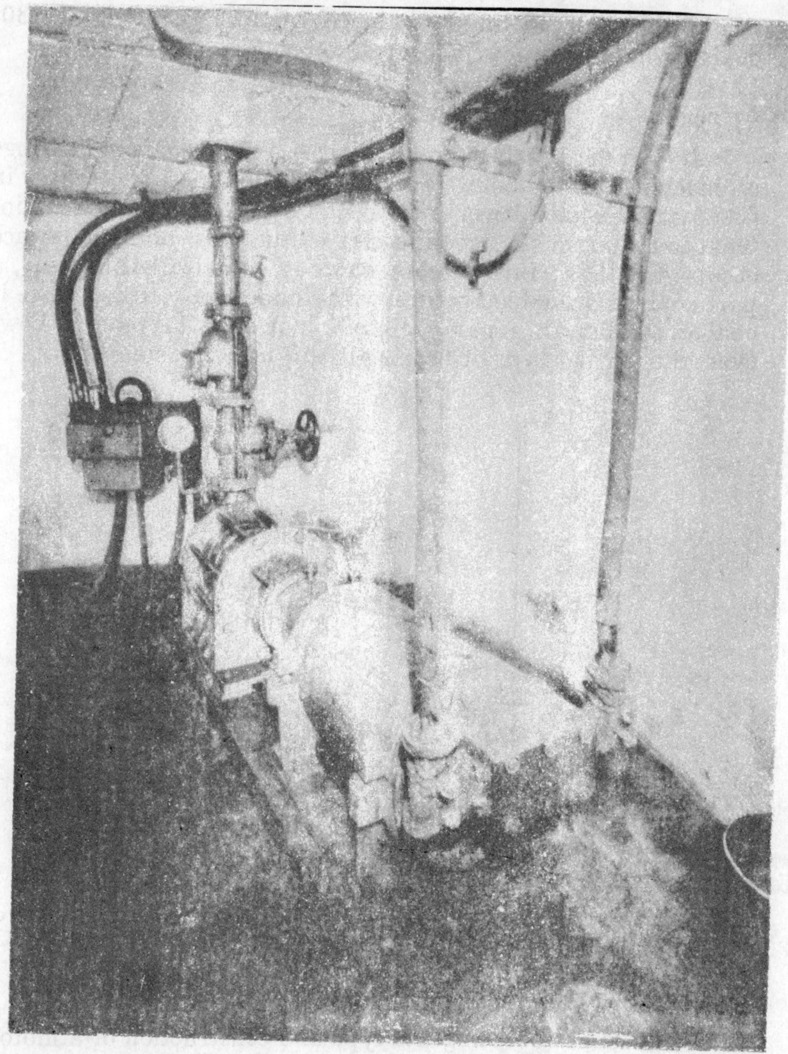

FIG 35—7 5 KW—1,460 REV/MIN, FLAME-PROOF MOTOR DRIVING A PUMP IN A COAL MINE
(*B T.-H. Co.*)

the latter are not gas-tight their cooling effect will prevent a flame being transmitted from the inside to the outside. It is not always necessary to provide the whole motor with a flame-proof enclosure; for instance, slip-ring induction motors can usually be provided with flame-proof slip-ring enclosures only, as shown in Fig. 35. A special standard specification, B.S.S. 270, 1930, deals with flame-proof enclosures.

Bearings

Ball or roller bearings are tending to replaçe journal bearings on machines up tc about 75 kW. Although more expensive in first cost they have lower friction losses, almost negligible maintenance requirements, even in dirty situations, and the space occupied is less; furthermore there is practically no wear, a particularly valuable feature with induction motors, since it enables smaller air gaps to be used. For noiseless motors, however, the journal type of bearing is still usally preferred.

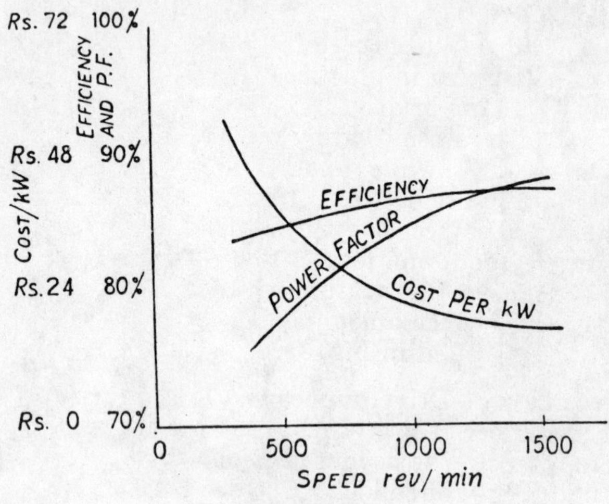

FIG 36.—EFFECT OF SPEED ON EFFICIENCY, POWER FACTOR, AND COST OF TYPICAL RANGE OF 15 kW SLIP-RING INDUCTION MOTORS

Transmission of Drive

In addition to choosing the type and construction of a motor, the method whereby its drive is transmitted to the driven machine must be carefully considered; this may be by direct coupling or by a gear, belt, chain, or rope drive. The choice is governed largely by the most economical speed of the motor, whether or not any form of clutch is required between the motor and driven shaft, and whether or not the motor can be conveniently situated in line with the driven shaft. For machine-tool drives the use of built-in motors, possesses many advantages.

Choice of Motor Speed.—The dimensions and, therefore, the cost of a motor of a given output are approximately inversely proportional to the speed, so that slow-speed motors tend to be more expensive in first cost, as shown by the curve in Fig. 36. Efficiency and, in the case of induction motors, power factor also decrease with a decrease in speed, as shown on the curves. When choosing a motor for a low-speed drive it is, therefore, frequently more economical to employ a high-speed motor and a reduction gear than a slow-speed direct-coupled motor. Manufacturers now make motors for low-speed drives with the gear incorporated in the motor frame, the total size and cost being less than that of the corresponding slow-speed motor ; gear efficiencies ranging from about 96 per cent. for a 5 to 1 ratio to about 80 per cent. for a 50 to 1 ratio can be obtained.

Belt Drive.—Within certain limits, which include the majority of cases occurring in practice, the leather belt gives the most economical form of drive. The maximum power which can be conveniently transmitted by means of belts is, however, about 150 to 220 kW, while another limit is imposed by the speed ratio and distance between pulley centres ; typical figures for the minimum distance between pulley centres for motors of 22 to 30 kW are about 6m. for a 6 to 1 ratio and about 1·5m for a 1½ to 1 ratio. Another feature which must be taken into account is belt slip, which amounts usually to 3 or 4 per cent. A belt drive is illustrated in Fig. 31.

Rope Drive.—Drive by means of ropes running over pulleys with a number of V grooves, as shown in Fig. 37, can be used where the power is beyond the limit for belt drive. Apart from some flexibility on sudden loads, which is an advantage, the slip is negligible. This latter feature enables rope drives to be used in cases where the speed ratio is too high for a belt drive, and they are coming into use on small and medium-sized machines for this purpose.

Chain Drive.—Although considerably more expensive than a belt drive, a chain drive has a higher efficiency and no slip: furthermore, it can be satisfactorily used for much greater speed ratios, the limit being about a 6 to 1 ratio with a distance between pulley centres of about 1½ to 2 times the diameter of the larger pulley.

Direct Coupling.—If the motor can be arranged to be in line with the driven machine a direct drive can be employed. In this case no protection is afforded to the motor against sudden shocks and heavy overloads, such as would be obtained by the slipping of a belt. Flexible couplings are frequently employed to overcome this difficulty. Another feature to be guarded against is the possibility of end thrust from the driven machine, such as with a worm drive or a centrifugal pump. A typical direct drive is shown in Fig. 38, which shows induction motors driving pumps.

FIG 37.—PROTECTED MOTORS WITH V-BELT DRIVE ON TO SHAFTING IN A TEXTILE FACTORY
(*English Electric Co.*)

Vertical Drive.—Fig. 38 also illustrates in the background a motor arranged with its axis vertical, an arrangement which is frequently found convenient.

Noise

A feature of importance in choosing a motor, as well as any other apparatus, is that of noise; extreme silence is, of course, necessary in motors for domestic purposes, use in hospitals, theatres, and other similar situations, but even for ordinary industrial purposes a reduction of motor noise is often desirable. The increasing use of steel-framed buildings, which transmit noise readily, tends to make the problem of greater importance than hitherto.

FIG. 38.—ENCLOSED VENTILATED MOTORS WITH DIRECT DRIVE ON TO PUMPS. NOTE ALSO A VERTICAL TYPE OF MOTOR IN THE BACKGROUND DRIVING A LIFT PUMP.
(*Crompton Parkinson*)

Units of Noise.—Whether or not a particular motor is considered noisy is to some extent a matter of opinion and depends on the note emitted, on the nature of the surroundings, and on the amount of other noise present, so that no hard-and-fast rules on the subject can be laid down. It is necessary to have some means of specifying the loudness, or intensity, of a noise, and several methods are available for doing this, notably by stating the rms value of the excess pressure of the sound wave above atmospheric pressure or by stating the power corresponding to this pressure. The characteristic of the ear is such that apparently equal changes in loudness correspond approximately to equal intervals on a logarithmic scale of the above pressure or power; this leads to another scale of loudness, in which equal intervals correspond to equal ratios of pressure or power. The unit on this scale is the bel, which can be defined by:

$$\text{Difference in loudness} = \log_{10} \frac{W_2}{W_1} \text{ bels (B)} \quad . \quad (17)$$

where W_1 and W_2 are the powers of the sound waves under consideration. In practice the decibel (one-tenth of a bel) is a more convenient unit and represents approximately the smallest difference in sound which the ear can detect.

Thus the difference in loudness between two sounds

$$= 10 \log_{10} \frac{W_2}{W_2} \text{ decibels (dB)}$$

Since power is proportional to the square of the pressure corresponding to the sound wave, i.e. $W = kP^2$, we can write:

Difference in loudness between two sounds

$$= 10 \log_{10} \frac{kP_2{}^2}{kP_1{}^2}$$

$$= 20 \log_{10} \frac{P_2}{P_1}$$

where P_1 and P_2 are the pressures corresponding to the sound waves concerned.

In order to get an absolute scale of loudness it is necessary to adopt some arbitrary pressure as our zero, this pressure being, for convenience, just below that which gives the minimum audible sound (threshold of hearing). The pressure adopted as standard in this country for this purpose is 0·00002 N/m². This corresponds almost exactly to a power of 10^{-12} W/m² at 20°C. and 760 mm. barometric pressure.*

The loudness of a sound expressed in decibel can now be calculated if the pressure is known; for instance, consider a sound wave exerting a pressure of 0.1 N/m². The difference in loudness between this and the zero will be:

$$20 \log_{10} \left(\frac{0{\cdot}1}{0{\cdot}00002}\right)$$

$$= 20 \log_{10} 5000 = 74 \text{ dB}$$

* This is 101 325 N/m².

The maximum sound which can be heard without serious discomfort or damage to the ear has a pressure of about 100 N/m^2 and therefore on the decibel scale is:

$$20 \log_{10} \frac{100}{0{\cdot}00002} = 20 \log_{10}(5 \times 10^6)$$
$$= 134 \text{ dB.}$$

The apparent loudness of a noise as heard by the ear depends to some extent on the frequency of the note emitted; as a standard, a 1,000 HZ note has been chosen, and the decibel defined as above but referring to a 1,000 HZ note is called a "phon." Thus a noise of 80 dB would, if the note emitted by the noise has a frequency of 1,000 HZ, be 80 phons; if the note had any other frequency it would still be referred to as 80 dB.

Fig. 39 shows a number of typical engineering noises and their intensities, expressed on a pressure scale and on a decibel scale. The importance of this table, so far as the question of choosing a motor is concerned, lies in the fact that the ear behaves in such a way that any sound more than about 15 dB below the general surrounding noise will be practically inaudible; thus for a fitting shop having a general noise level of about 80 dB a motor emitting 60 dB would be inaudible and there would be no object in going to any expense in obtaining a more silent motor than this.

The noise emitted by ordinary industrial motors lies roughly between the following limits:

3.7 kW., 500 rev/min totally enclosed squirrel-cage motor, 40-50 dB.

250 kW., 3,000 rev/min enclosed ventilated induction motor, 100 dB.

By paying special attention to the mechanical and electrical design it is possible, however, to produce motors up to 11 to 15 kW which are much more silent than the above.

Elimination of Noise.—Noise may be due to purely mechanical causes, such as resonance or vibration of the laminations, or it may be due to magnetic pulsations caused by an incorrect choice of the number of slots. The elimination of such features is a matter for the manufacturer, but the user can minimise their effects by preventing transmission of the vibrations to other parts of the building—the motor may be mounted on a heavy concrete or cast-iron block or alternatively on a flexible support provided by rubber pads or springs; in either case there

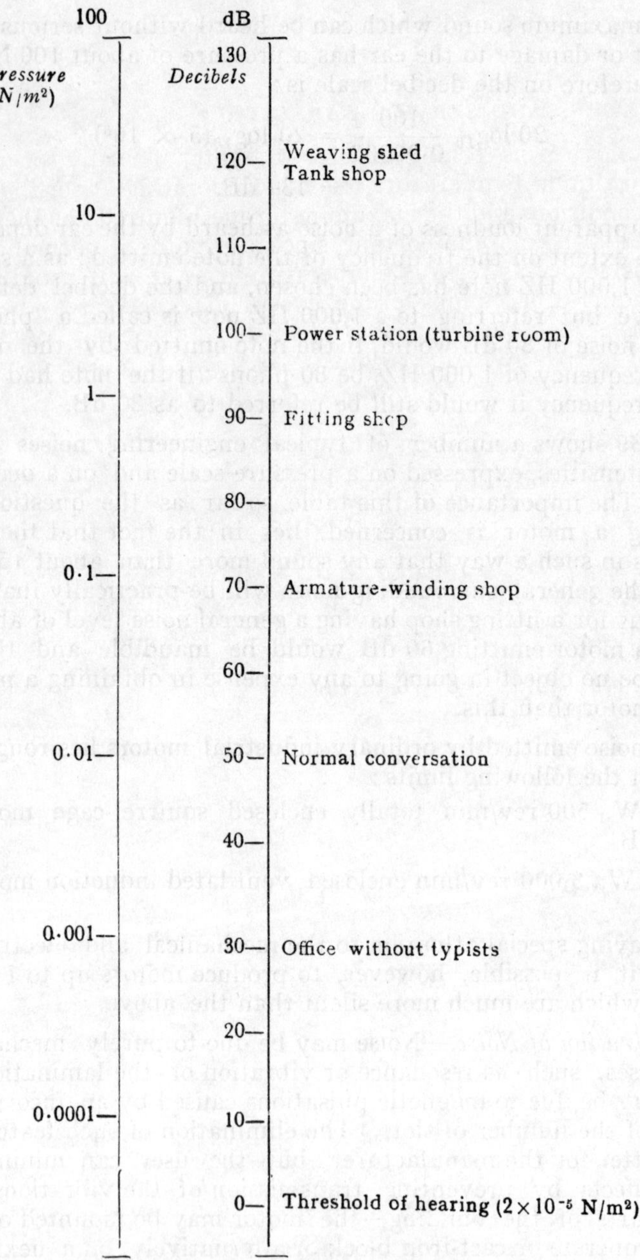

FIG. 39—TYPICAL ENGINEERING NOISES.

must be no rigid mechanical connection to the motor, such as wiring conduit.

6. RATING AND SERVICE CAPACITY

The factors governing the size of motor for any service are the maximum temperature rise when operating under the given load conditions and the maximum torque required; of these, the former is the more important, since if a motor of normal design is satisfactory as regards temperature rise it will usually give the required maximum torque, except in special cases where the load consists of heavy peaks followed by relatively long intervals of no load. The motor must also fulfil the required starting conditions as described in Section 2.

Temperature Rise

The temperature to which a motor may be allowed to rise is limited by the insulation. The maximum temperature rises which should not be exceeded by different types of motor are fully set out in the relevant Indian Standard Specifications (see Bibliography). In general it may be stated that motors equipped with Class A insulation, consisting of oil, impregnated cotton, silk, paper, or other organic material, should not be allowed to have a temperature rise of more than 40°C. as measured by a thermometer when running on continuous full load. For very arduous service, such as rolling-mill drives, motors equipped with Class B insulation (mica or asbestos with suitable binding material) are commonly used, and a limiting temperature rise of 50°C. can be adopted.

Since temperature rise is thus one of the chief features in fixing the size of a motor, its calculation becomes a matter of importance and may be carried out in the following way. It may be noted that these calculations refer not only to motors but also to any other electrical apparatus operating in accordance with the assumptions on which the calculation is based; a case of particular importance is that of the design of resistances for motor starting and control.

Heating of Motor.—The rise in temperature of a motor results from the heat generated by the losses, and an expression for this temperature rise is obtained by equating the rate at which heat is being generated by these losses to the rate at which it is being used up in raising the temperature of the motor and in dissipation from the surfaces exposed to cooling media.

Using the following symbols:

W = loss in the motor (in watts).

G = mass of motor (in kg).

s = average specific heat (*watt-seconds* to raise the temperature of unit mass through 1°C.).

$\therefore Gs$ = heat required to raise the temperature of motor through 1°C. (*watt-seconds*).

θ = temperature rise above cooling medium in °C.

θ_f = final temperature rise in °C.

A = cooling surface.

λ = rate of heat dissipation from cooling surfaces (watts per unit area per °C. rise in temperature above cooling medium).

$A\lambda$ = rate of heat dissipation in watts per °C. rise in temperature.

The following assumptions are made:

The loss W remains constant.

The heat dissipation is proportional to the temperature difference between the motor and the cooling medium.

The temperature of the cooling medium remains constant.

We therefore have:

Rate of heat generation in motor = Rate of heat absorption by motor + Rate of heat dissipation from cooling surface.

$$W = Gs\frac{d\theta}{dt} + A\lambda\theta$$

$$\therefore \quad \frac{d\theta}{\frac{W}{A\lambda}-\theta} = \frac{dt}{\frac{Gs}{A\lambda}}$$

Integrating, we have:

$$\log_e\left(\frac{W}{A\lambda}-\theta\right) = -\frac{A\lambda}{Gs}t + C \text{ (constant of integration)}$$

when $t = 0$, $\theta = \theta_1$ (initial temperature rise)

$$\therefore C = \log_e\left(\frac{W}{A\lambda}-\theta_1\right)$$

$$\therefore \log_e\left\{\frac{\frac{W}{A\lambda}-\theta}{\frac{W}{A\lambda}-\theta_1}\right\} = -\frac{\lambda A}{Gs}t$$

$$\theta = \frac{W}{A\lambda} - \left(\frac{W}{A\lambda} - \theta_1\right)_e - \frac{A\lambda}{Gs}t$$

When the final temperature rise, θ_f, is reached, all the heat generated is dissipated from the cooling surface, so that:

$$W = \lambda A \theta_f$$

$$\therefore \frac{W}{\lambda A} = \theta_f$$

The quantity $\frac{Gs}{\lambda A}$ is called the heating time-constant, T, of the motor and represents the time taken for it to heat up to 0.632 of its final value. $\left(0.632 = 1 - \frac{1}{e}\right)$.

Substituting these values in the above equation gives:

$$\theta = \theta_f - (\theta_f = \theta_1)e^{-\frac{t}{T}} \quad . \quad . \quad . \quad (18)$$

If starting form cold ($\theta_1 = 0$), this becomes:

$$\theta = \theta_f\left(1 - e^{-\frac{t}{T}}\right) \quad . \quad . \quad . \quad (18a)$$

Typical values of the heating time-constant lie between about 90 minutes for small motors of 7.5 to or 15 kW up to about 300 minutes for motors of several hundred kW.

Cooling of Motor.—In this case heat is being given out by the motor instead of being absorbed by it, but the original equation holds if it is remembered that $\frac{d\theta}{dt}$ will now be negative. If the initial temperature is now θ_2 and the final temperature θ_f', we can write, by substituting these for θ_1 and θ_f in the previous equation and rearranging in a more convenient form, since θ_2 will be greater than θ_f':

$$\theta = \theta_f' + (\theta_2 - \theta_f')e^{-\frac{t}{T'}} \quad . \quad . \quad . (19)$$

$T' = \frac{\lambda' A}{Gs}$ is the cooling time-constant. If the motor is stationary during the cooling period, λ' will not be the same as λ occurring during the heating period, as the cooling effect of the rotation of the motor will have ceased.

5

Also, if the machine is shut down so that there is no loss (W = 0 and $\theta_f' = 0$), the equation becomes :

$$\theta = \theta_2 e^{-\frac{t}{T'}} \quad . \quad . \quad . \quad (19a)$$

The curves of Fig. 40 show heating and cooling curves for a typical motor operating under different conditions. Curve A shows the temperature-rise curve obtained when the motor is run continuously on full load ; curve A is the corresponding cooling curve when the motor is shut down. Curve B represents conditions when the motor is operated on full load for a period of 17 minutes followed by a period of no load sufficiently long for the motor to cool to its initial temperature. Curve C represents the case of an intermittent load in which the interval between the full-load periods is not long enough for the motor to

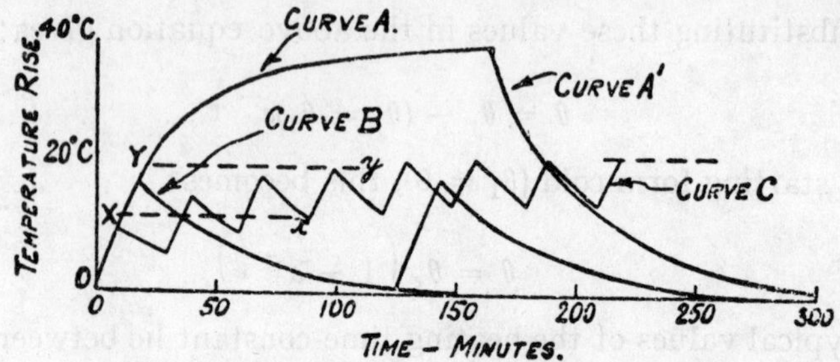

FIG. 40.—HEATING AND COOLING CURVES OF MOTOR OPERATING UNDER DIFFERENT CONDITIONS.

cool down to its initial temperature (10 min. on full load followed by 20 min. on no load). The second and third curves can easily be constructed if curves A and A are known, since they are made up of portions lying parallel to these two, e.g., the portion $x\,y$ is parallel to portion X Y.

It can be seen that the maximum temperature rise only approaches the limiting figure of 40°C. when the motor is run on a continuous load ; for intermittent loads a motor of a smaller size could have been used without exceeding the safe temperature rise, or, alternatively, the same motor could have given greater output.

Standard Ratings

The above considerations give rise to two alternative methods of rating or specifying the output of a motor, and these have been standardised by the Indian Standards Institution as follows :

Continuous Rating.—The output which a motor can give continuously without exceeding the temperature rise specified by the appropriate Iss. A continuously rated motor can also give 25 per cent. overload for 2 hours.

Continuous Maximum Rating.—Similar to continuous rating but not permitting any overload. It is only used for motors larger than 1.5 kW per rev/mim.

Short-time Rating.—The output which a motor can give for a specified period (1 hour, ½ hour, ¼ hour, etc.), without exceeding the specified temperature rise, the motor being assumed to start from cold.

Continuously Rated Motors.—For drives requiring fairly constant powers, such as fans, air compressors, etc., the choice of the correct size of motor is simple, since it is necessary merely to determine the power required and choose a motor having a continuous rating equal to this ; it is, however, worth while to take considerable trouble to find out exactly how much power the driven machine actually consumes, since if the motor chosen be too small it will be overloaded and will, therefore, overheat and deteriorate, while if it is too big the efficiency and power factor will probably be less than those of a motor of the correct size, since it would not be running at full load.

If there is no possibility of an overload, a motor with a continuous maximum rating can be selected; such a motor may run at a higher temperature (55°C. instead of 40°C.) and will therefore be smaller in dimensions and consequently cheaper.

Motors for Intermittent Loads.—The problem with intermittent loads is to choose a continuously or short-time rated motor which, when operating on the given load cycle, will not exceed the specified temperature rise. In many cases the 1-, ½-, or ¼-hour rating conditions may correspond approximately to the actual load conditions, in which case the choice is a simple matter and consists merely in choosing a motor rated at the required horsepower for the given period.

If, however, the load fluctuates in value over a given cycle, as in a rolling-mill or colliery-winding motor (Figs. 41 and 54), the only accurate method of procedure is to determine the heating and cooling curves of the range of motors under consideration and then plot a heating curve for each motor when operating on the given cycle: the smallest size of motor which does not exceed the safe temperature rise should then be chosen for the drive.

If it may be assumed that the heating of the motor be proportional to the square of the current (the basis of this assumption being that the load is proportional to the current and the loss is proportional to the square of the current), then the equivalent continuous rating can be found by taking the rms value of the load curve and choosing a motor having a continuous rating equal to this. This method is very frequently used, since the data for drawing accurately the heating and cooling curves of the motors are rarely available. Examples 5 and 6 illustrate calculations of this nature.

Example 5:—A 18·5-kw motor has a heating time-constant of 90 minutes and when run continuously on full load attaining a temperature of 45°C above the surrounding air. What would be the ½ hour rating of the motor for this temperature rise, assuming that it cools down completely between each load period and that the losses are proportional to the square of the load?

Solution :

When the final temperature is reached, all the losses are dissipated and the temperature rise attained is proportional to the losses:

If P is the ½ hour rating of the motor, then the losses at this load would be:

$$\text{Original losses} \times (P/18{\cdot}5)^2$$

The final temperature rise, θ_f if run continuously at P kW, is given by:

$$\frac{\theta'_f}{\theta_f} = \frac{\text{losses at P kW}}{\text{Original losses}} = \left(\frac{P}{18{\cdot}5}\right)^2$$

Where θ_f is the temperature rise at 18.5 kW

$$\therefore \theta_f' = \theta_f \left(\frac{P}{18{\cdot}5}\right)^2 = 45 \left(\frac{P}{18{\cdot}5}\right)^2 {}^\circ\text{C}$$

From equation 18(*a*), the temperature rise at any time is given by:

$$\theta = \theta_f \left(1 - e^{-\frac{t}{T}}\right)$$

∴ After 30 min, when temperature rise must not exceed 45°C

$$45 = 45 \left(\frac{P}{18{\cdot}5}\right)^2 \left[1 - e^{-\frac{30}{90}}\right]$$

$$= 45\left(\frac{P}{18{\cdot}5}\right)^2\left[1 - \frac{1}{1{\cdot}394}\right]$$

$$\therefore P^2 = \frac{(18{\cdot}5)^2}{0{\cdot}283}$$

$$\therefore P = 34{\cdot}8 \text{ kW or say } \mathbf{35\ kW}.$$

Example 6 :—A motor, driving a colliery winding equipment, has to deliver a load rising uniformly from zero to a maximum of 1500 kW in 20s during the accelerating period, 750 kW for 40s during the full speed period and during the acceleration period of

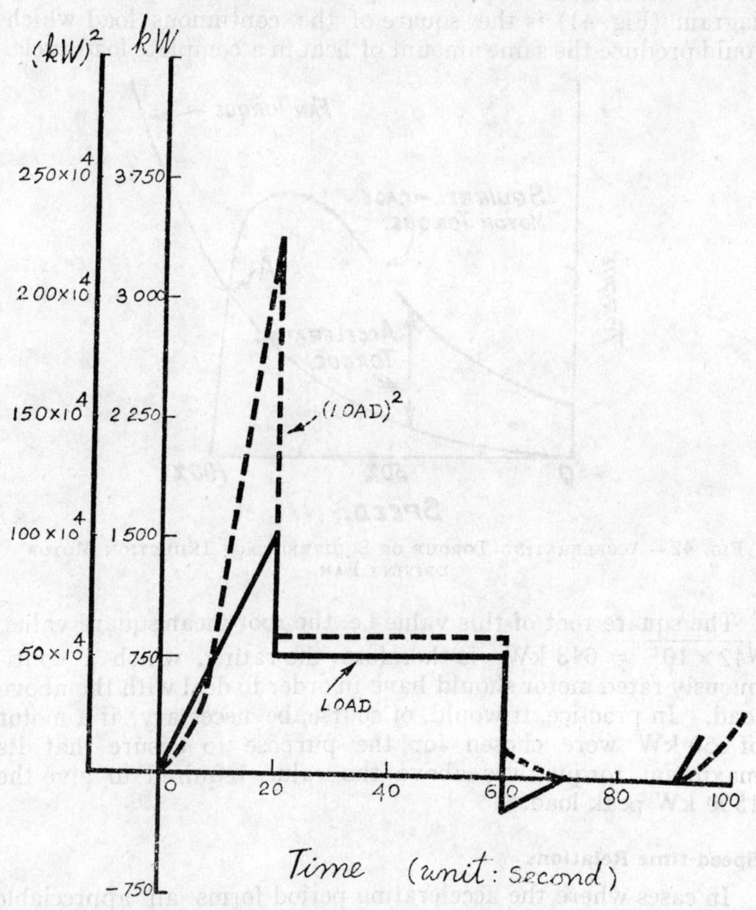

FIG. 41

10s, when regenerative braking is taking place, the kW returned to the supply falls from an initial value of 250 kW to zero. The interval for decking before the next load cycle starts is 20s. Estimate a suitable kilowatt rating for the motor.

Solution :

The load curve is shown by the full line in Fig. 41, the heat produced which governs the rating of the motor to be chosen is proportional to the square of the load, and the (load) curve is, therefore, plotted as shown by the dotted curve. The average value of this curve can be found, and this gives the average rate at which heat is produced ; this value (42×10^4) in the diagram (Fig. 41) is the square of the continuous load which would produce the same amount of heat in a complete load cycle.

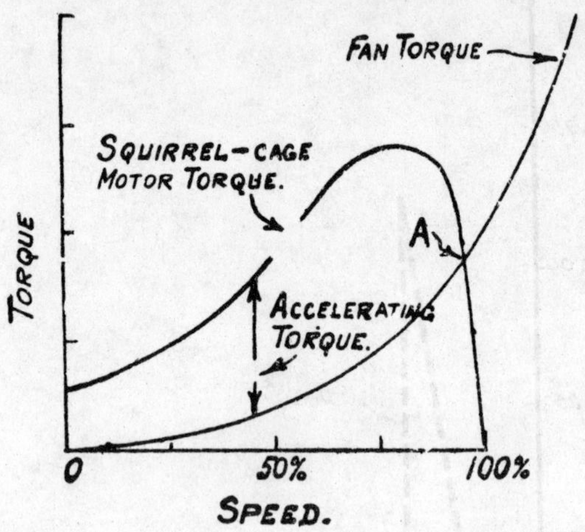

FIG. 42.—ACCELERATING TORQUE OF SQUIRREL-CAGE INDUCTION MOTOR DRIVING FAN.

The square root of this value i.e. the root mean square value, $\sqrt{42 \times 10^4} = 648$ kW, is therefore the rating, which a continuously rated motor should have in order to deal with the above load. In practice, it would, of course, be necessary, if a motor of 650 kW were chosen for the purpose to ensure that its maximum torque was above the value required to give the 1500 kW peak load.

Speed-time Relations

In cases where the accelerating period forms an appreciable proportion of the total time during which a motor is in operation it is necessary to investigate the time taken to accelerate the load in order that the most suitable type and size of motor may be chosen for the purpose; this is done by determining the speed-time relationships during acceleration and also, when electric braking is employed, during the braking period. These investigations are of particular importance when dealing with various forms of haulage problem, such as with mine winding gear, electric lifts, etc., but they also occur quite frequently in industrial practice.

Torque-speed Curve.—It is first necessary to obtain the torque-speed curve of both the motor and the load during the period concerned (accelerating or braking). The difference between the motor torque and the load torque represents the torque available for accelerating or retarding the moving parts. These torques are illustrated in Fig. 42 for the case of a squirrel-cage induction motor accelerating a fan. The load torque is proportional to the square of the speed, while the motor torque follows the usual shape for the squirrel-cage motor; at the point A the motor torque becomes equal to the load torque (having previously been greater), so that no further acceleration can take place, and this represents the maximum speed which the motor can attain under these particular conditions.

When dealing with haulage problems, it is convenient to use tractive effort applied to the rope or the driving wheels of the vehicle instead of torque, and speed is more conveniently measured in metres per second or some other linear unit than in rev/min.

If T is the torque at the motor shaft in N. m, the torque at the axle of the driving wheel or rope drum $= T \times G \times \eta$ N.m. where η is the efficiency of the gear and G is the gear ratio.

Tractive effort at periphery of wheel or drum:

$$= \frac{T \times G \times \eta \times 2}{D} \text{ newtons (N),}$$

where D = diameter of wheel or drum (in metres).

Similarly, if the motor speed is N rev/min, the peripheral speed of the driving wheel or drum is:

$$\text{speed} = \frac{\pi N D}{60G} \ m s^{-1}$$

—

Having determined the torque T_M or tractive effort T_E at any instant, the acceleration at that instant can be found from the well-known dynamical formulae:

Linear Motion

$$\text{Acceleration} = f = \left(\frac{T_E}{m}\right) m\ s^{-2}, \quad . \quad . \quad . \quad . \qquad (20a)$$

where T_E is in newtons (N),

m is mass of the moving parts in kilograms (kg)

Angular Motion

$$\text{Acceleration} = \alpha = \left(\frac{T_M}{I}\right) \text{rad}\ s^{-2}, \quad . \quad . \quad . \qquad (20b)$$

where T_M is in newton-metres (N.m)

I is moment of inertia of moving parts in kg. m²

Speed time Relation: Having thus determined the acceleration, the speed-time relation can be found as follows:

Linear Motion

$$f = \left(\frac{dv}{dt}\right), \text{ where } f \text{ is the linear speed } (ms^{-1})$$

$$t = \int \frac{1}{f}\, dv \text{ seconds (s)} \quad . \quad . \quad . \qquad (21a)$$

Angular Motion

$$\alpha = \frac{d\omega}{dt}$$

where ω is angular speed (rad/s)

$$t = \int \frac{1}{\alpha}\, d\omega \text{ seconds (s)} \quad . \quad . \quad . \qquad (21b)$$

In cases where the accelerating (or braking) torque or tractive effort is constant or is a simple function of the speed, the above integrations can be performed mathematically, as in Examples 7 and 8. In other cases they must be performed graphically, as in Example 14.

Speed-distance Curve.—In addition to finding the time taken it is often necessary to determine also the distance travelled or the number of revolutions made during acceleration or braking.

Linear Motion

$$v = \frac{ds}{dt}$$

where s = distance travelled

$$s = \int v dt \quad . \quad . \quad . \quad . \quad . \quad (22a)$$

Angular Motion

$$\omega = \frac{2\pi dr}{dt}$$

where r = number of revolutions made

$$r = \frac{1}{2\pi}\int \omega dt \quad . \quad . \quad . \quad . \quad . \quad (22b)$$

Again, the integrations may be carried out mathematically if v or ω are simple functions of t, or graphically in other cases (see Example 14).

Typical Figures for Stored Energy

It is convenient and usual to express the inertia of rotating machinery as stored energy per kW, typical figures for which are given in Tables II and III for motors and various driven machines. These are taken from much more detailed information given by Anderson.* Having a figure for stored energy per kW, the moment of inertia, I, can easily be found from :

Total stored energy = $\frac{1}{2}$ Iω^2 N.m (or J)

$$\therefore \mathrm{I} = \frac{\text{total stored energy} \times 2}{\omega^2} \text{ kg.m}^2$$

TABLE II

STORED ENERGY IN ROTOR

kW	J/kW	
	400-700 rev/min	1300-1500 rev/min
7·5	180	220
37	310	630
75	420	1250

* *J.I.E.E.* vol. 60, p. 619.

TABLE III
STORED ENERGY IN DRIVEN MACHINES

	J/kW
Lathes and drills	540
Shop shafting	1450-1800
Punching machines	3600
Disc saws for wood	3400-6800
Centrifugal hydro-extractor	110 000/145 000

Example 7 :—A-75-kW, 500-rev/min d.c. shunt motor is being used to drive machinery for which the figure for stored energy per kilowatt is 5400 joules. Estimate the time taken to start the motor if the load torque is equal to full load torque during the starting period and the current is limited to $1\frac{1}{2}$ times full-load current.

Solution :

$$\text{Full load torque} = \frac{75 \times 1000 \times 60}{2\pi \times 500} = 1430 \text{ N.m}$$

Torque during starting (assumed constant) = 2145 N.m.

Torque available for acceleration = 715 N.m

Stored energy = 5400 × 75 = 405 000 J

$$\omega = 500 \times \frac{2\pi}{60} = 52 \text{ rad/s}$$

$$\text{I} = \frac{2 \times 405\,000}{52^2} = 300 \text{ kg/m}^2$$

Assuming the current, and therefore, the torque, during the starting period to be constant, we have from equations (20b) and (21b):

$$\alpha = \frac{\text{T}}{\text{I}} = \frac{715}{300} = 2{\cdot}38 \text{ rad/s}^{-2}$$

$$t = \int \frac{1}{\alpha} d\omega$$

In this case, α is constant, so that the integration can be performed very simply :

$$t = \frac{1}{\alpha} \cdot \omega + \text{C}$$

$$\text{when } t = 0, \omega = 0 \quad \therefore \text{C} = 0$$

$$t = \frac{1}{2{\cdot}38} \times 52 = \mathbf{21{\cdot}8} \text{ s.}$$

Example 8 :—A-2 200-V, 110-kW, 750-rev/min synchronous motor driving rubber-making machinery having a total moment of inertia of 60kg.m² employs rheostatic braking for obtaining rapid stopping in cases of emergency. When the mill is running on full-load, estimate the time taken and the number of revolutions made before the motor is stopped after switching on a star connected braking resistance of 13 Ω per phase.

Solution :

$$\text{Full-load torque} = \frac{110\times1000\times60}{2\pi\times750} = 1400 \text{ N.m}$$

$$\text{Full-load line current} = \frac{110\times1000}{\sqrt{3}\times2\ 200\times0{\cdot}93}$$

$$= 31 \text{ A} \quad \text{(assuming 93\% efficiency and cos. } \phi = 1)$$

Approximate line current at start of braking period (neglecting impedance drops) ;

$$= \frac{2000}{\sqrt{3}\times13} = 98 \text{ A}$$

This is approximately 3 times full-load current and will produce approximately 3 times full-load torque assuming the excitation to be held constant. Therefore,

Initial electric braking torque = 4200 N.m

Total initial braking torque = 4200+1400=5600 N.m.

It has been shown (Eqn. 16) that with constant excitation, the electric braking torque is proportional to speed.

If T_F is the mechanical braking torque due to the load (assumed constant in this case) and T_E is the electric braking torque we have,

Total braking torque : $T_B = T_F + T_E = T_F + kW$

Now, $$\omega = \frac{750\times2\pi}{60} = 78{\cdot}5 \text{ rad/s}$$

$$T_E = 4200 \text{ N.m}$$

and therefore, $$K = \frac{4\ 200}{78{\cdot}5} = 53{\cdot}5$$

Thus, retardation $$\beta = \frac{T_B}{I} = \frac{T_F + K\omega}{I}$$

$$t = \int\frac{1}{\beta}\,d\omega$$

Since β is a simple function of ω this can easily be integrated:

$$t = \text{I}\int \frac{\text{I}}{\text{T}_\text{F}+\text{K}\omega}\, d\omega$$

$$= \frac{\text{I}}{\text{K}} \log_e (\text{T}_\text{F} + \text{K}\omega) + \text{C}$$

when t = O, $\omega = \omega_1$ (initial speed)

$$\therefore \text{C} = \frac{\text{I}}{\text{K}} \log_e (\text{T}_\text{F}+\text{K}\omega_1)$$

$$t = \frac{\text{I}}{\text{K}} \log_e \frac{(\text{T}_\text{F} + \text{K}\omega_1)}{(\text{T}_\text{F} + \text{K}\omega)}$$

$$= \text{time taken to reach speed } \omega$$

Putting in numerical values for the case when $\omega = 0$,

$$t = \frac{60}{53{\cdot}5} \log_e \left(\frac{5600}{1400}\right) = 1{\cdot}12 \log_e 4 = 1{\cdot}55 \text{ s.}$$

To find the number of revolutions we have: $r = \dfrac{1}{2\pi}\displaystyle\int \omega dt$

From the above expression for t:

$$\frac{\text{T}_\text{F}+\text{K}\omega_1}{\text{T}_\text{F}+\text{K}\omega} = e^{\frac{\text{K}}{\text{I}}t}$$

$$\therefore \omega = \frac{\text{I}}{\text{K}}\left\{(\text{T}_\text{F}+\text{K}\omega_1)e^{-\frac{\text{K}}{\text{I}}t} - \text{T}_\text{F}\right\}$$

$$\therefore r = \frac{1}{2\pi\text{K}}\int\left\{(\text{T}_\text{F}+\text{K}\omega_1)e^{-\frac{\text{K}}{\text{I}}t} - \text{T}_\text{F}\right\} dt$$

$$= -\frac{1}{2\pi\text{K}}(\text{T}_\text{F}+\text{K}\omega_1)\frac{\text{I}}{\text{K}}e^{-\frac{\text{K}}{\text{I}}t} - \frac{\text{T}_\text{F}}{2\pi\text{K}}t + \text{C}$$

when $t = 0, r = 0, \therefore \text{C} = \dfrac{\text{T}_\text{F}+\text{K}\omega_1}{2\pi\text{K}} \cdot \dfrac{\text{I}}{\text{K}}$

$$\therefore r = \frac{\text{I}}{\text{K}} \cdot \frac{\text{T}_\text{F}+\text{K}\omega_1}{2\pi\text{K}}(1 - e^{-\frac{\text{K}}{\text{I}}t}) - \frac{\text{T}_\text{F}}{2\pi\text{K}}t$$

Putting in the numerical values:

$$r = 1{\cdot}12 \times \frac{5600}{2\pi\times53{\cdot}5}(-e^{-0{\cdot}893\times1{\cdot}55}) - \frac{1400}{2\pi\times53{\cdot}5} \times 1{\cdot}95$$

$$= 7{\cdot}55 \text{ revs.}$$

As the actual rollers of rubber-making machinery are geared down to a very low speed, this number of revolutions of the motor will correspond to only 25mm or 50mm movement of the rollers.

FIG. 43.—DRUM-TYPE INDUSTRIAL CONTROLLER, SHOWING BARREL (ON RIGHT) AND CONTACT FINGERS THE ARC SHIELD (ON LEFT) HAS BEEN SWUNG CLEAR OF THE CONTACTS FOR INSPECTION. (*English Electric Co.*)

7. CONTROL GEAR

For the starting, reversing, speed control, and braking of electric motors, as described in previous sections of this chapter, suitable switches are required for opening and closing the necessary circuits and for opearting rheostats. This apparatus, together with the protective equipment for guarding against faults or careless usage, is known as the control gear, and may be classified according to the method of operation as follows :

Hand-operated Equipment, in which the switches and rheostats are operated manually, as in the ordinary face-plate motor starter or field rheostat.

Master Controller Equipment, in which the switches are operated by solenoids, these being controlled by a small hand-operated master switch or controller.

Fully Automatic Equipment, in which an operation is initiated by the closing of a single master switch or push button, after which the correct sequence of operations is carried out automatically.

In all cases protective equipment must also be provided according to circumstances, as described later on.

Hand-operated Equipment

The use of hand-operated equipment is limited partly by the voltage, which should not exceed about 600 unless special safety precautions are taken, and partly by the current-carrying capacity of switches of a design suitable for operation by hand.

Face-plate Starters.—The face-plate starter is familiar as a means of starting d.c. and slip-ring induction motors up to about 37 or 45kW. Its application is limited to motors up to this size by the current-carrying capacity of the contacts, and also by its susceptibility to damage due to arcing.

Drum-type Controllers.—When heavier currents have to be dealt with, a more robust and convenient arrangement consists of a drum upon which are mounted contact strips. Heavy contact fingers bear on these strips, the latter being arranged in such a manner that when the drum is rotated the proper sequence of connections between the different contact fingers is made. By a suitable arrangement of the contact strips on the drum, a controller of this type can be used for reversing, braking, and certain forms of speed control, as well as for plain motor starting. The construction of a drum-type controller is shown in Fig. 43, while Fig. 44 shows a controller mounted on site for operating a motor driving haulage gear at a colliery. The conventional method of representing the connections diagrammatically is shown in Fig. 45 (*a*) : the drum is assumed to be spread out flat with the contact strips shown in thick black lines. The contact fingers are shown on the left, and as the drum is rotated these may be assumed to occupy successively the positions, 1, 2, 3, etc., for forward operation, and 0·3, 6·0, 0·9 metre, etc., for reverse operation. The particular case illustrated is for the starting of a series motor in either direction, with the resistance cut out in four steps, and the circuit connections for each controller position are shown in the schematic diagram of Fig. 45(*b*). The contact fingers are of heavy copper section, and are separated by heat-resisting shields, in which is incorporated a magnetic blow-out coil to assist in extinguishing the arc, so that heavy currents can be dealt with, and the whole construction is such as to be able to withstand

FIG. 44—TOTALLY ENCLOSED MOTOR WITH DUST-PROOF SLIP-RING COVER GEARED TO HAULAGE EQUIPMENT AND OPERATED BY A DRUM-TYPE CONTROLLER.

(*Crompton Parkinson*)

hard usage. The most common application of the drum-type controller is for the control of trams, but it is also widely used for the operation of cranes, hoists, machine tools, and heavy industrial drives requiring powers up to about 112·5 kW.

Plural Starting.—In cases where there are several motors situated fairly close to each other, as may occur on board ship or in a boiler house, it is possible to use a single starter for all the motors, selector switches being provided to connect it to any desired motor. Such a scheme can be used where the size of the largest motor of the group does not exceed about 10 times that of the smallest, and it effects an obvious saving in capital cost of starting equipment, although this is partly offset by extra costs of wiring.

Control of Squirrel-cage Induction Motors.—Starting of squirrel-cage induction motors is carried out by direct switching, by a star-delta switch, or by an auto-transformer, as described in Section 2 of this chapter. For any of these methods a simple type of switch can be used for any of the sizes for which the squirrel-cage motor is normally used.

Field Rheostats.—Shunt or separately excited field circuits of d.c. machines and field circuits of synchronous machines carry currents which do not usually exceed about 10 A in the

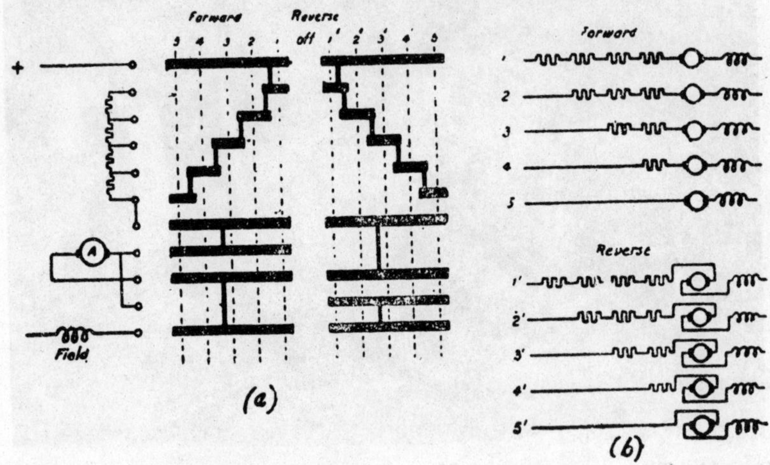

FIG. 45.—HAND-OPERATED CONTROLLER FOR STARTING D.C. SERIES MOTOR.

largest sizes, and field rheostats of the face-plate type are standard practice. To obtain fine control (i.e. small steps of resistance) as many as 50 steps of resistance may be required.

Liquid Rheostats.—Instead of the usual grid or wire resistance, which is varied in a definite number of steps, a liquid resistance is sometimes employed consisting of two movable electrodes in a wooden or earthenware vessel containing water with a small amount of soda in solution ; the resistance is varied by raising or lowering the electrodes, thus producing a smooth resistance variation. A single electrode in a metal tank, the latter serving as the other electrode, can be used in cases where it is permissible to earth one electrode, or where the tank can be insulated from earth. Owing to its simplicity, this type of rheostat can easily be constructed for temporary use; it has the advantage that the resistance is varied smoothly instead of in steps, but against this must be set the fact that the actual value of the resistance for a given position of the plates changes with temperature and with the chemical state of the water; evaporation also occurs, which must be made up from time to time. As the heat-dissipating capacity is less than that of a grid resistance, a liquid rheostat will be more bulky, and it is therefore not widely used except in very large sizes, where it is practicable to provide artificial cooling by circulating the liquid through a cooler; in such cases the electrodes generally remain stationary and the liquid is pumped into or out of the tank. Electrolytic corrosion of the electrodes and electrolysis of the water limit the use of the liquid rheostat for d.c. circuits, but it is frequently used for starting induction motors of 750—1500kW such as are required for the drive of colliery winding gear or rolling mills.

Design of Resistance of Elements.—The method of determining the values of the steps of resistance required for starting and control of motors is described in textbooks on Electrical Technology or Electric Machinery. The calculation of the other important factor arising in the design, namely, the temperature rise, is carried out exactly as described earlier for a motor.

Master Controller Equipment

The master controller is similar in construction to the drum-type hand-operated controller, but instead of dealing with the main currents it only controls the energising currents of solenoid-operated switches, such switches being commonly known as contactors. In Fig. 46 are shown the connections of an equipment of this type which performs the same functions as the hand-operated equipment shown in Fig. 45. The diagram is schematic in that the operating coils are all shown, for ease in tracing out the connections, adjacent to the master controller, whereas they are, of course, actually a part of their respective contactors and connected by suitable leads to the appropriate contacts on the controller. The sequence chart shown on the right of the diagram illustrates the usual method of showing at a glance which of the contactors are closed for any position of the controller; a cross in the square opposite the contactor number and in any controller position indicates that the contactor of that number is closed with the controller in that position—for instance, in the forward controller position 3, contactors 1, 3, 5, and 6 are closed.

The operating currents of the contactors are usually not more than about half an ampere, and with d.c. equipments the supply for these can often be conveniently obtained from the same source of supply as that for the motor, as shown in the diagram; contactors for a.c. motors, however, are usually operated by a special source of direct current obtained either from a battery or a rectifier, since the design and operation of a.c. contactors present certain difficulties, due to vibration and noise. The connections between the controller and the contactors only have to deal with very small currents, so that the

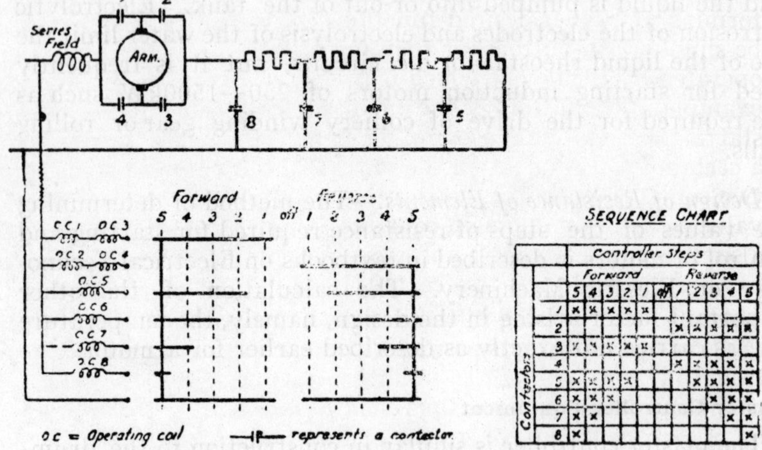

Contactors	Forward 5	Forward 4	Forward 3	Forward 2	Forward 1	Off	Reverse 1	Reverse 2	Reverse 3	Reverse 4	Reverse 5
1	×	×	×	×	×						
2							×	×	×	×	×
3	×	×	×	×	×						
4							×	×	×	×	×
5	×	×	×	×				×	×	×	×
6	×	×	×						×	×	×
7	×	×								×	×
8	×										×

FIG. 46.—STARTER WITH MASTER CONTROLLER FOR D.C. SERIES MOTOR.

controller can easily be placed at some distance from the motor, as in the case of a passenger lift, where the controller is placed in the lift itself and connected through a flexible cable to the control gear placed at the top of the lift shaft. Another feature is the possibility of employing duplicate controllers so that the motor may be operated from two or more points; suitable interlocks must, of course, be provided to prevent more than one being in use at the same time.

The master controller equipment thus possesses many advantages over the simple hand-operated control gear, and it can be used for dealing with motors up to any size; a certain amount of skill and care are, however, required for its operation, just as with the hand-operated equipment.

Fully Automatic Equipment

From the operational point of view, fully automatic equipment is the simplest of the three types mentioned, although electrically it is the most complicated and expensive. To start an automatically controlled motor the operator merely has to close a control switch, which causes the main contactors to operate, after which the succeeding contactors (accelerating contactors) close in their correct sequence and with suitable time intervals to cut out the steps of starting resistance or make other changes in connections. Stopping is performed by closing a second switch, which de-energises all the contactors; other switches can also be provided for raising or lowering the speed or performing any other desired function. The control switches may be simple push-buttons, or they may be the contacts of a relay operated by the device which it is desired to control; a common example of the latter is the float switch frequently used for starting and stopping a pump when the water in a tank reaches a certain level—a float on the surface of the water short-circuits two contacts when the level reaches a certain predetermined value and causes the main contactor of the pump motor to close; a similar device operates and stops the motor when the water has been pumped out to a certain level.

Any number of push-buttons or control relays may be provided and situated in various positions so that control may be obtained from different points. In addition to providing the simplest possible means of control, thus enabling the motor to be operated by unskilled labour, or, in the case of a machine tool, enabling the operator to concentrate on the work in hand, the automatic equipment possesses another important advantage—the accelerating contactors can be arranged to give the maximum possible acceleration consistent with safety whatever the load on the machine, thus protecting the equipment against excess currents and also saving time by always accelerating the motor as quickly as possible. This feature prevents overloading of the starting resistances and they need not, therefore, be so liberally rated as in the case of a hand-operated equipment. These advantages are tending to increase the applications of fully automatic equipment, in spite of the fact that it costs about three times as much as the corresponding manual equipment. A typical automatic control panel is shown in Fig. 47.

Accelerating Contactors.—The most common application of automatic equipment is for the starting of motors by cutting out steps of resistance. Several methods are available for ensuring operation of the appropriate contactors in the correct sequence and with the correct time interval.

(i) *Current-limit Relays.*—The diagram in Fig. 48 illustrates the principle of equipment for the fully automatic starting of a d.c. series motor with the accelerating contactors controlled on the current-limit principle; the operations performed are exactly

FIG. 47.—TYPICAL AUTOMATIC CONTROL PANEL.

similar to those of the equipments illustrated in Figs. 45 and 46. Pressing either the forward or reverse start-button energises the operating coil of one of the pairs of main contactors A or B. When one of these has closed, the motor will start in the required direction, forward or reverse, and the rush of current will cause relay C to lift; as the motor speeds up the current falls until at a predetermined value relay C falls and closes the operating-coil circuit of the second accelerating contactor D, thus causing it to close and cut out the first step of resistance ; as the current falls again the process is repeated with the next contactor, and so on until all the contactors have closed. The start-button, after being pressed, must, of course, remain closed so long as the motor is required to run.

Stopping is carried out by the stop-button, which de-energises the operating coils of the main contactors, causing these to open the main circuit and also the operating-coil circuits for the accelerating contactors; pressing the stop-button must also release, by a mechanical or electrical interlock, the start-button so that it returns to the open position.

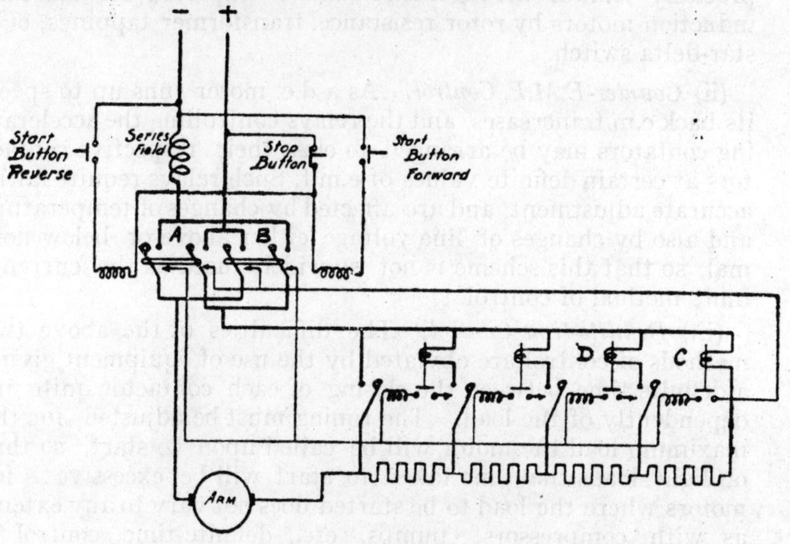

FIG. 48.—FULLY AUTOMATIC STARTER FOR D.C. SERIES MOTOR

A *self-sealing* contact is usually added to the main contactor; this is a contact which closes when the main contactor closes and short-circuits the start button, thus enabling this to be released. Such a device is shown in the equipment illustrated in Figs. 50 and 51.

It is evident that the relay C must lift before the current has had time to rise in the operating coil of the succeeding contactor; this does not usually introduce any difficulty, on account of the relatively high time constant of the operating coil, but sticking of the relay C might cause maloperation, and various modifications of the above simple arrangement have been developed to avoid such a contingency.

With any current-limit arrangement, the time between the closing of successive contactors depends upon the rate at which the current falls. With a lightly loaded motor this will fall quickly and the motor will start quickly, whilst with a heavy load the starting period will be longer ; this is a desirable state of affairs, and the chief danger lies in trying to start a load which is so heavy that the current never falls to the lower limit at which the relays C, D, etc., fall : some or all of the resistance will then be left in circuit and will inevitably be burnt out.

Although the above description applies to d.c. motors, a precisely similar arrangement can be employed for starting induction motors by rotor resistance, transformer tappings, or a star-delta switch.

(ii) *Counter-E.M.F. Control.*—As a d.c. motor runs up to speed its back e.m.f. increases, and the relays controlling the accelerating contators may be arranged to close their respective contactors at certain definite values of e.m.f. Such relays require fairly accurate adjustment, and are affected by changes of temperature and also by changes of line voltage either above or below normal, so that this scheme is not so widely used as the current-limit method of control.

(iii) *Definite-time Control.*—The difficulties of the above two methods of control are obviated by the use of equipment giving a definite time between the closing of each contactor quite independently of the load. The timing must be adjusted for the maximum load the motor will be called upon to start, so that on light loads the time taken to start will be excessive : for motors where the load to be started does not vary to any extent, as with compressors, pumps, etc., definite-time control is eminently suitable. Various ingenious devices have been used for providing the definite time-interval. A small vessel similar to an egg boiler and containing mercury may be attached to the contactor and tilted when the contactor closes so that mercury runs through the neck into the lower half of the chamber ; on reaching a certain level it covers two contacts in the energising circuit of the succeeding contactor. Another system employs a clockwork mechanism, which is started by the closing of a contactor and which energises the succeeding contactor after a certain fixed time.

(iv) *Motor-operated Controller or Camshaft.*—The contactors may be operated by a drum controller, as in the master controller type of equipment, except that the controller is driven by an electric motor; alternatively, the motor may drive a camshaft which acts directly on the contactors. In either case the auxiliary motor is started by means of a push-botton and automatically stopped, when at the end of its travel, by a special contact on the shaft. Stopping of the main motor is carried out by a second push-botton, which de-energises the contactors and causes the controller or camshaft to return to the starting position. With this equipment a definite time-interval between the closing of the successive contactors is obtained.

Protective Devices and Interlocks

Protective devices must be incorporated in the control equipment to guard against overloads or other conditions dangerous to the motor or the driven machine, and also to guard against faulty or careless operation of the equipment itself. The conditions against which the motor should be protected are

Overload.—Applicable to all types of motor to prevent the motor from overheating.

Low Voltage.—Applicable to all types of motor to prevent full voltage being applied to it with the starter in the full-on position after a temporary failure of the supply.

Overspeed.—Occasionally desirable with d.c. and some a.c. commutator motors.

Overheating of Bearings or other Mechanical Parts.—Desirable in large motors which have to operate for long periods without attention.

In addition to the above it is possible to install apparatus to shut down the motor in case of any trouble on the driven machine. In a belt-conveyor system, for instance, where different sections of the conveyor are driven by different motors, a stoppage of any motor is made to shut down all the others to prevent accumulation and possible damage to the conveyed goods.

Overload Protection.—Overload protection is necessary to prevent overheating of the motor and its supply cables due to excess currents. An excess current lasting for only a second or two will not normally do any serious damage in this respect, so that whatever overload device is employed should possess a time lag to ensure that it operates only for a sustained overload. The characteristics of the two usual types of time lag are illustrated in Fig. 49. A definite time lag, produced usually by some mechanical device, as described on page 86, will cause the motor to be tripped out of circuit when a certain predetermined value of current has been exceeded for a certain length of time. Apparatus having an inverse time lag will trip the motor out after a very short interval on a heavy overload but after a relatively long interval on a small overload; this is obviously a more satisfactory characteristic for most purposes, since the temperature of the motor will rise much more quickly on a heavy overload. This inverse-time characteristic is possessed by certain special types of relay, by a fuse, and also by an ordinary solenoid relay fitted with an oil dashpot.

It is not practicable to obtain time lags of more than a minute or so with the above devices, so that the time lag is usually very much less than the time taken to heat up the motor.

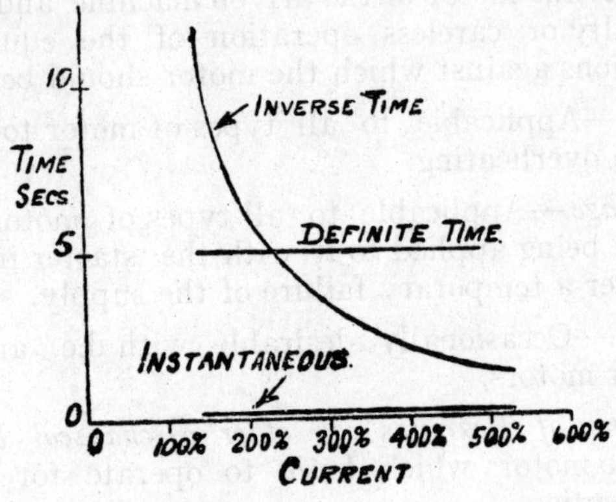

FIG. 49.—OVERLOAD RELAY CHARACTERISTICS.

Improved protection can be obtained by the use of a thermal relay, which operates by virtue of the expansion of a special metal strip due to heat generated by the motor current. When this strip attains a certain predetermined temperature, it is arranged to close two contacts which shut down the motor; if the rate of heating and cooling of the strip is made equal to that of the motor, then as soon as the motor reaches its maximum safe temperature the thermal relay will also have attained this temperature (or a value proportional to it) and it can be made to shut down the motor at this value. In practice very satisfactory operation can be obtained with this type of equipment.

Overload relays or fuses need only be placed in two of the three phases of a three-phase machine if the neutral of the system is not earthed, but should be placed in all three phases if it is earthed. Although an overload relay arranged to trip the main switch is more expensive than a fuse, it has the advantage that it automatically resets itself when the switch is reclosed.

Low-voltage Release.—This protection is necessary, partly to prevent heavy currents and possible damage to the motor and its driven machine if full voltage were applied after a temporary shutdown, and partly to protect the operator of the equipment, who may take advantage of the shut-down to make some adjustments in the driven machine and who might, therefore, be seriously injured if it were to restart unexpectedly. The low-voltage release consists usually of a simple solenoid held up by the voltage of the supply and which, if this fails, causes the starting equipment to return to the " off " position.

Overspeed Protection.—A centrifugal device operates at a certain predetermined speed, usually about 20 per cent. above normal, and causes the motor to be shut down.

Overheating of Bearings.—Thermocouples can be placed in the bearings or in other desired situations and arranged so that when the temperature reaches a certain figure relays are operated which cause the motor to be shut down or alarm bells to be rung.

Protection against Maloperation of Control Gear.—In addition to the features cited above to guard against faults on the motor or driven machine, protection must be provided against careless manipulation of hand-operated gear or faulty operation of automatic equipment due to sticking of relays or contactors or to dirty contacts.

The chief danger with hand-operated gear is the moving of the starting handle too quickly. If it is to be operated by unskilled labour a mechanical ratchet is often provided to prevent the handle being moved more than one step at a time. Another danger, arising with d.c. machines, is attempting to start with a weak field. This results in an unnecessarily heavy current to provide a given torque, and mechanical or electrical interlocks may be provided as protection. The mechanical interlock may consist of a metal plunger, operated by the arm of the field rheostat, which prevents movement of the starting handle except when the rheostat is in the full-field position ; with an electrical interlock the plunger is controlled by a solenoid, which is energised only when the field is fully on. Similar interlocks should be provided in the equipment for a.c. commutator motors employing speed control by brush shifting : unless the brushes are in the low-speed position, the main switch should be prevented from closing.

With fully automatic equipment there is a danger of one or more of the accelerating contactors remaining closed after being de-energised, due to dirt having clogged their movement; this can be prevented by placing auxiliary contacts on the moving arm which are closed when the contactor is open. These contacts are connected in series with the start-button, so that the latter is in-operative if any of the contactors have remained closed.

In the automatic equipment illustrated in Fig. 47 it would be desirable to provide an interlock to prevent both forward and reverse start-buttons being operated at the same time, since closing both A and B contactors would short-circuit the supply.

Example of Automatic Control Equipment.—A typical example of a push-button-controlled motor is shown in Fig. 50. This gives the connections of a hoist with two skips, one of which is being raised while the other is being lowered, the whole being driven by a three-phase induction motor. Pressing the middle push-button causes the motor to start and raise skip 1. On reaching the end of its travel the skip operates the limit switch 15, which cuts off the supply. Pressing the lower button causes the motor to start in the opposite direction, thus lowering skip 1 and raising skip 2. Pressing the upper button will cause the motor to stop at any time. The second group of push-bottons (shown dotted) is connected in parallel with the first and enables control to be obtained from another point if desired. The other group of dotted connections provides for fully automatic operation: the limit switch in this case stops the motor and also energises a time-limit relay, which restarts the motor in the opposite direction after a predetermined time interval; this is repeated at the other end of the travel so that operation goes on continuously without any attention.

Wiring and Schematic Diagrams.—The diagram of Fig. 50 shows all the equipment in its correct geographical position, and is the type of diagram which would be required by a wireman when connecting up the apparatus. For tracing out the circuits in order to see how the apparatus operates, a simpler form of diagram, known as a schematic diagram, is preferable—in such a diagram each circuit, e.g., the main circuit, the control circuit, and the protective gear circuit, is shown separately and the various items are shown in such a way as to make the simplest

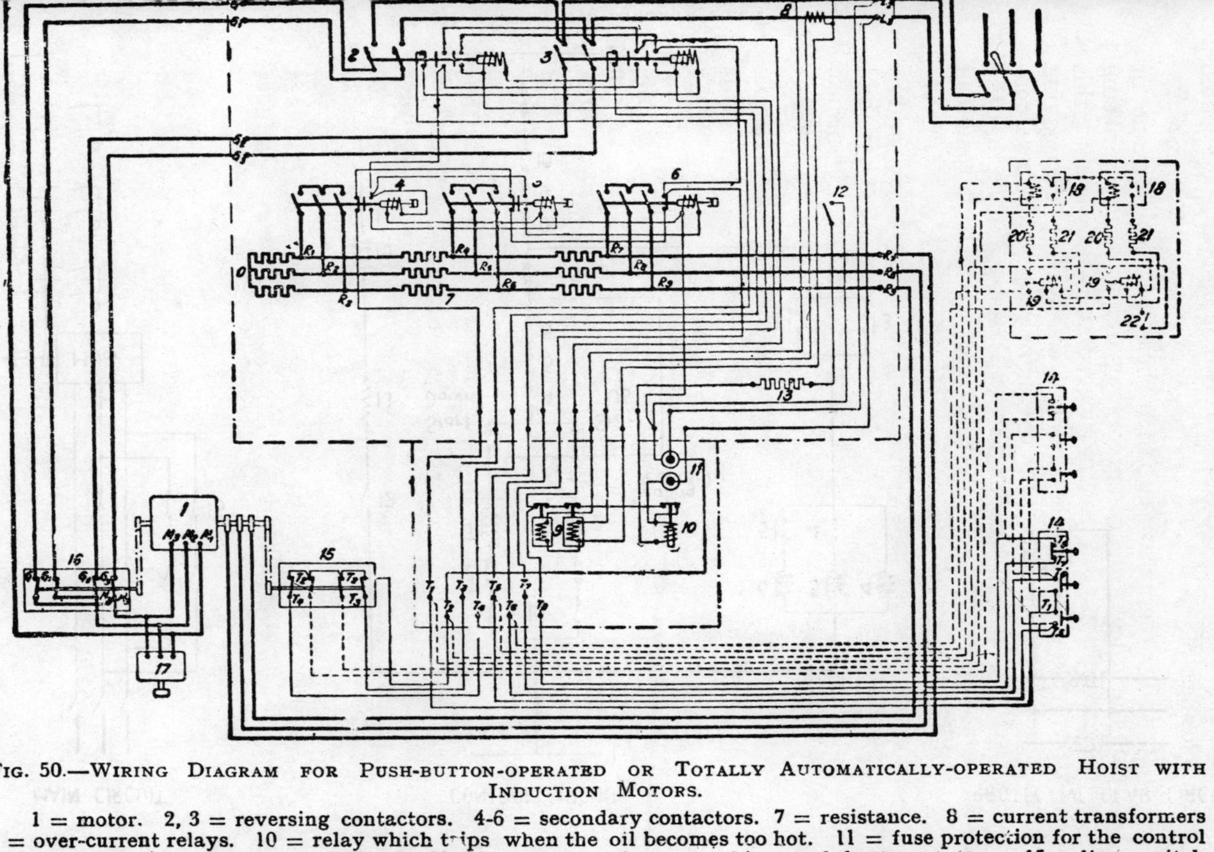

FIG. 50.—WIRING DIAGRAM FOR PUSH-BUTTON-OPERATED OR TOTALLY AUTOMATICALLY-OPERATED HOIST WITH INDUCTION MOTORS.

1 = motor. 2, 3 = reversing contactors. 4-6 = secondary contactors. 7 = resistance. 8 = current transformers 9 = over-current relays. 10 = relay which trips when the oil becomes too hot. 11 = fuse protection for the control circuit. 12 = thermal contact for 10. 13, 20, 21 = series resistances. 14 = push-button station. 15 = limit switch 16 = emergency limit switch. 17 = brake magnet. 18 = definite-time relays. 19 = auxiliary relays. 22 = switch for operating current to 18.

ASEA Electric, Ltd.

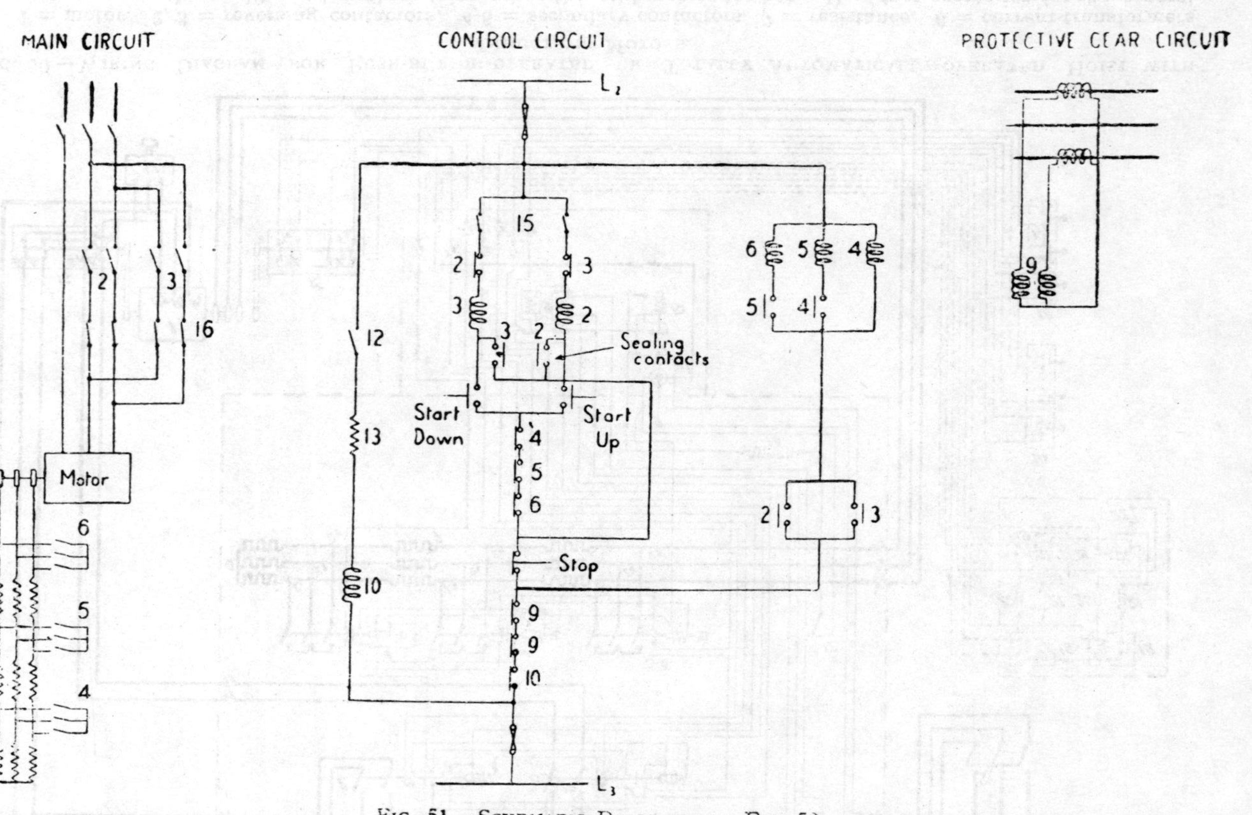

FIG. 51.—SCHEMATIC DIAGRAM FOR FIG. 50.

possible diagram, as in Fig. 51, without any reference to their actual geographical positions on the control panel. Parts of the same item may appear on different parts of the same diagram—thus the operating coil of main contactor 2 appears far removed from its contacts, correlation between the two being obtained by the proper numbering.

When drawing the schematic diagram of a control circuit, it is generally desirable to start with one line terminal (positive in the case of d.c. circuits) at the top of the paper and to proceed through the various items of equipment to the other line terminal at the bottom of the paper, the various circuits being kept vertical as far as possible.

Automatic Regulating Equipment

It frequently happens that an industrial process requires that a certain quantity, such as the speed of a motor, the temperature of an oven, or the tension in a wire, must be held at some specified value, usually constant, although in certain cases a predetermined cycle of variation may be required.

Electrical devices are widely used for providing such regulation, and operate on the closed-cycle or feed-back principle. The essential features of such an arrangement are as follows

(i) An actuating device for providing a control signal dependent on the deviation of the controlled quantity from its specified value.

(ii) An operating device which controls the power supply feeding the apparatus to be regulated in such a way as to counteract any deviation.

(iii) A connecting-link which will transfer the actuating signal in an appropriate manner to the operating device.

To ensure sensitivity the connecting-link should amplify the actuating signal so that the smallest departure from the specified value will be sufficient to initiate the correcting effect of the operating device; it must also have a very rapid response, so that there is a negligible time delay between the occurrence of the actuating signal and the correcting effect.

The thermionic valve, usually of the gas-filled type since this can deal with larger currents than the vacuum type, often forms a convenient connecting-link, since it has well-known amplification properties and has a negligible time lag. Where larger powers are required than can conveniently be dealt with by a valve, a rotating machine, known as an *amplidyne*, can be used.

Automatic Tension Control.—As an example of a regulating equipment using a triode gas-filled valve (thyratron) as the link between the actuating signal and the operating device, a simple arrangement for maintaining a constant tension in a wire during a reeling process is described. The arrangement is shown diagrammatically in Fig. 52.

Since it is desired to keep the tension constant, any deviation from the desired value must form the actuating signal. This deviation must, therefore, be converted to an electrical change, and this is done by means of a solenoid whose iron core is con-

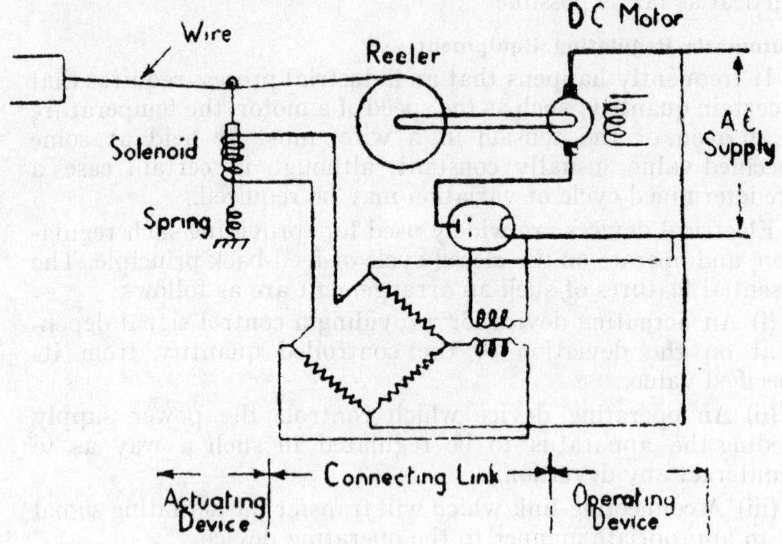

FIG. 52.—AUTOMATIC WIRE-TENSIONING APPARATUS

trolled by the tension in the wire as shown—the variation in reactance resulting from any movement of the core results in a phase shift of the output voltage of the impedance bridge circuit of which the solenoid forms one arm. Since this output voltage is applied to the grid of the valve, it will cause a variation in the current supplied to the d.c. motor with a consequent variation of its torque to rectify the original deviation of the tension from the specified value.

The Amplidyne Regulator—Where larger outputs are required from the connecting-link, an amplidyne regulator may be used instead of a valve; this machine is a development of the metadyne, described on page 30, and consists of a d.c. armature having (for a 2-pole machine) two sets of brushes one of which is short-circuited, as shown in Fig. 53 ; the machine is driven by any suitable constant-speed motor. A current in the control winding sets up a flux, Φ_c, which causes a relatively heavy current to flow in the short-circuited brushes ; this short-circuit current sets up a flux, Φ_A, which may be as much as 10 times Φ_c and which generates an e.m.f. across the output brushes. The compensating winding is necessary to prevent the current in the output circuit from demagnetising the flux Φ_c and must be designed so that its m.m.f. just neutralises that of the armature winding. A power amplification of as much as 10,000 to 1 between the input and output circuits can be obtained, so that when used as the connecting-link in a regulator there is ample sensitivity. The control winding can be given a sufficiently high ratio of resistance to inductance to ensure a short-time constant and rapid response and, although this cannot be as high as that of a valve, it is sufficient to enable the amplidyne to be used for a wide variety of industrial control purposes.

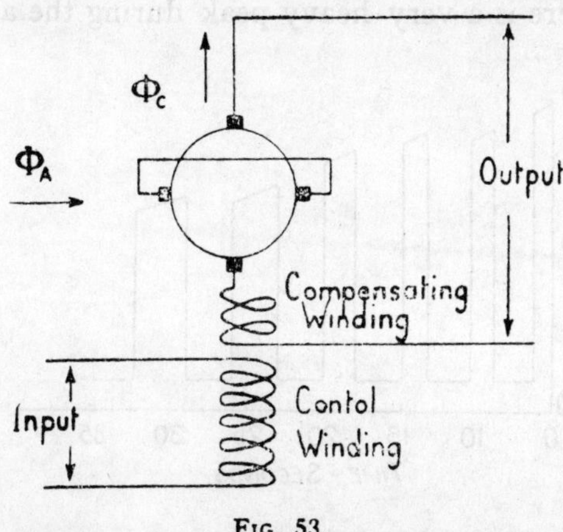

FIG. 53.

8. LOAD EQUALISATION

In many industrial drives the load fluctuates between wide limits in the space of a few seconds, and it is desirable to smooth out the large peak demands of current, which would otherwise be taken from the supply and produce heavy voltage drops in the system, or alternatively would require very large-section cables.

The process of smoothing out these fluctuating loads is commonly referred to as *load equalisation*, and involves the storage of energy during the light-load periods which can then be given out during the peak load, so that the demand from the supply is approximately constant.

Typical Fluctuating Loads.—Fig. 54 illustrates the load curve of a non-continuous rolling mill, e.g. a mill for rolling steel billets to rails or other sections: it can be seen that the load varies from a very heavy peak, lasting for a few seconds while the billet is actually between the rolls, to a light-load period during which the driving motor has to supply only the friction loss in the rolls.

The load of a colliery winding gear is illustrated in Fig. 41. It is seen that there is a very heavy peak during the accelerating

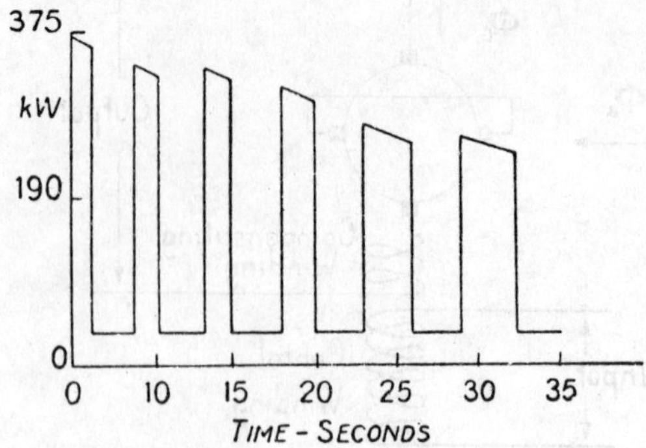

FIG. 54.—TYPICAL ROLLING-MILL LOAD

period, and also a small peak during the braking period, when power may be returned to the supply by regeneration.

Other examples occur in certain large machine tools, such as planing machines, in which it is desirable to hold the tool stationary and move the work backwards and forwards under the tool. There is thus a high load during the accelerating period followed by a constant load during the cut and finally a reversal and rapid return of the work to the starting-point. It is evident that heavy peak loads will be drawn from the supply unless some equalising arrangement is employed.

Use of Flywheels

The method of load equalisation most commonly employed is by means of a flywheel. During peak loads the flywheel decelerates and gives up some of its stored energy, thus reducing the load demanded from the supply, and during the light-load periods load is taken from the supply to accelerate the flywheel and replenish its stored energy ready for the next peak. Where the driving motor always has to run in the same direction and does not have to be frequently started and stopped, the flywheel can be mounted on the motor shaft; the motor must, of course, have a drooping speed characteristic in order that there may be a drop in speed as the load comes on to enable the flywheel to give up its stored energy. For a reversing drive, such as is required for a colliery winder, the reversing and speed control are generally carried out by the Ward-Leonard control system, and the flywheel can then be mounted on the shaft of the motor-generator set. When used with a flywheel in this way, this method of control is often referred to as the Ward-Leonard-Ilgner system.

Flywheel Calculations

The behaviour of a flywheel set may be determined as follows:

Let:

T_l = load torque, assumed constant during the time for which the load is applied.

T_f = torque supplied by the flywheel.

T_0 = torque required on no-load (friction torque, etc.).

T_m = torque supplied by the motor at any instant.

ω_0 = no-load speed of the motor in radians per second.

ω = speed of the motor at any instant in radians per second.

s = slip of the motor from its no-load speed ($s = \omega_0 - \omega$).

I = moment of inertia of the flywheel.

t = time in seconds.

g = acceleration due to gravity.

When the SI system of units is employed the torques should be expressed in *N.m.* the moment of inertia in kgm^2 and g will be $9{\cdot}806\ ms^{-2}$

Load Condition—Flywheel Decelerating.—In this case the flywheel is giving up its energy, so that the torque which the motor has to supply is given by:

$$T_m = T_l - T_f$$

It is necessary, therefore, to find the value of T_f, the torque supplied by the flywheel in terms of its moment of inertia, and the drop in speed.

The energy stored by the flywheel when running at a speed ω is $\frac{I}{2}\omega^2$. If the speed is reduced from ω_0 to ω the energy given up is $\frac{I}{2}(\omega_0{}^2 - \omega^2) = \frac{I}{2}(\omega_0 + \omega)(\omega_0 - \omega)$

But $\frac{\omega_0 + \omega}{2}$ is the mean speed during the interval, and since we are contemplating speed drops of not more than about 10 per cent., this may be assumed to be equal to the speed ω. Also $\omega_0 - \omega$ is the slip s, so that the above expression for the energy given up becomes:

$$\text{energy} = I\omega s$$

The power given up is the rate at which energy is given up as the speed varies, i.e.:

$$\text{power} = I\omega \cdot \frac{ds}{dt}$$

Torque is $\frac{\text{power}}{\omega}$, so that the torque supplied by the flywheel is:

$$T_f = I \cdot \frac{ds}{dt}$$

The equation for the torque thus becomes:

$$T_m = T_l - I \cdot \frac{ds}{dt}$$

An examination of the torque-speed curves of d.c. or induction motors will show that for slips up to about 10 per cent. the slip is proportional to torque, i.e. $s = KT_m$.

The equation can therefore be written:

$$T_m = T_l - I \cdot K \cdot \frac{dT_m}{dt}$$

This equation is exactly similar in form to that given on page 64 for the heating of a motor, and the solution is therefore:

$$\text{Motor torque} = T_m = T_l - (T_l - T_0)e^{-\frac{1}{IK}\cdot t} \qquad (24)$$

The motor torque (and therefore the current taken from the supply) thus rises exponentially, as shown in Fig 55. The torque produced by the flywheel is the difference between this motor torque and the load torque. Since $s = KT_m$ the speed can also be calculated and is shown in Fig. 55.

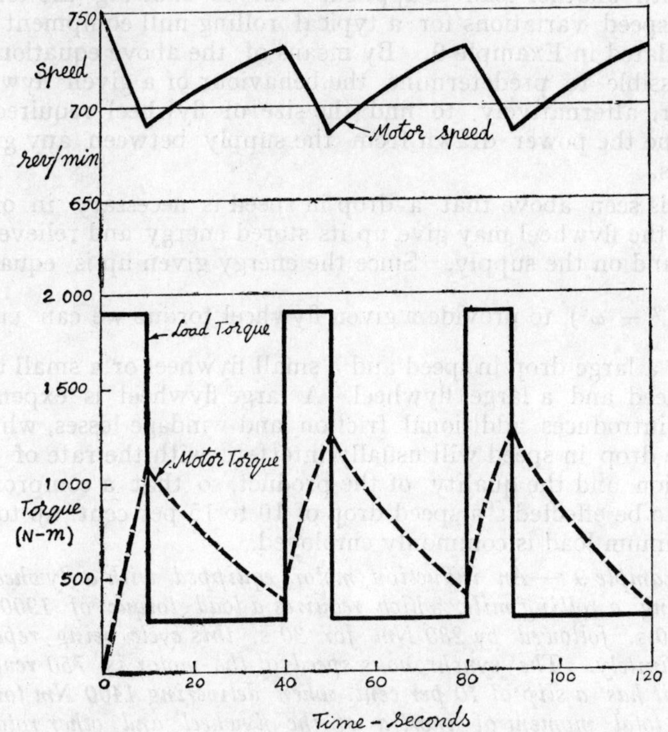

FIG. 55

No-load Condition—Flywheel Accelerating.—Suppose now that the load is removed and the motor accelerates the flywheel to its normal speed. We now have

$$T_m = T_0 + T_f$$
$$= T_0 - I \cdot \frac{ds}{dt}$$

the negative sign occurring because ds/dt is now negative.

This equation may be solved as before, and gives the result :

$$T_m = T_0 + (T_m{}' - T_0)\, e^{-\frac{1}{IK}t} \quad . \quad . \qquad (25)$$

where $T_m{}'$ is the motor torque at the instant when the load is removed.

As the set speeds up, so the motor torque falls according to an exponential law until the set is running at its no-load speed or until another load is applied. Curves showing the torque and speed variations for a typical rolling-mill equipment are calculated in Example 9. By means of the above equations, it is possible to predetermine the behaviour of a given flywheel set or, alternatively, to find the size of flywheel required to confine the power drawn from the supply between any given limits.

It is seen above that a drop in speed is necessary in order that the flywheel may give up its stored energy and relieve the demand on the supply. Since the energy given up is equal to $\frac{I}{2}(\omega_0^2 - \omega^2)$, to provide a given flywheel torque we can either have a large drop in speed and a small flywheel or a small drop in speed and a large flywheel. A large flywheel is expensive and introduces additional friction and windage losses, while a large drop in speed will usually interfere with the rate of production and the quality of the product, so that a compromise has to be effected: a speed drop of 10 to 15 per cent. up to the maximum load is commonly employed.

Example 9:—An induction motor equipped with a flywheel is driving a rolling mill, which requires a load torque of 1900 Nm for 10 s. followed by 280 Nm for 30 s, this cycle being repeated indefinitely. The synchronous speed of the motor is 750 rev/min and it has a slip of 10 per cent. when delivering 1400 Nm torque. The total moment of inertia of the flywheel and other rotating parts is 2100 kg.m² Draw curves showing the torque exerted by the motor, and the speed for three complete cycles, assuming that the initial torque is zero.

Solution.

The load torque on the motor is given by the full curve in fig. 55. The slip of the induction motor may be assumed proportional to torque so that the constant K in the expression for the torque may be found as follows:

At 1400 Nm torque the slip = 10%

$$= \frac{10}{100} \times 750 = 75 \text{ rev/min}$$

$$= 75 \times \frac{2\pi}{60} = 7{\cdot}85 \text{ rad/s}$$

$$7{\cdot}85 = K \times 1400$$

$$K = 0{\cdot}0056.$$

During the load period, the flywheel decelerating, we have, from equation (24)

$$T_m = T_l - (T_l - T_0)e^{-\frac{t}{IK}}$$

$$\frac{1}{IK} = \frac{1}{2100 \times 0{\cdot}0056} = 0{\cdot}085$$

Thus, after 5s, ($t=5$), $T_m = 1900 - (1900-0)e^{-0{\cdot}085 \times 5}$

$$= 1900 - \frac{1900}{1{\cdot}53} = 660 \text{ Nm}$$

At this torque,

$$\text{slip} = 0{\cdot}0056 \times 660 = 3{\cdot}7 \text{ rad/s}$$
$$= 35{\cdot}2 \text{ rev/min.}$$

$$\therefore \text{Speed} = 750 - 35{\cdot}2 = 714{\cdot}8$$

After 10s, i.e. at the end of the first peak-load, period :

$$T_m = 1900 - (1900 - 0)e^{-0{\cdot}085 \times 10}$$

$$= 1900 - \frac{1900}{2{\cdot}34} = 1088 \text{ Nm}$$

$$\text{Slip} = 0{\cdot}0056 \times 1088 = 6{\cdot}08 \text{ rad/s}$$
$$= 58 \text{ rev/min}$$

$$\therefore \text{Speed} = 750 - 58 = 692 \text{ rev/min.}$$

The torque at other times during the first peak period can be calculated in a similar way and the dotted curve of Fig. 55 plotted for this period and also the speed curve. The difference between the load torque and the motor torque at any instant represents the torque being supplied by the flywheel at that instant. Consider now the off-peak period, when the load is only 280 Nm.

From equation (25), the motor torque is given by :

$$T_m = T_0 + (T'_m - T_0)e^{-\frac{t}{IK}}$$

where T_m' is the motor torque at the beginning of the period : in this case T'_m = 1088 N.m. After 15 s,

$$T_m = 289 + (1088 - 280)e^{-0{\cdot}085 \times 15}$$

$$= 280 + \frac{808}{3{\cdot}57} = 506 \text{ N.m}$$

$$\text{Slip} = 0{\cdot}0056 \times 506 = 2{\cdot}84 \text{ rad/s}$$
$$= 27 \text{ rev/min}$$

$$\therefore \text{speed} = 723 \text{ rev/min.}$$

After 30s, at the end of the off-peak period:

$$T_m = 280 + (1088 - 280)e^{-0.085 \times 30}$$

$$= 280 + \left(\frac{808}{12.8}\right) = 343 \text{ N.m}$$

$$\text{slip} = 0.0056 \times 343 = 1.92 \text{ rad/s}$$

$$= 18.4 \text{ rev/min.}$$

$$\therefore \text{Speed} = 731.6 \text{ rev/min.}$$

These quantities can be plotted and we can proceed to deal with the second peak load period, remembering that the initial motor torque T_0 is now 343 N.m.

At the end of this period, we have thus.

$$T_m = 1900 - (1900 - 343)\, e^{-0.085 \times 10}$$

$$= 1900 - \frac{1557}{2.34} = 1235 \text{ N.m}$$

$$\text{Slip} = 0.0056 \times 1235 = 6.92 \text{ rad/s}$$

$$= 66 \text{ rev/min}$$

$$\therefore \text{Speed} = 684 \text{ rev/min}$$

At the end of second off-peak period:

$$T_m = 280 + (1235 - 280)\, e^{-0.085 \times 30}$$

$$= 280 + \frac{955}{12.8} = 354.6 \text{ N.m}$$

$$\text{Slip} = 0.0056 \times 354.6 = 1.99 \text{ rad/s}$$

$$= 19 \text{ rev/min}$$

$$\therefore \text{Speed} = 731 \text{ rev/min}$$

The initial condition at the beginning of the third peak load are thus practically the same as at the beginning of the second, so the motor torque in this and all succeeding load cycles will follow a similar curve to that in the second period.

The kilowatts delivered by the motor can easily be calculated if desired:—

$$\text{kW} = \frac{2\pi \times \text{rev/min} \times \text{torque}}{60 \times 1000}$$

and it will evidently follow an approximately similar shape of curve to that of the torque. It can be seen therefore that the peak-load demand required from the supply is very considerably reduced by the use of a flywheel. The increasing size of power systems makes the drawing of heavy peak loads cause less trouble than in earlier days, but there are still many situations when flywheels are desirable.

Speed Reduction and Slip Regulators

With the exception of the special case mentioned below, the synchronous motor is ruled out for use with a flywheel, as it runs at a constant speed, but d.c. shunt motors and induction motors are eminently suitable. The speed drop with a normally designed d.c. or induction motor is, however, only about 5 per cent. up to full load, and some means of artificially increasing it must therefore be adopted.

D. C. Compound Motor.—The speed-torque characteristic of a d. c. motor can very easily and economically be made steeper by adding a series winding to the field system arranged so that the flux is increased as the load comes on. The additional cost of this is small and it involves a negligible extra loss.

Induction Motor with Permanent Rotor Resistance.—There is no way of reducing the speed of an induction motor which is analogous to the use of a series winding with a d.c. motor, and the simplest method is to add resistance permanently to the rotor circuit. This suffers from the obvious disadvantage that power is lost in the resistance under all conditions, but on account of its small initial cost and its simplicity it is commonly used.

Induction Motor with Variable Rotor Resistance.—To overcome the wastage of energy which occurs with the permanent rotor resistance, it is possible to use a variable resistance which automatically increases as the load comes on, such an equipment being known as an automatic slip regulator. This equipment also has the important advantage that, theoretically, the resistance may be so varied that the load taken from the supply can, instead of being as shown in Fig. 55, be made absolutely constant. It is not possible to realise this exactly in practice, but a very much improved equalisation can be obtained. Two types of resistance are in common use—the liquid resistance with movable electrodes, and a metal resistance varied in steps by contactors. The movement of the electrodes with the former arrangement is controlled by a torque motor, i.e. a motor with the windings in series with the supply (or supplied through a current transformer) so that the torque exerted is proportional to the current. This motor acts against a spring, so that it cannot make a complete revolution, and is connected to the movable electrodes of the liquid resistance; as soon as the current reaches a predetermined value, resistance is inserted and an increased drop in speed obtained. With contactor-controlled resistances a similar operation is obtained, each step of resistance being cut in at a predetermined value of current. The liquid resistance has the advantage of a smooth resistance variation, but is inclined to be rather sluggish and therefore not suitable for rapidly fluctuating loads, such as rolling mills, although it is commonly used for colliery winders.

Induction Motor with A. C. Commutator Motor.—To eliminate the loss of energy in the resistance which occurs with the above method of control, the speed variation may be carried out by an a.c. commutator motor, as described in Section 3. The additional complication and higher initial cost, however, have prevented the adoption of this method in the majority of cases.

The Hydraulic Slip Regulator.—Instead of obtaining the slip electrically, as described above, a hydraulic slip regulator is employed in some cases; this is connected between the driving motor and the flywheel and consists of a casing containing an impellor and a runner—the former is connected to the driving motor and the latter to the flywheel. When the casing is filled with oil under pressure, the runner is driven by the impellor with a slip of only 2 or 3 per cent., and if oil is released the slip increases; a torque motor similar to that used with liquid regulators is employed to control the supply of oil so that slip is increased as the load comes on. This arrangement enables a constant-speed motor, such as the synchronous motor with its good power factor characteristics, to be employed as the driving motor.

9. PARTICULAR APPLICATIONS OF ELECTRIC DRIVE

In addition to the general problems, already discussed, which are common to the majority of electric drives, each industry has its own special problems. Space does not permit of a discussion of more than a few of these, but the more important applications are described and these illustrate the type of problem which has to be met.

General Factory Drive

Electric drive for factories can usually show considerable advantages over the older method of mechanical drive with a steam engine and shafting, and it is being almost universally adopted.

The chief factors leading to this are:

Economy in Running Cost.—It is frequently found that the cost of electrical energy is less than that of the coal and attendance required for a steam drive.

Flexibility in Layout of Factory.—Motor-driven machines can be placed in the most suitable position for giving maximum production, whereas belt-driven machines must be located in a definite position relative to the line shafting. Furthermore, it is a relatively simple matter to alter their position should a change in production methods be desirable. This feature is particularly apparent when the motors are built in as an integral part of the driven machine.

Ease of Control.—Each motor or group of motors can be placed under the direct control of the machine operator.

Reduction of Waste Power.—It is a very simple matter to install temporary meters for measuring the power taken by any circuit, so that any wasteful process can easily be detected.

Improvement of Amenities of Factory,—By reduction or elimination of overhead shafting and belting a considerable amount of dirt is avoided, which helps to improve the manufactured product and improves the amenities and safety of the worker, and at the same time enables adequate arrangements to be made for providing suitable lighting.

Constancy of Speed.—A steam engine can be governed to within 1 or 2 per cent., but the variable slip of belts under changing load conditions may cause variations in the speed of the driven machines of up to 10 per cent. This can be avoided by the use of electric drive, with consequent increased production and improved products.

It is thus seen that electric drive possesses features which tend to cheapen production and improve the manufactured product, so that even if power costs were greater with electric drive than with steam drive, a case could still be made out in favour of electrification. It may be noted here that although it is important to keep power costs down to as low a figure as possible by using equipment having the highest possible efficiency, these costs usually lie between about 1 and 10 per cent. of the total cost of the manufactured product, and any features which cheapen production are of relatively greater importance.

Group and Individual Drive.—The power for machines in factories may be obtained either by individual drive, in which each machine has its own separate motor, or by group drive in which a single larger motor drives a number of machines through a short length of shafting. Individual drive is taken to its limit in certain machine tools where each movement of the tool has a separate motor, while the limiting case of group drive occurs in certain old factories changed over from steam to electric drive simply by replacing the steam engine by an electric motor of corresponding output, all the old shafting and belting being retained. The usually accepted meaning of the

FIG. 56.—GROUP DRIVE IN MACHINE SHOP. EACH LINE OF SHAFTING IS DRIVEN BY A SINGLE 30 kW. MOTOR SITUATED AT THE FAR END.
(*Crompton Parkinson*)

term "group drive" refers, however, to anything between a group of two or three machines of similar size situated close together, and all the machines on one floor of a factory. Illustrations of typical group and individual drives are shown in Figs. 56 and 57.

The various salient features which have to be considered when choosing the type of drive for any particular case are outlined below.

Individual Drive.—Each operator has complete control of his power unit, enabling him to vary its speed if necessary and to shut it down when not in use, thus eliminating no-load losses.

The motor and its control unit can be built as an integral part of the machine, resulting in a neat appearance and tending to cleanliness and safety.

The machines can be placed in any desired position and can very easily be moved.

FIG. 57.—INDIVIDUAL DRIVE OF LOOMS IN A TEXTILE FACTORY. (*Crompton Parkinson*)

Complete elimination of all shafting and its attendant maintenance and losses. If a new factory is being considered the superstructure can be made much lighter and less expensive.

Group Drive.—The cost of a single large motor will be smaller than a number of smaller units of the same total horse-power, as shown by the curve on Fig. 58.

As all the machines may not be on full load at the same time the kW-power of the group-drive motor can often be less than the sum of the kW-powers of all the individual motors, again tending to reduce the cost.

The efficiency and power factor of a larger group-drive motor will be higher provided it is always run fairly near its full load (see Fig. 58).

Losses will occur in the shafting amounting to between 0·1 and 0·5 kW. per 3m. run, or more if the shafting is not well maintained.

The savings in capital cost obtained as a result of using a single large motor will be partially offset by the cost of the shafting.

In any particular case, careful attention will have to be given to each of the above factors, and to any other special considerations which may occur, so that no hard-and-fast rules can be

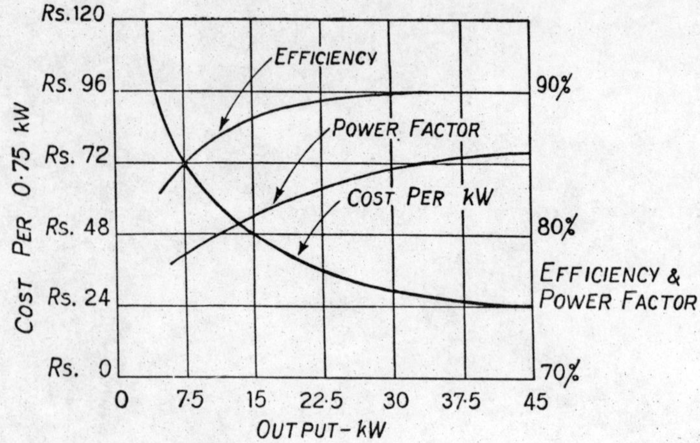

Fig. 58.—Efficiency Power Factor and Cost of Typical Range of 750 r.p.m. Induction Motors

laid down regarding the correct choice. The general tendency is, however, to use individual drive for new factories where some saving in the cost of the superstructure may thereby be obtained and group drive when converting existing factories and use can be made of some of the existing line shafting.

Integral Construction of Driving Motor.—Most motor manufacturers now co-operate with the machine-tool makers to enable the driving motor and its control gear to be built as an integral part of the machine. This method of construction is particularly applicable when using the squirrel-cage induction motor, since the rotor, being practically indestructible, can be solidly mounted on the driving spindle of the machine, while the stator is simply a steel shell supporting the windings and can easily be built into the machine tool by the manufacturers. The advantages of this arrangement are an improvement in the appearance of the machine, thus adding to the amenities of the factory and facilitating cleaning, while the operator has his control gear conveniently at hand instead of his having to walk a distance of possibly several yards to it.

High-speed Drives.—Drives for certain forms of spinning machinery, woodworking tools, and drilling and grinding machines in metal-working industries, particularly when using portable tools, have to be at speeds between 6,000 and 15,000 or even 20,000 rev/min. D.c. or a.c. series motors can be used for such drives, but, on account of the shape of their speed-torque characteristics, a high full-load speed means an exceptionally high speed on no-load, and such motors are not, therefore, entirely satisfactory. The induction motor has the required speed characteristic, but on a 50 Hz system the maximum speed possible is 3,000 rev/min, so that for the higher speeds either gearing must be employed or a high-frequency supply must be used. The introduction of the relatively simple and inexpensive induction type of frequency convertor has made the latter method an economic proposition, even in cases where only a single motor has to be supplied ; the convertor consists simply of an ordinary induction motor with a 50 Hz supply on its primary and with its secondary driven by an auxiliary squirrel-cage motor in the opposite direction to that of the rotating field on the primary. The high frequency is then taken from the slip-rings, as shown in Fig. 59. If the speed of the rotating field of the primary is $n_1 = \frac{f_1}{p}$ revs second, f_1 being the supply frequency and p the number of pairs of poles on the main machine, and if n_r is the speed at which the rotor is driven, then the relative speed of the rotor conductors and the rotating field is n_1+n_r rev/sec. and the frequency of the e.m.f.'s set up in them will be $f_2 = p(n_1+n_r)$ Hz.

Alternatively, to obtain a given frequency f_2, the speed at which the rotor must be driven is:

$$n_r = \frac{f_2 - pn_1}{p} = \frac{f_2 - f_1}{p}. \qquad (26)$$

Unless f_2 is at least twice f_1, the speed n_r will be so low, necessitating a large machine, that a motor-alternator set will usually be a more economcal proposition.

Paper-mill Drive

The drive of a paper mill is interesting in that it illustrates the advantages of electric drive in a case where very special speed-control arrangements are required.

The raw materials used in the manufacture are rags, esparto grass, and wood, and after a preliminary breaking up, these are boiled with solvents to dispose of impurities and then beaten up to a pulp, or " stuff," which contains about 99½ per cent. of water. This stuff is pumped to storage tanks on the paper-making machine proper. The driving motors for the pulping machinery and the pumps will be ordinary standard motors ranging from 1·5 or 2.2 kW up to 22 kW or more if group drive is employed.

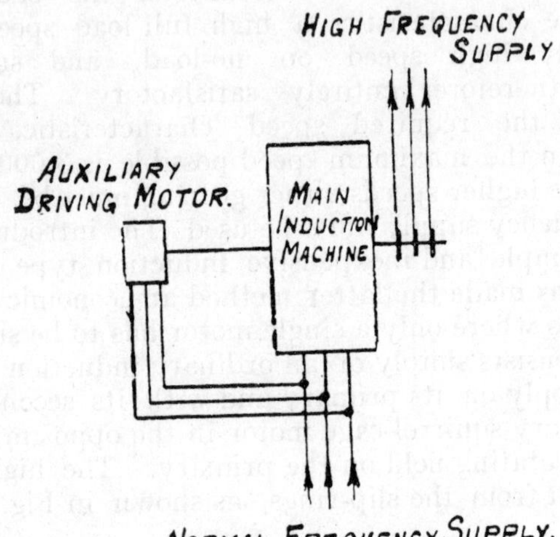

FIG. 59.—CONNECTIONS OF INDUCTION-TYPE FERQUENCY CONVERTOR

From the storage tanks the stuff passes through strainers on to the first section of the paper-making machine itself, and it is this which requires the special speed-control arrangements. This first section consists of a moving wire mesh having a width equal to the final width of the paper, which may be anything up to 6·25m and it travels at speeds of up to 300m per minute, driven by the couch motor. About 25 per cent. of the water content of the stuff passes through the wire mesh, a process which is assisted by vacuum boxes placed beneath it, so that when it leaves the mesh it begins to take on the appearance of paper and is sufficiently strong to be passed on to a moving belt which passes between a series of heated press rolls. From here it travels successively through groups of drying rolls, calenders, and smoothing rolls, and passes finally on to a reeler as the finished product. The driving of these various groups of rolls presents a difficult problem, since it is necessary:

(i) To be able to vary the speed of the entire equipment to suit different types of paper;

(ii) To ensure that the relative speed of every part remains absolutely constant, otherwise tearing of the paper will inevitably result.

(iii) To be able to adjust the speed of any one group of rolls relative to the others in order to allow for the draw of the paper, i.e. difference in speed at various parts of the machine due to its elongation as it dries this difference may amount to

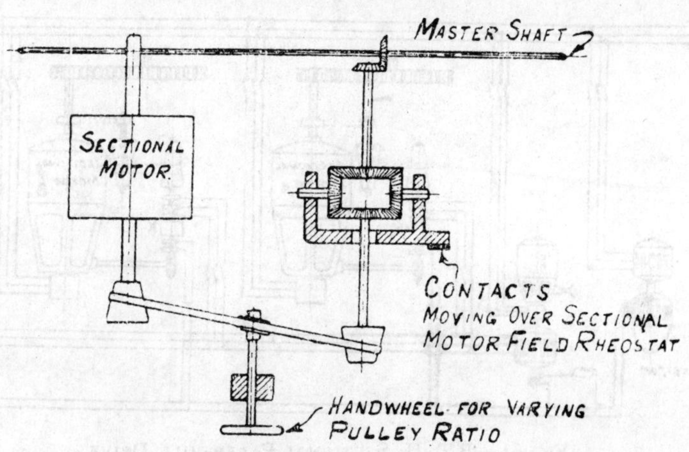

FIG. 60.—HARLAND SECTIONAL PAPER-MILL DRIVE

8 or 9 per cent. between the two ends and must be found by trial for any particular paper.

Early types of machine employed a steam engine and complicated system of belts and cone pulleys to transmit the drive to each section, but increased powers and higher speeds made it extremely difficult to meet the above requirements with this method, and the modern type of electric "sectional" drive was developed. A separate motor is employed to drive each group of rolls, as many as twelve or sixteen motors, all interdependent in accordance with the above requirements, being employed in some cases. Several schemes have been developed for controlling the speed of these motors in the required manner, and two of these, one using d.c. motors and the other using a.c. motors, are described below.

Harland Drive (*D.C. Motors*).—A master shaft runs the whole length of the paper-making machined and mounted on this at each sectional motor is a bevel gear attached to one wheel of a differential gear, as shown in Fig. 60 ; the other wheel of the differential is belt-driven from the shaft of the sectional motor. So long as the speed of these two wheels is the same, the frame of the differential will remain stationary, but any change in their relative speeds will cause the frame to rotate and operate a field rheostat in the sectional motor circuit, to counteract that change. Thus if the speed of any one of the sectional motors should deviate from normal for any reason the rheostat will be

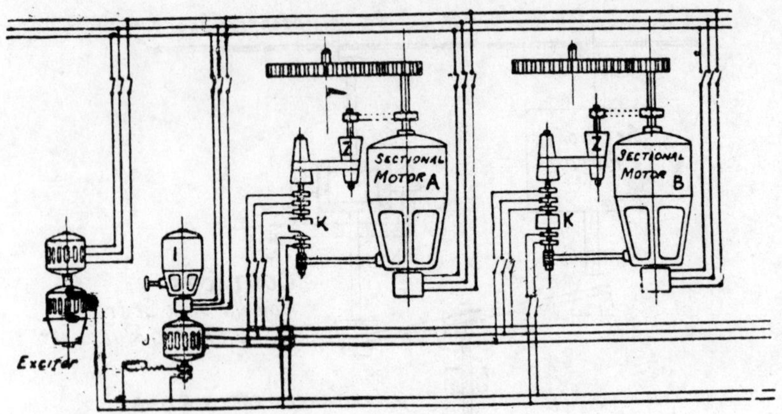

Fig. 61.—B.T.-H. Sectional Paper-mill Drive.

operated and immediately bring it back so that condition (ii) is fulfilled. If the speed of the master shaft is varied, the rheostats of all the motors will be operated and the speed of the entire equipment will be varied, thus fulfilling condition (i). To enable the speed of any one motor to be varied independently of the rest, the belt drive from the motor shaft to the differential is arranged on cone pulleys, so that the pulley ratio can be altered by operating the hand wheel shown.

B. T.-H. Co.'s Drive (*A.C. Motors*).—The driving motors in this case are Schrage motors and the mechnical control of the Harland drive is replaced by a purely electrical control, as shown in Fig. 61. Attached to each sectional motor is a small synchronous motor, K, whose stator and rotor are both free to rotate ;

the rotors of these motors are driven from their respective sectional motor shafts via the cone pulleys, Z, while the stators, which are attached to the brush-shifting gear of the sectional motor, are supplied with 3-phase a.c. from a master alternator, J. Normally the speed of the rotor and of the rotating field of the stator of the synchronous motor will be the same, and there will, therefore, be no torque on the stator ; a change in speed of the sectional motor will upset this condition and produce a torque, thus causing a rotation of the brush gear to counteract the change. A change in speed of the whole equipment is brought about by varying the speed of the master alternator (also driven by a Schrage motor), thereby varying the speeds of the rotating fields of all the synchronous motors, and causing them to begin to rotate in order to maintain synchronism, with a consequent shift of the brush gear of all the sectional motors. Variation of the speed of an individual motor is carried out by means of its cone pulleys, 7., as in the Harland drive.

Electric Ship Propulsion

The many advantages of electric motors for industrial drives and also for the driving of auxiliaries on shipboard have led to its adoption for ship propulsion. The prime mover (steam turbine or Diesel engine), instead of driving the propellor shaft directly or through a reduction gear, drives an a.c. or d.c. generator, which supplies a.c. or d.c. motors mounted on the propellor shafts. The success achieved by early experiments in electric ship propulsion has led to its use for all classes of vessel, ranging from small tugs and ferry boats to the 84,400 tonne liner *Normandie*.

Salient features of Electrical Propulsion.—The chief advantages of electric propulsion may be briefly summarised as follows.

(i) Propellor and Prime Mover Speeds.—The speeds of the prime mover and of the propellor can be chosen quite independently in order that each shall give the most efficient operation without any limitations such as are imposed by their having to be coupled either directly or through reduction gearing. The most economical speed for the propellor is usually between about 100 and 200 rev/min., while for a steam turbine it is about 3,000 rev/min or even higher, and for a Diesel engine it is usually between 400 and 800 rev/min. It may be noted, however, that very low propellor speeds mean motors of very large physical dimensions to provide a given power if they are to be direct-coupled.

(ii) Economy at Low Speeds.—Where two or more prime movers are employed, all the propellor motors can be supplied from one of these at low speeds, thereby considerably increasing the efficiency ; this is of particular importance for voyages in which the ships have to steam at half-speed for considerable distances, as on the Indian route, and it is also of importance for warships, where an economical cruising speed of about half the maximum " fighting " speed is required.

(iii) Economical Design and Operation of Prime Movers.—Speed control and reversing can be carried out on the motors, so that the prime movers can always operate in the same direction and at a constant speed, thus eliminating the use of a reverse turbine or the complicated equipment necessary for reversing a Diesel engine. Furthermore, the full power of the ship is almost instantaneously available for reversal, which may be extremely valuable in cases of emergency.

(iv) Ease of Control.—The most important advantage of electric propulsion is the simplicity and scope of the control equipment, since it is entirely, or almost entirely, electrical, and can if desired be carried out directly from the bridge instead of by signals communicated to the engine room.

In addition to the above there are other features which are of importance with electric propulsion, namely, the greater flexibility in the layout of the plant, since the position of the prime movers is not fixed by that of the propellor shafts, and also there is, in the majority of cases, a smaller tendency to vibration than with direct or geared drive.—There is no outstanding saving in the weight or space occupied—in fact, for small high-speed vessels, such as destroyers, the weight of electric equipment will be greater than that of alternative systems and precludes its use for this service.

Types of Drive.—Both a.c. and d.c. have been widely used ; for reasons outlined below a.c. is more suitable for large ships requiring above about 2500 kW., and using steam turbines as the prime mover, while Diesel engines with d.c. equipment are generally employed for smaller vessels.

Propellor Load Characteristics.—The most severe duty on the motors occurs when reversing the ship, and to examine the requirements of the motors for this purpose it is necessary to study the characteristics of the propellor. The motors are reversed by one of the usual methods, but the ship, owing to its large inertia, continues to travel for a considerable distance before coming to rest, and during this time the water is exerting a torque on the propellor tending to rotate it in the original (forward) direction, in order to reverse the propellor, therefore, the motors must exert a reversing torque greater than this. The curves of Fig. 62 show the speed-torque characteristics of a typical propellor; the ordinate at any speed represents the torque which the motor must exert in order to drive the propellor at that particular speed. Curve A shows the speed-torque curve obtained when the ship is stationary, while curve B represents the curve obtained when the ship is travelling at full speed ahead; the latter is, of course, the curve which is of importance when reversing from full speed. As soon as the

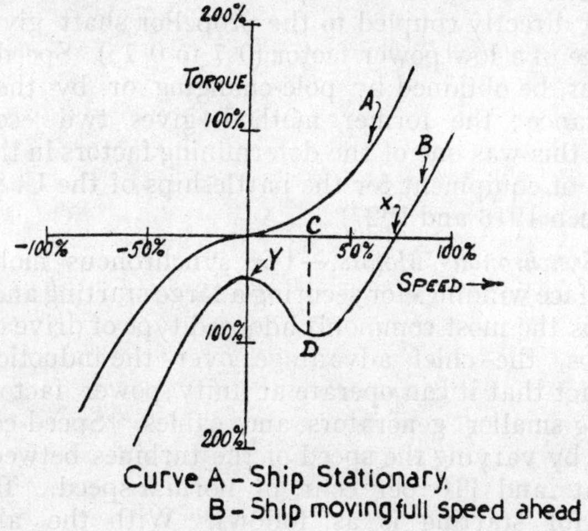

FIG. 62—PROPELLOR SPEED-TORQUE CHARACTERISTICS.

motors are switched off preparatory to being reversed the driving torque falls to zero, corresponding to point X, and the inertia of the ship drives the propellor at about 70 per cent. of its full speed. At any propellor speed below this the water exerts a torque on the propellor tending to increase its speed to this 70 per cent. value, the magnitude of this torque being as shown by the curve (e.g. ordinate C D). To ensure that the propellor speed does actually decrease, however, the motor must exert a reverse torque greater than this value, and it can be seen therefore that it must be able to exert a reverse torque of about full-load torque at about 35 per cent. of full speed and a torque of about 40 per cent. of full load at standstill (point Y).

If the motor is not capable of exerting these torques, it will not be able to reverse the propellor until the speed of the ship has dropped to a much lower value.

Turbo-electric Drive.—For large ships requiring 2500 kW. and upwards, the steam turbine is the standard type of prime mover and, on account of the size, 3-phase alternators driving induction or synchronous motors are employed when electric propulsion is required. To keep currents down to a reasonable figure a voltage of between about 2,200 and 6,600 is usually chosen.

Use of the Induction Motor.—Although the induction motor possesses desirable characteristics from the point of view of starting and reversing, the low speed at which it must necessarily run if directly coupled to the propellor shaft gives it the disadvantage of a low power factor (0·7 to 0·75). Speed control can. however, be obtained by pole-changing or by the use of rotor resistance; the former method gives two economical speeds, and this was one of the determining factors in the choice of this type of equipment for the battleships of the U. S. Navy (built between 1918 and 1927).

Use of Synchronous Motors.—The synchronous motor with heavy pole-face windings for securing a large starting and reversing torque is the most commonly adopted type of drive of turbo-electric ships, the chief advantage over the induction motor being the fact that it can operate at unity power factor, thereby requiring smaller generators and cables. Speed control is carried out by varying the speed of the turbines between about 20 per cent. and 110 per cent. of normal speed. The usual procedure for starting is as follows. With the alternator running at $\frac{1}{5}$ to $\frac{1}{4}$ of full speed and with $1\frac{1}{2}$ to 2 times normal excitation, the main contactors are closed and the synchronous motors start as squirrel-cage induction motors, using the pole-face winding. When nearly synchronous speed is reached, the motor excitation is switched on and the motors pull into step as synchronous motors; the alternator excitation is reduced to normal and the alternators are then run up to the desired speed.

Diesel-electric Equipment.—The limitations in output of the Diesel engine limit its use to the propulsion of merchant ships of up to about 15,000 tonnes, and to ferry boats, tugs, and other small craft. When electric drive is required for the smaller vessels, the relatively small outputs to be dealt with permit the use of voltages up to about 650, and this, together with the relatively low speed at which a Diesel engine usually runs (400 to 800 rev/min.), makes possible the use of direct current, so that speed control and reversing can be carried out by variation of the generator field on the Ward-Leonard principle. A very much greater flexibility can therefore be obtained with Diesel-electric propulsion than with direct Diesel drive, and this is usually a determining factor in the choice of electric equipment for tugs and small river craft; the additional losses in the electrical equipment are more than offset by the greater economy in operating the Diesel engine, since this can be run at a constant speed and does not have to be started, stopped, or reversed when manœuvring.

For larger vessels a.c. is used to give greater efficiency although manœuvrability is less; it is convenient and economical to employ several Diesel engines and alternators to supply a single propellor motor, so that special means have to be adopted for keeping the alternators in synchronism under all conditions of speed and while carrying out switching operations.

For dredgers, firefloats, etc., where a considerable amount of power is required when the vessel is at anchor, a change-over switch can be provided to enable the main generators to supply either the propulsion motors or the driving motors of the auxiliary equipment.

CHAPTER I

QUESTIONS

1. A delta-connected, 400-V, 22-kW, 750 rev/min. squirrel-cage motor takes a full-load current of 40 A and has a full-load slip of 4·5%. The impedance per phase is 3·9Ω. Determine the starting torque and the starting current taken from the supply, if the motor is started by:

(*a*) direct switching;

(*b*) an auto-transformer starter with a 70% tapping;

(*c*) a star-delta starter;

(*d*) a series-parallel switch which connects sections of the winding in series at starting and parallel when running.

2. A 3-phase, 15-kW, 400-V, 500-rev/min. squirrel—cage motor driving a machine tool has a full-load efficiency of 0·85 and a full-load power factor of 0·88. The motor takes a short-circuit current of 125 A at 0·25 lagging power factor (motor held stationary and full voltage applied to stator). The full-load

slip is 5%. It is desired to ensure that the starting torque shall be not less than half full-load torque. What will be the minimum starting current to be taken from the supply to enable this torque to be obtained if the motor is started by:

(*a*) an auto-transformer?

(*b*) a series resistance in the stator circuit? What will be the value of the tapping on the transformer and the magnitude of the resistance to be added to each phase?

3. A d.c. shunt motor takes 50 A from a 200-V supply and runs at 1000 rev/min., when delivering an output of 9.3 kW. The armature resistance is 0.1Ω. What resistance must be inserted in the armature circuit to reduce the speed to 850 rev/min. and what will be the loss in this resistance if the motor is driving:

(*a*) a centrifugal pump for which the torque required is proportional to the square of the speed?

(*b*) a reciprocating pump requiring a constant-torque at all speeds?

4. A fan is driven at 300 rev/min. by a series motor having a total resistance of 1.5Ω; the motor is supplied at 200V and takes 15 A. If the flux may be assumed proportional to the current, what voltage will have to be applied to the motor in order to drive the fan at 400 rev/min.? At what speed would it run if connected to a 400-V supply? What would be the effect of saturation of the magnets on the figures obtained above?

5. A 230-V, d.c. shunt motor runs at 900 rev/min. on no-load with full field and has an armature resistance of 0.7Ω. The armature current to give full-load torque is 15 A. If a resistance of 6Ω is put in series with the armature and a resistance of 5Ω in parallel with it, determine the speed-torque characteristic. Find also the current drawn from the supply and the approximate efficiency when delivering full-load torque.

6. A 50-Hz, pole-changing induction motor can be connected to have either 4 or 8 poles. At what two speeds will it run on no load? If it is used for driving:

(*a*) a fan taking 15 kW at the lower speed,

(*b*) a lift requiring 15 kW at the lower speed. What will be the approximate output (kW) delivered by the motor at the higher speed in each case?

7. Two mechanically coupled 50-Hz induction motors have 8 and 6 poles respectively, and can be connected in cascade.

What possible no-load speeds are available and how would you connect the motors to obtain these speeds?

8. A 400-V, 22-kW, 500-rev/min., d.c. shunt motor has an armature resistance of 0.3Ω and takes a normal full-load current of 70 A. What value of starting resistance is required, if the starting current is to be limited to 90 A?.

If the motor is to be braked by plugging when running on full-load, how much resistance, additional to the starting resistance must be added to the circuit to prevent the initial braking current from exceeding 100 A? What will be the initial braking torque under these conditions and the braking torque when the speed has fallen to 250 rev/min.?

9. A 460-V, d.c. shunt motor having an efficiency of 85% operates a hoist having an efficiency of 70%; the diameter of the drum of the hoist is 0.6 m and the gear ratio is 60 : 1. Calculate the current taken from the supply in order to raise a load of 225 kg. mass at 3 ms^{-1}. If rheostatic braking is to be employed, what resistance must be put in the armature circuit in order to lower the load at the above speed? Neglect the resistance of the armature.

10. The following figures give the magnetisation curve of a d.c. series motor running at 640 rev/min. The total resistance of the motor is 0.8 Ω.

Current (A)	20	40	60	80
Emf (V)	215	381	485	550

When connected for rheostatic braking against a load giving a torque of 270 N.m., it is desired to limit the motor speed to 600 rev/min. What resistance must be connected across the motor terminals?

11. A 18.5—kW 750-rev/min., 400-V, 3-phase, squirrel-cage induction motor has a rotor resistance of 0·08Ω per phase, and a rotor reactance at standstill of 0.6Ω per phase. The maximum torque of the motor is 610 N.m. Draw the torque-slip curve for the motor upto a slip of 200%. If the motor is braked by plugging, what will be the initial braking-torque and the torque at stand-still?

12. A motor driving some haulage equipment for a mine has to deliver a load, which follows the following cycle:

37.0 kW for 10 min ;
No load for 4 min ;
18.5 kW for 10 min ;
No load for 6 min,

the cycle being repeated indefinitely. Estimate a suitable size of continuously rated motor for the purpose.

13. A motor has a heating-time-constant of 70 min. and a cooling-time-constant when stationary of 90 min. When run continuously on full-load of 18.5 kW, the final temperature-rise is 40°C. What load could the motor deliver for 10 min. if this is followed by a shut-down period long enough for it to cool without the temperature-rise exceeding 40°C ? If it is on an intermittent load of 10 min. on-load and followed by 15 min. shut-down, what is the maximum value of the load which it could supply during the on-load period, without the maximum temperature rise exceeding 40° C ? Assume losses to be proportional to the square of the load.

14. A motor is operating some haulage equipment which has to accelerate a train of 20000 kg mass up a gradient of 6% with an acceleration of 0.15 ms^{-2}. The maximum speed is 24 km/h. The motor drives, through a gear ratio having a 6 : 1 ratio, a rope drum 1.2 m in diameter. The gear efficiency is 88% and the tractive resistance of train 60 N/1000 kg. What must be the full-load speed of the motor and what torque must it be capable of exerting during the accelerating period ?

15. A 75-kW, 500-rev/min. d.c. shunt motor is driving through gears, a grinding mill having a moment of inertia of 1250 $kg.m^2$. If the current taken by the motor must not exceed twice full-load current during the starting period, estimate the minimum time taken to run the mill upto full-speed.

16. A 500-rev/min. synchronous motor and its driven machine have a total moment of inertia of 420 $kg./m^2$ and a frictional torque of 136 N.m. If this motor is braked by the following methods, calculate the time taken for it to come to rest and the number of revolutions made during the braking process ; draw also the speed-time curve during the braking period.

(*a*) Braking carried out by plugging, which produces a constant braking torque of 1360 N.m.

(*b*) Rheostatic braking employed, the field-current and braking-resistance being kept constant at a value, which gives an initial electric braking torque of 5440 N.m.

17. A 18.5-kW, squirrel—cage motor of question 11 is used to drive a fan requiring a torque of 340 N.m. at a speed of 750 rev/min. At what speed would the fan be driven, the fan torque being proportional to the square of the speed? How long would the motor take to accelerate the fan to this speed, assuming it to be started by direct switching and the motor and fan to have a total moment of inertia of 168 kg. m^2?

18. A motor equipped with a flywheel has to supply a load torque of 810 N.m. for 10 seconds followed by a no-load period long enough for the flywheel to regain its full-speed. If it is desired to limit the motor torque to 610 N.m, what should be the moment of inertia of the flywheel? The no-load speed of the motor is 600 rev/min. and it has a slip of 8% at a torque of 610 N.m.

19. Motors are required for the following drives:

(*a*) Lathe	(*h*) Fan
(*b*) Emery wheel	(*i*) Reciprocating pump
(*c*) Milling machine	(*j*) Centrifugal pump
(*d*) Circular saw	(*k*) Electric generator
(*e*) Cement kiln	(*l*) Air-compressor
(*f*) Hoist	(*m*) Church organ
(*g*) Rolling mill.	

State, with reasons, what type of motor you would consider suitable for these drives if:

(*i*) only a d. c. supply were available;

(*ii*) only a 3-phase supply were available;

(*iii*) either a d. c. or a 3-phase supply were available.

Indicate any special electrical or mechanical features, which should be incorporated.

20. Draw a connection diagram of the equipment for automatically starting:

(*a*) A squirrel-cage induction motor by means of an auto-transformer;

(*b*) A slip ring induction motor by means of resistance in the rotor circuit. Include any safety devices which you consider desirable.

CHAPTER II

ELECTRIC TRACTION

1. GENERAL FEATURES

THE chief factor underlying the electrification of railways or other traction services is one of economics. If operation by electric traction can be shown to be cheaper than by any alternative method, and if the necessary additional capital can be raised, then electrification is invariably carried out, since there are now no technical difficulties to prevent its adoption.

In certain cases other reasons have led to the use of electric traction on railways ; for instance, in New York the use of steam locomotives is prohibited by law on account of smoke emission, while in other countries with abundant water-power resources it is desirable to avoid the import of coal. Experience shows that the traffic which can be handled over an electrified railway may be anything up to double the amount possible with steam operation, so that electrification may save a large expenditure in doubling of track or provision of increased terminal facilities.

Requirements of an Ideal Traction System

The most important requirements of the driving equipment for traction service are as follows :

(i) Maximum tractive effort should be exerted at starting in order that rapid acceleration may be attained.

(ii) The equipment should be capable of overloads for short periods.

(iii) The wear caused on the track should be a minimum.

(iv) The locomotive or train unit should be self-contained and able to run on any route.

(v) Braking should be possible without excessive wear on brake shoes, and if possible the braking energy should be regenerated and returned to the supply.

No single system embodies all these requirements, and the salient features of the systems in common use or under consideration are briefly discussed below.

Systems of Traction

Direct Steam-engine Drive.—The steam car for road transport has disappeared, but for railway work the steam locomotive is still the most widely adopted method of propulsion. The reciprocating engine is invariably employed on account of its inherent simplicity, the simplicity of the connection between the cylinders and the driving wheels, and the ease with which the speed can be controlled. Owing to the difficulty of installing a condenser on a locomotive, such engines run non-condensing and therefore have an efficiency of only 6 to 8 per cent.; disadvantages of the steam locomotive are its strictly limited overload capacity and the fact that it is only available for hauling for about 60 per cent. of its working day, the remainder of the time being spent in preparing for service and in maintenance and overhaul; furthermore, there is considerable wear on the track caused by unbalanced reciprocating parts and corrosion of steel structures by the smoke emitted.

A few locomotives employing steam turbines have been built which use a condenser and which have reduction gearing between the turbine and driving wheels; although such locomotives have an efficiency of 10 to 15 per cent. their high initial and maintenance costs have not so far justified their general use.

Experimental gas-turbine locomotives have also been built.

Direct Internal-combustion Engine Drive.—The efficiency of an internal-combustion engine at its normal speed is about 25 per cent., but the overload capacity is limited, and operation at any but the normal speed, usually between 600 and 2,000 rev/min, is very uneconomical. Furthermore, the torque available is approximately constant at all speeds, so that an engine which is capable of giving the high starting torque required will not be used to its full capacity when running at full speed unless some form of gear or other torque convertor is employed. For road and light railway work a gear-box is provided for this purpose and also to give speed control, but such an arrangement is not altogether satisfactory for heavy railway work.

Steam-electric Drive.—To avoid the necessity for a reduction gear with the turbo-locomotive, the turbine can be made to drive a generator which supplies current to suitable motors. Such locomotives have been built experimentally, but the mechanical difficulties have so far prevented their general adoption.

Internal-combustion Electric Drive.—Replacement of the reduction gear and gear-box of the direct internal-combustion engine drive by an electric generator and motors has found considerable favour for railway work, and locomotives of this type, usually employing a Diesel engine, are becoming widely used. The maintenance cost is fairly heavy, but the time which such a locomotive must be out of service for maintenance and overhaul is, on an average, only 5 to 10 per cent. of its working day. The weight of such a locomotive is high, but its use is justified where coal is scarce and water bad. It is being increasingly used both for high-speed main-line work and for shunting service.

Battery-electric Drive.—Direct-current motors are here used for driving, but are supplied from a secondary battery carried on the vehicle. The scope of such vehicles is limited by the small capacity of the battery which can be carried and the necessity for frequent charging, but they are well suited, and frequently used, for shunting, for traction in industrial works and mines, and for certain forms of road transport.

Track Electrification.—This is the most widely used and most important form of electric traction; electric energy is supplied to the vehicle from a contact wire suspended above the track or from an additional rail laid alongside it. The amount of equipment on the vehicle is thus much less than in the other forms, since there is no prime mover and no storage of fuel or energy; the efficiency of the vehicle is, therefore, 85 to 90 per cent., although, of course, the overall efficiency of the whole system, including the power station, transmission and distribution equipment, and the contact wire, is only 10 to 15 per cent. By the concentration of all prime movers in a few large generating stations, the maintenance cost is much reduced and a lower grade of fuel can be burned, while if the traction company purchases its energy in bulk from a supply undertaking it is relieved of all responsibility in this respect. The maintenance of the electrical equipment on the vehicle is very small, and such vehicles can, if desired, be kept in service for 95 per cent. or more of the working day. The only serious technical disadvantage of track electrification as against the use of self-contained power units is the fact that a breakdown of the electric supply causes a complete stoppage of the system. Such an occurrence is, however, sufficiently rare nowadays to be a negligible factor in making a comparison.

Systems of Track Electrification

Alternating or Direct Current.—Current may be supplied to the contact rail or wire in the form of direct current, single-phase a.c., or 3-phase a.c. Direct current at about 600 V is universally employed for tramways and for many suburban railways, while 1,500 or 3,000 V. d.c. is used for main-line railways in many countries. For d.c. working, series motors are generally used, although the compound motor is coming into favour for tramways or trolleybuses where regenerative braking is desired. When single-phase a.c. is employed the pressure at the contact wire is 16,000 to 20,000 V at $16\frac{2}{3}$ or 25 Hz, and is stepped down by means of a transformer on the locomotive to a low voltage suitable for supplying to single-phase series motors. With both the d.c. and the single-phase systems only one contact wire is normally employed, the current returning by the running rails. The 3-phase system also employs a high contact-wire voltage, and this is applied to an induction motor on the locomotive. Here two contact wires must be employed, the track rails forming the third phase, and this leads to insulation difficulties at junctions. The induction motor is simple and robust, but is not convenient for obtaining speed control.

The a.c. systems with their high contact-wire voltage have to deal with much smaller currents for a given power than would a d.c. system for the same service, and the efficiency of the distribution system between the incoming a.c. supply and the locomotive is therefore higher. For the single-phase system a low frequency is required to secure satisfactory motor characteristics, and it cannot therefore be supplied directly from the ordinary industrial network ; in some cases it is supplied from a separate system employing single-phase generating stations, while in others it is supplied from the industrial net work through frequency convertors changing from 3-phase, 50 Hz to 1-phase, $16\frac{2}{3}$ or 25 Hz. The 3-phase system can be supplied directly from the industrial network without any rotating convertors, and therefore has a high efficiency. This system was originally adopted by the Italian State Railways and has proved satisfactory in practice on many miles of line in Northern Italy ; no important extensions of it are, however, being made on account of the contact-wire and speed-control difficulties previously mentioned.

With regard to the relative merits of the d.c. and the single-phase systems, it is generally accepted that so far as locomotive equipment is concerned the d.c. motors have better characteristics, lower maintenance costs, and a smaller weight per horse-power than corresponding a.c. motors, while the a.c. system is preferable from the point of view of the distribution and contact-wire system. For suburban services and road transport, where stops are frequent and distribution distances small, the d.c. system at 600 or 1,500 volts is almost invariably employed. For main-line railways, however, opinion in different countries is divided. Great Britain, France, and Italy have standardised d.c. at 1,500 or 3,000 V, the power supply being taken from the industrial network through rotary-convertor or mercury-arc rectifier substations. In Scandinavia the single-phase system at 16,000 V., $16\frac{2}{3}$ Hz, supplied through frequency-convertor substations from the 50 Hz industrial network, is employed, whilst in Germany, Austria, and Switzerland the single-phase 16,000 V., $16\frac{2}{3}$ Hz system supplied from special single-phase generating stations is standard. In other countries, including the U.S.A., the tendency is to employ direct current.

Attempts have been made, however, to combine the advantages of both systems by the use of a motor generator or mercury-arc rectifier on the locomotive, so that the high efficiency of the a.c. distribution system may be obtained together with the desirable characteristics of the d.c. motors. Another method, known as the Kando system, and adopted in Hungary, employs a phase convertor on the locomotive to convert from the single-phase 16,000-V., 50-Hz supply on the trolley wire to a polyphase supply for driving an induction motor. This enables the traction supply to be taken from the industrial supply system without the complicated overhead trolley-wire equipment of the ordinary 3-phase system.

Overhead Contact Wire or Contact Rail.—Where the contact voltage is 1,500 V. or more an overhead wire is almost invariably used, while below this value either an overhead wire or the contact rail may be employed. For tramway work the overhead construction is universal, except in a very few instances where it was considered that the overhead wire would be unsightly and an expensive slot construction was adopted; the conductor rails are, in this case, laid beneath the road surface and contact is made with them by means of a plough passing through a slot in the roadway. Suburban railways at 600 V. use the contact rail, as this gives a cheaper construction than the overhead wire for this voltage and does not cause undue danger to the permanent-way staff. The running rails are employed as the return conductor except in special cases where it is necessary to reduce stray earth currents to a minimum; the rails must, of course, be specially bonded at the joints when used for this purpose.

Locomotives or Motor Coaches.—One advantage of electric traction for railway work lies in the fact that motors may be placed on two or more of the vehicles of a train and all controlled from one point. Such an arrangement, known as the multiple-unit or motor-coach system, is emloyed for suburban traffic, a normal train unit consisting of one or two motor coaches and one or two trailer coaches having no motors ; during rush hours two or three such units can be coupled to form a train and the whole controlled by a single motorman in the front motor coach. By adopting this system the available motive power is used to the best advantage, and a large proportion of the total train weight is available as adhesive weight, enabling the rapid acceleration necessary for a suburban service to be attained. For main-line work and for goods traffic an electric locomotive hauling the train in the same way as a steam locomotive is preferable on account of the great diversity of rolling stock and the cost which would be incurred in equipping it for multiple-unit operation.

2. THE TRACTION MOTOR

The motor is common to all systems of electric traction, and as the conditions under which it operates are very different and much more arduous than those occurring in most industrial drives, a special type of motor, known as a traction motor, has been developed.

General Features of Traction Motors

The following are the chief requirements of a satisfactory traction Motor.

Electrical Features:

- High starting torque.
- Series speed-torque characteristic.
- Simple speed control.
- Possibility of dynamic or regenerative braking.
- Good commutation under rapid fluctuations of supply voltage.

Mechanical Features:

- Robustness and ability to withstand continuous vibration.
- Minimum weight and overall dimensions.
- Protection against dirt and damp, particularly if mounted beneath the locomotive or motor coach.

No type of motor completely fulfils all these requirements, and of the various types which have been tried the only ones which have been found satisfactory in practice are the series and compound motors for d.c. systems, the a.c. series motor for single-phase systems, and the induction motor for 3-phase systems.

Speed-torque Characteristic.—If a vehicle has two motors connected to different driving axles, the relative speeds of the motors will, of course, be fixed by the relative speeds of these axles. Assuming no slip, the peripheral speed of all the driving wheels will be the same, but should there be a slight difference in the diameter of these wheels, due to differences in the wear, there will be a corresponding difference in the speeds of the driving axles to which they are connected, and also, therefore, a difference in speed of the motors. Suppose the motor speeds are

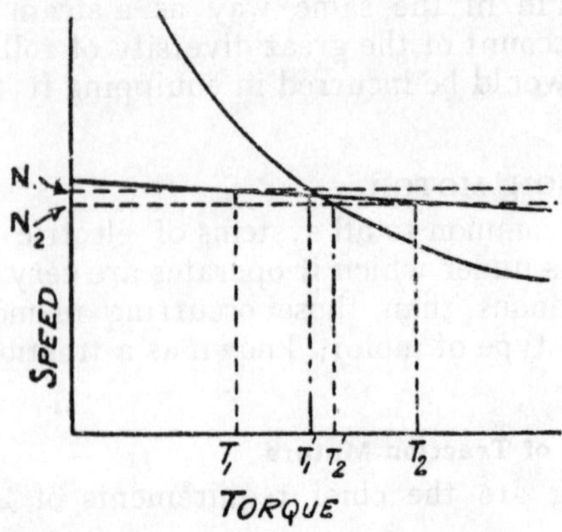

FIG. 63.—EFFECT OF SPEED DIFFERENCE ON MOTORS IN PARALLEL.

N_1 and N_2, as shown in Fig. 63. If the motors have the shunt characteristics indicated, that having the speed N_1 (with the worn driving wheels) will be exerting only about half as much torque as that exerted by the motor running at a speed N_2 (torques T_1 and T_2); since it is obviously desirable that all motors of a train should share the load equally, such a state of affairs is not satisfactory. With a series characteristic, however, it can be seen that a slight difference in the two speeds has a very small effect on the relative torques provided by the two motors (T_1' and T_2). Motors with a shunt characteristic can be used if all the driving axles are coupled by a connecting rod so that there is no possibility of a difference in speed. Such a scheme is used on 3-phase locomotives driven by induction motors; motor-coach operation with motors having a shunt characteristic is, however, impossible, and even the coupling of two such locomotives to draw a heavy train is often impracticable. The conditions existing are illustrated by Example 10.

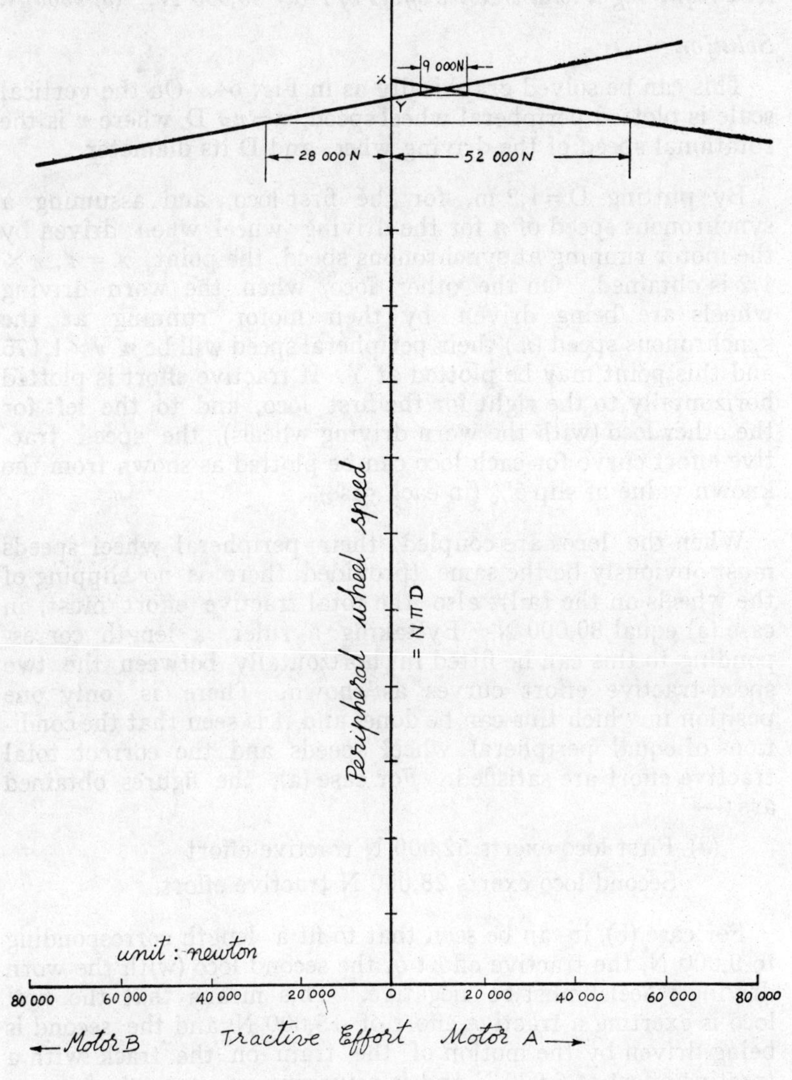

Fig. 64

Example 10 : Two 3-phase locomotives employing induction motors are being used to haul a train. The driving wheels of one loco are 1.2 m in diameter, while the wheels of the other have been worn down to a diameter of 1.175 m. Both the motors have a slip of 5% when exerting 44500 N tractive effort. How will the locos share a load requiring a total tractive effort of : (a) 80,000 N ; (b) 9000 N.

Solution :

This can be solved graphically as in Fig. 64. On the vertical scale is plotted peripheral wheel speed, $v = n\pi D$, where n is the rotational speed of the driving wheel and D its diameter.

By putting D = 1.2 m, for the first loco, and assuming a synchronous speed of n for the driving wheel when driven by the motor running at synchronous speed, the point $\times = n'.\ \pi \times 1.2$ is obtained. On the other loco, when the worn driving wheels are being driven by their motor running at the synchronous speed (n') their peripheral speed will be $n'.\pi \times 1.175$ and this point may be plotted at Y. If tractive effort is plotted horizontally to the right for the first loco, and to the left for the other loco (with the worn driving wheels), the speed tractive effort curve for each loco can be plotted as shown from the known value of slip 5% (in each case).

When the locos are coupled, their peripheral wheel speeds must obviously be the same (provided there is no slipping of the wheels on the rail) ; also the total tractive effort must, in case (a) equal 80,000 N. By taking a ruler, a length corresponding to this can be fitted in horizontally between the two speed-tractive effort curves as shown. There is only one position in which this can be done, and it is seen that the conditions of equal peripheral wheel speeds and the correct total tractive effort are satisfied. For case (a), the figures obtained are :—

(*a*) First loco exerts 52,000 N tractive effort
Second loco exerts 28,000 N tractive effort.

For case (b), it can be seen that to fit a length corresponding to 9,000 N, the tractive effort of the second loco (with the worn driving wheels) must be negative. This means that the first loco is exerting a tractive effort of 15,000 N and the second is being driven by the motion of the train on the track with a tractive effort of 6,000 N and is returning an amount of power corresponding to this value to the supply.

It is thus seen that there is a danger of seriously overloading one locomotive when hauling heavy loads under these conditons.

If the slips of the motors on the two locos had been slightly different, the problem could have been treated in exactly the same way, but the slopes of the two speed-tractive effort curves would, in this case, have been different. It may be noted also that, when drawing the diagram, a false zero can be used for the peripheral speed scale, so that the slopes of the speed tractive effort curves will be greater and measurements therefore easier to read.

Overload and Tractive Effort.—A further point in connection with the speed-torque characteristic is the relation between the torque required by the train and the h.p. drawn from the supply.

With the d.c. series motor, assuming that the flux is proportional to the current, we may write:

$$\text{Speed } n \propto \frac{V}{\Phi} \propto \frac{V}{I} \propto \frac{1}{I} \text{(if V is constant)}$$

$$\text{Torque } T \propto I\Phi \propto I^2$$

$$\therefore \quad I \propto \sqrt{T}$$

$$\therefore \quad n \propto \frac{1}{\sqrt{T}}$$

But $$kW \propto Tn \propto T \times \frac{1}{\sqrt{T}} \propto \sqrt{T} \qquad (27)$$

The power taken from the supply thus increases with the torque required by the train, but only as the square root of this quantity. Actually, of course, on account of the saturation of the magnetic circuit, the kW will increase slightly more than this.

Similar conditions apply to the a.c. series motor, but with the induction motor (or the d.c. shunt motor if such were used) where the speed is approximately constant and independent of the torque we have:

$$kW \propto Tn \propto T \qquad . \quad . \quad . \quad . \qquad (28)$$

i.e. the kW taken from the supply is proportional to the first power of the torque required. A given overload, as measured by an increased tractive effort to be provided for the train, will thus require a much greater input from the supply when induction motors (or shunt motors) are used than when series motors are employed.

Rating.—Traction motors are subject to an intermittent load, particularly when used for tramway and suburban services, since apart from actual stops there are periods of coasting, when they are delivering no power. The usual procedure therefore is to give traction motors a 1-hour rating, as well as a continuous rating—these ratings are fully defined in I.S.S. The continuous rating of an ordinary self-ventilated motor is usually about $\frac{1}{3}$ to $\frac{1}{4}$ of its 1-hour rating, while if forced ventilation is used the continuous rating may be 80 per cent. of the 1-hour rating.

Ventilation.—Since it is necessary to keep down the size and weight of a traction motor, efficient cooling is essential. On account, however, of the arduous conditions under which motors operate, particularly when mounted under the frame of the vehicle, as with motor coaches and road vehicles, some form of enclosure is necessary to prevent the ingress of dirt and moisture. Small motors can be totally enclosed, but for tramway or railway work some form of ventilation is necessary ; either self-ventilation or forced ventilation may be employed, the former using a fan mounted on the motor shaft which blows a current of air through suitable ducts in the motor, while the latter uses an external fan. In either case care must be taken in designing the ducts to prevent their becoming choked with dirt, and axial rather than radial ducts are always employed. The use of forced ventilation has a decided advantage in that it is operative when the vehicle is stationary, and it is almost invariably used on locomotives ; for motor coaches and road vehicles, however, the noise of the fan precludes its use and self-ventilation is the usual practice.

Applications of the Different Types of Motor

Although the d.c. series, the a.c. series, and the induction motor are all used for traction work, they are not equally suitable for all types of service.

The D.C. Series Motor.—The simplicity and robustness of the d.c. series motor render it suitable for all types of traction service, but more particularly for suburban work, where high starting torques and rates of acceleration are essential. Motors of 45 to 75 kW, mass 5.4 to 7.2 kg per kW are available for trams and trolley buses, although masses of 12 or 18 kg per kW are more usual for the larger motors required for railway work. Commutation is excellent up to twice full load, thus cutting down brush replacements and commutator grinding to a minimum.

The A.C. Series Motor.—Although very many types of single-phase motor have been used for traction work, the only survivor is the compensated series motor, and this can be built in sizes up to several hundred kW, e.g. the 500 kW motors for the 9000 kW locomative for the Swiss Federal Railways. The voltage is limited to about 300 volts and the weight is $1\frac{1}{2}$ to 2 times that of a d.c. motor. The power factor at starting is low, so that for a given current the starting torque is much lower than that of a d.c. motor, and a.c. series motors are not therefore well suited for suburban work with frequent stops. For main-line work, however, they are used on all the single-phase lines in Germany, Switzerland, Scandinavia, and America, and give eminently satisfactory service.

The Induction Motor.—Although the induction motor is inherently the simplest of the available types, the complication of the pole-changing or other equipment necessary to obtain speed control and the large rheostats required for starting offset this advantage to a considerable extent. Furthermore, on account of its flat speed-torque characteristic, it cannot be applied to multiple-unit working. Except for the Kando system adopted in Hungary and the existing sections of the Italian State Railways, it is not likely to be used to any extent in the future.

3. THE LOCOMOTIVE

The mechanical problems which are of chief importance to the electrical engineer in connection with the locomotive are the wheel arrangement and general disposition of the equipment to secure good riding properties and the transmission of the drive from the motor armatures to the driving axles.

Wheel Arrangement and Riding Qualities

The maximum tractive effort which can be exerted by a locomotive without slipping of the driving wheels is generally about 15 per cent. to 25 per cent. of the weight on these wheels, this factor being known as the coefficient of adhesion. To haul a given train, therefore, a certain minimum weight of locomotive must be provided. The maximum allowable mass on each driving axle is limited by the strength of the track, bridges, etc., to between 15 and 30 tonnes, depending on the circumstances; if this figure is known, the number of driving axles can thus be fixed - for example, the locomotives for the South African Railways have to produce a maximum tractive effort of 294 kN. Assuming a coefficient of adhesion of 15 per cent., the minimum mass of locomotive has to be :

$$\frac{294 \text{ kN}}{0{\cdot}15} \times \frac{1}{9{\cdot}81} = 196 \times 10^3 \text{ kg}$$

The maximum allowable mass per driving axle for the track concerned is 18 tonnes, so that at least 11 driving axles must be provided. Actually, a train requiring the above tractive effort is hauled by three locomotives each having 4 driving axles, making 12 in all. Each of these locomotives is arranged

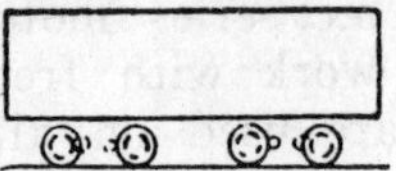

(*a*) SOUTH AFRICAN RAILWAYS 900 kW; B_0-B_0 GOODS & PASSENGER LOCO. NOSE SUSPENDED MOTORS. MAX. SPEED 72 km/h. (3′-6″ GAUGE). 3000 V.D.C.

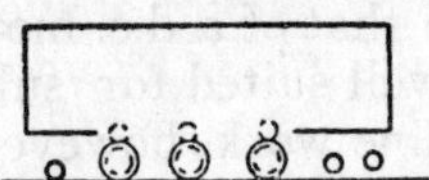

(*b*) GREAT INDIAN PENINSULA RAILWAY 1575 kW, 1-C_0-2 EXPRESS PASSENGER LOCO. MAX. SPEED 112km/h. 15000 V.D C.

(*c*) P.L.M. RAILWAY. 4080kW, 2-C_0+C_0-2 EXPRESS PASSENGER LOCO. MAX. SPEED 130 km/h. 1500 V.D C.

(*d*) SWEDISH STATE RAILWAYS 1245 kW, 1-C-1 GOODS & PASSENGER LOCO. MAX. SPEED 96 km/h. 1-PH. 16000 V. 16 2/3 Hz.

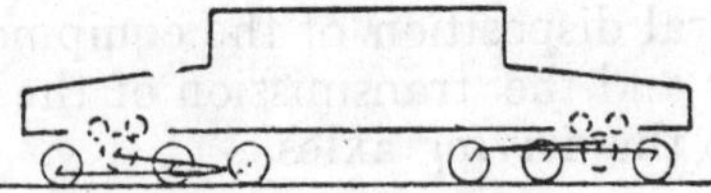

(*e*) GREAT INDIAN PENINSULA RAILWAY 1950 kW C+C. GOODS LOCO. COLLECTIVE DRIVE WITH CONNECTING ROD. MAX. SPEED 56 km/h. 1500 V.D.C.

(*f*) ITALIAN STATE RAILWAYS 2025 kW 0-E-0 GOODS LOCO. COLLECTIVE DRIVE WITH MODIFIED SCOTCH YOKE (BIANCHI SYSTEM). MAX. SPEED 50 km/h. 3-PH. 3700V. 16 2/3 Hz.

FIG. 65.—TYPES OF LOCOMOTIVE DRIVE

as shown in Fig. 65(*a*). With d.c. locomotives, the electrical equipment of which is relatively light, it is often desirable to place the whole of the locomotive weight on driving wheels to obtain the required tractive effort; with a.c. locomotives, however, where the weight per kW is much higher, the required tractive effort can often be obtained by placing only a portion of the weight on the driving wheels and supporting the rest on trailing axles, as shown in Fig. 65(*d*). These trailing axles, however, tend to improve the riding qualities of high-speed locomotives, and are often used on d.c. locomotives for this purpose (Figs. 65 (*b*) and (*c*)).

Individual and Collective Drive.—A point about which there has been a great deal of controversy is whether each driving axle should have its own motor (individual drive) or whether a single motor should drive all the axles through connecting rods, as in a steam locomotive (collective drive). The latter are illustrated in Figs. 65 (*d*), (*e*), and (*f*), and Fig. 66. It appears at first sight to be a retrograde step to introduce any reciprocating masses into the drive, since we have in the electric motor a smooth rotational drive in the first place, but there are points in favour of the collective drive which have led to its adoption in certain cases. Firstly there is less tendency for the wheels to slip if they are all coupled, and secondly the motor can be mounted well up in the main body of the locomotive, thereby raising the centre of gravity, which reduces wear on the track and also enables the motor designer to have a free hand with regard to dimensions. Difficulties arise, however, due to stresses and vibrations in the connecting rods, particularly at high speeds, and the general tendency at the present time is to employ individual drive for high-speed locomotives and collective drive only for low-speed goods locomotives.

General Riding Qualities.—It is only recently that high-speed electric locomtives have been built, all the early electrification having been of a suburban nature or in mountainous districts, so that no very definite rules can be laid down regarding the behaviour of electric locomotives under high-speed conditions. It is generally accepted, however, that a leading or trailing bogie improves the behaviour, and that the centre of gravity should be fairly high, figures between about 0·61m and 1·07m. above rail level being common practice.

Classification by Wheel Arrangement.—Electric locomotives can be classified by the method usually employed for steam locomotives, that is, by numbers representing the number of driving wheels—e.g. 4-4-0 for an Atlantic-type locomotive with a two-axle leading bogie, two driving axles, and no trailing bogie ; the number of possible arrangements is greater, however, with an electric than with a steam locomotive, and a more comprehensive system employing both numerals and letters is in common use. Trailing axles are represented by numbers and driving axles

FIG. 66.—1245 KW LOCOMOTIVE HAULING TRAIN ON SWEDISH STATE RAILWAYS
(16,000 V., $16\frac{2}{3}$ Hz.)
(*ASEA Electric, Ltd.*)

by letters; a two-axle trailing bogie is thus represented by the figure 2. Driving axles are represented by the letters A, B, C, etc., according as to whether there is a single independent axle, two coupled axles, or three coupled axles; two or more individually driven axles on the same bogie or truck are represented by B_0, C_0, etc. The application of this system can be seen by reference to the diagrams in Fig. 65.

Transmission of Drive

In order to obtain reasonable freedom from vibration in any type of locomotive and to prevent damage to the track, springs must be interposed between the driving axles and the locomotive frame, and as much as possible of the weight of the locomotive must be spring-borne. In the electric locomotive, if the motor is supported on the frame in order to secure this condition, it is obvious that there will be relative motion between the motor armature and the driving axle due to the compression and extension of the springs, and the drive between the two must, therefore, be flexible. The problem does not arise in the steam locomotive, as the piston (attached to the driving axle) is free to move in the cylinder (attached to the frame). The provision of a satisfactory form of flexible drive is one of the most difficult problems of the electric locomotive, and many devices have been tried with varying success.

Direct Drive.—The simplest method of drive is to mount the armature of the motor directly on the driving axle with the field rigidly attached to the frame, as shown in Fig. 67. The pole pieces of the motor are approximately flat, so that the armature can move relatively to them without affecting the operation. It

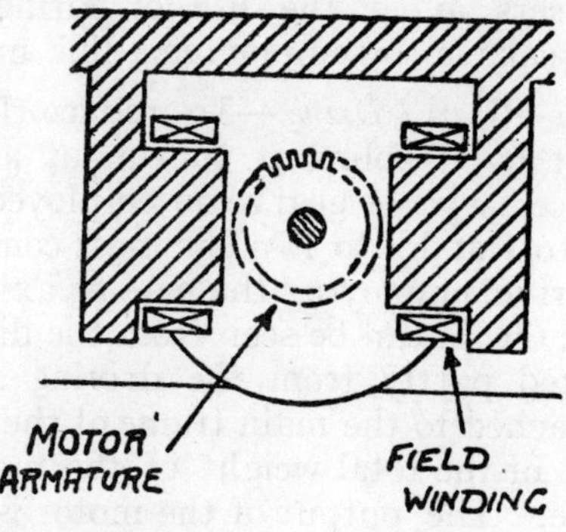

Fig. 67.—Direct Drive.

is evident that a two-pole motor must be employed and that its size is limited by the diameter of the driving wheels; furthermore, if a reasonably large driving wheel is to be used, the motor will have to run at a low speed. These facts, together with the relatively large unsprung weight of the armature, limit the applications of this method, although a number of d.c. locomotives of the New York Central railway employ this arrangement.

Direct Quill Drive.—The quill is hollow shaft surrounding the driving axle and attached to it by means of springs or some other flexible device, as shown in Fig. 68, which allows relative motion between it and the axle. The motor armature is mounted on the quill, and it may therefore be entirely spring-borne. This

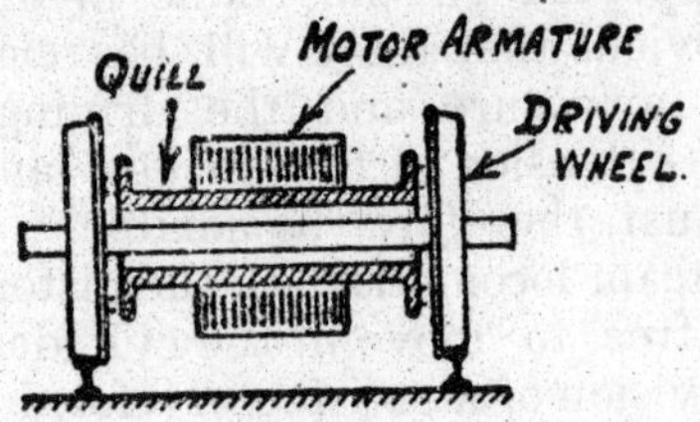

FIG. 68.—QUILL DRIVE. FLEXIBLE CONNECTION BETWEEN QUILL AND DRIVING WHEEL.

arrangement reduces the unsprung weight to a minimum and enables a normal design of motor to be used, although its size and speed are still governed by the diameter of the driving wheels.

One class of devices for obtaining a flexible connection between the flange of the quill and the driving wheel employs springs; other manufacturers avoid the use of springs and possible troubles due to breakages by employing a link motion.

Nose Suspension—Geared Drive.—To reduce the size of motor for a given output by enabling it to run at a higher speed a geared drive is necessary, the gear ratio employed being usually between about 3 to 1 and [illegible] to 1. The most common of all the types of geared drive, employing the nose or axle suspension, is illustrated in Fig. 69. It can be seen from the diagram that the motor is supported partly from the driving axle and partly from a spring attached to the main frame of the vehicle; about 50 or 60 per cent. of the total weight of the motor and gear is thus spring-borne. The output of the motor is limited by the space available to about 337.5 kW for normal-gauge vehicles, and there is a relatively large unsprung weight, so that the method is not suitable for large locomotives, although it is almost invariably employed for motor coaches and tramways.

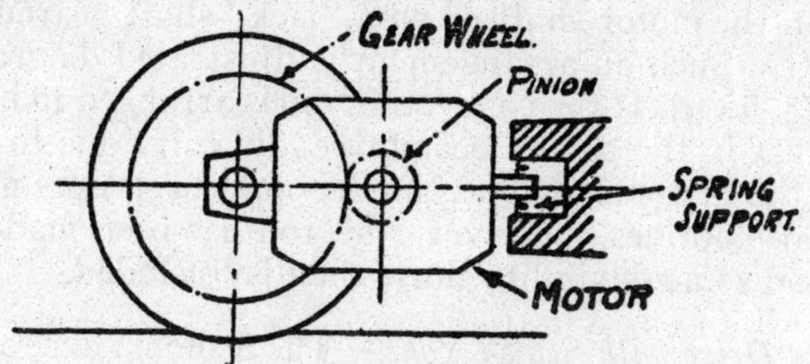

FIG. 69.—NOSE SUSPENSION.

Geared Quill Drive.—When it is desired to place the motor higher in the frame than is possible with the nose suspension in order to enable a larger motor to be used or to raise the centre of gravity and reduce the unsprung weight, a geared quill drive can be used. A quill surrounds the driving axle, as in the direct quill drive, but instead of the motor armature being mounted directly on this, only the gear is mounted on it. One of the methods previously mentioned can then be employed for providing a flexible connection between the quill and the axle.

Brown Boveri Individual Drive.—An arrangement adopted with considerable success on both high-and low-speed locomotives by Messrs. Brown Boveri is illustrated diagrammatically

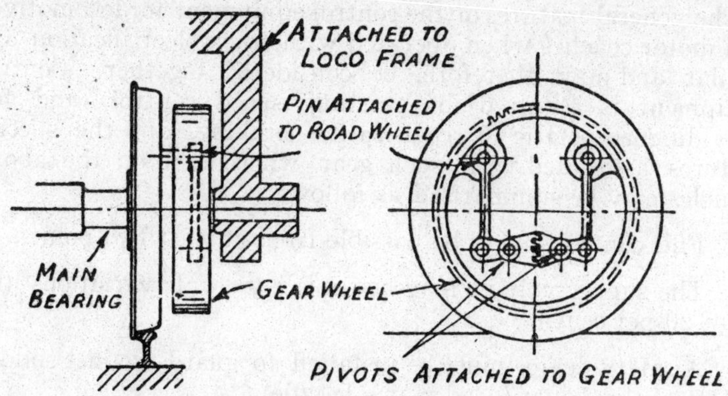

FIG. 70.—BROWN BOVERI INDIVIDUAL DRIVE.

in Fig. 70. The special link arrangement allows of flexibility between the gear wheel and the driving wheel.

Collective Drive with Connecting Rod.—Where a collective drive is considered desirable, a common method is to drive with coupled wheels by means of a connecting rod attached to a crank mounted on the motor shaft or on a "jack" shaft geared to the motor shaft. Such an arrangement is illustrated diagrammatically in Fig. 65 (*e*). If the connecting rod is arranged to be nearly horizontal, as in the steam locomotive, difficulty due to relative motion of the motor shaft and the driving wheels does not arise. In a few locomotives, however, the rod has been made nearly vertical, and some flexibility must then be included.

Collective Drive with Scotch Yoke.—The Scotch Yoke, or Kando type of drive, is illustrated in Fig. 65(*f*), and employs a triangular framework with the apex attached to the coupling rod and the other two corners attached to cranks on two motor shafts. Vertical play is allowed in the bearings to secure the necessary flexibility between the motor shaft and driving wheels. Early designs gave a certain amount of trouble due to breakage of the yokes, as very high and incalculable stresses are liable to be set up ; these have been overcome in later designs by employing stronger frames or, preferably, by using an articulated framework, as in the Bianchi drive used on the 3-phase locomotives of the Italian State Railways.

4. CHARACTERISTICS AND CONTROL OF LOCOMOTIVES AND MOTOR COACHES FOR TRACK ELECTRIFICATION

The general features of the control equipment for locomotives and motor coaches when operated with track electrification are similar and may, therefore, be considered together. Control equipment is required for starting, speed control, and for providing rheostatic or regenerative braking, and the special features associated with such gear when used on the above vehicles may be summarised as follows :

Full control should be possible from at least two points.

The supply voltage may be subject to wide variations (up to $\pm$ 20 per cent.).

A safety device must be installed to guard against sudden illness of the driver (dead man's handle).

As with industrial equipment, it may be operated by hand, by master controller, or it may be fully automatic, although the use of a master controller is the general practice.

D. C. Equipment—Starting and Speed Control

It was pointed out in Chapter I that the speed of a d.c. series motor may be varied by field control or by variation of the voltage applied to the motor. On account of design difficulties arising with traction motors, field control is usually limited to one or two tappings on the field, giving speeds of about 115 per cent. and 130 per cent. of normal. Speed variation below normal and starting must be carried out by voltage control,

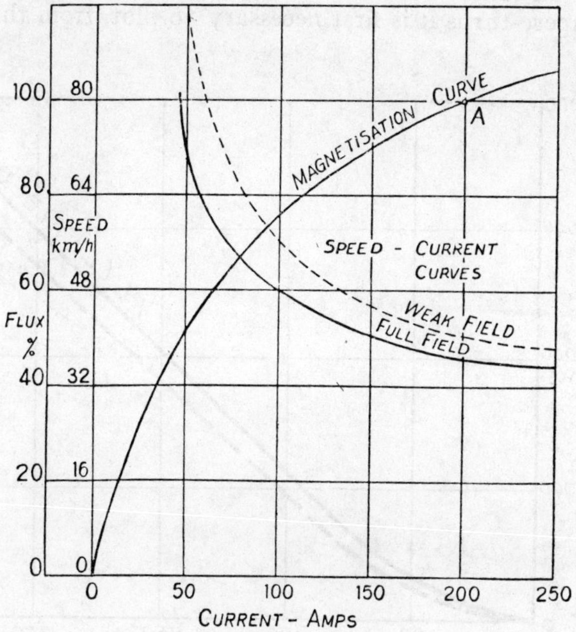

FIG. 71.—EFFECT OF FIELD WEAKENING ON SPEED-CURRENT CHARACTERISTICS. (EXAMPLE 11.)

employing either a series resistance or the series-parallel connection or, in most cases, a combination of the two. The effect of field weakening on the speed-current and speed-tractive effort curves is illustrated by Example 11.

Example 11 : The following figures give the speed-current and speed-tractive effort of a motor coach when running with the motors having all their field turns in circuit. What will be the corresponding characteristics if run on a field tapping, which cuts out 30% of turns.

Current (A) . .	50	100	150	200	250
Speed (km/h) .	74	48·2	41·3	37·5	35·4
Tractive effort (N)	1330	4670	8250	11850	15550

Solution :

The speed current curve in the full field position is shown in fig. 71. In order to determine the effect of a reduction of the field ampere-turns it is first necessary to plot, from this curve,

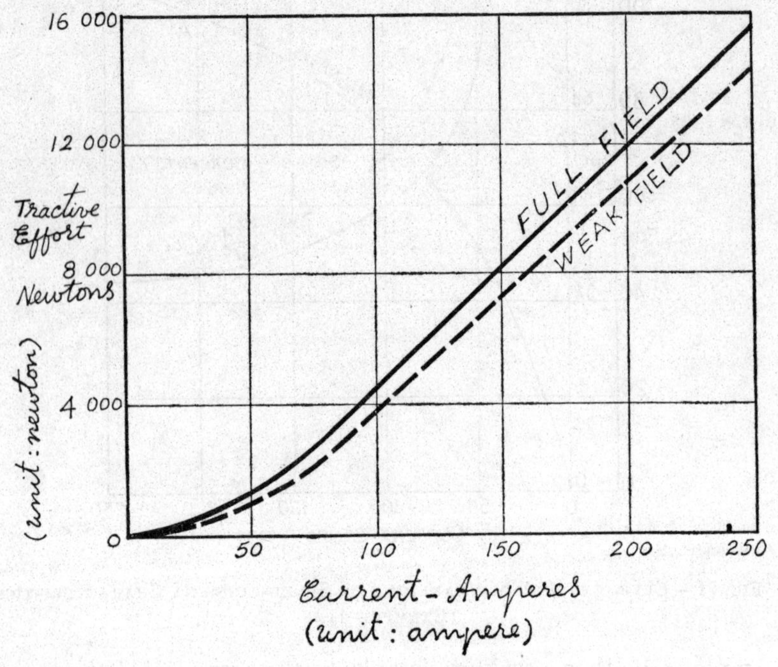

Fig. 72

the magnetisation curve, i.e. the relation between flux and current. Suppose the flux at a current of 200 A is 100% as given by point A on fig. 71. The speed at this current is 37.5 km/h. Consider now a current of 100 A: the speed is 48.2 km/h.

From equation (6), neglecting the resistance drop, we have

Therefore, since V is constant, $\phi \propto \frac{1}{n}$

Flux at the new speed $\phi' = 100 \times \frac{37 \cdot 5}{48 \cdot 2} = 77 \cdot 7\%$

The current at this speed is 100 A, so that another point on the magnetisation curve has been found.

Other points can be found in a similar way and the complete magnetisation curve drawn as shown.

Now, reducing the field turns, by 30% will reduce the ampere-turns by this amount, and the effect so far as the flux is concerned, is similar to reducing the current by 30%.

Consider now a current of 100 A (the flux with full field is 77.7%). If the current is reduced by 30% to 70 A, the new flux will, from the magnetisation curve, be 64%.

With a current of 100 A; therefore, the flux on the weak field tapping is only 64% as compared with 77.7% when a full field.

As speed $\propto \frac{1}{\phi}$ the new speed at 100 A will be:

$$48 \cdot 2 \times \frac{77 \cdot 7}{64} = 58 \cdot 5 \text{ km/h.}$$

and as a tractive effort $\propto$ I Φ, the new tractive effort at 100 A will be:

$$4670 \times \frac{64}{70 \cdot 7} = 3850 \text{ N.}$$

A similar procedure can be carried out for other values of current, and the new curves plotted as shown dotted in Figs. 71 and 72.

Series-parallel Control.—This method of control presupposes the use of at least two motors, and these are connected in series at starting and for low speeds and in parallel for full-speed running. With a two-motor equipment, therefore, half normal voltage will be applied to each motor at starting, and they will run up to approximately half-speed, at which instant they are switched into parallel and full voltage is applied to each. In pratice, in order to limit the starting current to reasonable values, it is necessary to use series resistance in addition. This is inserted at starting and gradually cut out with the motors in the series connection and then reinserted when the motors are switched into parallel and again gradually cut out. It is of course not economical to use the resistances for speed control, but the series-parallel control gives two economical running speeds without any resistance in circuit, i.e. about half and full speed, while if used in conjunction with one or two field tappings, additional economical speeds can be obtained.

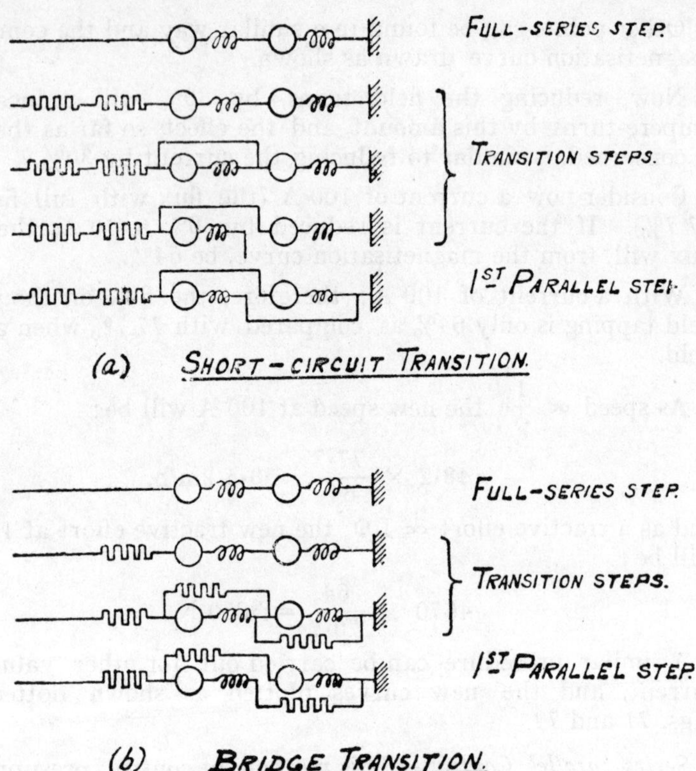

FIG. 73.—SERIES-PARALLEL CONTROL—TRANSITION STEPS.

The chief difficulty with series-parallel control is to obtain a satisfactory method of transition from series to parallel without interrupting the torque or allowing any heavy rushes of current. In all but very small units it is quite inadmissible to open the circuit to effect the change-over, and two other methods, the "short-circuit" and the "bridging" methods, are usually adopted. The connections of the short-circuit method are shown in Fig. 73 (*a*). one motor is short-circuited and the total torque is reduced by about 50 per cent. during the transition period, causing a noticeable jerk in the motion of the vehicle. The bridging method illustrated in Fig. 73 (*b*) is more complicated, but the resistances which are connected in parallel with, or "bridged" across the motors are of such a value that the current through the motors is not altered in magnitude and the total torque is therefore held constant. The bridging method is generally employed for railway work, but the simpler short-circuit transition is often used for trams.

Another important feature of the series-parallel method of control is the saving of energy lost in resistances during the starting period as compared with plain resistance starting with both

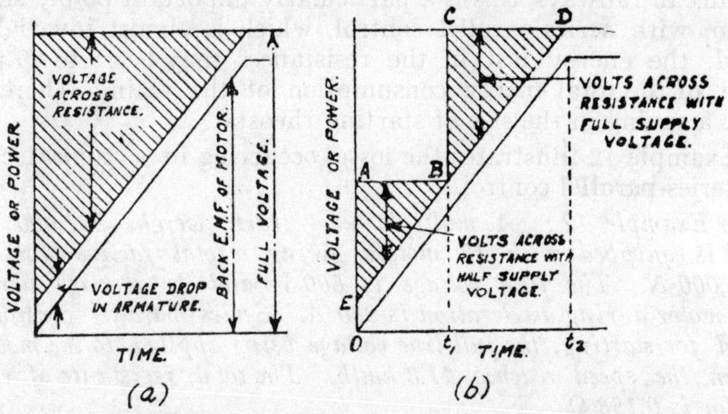

FIG. 74—SERIES-PARALLEL CONTROL—ENERGY LOSS.

motors in parallel. This is illustrated in Fig. 74, where it is assumed that the resistances are so varied that the maximum allowable current flows through both motors during the whole of the accelerating period ; the starting torque will, therefore, be the same whether the series-parallel or plain resistance method is used. In the latter case, assuming that the motor speeds up uniformly, the back e.m.f. will increase uniformly with time, as shown in Fig. 74 (*a*), while the voltage across the starting resistance of each motor will decrease uniformly. Since current is assumed constant the ordinates of Fig. 74 can also be considered to represent power and the shaded area represents the energy lost in the starting resistance for each motor. With series-parallel starting, again assuming uniform acceleration, the conditions will be as shown in Fig. 74 (*b*). Between O and t_1

the two motors are in series, and at time t_1 half the voltage is across each motor with no resistance in circuit. In reaching this condition the energy wasted per motor is shown by the area EAB. The motors are now switched into parallel with the appropriate amount of resistance reinserted, and acceleration continues to the time t_2, when the motors are in parallel with no resistance in circuit ; the shaded area BCD represents the loss of energy per motor during the latter part of the accelerating period, when the motors are in parallel. By comparing the two diagrams it can be seen that the amount of energy wasted in starting is only about half as much with series-parallel control as it would be with plain resistance starting. In situations where starting is frequent, as with tramways or suburban railways, this is a particularly important point, since even, with series-parallel control, which is almost invariably used, the energy lost in the resistances may be 15 to 20 per cent. of the total energy consumption of the train. There is also a saving in the size of starting rheostat.

Example 12 illustrates the losses occurring in a typical case of series-parallel control.

Example 12 : A multiple unit train weighs 391,000 kg. and is equipped with 12 motors giving a total tractive effort of 171,000 N. The line voltage is 600 V and the average current per motor during acceleration is 380 A. Series parallel control is used for starting, the full line voltage being applied to the motors when the speed reaches 41.8 km/h. The total resistance of each motor is 0.158 Ω.

Determine the total energy supplied during the starting period, the energy lost in the starting resistances, the energy lost in the motor, resistance and the useful energy applied to the train.

Solution :

Acceleration of train (from Eqn. 21a)

$$= \frac{171\ 000}{0{\cdot}277\ 8 \times 391\ 000} = 1{\cdot}575 \text{ km per hour per second}$$

$$\text{Time taken to reach } 41{\cdot}8 \text{ km/h} = \frac{41{\cdot}8}{1{\cdot}575} = 26{\cdot}55 \text{ s.}$$

Speed $\propto$ back e.m.f. of motors $(V - IR)$

In full series position, back e.m.f.

$$= 300 - 380 \times 0{\cdot}158 = 244 \text{ V.}$$

In full parallel position, back e.m.f.

$$= 600 - 380 \times 0{\cdot}158 = 540 \text{ V.}$$

Speed in full parallel position $= 41{\cdot}8$ km/h

Speed in full series position $= 41{\cdot}8 \times \frac{240}{540} = 18{\cdot}6$ km/h.

Time taken to reach this $= \frac{18{\cdot}6}{1{\cdot}575} = 11{\cdot}8$ s.

Time running in parallel position, upto $41{\cdot}8$ km/h

$$= 26{\cdot}55 - 11{\cdot}8 = 14{\cdot}75 \text{ s.}$$

Total Energy Input

Series position (6 circuits of 2 motors each, in parallel)

$$= 6 \times 600 \times 380 \times 11{\cdot}8 = 16{\cdot}25 \times 10^6 \text{ Ws.}$$

parallel position (12 motors in parallel)

$$= 12 \times 600 \times 380 \times 14{\cdot}75 = 40{\cdot}4 \times 10^6 \text{ Ws.}$$

$$\text{Total} = 56{\cdot}55 \times 10^6 \text{ Ws.}$$

$$= \mathbf{15{,}750} \text{ Wh.}$$

Energy wasted in starting resistances

Series position:

$$= 6 \times \tfrac{1}{2} \times 240 \times 330 \times 11{\cdot}8 = 3{\cdot}23 \times 10^6 \text{ Ws.}$$

parallel position:

$$= 12 \times \tfrac{1}{2} \times 300 \times 380 \times 14{\cdot}75 = 10{\cdot}1 \times 10^6 \text{ Ws.}$$

$$\text{Total} = 13{\cdot}33 \times 10^6 \text{ Ws.}$$

$$= \mathbf{3700} \text{ Wh.}$$

Energy lost in motor resistance

$$W = 12 \times 380^2 \times 0{\cdot}158 \times 26{\cdot}55 = 7{\cdot}27 \times 10^6 \text{ Ws.}$$

$$= \mathbf{2020} \text{ Wh.}$$

Useful Energy

K.E. of train at 41.8 km/h

$$= \tfrac{1}{2} \times \frac{26{\cdot}55}{3600} \times \frac{171\ 000 \times 41{\cdot}8}{360\ 0}$$

$$= \frac{1000}{3600} \text{ Wh.}$$

$$= \mathbf{7325} \text{ Wh.}$$

Metadyne Control.—The metadyne system of control described in Chapter I is also applicable to traction work. It requires no starting resistances, and therefore effects a considerable saving of energy over the ordinary series-parallel system, particularly for suburban services. Another important advantage is the fact that regenerative braking can be obtained down to zero speed. The savings due to these items may easily counterbalance the additional cost of the more complicated equipment required and its additional maintenance. It may be noted that the London Passenger Transport Board have a number of trains equipped with metadyne control.

A.C. Equipment—Starting and Speed Control

Single-phase Motors.—As pointed out previously, the maximum voltage for which a 1-phase series motor can be designed is about 300, so that a transformer always forms an essential part of the locomotive equipment. A variable voltage for both starting and speed control can therefore be obtained by means of tappings on the transformer—each tapping gives an economical running speed and no resistances with their attendant losses are required. The transformer tappings are usually arranged on the low-voltage side in order to avoid insulation difficulties, but 11,000-V locomotives have been built with high-voltage tappings, which enable a lighter construction to be used on account of the much lower currents which have to be dealt with. Between 6 and 12 tappings are usually provided, giving a corresponding number of economical speeds. On-load tap-changing equipment must, of course, be provided similar in principle to that used on transformers for ordinary power purposes.

Induction Motors.—Either cascade connection or pole-changing may be used for speed control; some types of locomotive in use on the 3-phase sections of the Italian State Railways employ cascade connection for the two-speed goods locomotives (24 and 50 km/h) and a combination of cascade connection and pole-changing for the four-speed passenger locomotives (37, 51, 74 and 102 km/h). Starting is carried out by means of liquid resistances in the rotor circuit.

Electric Braking

By electric braking is meant the dissipation of the braking energy electrically instead of converting it to heat at the brake shoes; the traction motors operate as generators driven by the momentum of the train and in rheostatic braking supply the energy to resistances mounted on the vehicle, while in regenerative braking the energy is returned to the supply system.

Although electric braking cannot replace the ordinary vacuumor air-brake equipment, since it cannot hold a train stationary, it forms a very valuable adjunct to it, as it provides an additional factor of safety and also reduces wear of brake shoes and the production of brake-shoe dust, particularly where long gradients have to be negotiated. If regenerative braking is employed, the total energy consumption may be reduced by as much as 15 or 20 per cent. if conditions are favourable.

The requirements of a braking system on a main-line locomotive differ from those of motor coaches operating on a suburban system in that the former usually needs braking to hold the train at the steady speed on a long down grade, whereas with the latter braking is primarily required for stopping the train. Rheostatic braking is employed in both cases, but regenerative

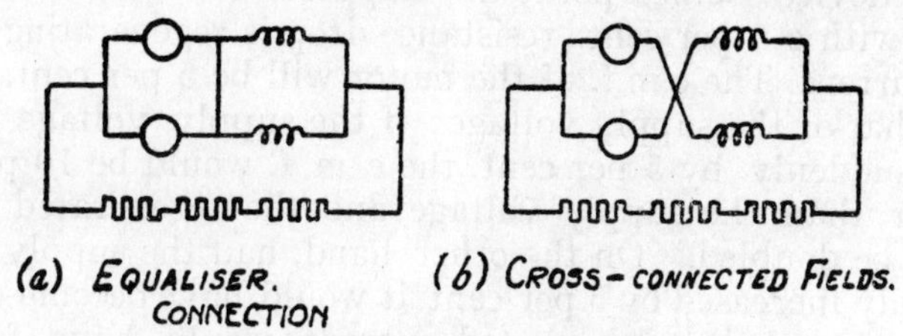

FIG. 75.—RHEOSTATIC BRAKING CONNECTIONS.

braking, owing to the complication of providing for it with d.c. series motors, is chiefly confined to main-line electrification.

Rheostatic Braking with D.C. Series Motors.—Rheostatic braking with a single series motor has been described previously in connection with the drive of cranes, hoists, etc. For traction work where two or more motors are employed, these are connected in parallel for braking, as shown in Fig. 75, because the series connection would produce too high a voltage. To ensure that the two machines share the load equally an equalising connection may be used for this purpose, as in Fig. 75 (*a*); if this were not done the machine whose excitation built up first would send a current through the second machine in the opposite direction, causing it to excite with reversed voltage, so that the two machines would be short-circuited on themselves. A large braking torque would be produced in this way, but it would be quite uncontrollable and the currents would be dangerously high. An alternative method of avoiding this condition is to cross-connect the fields, as shown in Fig. 75(*b*).

Regenerative Braking with D. C. Series Motors.—The series motor cannot be used for regenerative braking in the same simple way as the shunt motor (page 48) for the following two reasons:

(i) Since the motor current reverses when regeneration takes place the series field also, reverses thereby reversing the back e. m. f. and setting up a short-circuit condition. To change from motoring to regeneration therefore involves a reversal of the field connections, and to judge the correct instant at which to do this would require considerable skill on the part of the operator.

(ii) A small change in the supply voltage, such as frequently occurs in traction systems, will cause a large change in the regenerated current or even a short-circuit unless some compensating device is incorporated. Suppose, for instance, that a motor with a 5 per cent. resistance drop is regenerating at full-load current. The e.m.f. of the motor will be 5 per cent. greater than that of the supply voltage; if the supply voltage were to drop suddenly by 5 per cent. the e. m. f. would be 10 per cent. greater than the supply voltage and the regenerated current would be doubled. On the other hand, had the supply voltage suddenly increased by 5 per cent. it would have become equal to the e.m.f. and the regenerated current would have fallen to zero; had the supply voltage increased by more than 5 per cent. the current would have reversed. The series motor is thus quite unsuitable for regenerative braking, and if such braking is to be employed the motors must be reconnected as shunt or separately-excited machines.

One method of connection is to arrange the motors as shunt machines during regeneration, with the series fields connected across the supply in series with suitable resistances. If there were only one motor it is obvious that the conditions would be exactly as for rheostatic braking, since all the regenerated current would have to pass through the field circuit and the energy would be wasted in the resistances; if, however, the armatures can be connected in parallel and the fields in series, as in Fig. 76, then the current from one motor will be sufficient to excite the fields, and that from the others can be returned to the supply. Such an arrangement is quite stable; any change in line voltage produces a change in excitation, which produces a corresponding change in the e.m.f. of the motors so that inherent compensation is provided. This system is employed frequently by Brown Boveri, a typical example being on the

$B_0 - B_0 - B_0$, 750 kW locomotives for the Montreux-Bernese Oberland Railway, where the six motor armatures are connected, for regeneration, in three parallel groups of two in series, while all six fields are connected in series across the supply and in series with a suitable resistance.

An alternative method, which obviates the loss of power in the resistances in the field circuit, is to use a separate exciter for the field windings, this exciter being either axle-driven or driven by a motor operated from the auxiliary supply. Many devices have been employed to secure compensation against line-voltage

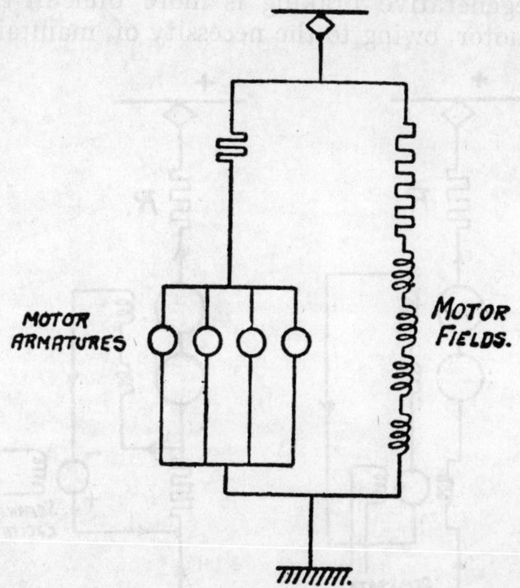

FIG. 76—REGENERATIVE BRAKING—SHUNT CONNECTION.

variation, most of which utilise some form of differential winding on the exciter. One such method is illustrated in Fig. 77 (*a*); a separate motor-driven exciter has a separately excited winding and also a series winding connected in the main motor circuit in such a way that it opposes the separately excited winding during regeneration. It can thus be seen that a reduction in line voltage, which will tend to increase the regenerated current, will weaken the exciterfield and counteract the change; the stabilising resistance R also assists in this action.

Another method, employed on the locomotives of the South African Railways, utilises a stabilising resistance and exciter connected as in Fig. 77 (*b*). The current through the stabilising resistance is the sum of the exciter current and the regenerated current, and any increase in the latter means that there will be a greater voltage drop in the resistance and therefore less current through the exciter circuit, again counteracting the effect of line voltage variations.

Electric Braking with A.C. Series Motors.—Both rheostatic and regenerative braking can be employed, the former being obtained by the machines operating as generators excited from the supply or self-excited as d.c. machines and loaded on resistances. Regenerative braking is more difficult than with the d.c. series motor, owing to the necessity of maintaining a high

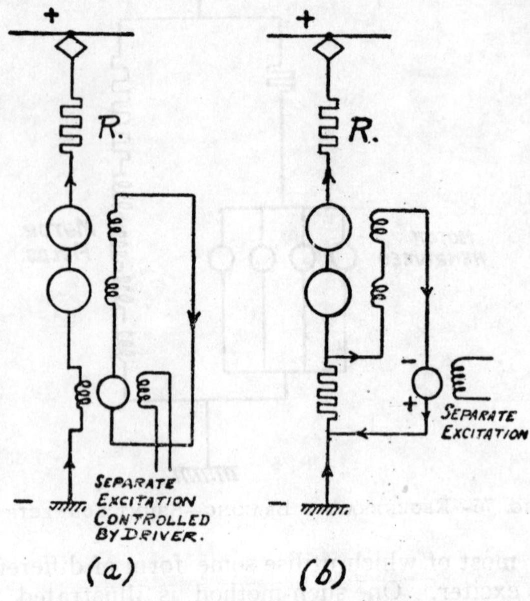

FIG. 77.—REGENERATIVE BRAKING WITH SEPARATE EXCITER.

power factor in order to secure a reasonable braking effect. To obtain this the fields must be separately excited and provided with a phase-shifting device to secure the correct phase angle.

Electric Braking with Induction Motors.—No additional control equipment is required to give regenerative braking with induction motors, since this occurs inherently if the motors run at above the synchronous speed corresponding to the number of poles.

Regenerative Braking and Power Supply.—An essential feature of regenerative braking is the ability of the power supply system to absorb the regenerated power. With a.c. systems and with d.c. systems employing rotary convertors or motor generators in the substations this does not present any difficulty, as the transforming and converting apparatus is inherently reversible. When, as is now becoming common practice, mercury-arc rectifiers are employed, which can only transmit power in one direction, regeneration is impossible. Recent developments in grid control of these rectifiers have, however, led to the possibility of their being operated inverted ; the necessary additional equipment consists either of a separate unit to deal with regenerated energy or automatic switching arrangements to change one or more of the ordinary rectifiers over to inverted operation.

Control Equipment

Although small industrial locomotives employ plain drum controllers similar to those used for industrial work, the currents

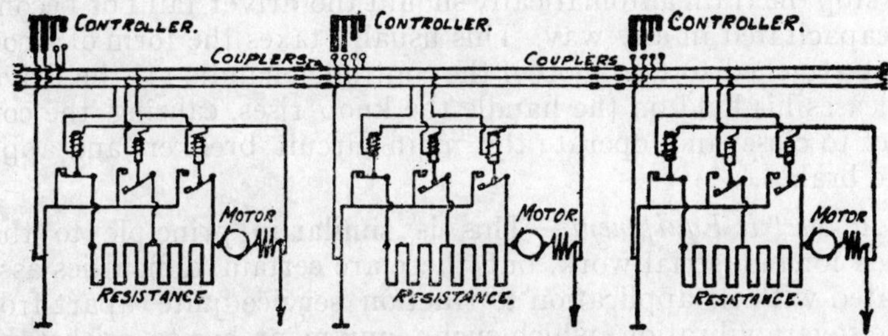

FIG. 78.—MULTIPLE-UNIT CONTROL.

dealt with in railway work are too heavy for this type of equipment and the master controller system is used, as described in Chapter I (page 80). This system lends itself easily to the multiple-unit method of control, in which any number of locomotives or motor coaches can be completely controlled from a master controller situated at either end of any one of them. A diagram illustrating the principle is shown in Fig. 78, where all three motors can be controlled by any one of the controllers. It is seen that control circuits must be carried from vehicle to vehicle, and this is done by means of flexible jumpers plugged into sockets at the ends of the coaches.

Three types of master controller equipment are in common use :

(i) All-electric equipment.

(ii) Electro-pneumatic equipment.

(iii) Camshaft equipment (with electric or pneumatic drive).

In any of these the operation may be entirely by hand or it may be semi-automatic; in the former the closing of the accelerating contactors is governed by the position of the controller handle, so that the rate of acceleration is completely under the control of the driver. With the semi-automatic arrangement the position of the handle governs the number of contactors which will close, but the sequence in which they operate and the time-interval between their individual operations are governed by time-lag devices, as in fully automatic equipment. The latter method is sometimes used for suburban services, as a consistently uniform acceleration is ensured with a minimum energy consumption, but the former is preferable in locomotives, where there is a probability of wide divergences in the loads hauled and the possibility of wheel slip.

With all types a *Dead Man's Handle* device is required in order to stop the train automatically should the driver faint or become incapacitated in any way. This usually takes the form of a contact attached to the knob of the controller handle; if the driver releases his hold on the handle the knob rises, causing the contact to close and operate the main circuit breaker and apply the brakes.

All-electric Equipment.—This is similar in principle to that used for industrial work, but there are certain difficulties associated with its application to traction service quite apart from the severe vibration which such equipment has to withstand. The chief of these are the impracticability of building contactors to operate at full voltage if above 600 V., and also the wide fluctuations in supply voltage which are liable to occur and which make the design of suitable contactors somewhat troublesome. The difficulties can be overcome by using a special low-voltage generator to give a supply at 100 V. or lower for the operating circuits, and although such a scheme is sometimes used, the modern tendency is to use one of the alternative systems. The multiple-unit equipment shown in Fig. 78 operates on the all-electric principle.

Electric-pneumatic System.—The contactors are closed and opened by compressed air, and the valves admitting air to the operating cylinders are worked electrically by solenoids energised from the master controller. This system leads to simplicity in the electrical connections and enables the control system to be quite independent of the supply. Furthermore, the use of compressed air enables a larger mechanical force to be obtained with smaller and simpler equipment than by any other method. As in many cases compressed air is necessary for other purposes (brakes or pantograph operation), its supply does not involve any additional complication. A low-voltage supply is, of course, required for operation of the air valves, and this is obtained from an auxiliary motor-generator set, which is usually also necessary for other purposes.

Camshaft Control.—The contactors are operated directly by means of cams mounted on a camshaft driven by an electric or a pneumatic motor. This type of control has the advantage of extremely simple electrical connections, and is being widely adopted. The position of the master controller handle governs the angle through which the camshaft is turned, and therefore fixes the number of contactors which are closed.

Auxiliary Equipment

In addition to the main traction motors, a considerable amount of auxiliary equipment has to be installed on a locomotive or motor coach, the total output of which may amount to 5 or 6 per cent. of that of the main motors. Any or all of the following may have to be provided :

Motor-generator Set.—For supplying a low voltage for lighting, control system, and other purposes. Between 30 and 100 V is usually employed. The set must be of special design so that fluctuations of the line voltage do not have any effect on the low-voltage supply. Using this for lighting avoids light flicker, which would occur if the lighting were supplied from the $16\frac{2}{3}$ or 25 Hz supply.

Battery.—To supply auxiliary power in cases of emergency and to operate the control gear in case of a supply failure, a battery is usually connected in parallel with the motor-generator set.

Air Compressor.—For supplying compressed air for operation of electro-pneumatic control gear, brakes, and pantograph-operating gear. At 1,500 V or under, the motor of the compressor can be supplied direct from the line, otherwise it is usually driven from the auxiliary generator.

Heating Equipment.—Electric heating for the locomotive and possibly for the train may be required. This may be supplied directly from the line up to 3,000 V. Where an electric locomotive has to haul steam-heated rolling stock an electrically heated boiler is often provided.

Pantograph-operating Equipment.—Raising and lowering the pantograph is usually carried out by compressed air and suitable switches for controlling the solenoid-operated valves of the air supply must be provided.

Traction Motor Blowers.—Separate motors and fans are sometimes provided for cooling the traction motors. These motors can usually be driven direct from the supply.

5. TRAMWAYS AND TROLLEYBUSES

The tramway supplied from an overhead trolley wire was a familiar sight in most large towns, but in recent years it has been largely replaced by the internal-combustion-engined omnibus or the trolleybus, the latter being an electrically operated pneumatictyred vehicle obtaining its supply from two overhead contact wires.

Although the overhead equipment required by the trolleybus is more expensive and more unsightly than that for the tram, this disadvantage is usually more than offset by the elimination of the necessity for a track in the roadway, which is costly to maintain and also constitutes a source of danger to other road users; furthermore, the trolleybus is able to manoeuvre in traffic over a width of several feet on each side of the centre line of the trolley wires.

Experience shows, however, that for the very dense traffic of large cities the ordinary tramway is the most economical means of transport available. The trolleybus is most suited for medium traffic densities, and many outlying tramway routes can be advantageously converted to trolleybus operation when the time comes for capital to be expended on track renewal.

Although the i.c -engined omnibus is more expensive to maintain and operate than a trolleybus, urban and rural services operating with a service interval of more than 15 or 20 minutes are most economically dealt with by this type of vehicle, as the cost of the overhead equipment for a trolleybus service would be too great relative to the number of passengers carried and the revenue obtained.

Tramways

The chief features in connection with the electrical equipment of a tram are the provision of at least two driving axles in order to secure the necessary adhesion and the fact that control must be possible from either end. Apart from this the equipment is generally similar to that required for railway work, although of course the output is much smaller, not usually exceeding 45 kW or 55 kW. Direct current at about 600 V is almost universal and is conducted from overhead contact wires by a trolley or bow collector, as described in Section 6 of this chapter. The running rails form the return path. The use of two or more driving axles lends itself to the use of two motors with series-parallel control, with, in more modern equipments, a field tapping to give higher speeds without sacrificing any starting torque.

Two drum-type controllers, one at each end, are usually employed for control of the vehicle. These controllers are connected in parallel, but have suitable interlocking arrangements to prevent their being used simultaneously. With the increasing outputs required by present-day tramcars the controller is tending to become so large that its operation is fatiguing to the driver, and master controller equipment similar to that already described for use on railways is employed in recent designs.

Regenerative Braking.—The conditions for regenerative braking are not usually so favourable with tramways as with railways, but it has been applied in a number of cases both in hilly districts and on level routes where energy is only regenerated when stopping. Although regeneration with series motors can be employed the complication renders it impracticable, and the compound motor, which can be satisfactorily used for tramway service, is generally employed where regenerative braking is required. Control of the braking torque is carried out by variation of the shunt field and regeneration down to about 20 km/h can be obtained. Below this speed rheostatic braking is used.

The Trolleybus

The chief features wherein the trolleybus differs from the tramcar are :

(i) As the total weight is limited, that of the electrical equipment must be cut down to the minimum possible value.

(ii) The adhesion between a rubber-tyred wheel and the roadway is sufficiently high to enable only a single driving axle, and therefore a single motor, to be used.

(iii) Only one driving position is required, but starting, stopping, and speed control must be carried out by means of a foot-operated pedal in order that the driver shall have his hands free for steering and hand-brake operation.

(iv) As the vehicle is insulated from earth by the rubber-tyred wheels precautions must be taken to prevent the setting up of any potential difference between the vehicle framework and the road-way.

Transmission.—As mentioned above, only a single driving axle is necessary, invariably the rear axle, but, as with the ordinary motor car, some form of differential action must be incorporated between the two wheels in order to prevent wheel slip at curves.

Either one or two motors may be employed : a single motor is preferable from the point of view of weight and cost and is the usual practice. Two motors, however, one coupled to each driving wheel, have been used in some cases, and this arrangement

FIG. 79 —GENERAL ARRANGEMENT OF SUNBEAM-B.T.-H. TROLLEYBUS CHASSIS (*B T.-H. Co.*)

eliminates the need for a differential gear and also enables low economical running speeds to be obtained by series-parallel control.

The motor may be installed under the bonnet of the vehicle, where it is easily accessible, or under the centre of the car body, which eliminates a long shaft between the motors and the differential gear. Illustrations of typical layouts are shown in Figs. 79 and 80.

Motors.—In addition to the general requirements for a traction motor mentioned on page 127, a motor for a trolleybus is more severely limited with regard to its dimensions and weight since the overall weight and size of the vehicle is governed by Ministry of Transport Regulations, and any saving in the motor results in greater passenger-carrying capacity. Noise must also be considered, since vehicle noise is much less than with rail-traction equipment. A further feature is the practical necessity, in order to save brake lining wear, of employing rheostatic or regenerative braking.

The motor output required is generally between about 45 kW and 75 kW., and a compound-wound motor is usually employed, the shunt winding ampere-turns assisting those of the series winding when motoring. Speed control is effected by resistance in the shunt field and tappings or a divertor on the series field. During rheostatic braking the series field opposes the shunt field and can be disconnected entirely if required; braking down to about 6.5 km/h. can be obtained. If arrangements are made for regenerative braking, it occurs automatically due to the shunt field at speeds above about 20 or 25 km/h.

Mass as low as 5 kg. per kW. is obtainable by the use of high peripheral speeds of 61 m/s for the armature and 48.25 m/s for the commutator, these being obtained as a result of improvements in material and, more particularly, in methods of manufacture.

Control Equipment.—Foot-operated master controllers are employed, with two pedals, one controlling starting, speed variation, and regenerative braking, and the other controlling the rheostatic and mechanical brake or compressed-air brakes. The contactors are operated from the 600-V trolley supply, although in some cases the braking contactors are supplied from a low-voltage battery source to ensure that they shall still be operative if the supply fails.

Automatic circuit-breakers are fitted which trip and disconnect the supply if a fault occurs. An over-current relay is also provided which trips the circuit-breakers; this relay is set for a lower current value than the circuit breakers and is intended to operate when the current reaches a value which would damage the motors or the contactors. When regenerative braking is used an over-voltage relay is necessary to open the circuit-breakers if the voltage rises above 12 to 15 per cent. above normal due to there being no load to absorb the regenerated energy.

Low-voltage lighting is necessary and is provided from a motor-generator set running in conjunction with a battery. Batteries are also sometimes provided for operating the vehicle at a low speed in case of power supply failure or for manoeuvring in the depot.

The frame of the vehicle is isolated from all electrical circuits, and it is necessary to take precautions against the possibility of its becoming alive, due to leakage, and causing electric shocks to passengers when boarding or alighting. If one pole of the supply is earthed and a leakage to the frame occurs near to the other pole, the frame will become alive to earth at the full system voltage; if both poles of the supply are isolated from earth (as is usually the case) any current flowing through a person alighting will also have to flow through the insulation resistance of one pole of the supply; this may be between 10,000 and 100,000Ω, so that this condition is less dangerous although

FIG. 80.—MOTOR AND RESISTANCES ON SUNBEAM-B.T.-H. TROLLEYBUS CHASSIS (*B.T.-H. Co.*)

unpleasant. To guard against such dangers every trolleybus must have its insulation resistance tested once per day, preferably when coming off service as the circuits are then hot and damp and, therefore, in their worst condition; all metal work on the platform must also be covered with insulating material.

6. TRACK EQUIPMENT AND COLLECTOR GEAR

With all systems of track electrification the running rails usually form the return path for the current from the train, but the outward path may be by means of a conductor rail laid along-side the running rails or an overhead wire. Suburban railways at 600 V. usually employ the conductor-rail system on account of its relative cheapness, since it is not considered necessary to protect the rail from accidental contact by platelayers, etc., except at stations and in sidings; the conductor rail also possesses the advantages of easier inspection and maintenance and its supporting structures do not interfere in any way with vision of signals. For 1,500 V. and over, however, considerations of safety make the overhead system almost universal.

Conductor-rail Equipment.

The Conductor Rail.—The conductor rail is mounted on insulators at the side of the track, as shown in Fig. 81, the

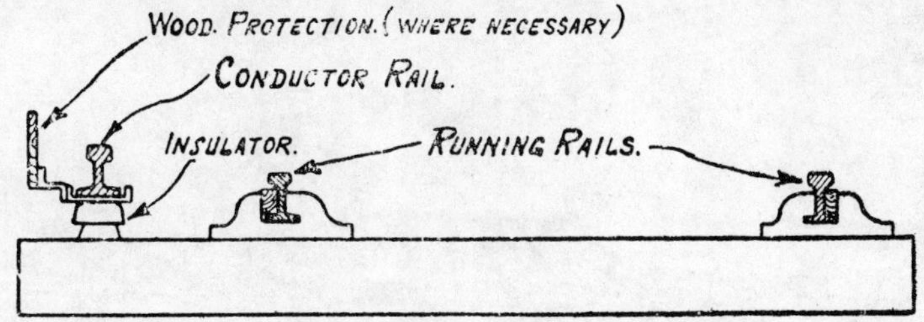

FIG. 81.—STANDARD CONDUCTOR-RAIL EQUIPMENT.

contact surface being uppermost in the majority of cases, although the Manchester-Bury 1,200-V. line employs a rail with a side-running contact; as shown in Fig. 82, and certain

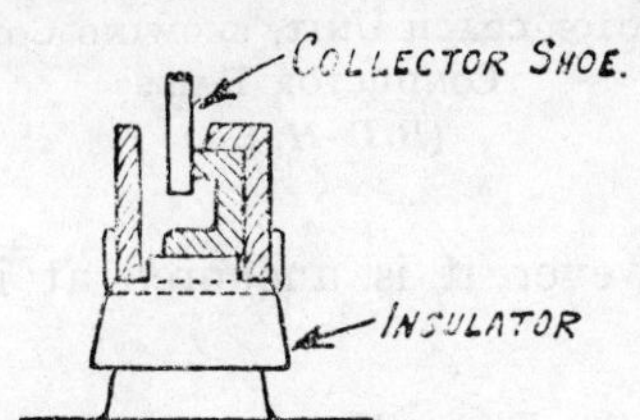

FIG 82.—CONDUCTOR RAIL—SIDE-RUNNING CONTACT.

American railways use an under-running contact. These constructions render the rail easier to protect against accidental contact and also render it less likely to obstruction from ice and snow. A special steel having a low carbon and manganese content to reduce the resistance is employed—a typical rail with about 0·05 per cent. carbon and about 0.02 per cent. manganese has a resistance of about $12{\cdot}0 \times 10^{-8}$ Ohm-m, at 18°C, which is about seven times that of copper* and about one quarter or one-fifth of that of the running rails. Special arrangements must be made at the joints to reduce the voltage drop, and copper bonds consisting of short lengths of flexible conductor are bolted or welded to the rails. To allow for movement due to expansion and contraction and also due to movements of the sleepers as the train passes over them the conductor rail is not fixed rigidly to the insulators. To prevent creepage due to friction of the

FIG. 83 —600-V. MOTOR-COACH UNIT, SHOWING COLLECTOR SHOE AND CONDUCTOR RAILS
(*B.T -H. Co.*)

collector shoes, however, it is anchored at intervals of 275 or 365 meters.

The Collector Shoe.—For collecting the current from the rail a flat steel shoe about 203 mm. long and 76 mm. wide is employed, which presses on to the rail with a force of 133·5 N or 178 N. For systems with the contact surface of the rail uppermost the pressure is obtained by gravity, but with side and under-running contacts springs are employed. The current which can be collected is about 300 to 500A. per shoe, although under good

* For Copper at 18°C, the value is $1{\cdot}75 \times 10^{-8}$ Ohm-m.

conditions as much as 2,000A. have been satisfactorily dealt with. As it is not always convenient to have the conductor rail on the same side of the track, shoes must be provided on both sides of the locomotive or train, and also, since there must be gaps in the rail at points and crossings, at least two shoes must be provided on each side so that there will be no likelihood of the current being interrupted. The shoe must not fall more than one or two inches when not in contact with the rail or it will foul the running rails at crossings.

The collector shoe and conductor-rail equipment are shown on Fig. 83, which illustrates a typical motor-coach equipment. In this illustration there is a second conductor rail between the tracks—this is used instead of the rails as the return path for the current.

Overhead Equipment

The overhead contact-wire equipment as employed for tramways and trolleybuses and for railways of 1,500 V. and over is more difficult to design than the conductor-rail equipment on account of the greater difficulty of ensuring that the collector and contact wire remain in contact at a fairly even pressure.

The materials used for the contact wire are hard-drawn copper, cadmium copper, or silico-bronze, particulars of which are given in Table IV. In spite of its higher electrical resistance, silicobronze is in fairly common use on account of its higher tensile strength and also its greater wear-resisting properties.

TABLE IV

	Ultimate strength (N/m^2)	Sp. resistance (ohm—m)	Temperature coefficient (per °C)	Modulus of elasticity : E (N/m^2)
H D. copper	37×10^7	$1{\cdot}76 \times 10^{-8}$	$16{\cdot}6 \times 10^{-6}$	124×10^9
cadmium copper	$41{\cdot}7 \times 10^7$	$2{\cdot}035 \times 10^{-8}$	$16{\cdot}6 \times 10^{-6}$	124×10^9
Silico-bronze	$49{\cdot}4 \times 10^7$	$3{\cdot}86 \times 10^{-8}$	$17{\cdot}0 \times 10^{-6}$	124×10^9

The actual quality of the wire is laid in ISS, which also specifies eight standard sizes ranging from the smallest, having a cross-sectional area equal to No. O.S.W.G. (53.57 mm^2) upto a size of 193.5mm^2. To facilitate connection to the supports the wire is grooved as shown in Fig. 84 : the dimensions of the groove are also laid down in the B.S.S. or I.S.S.

Single wire construction :—For street traction, the contact wire is usually supported from poles or other convenient supports at intervals of 25 to 40 m at a height of not less than 6 m the latter figure being one of the requirements of the Ministry of Transport. It is evident that there will be an appreciable sag of the wire between the supports, but at speeds up to about 48 km/h this does not cause trouble.

Collection of current is carried out either by a trolley pole with a wheel collector or by a bow collector, as described in a later section.

Calculation of Sags and Tensions of Single Contact Wire.—The contact wire, between its supports, takes up the form of a catenary, but, since the sag normally allowed is not more than 1 or $1\frac{1}{2}$ per cent. of the span, the curve which it takes up may be assumed to be a parabola having the equation:

$$y = \frac{w}{2T} \cdot x^2$$

where y and x are as shown in Fig. 85 $w=mg$, where m is the mass of the wire per metre run, T is the tension in the conductor (assumed the same at all points), and l is half the span length.

The sag at the centre of the span is obtained by putting $x=l$ in the above, so that :

$$\text{sag} = d = \frac{mgl^2}{2T} = \frac{mgl^2}{2fa} \quad \cdot \quad \cdot \quad \cdot \quad (29)$$

where f = stress, a = cross-sectional area.

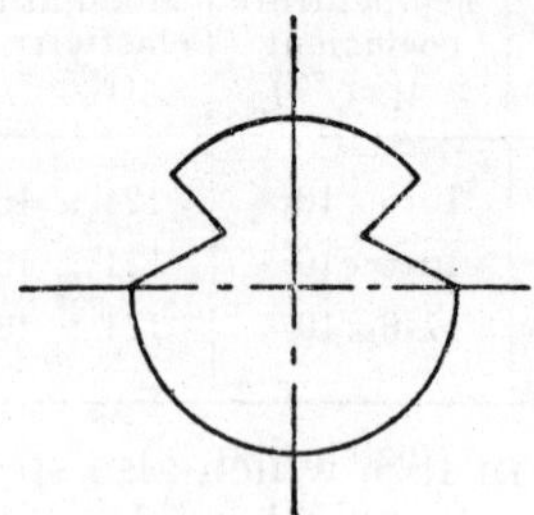

FIG. 84.—STANDARD TROLLEY-WIRE SECTION.

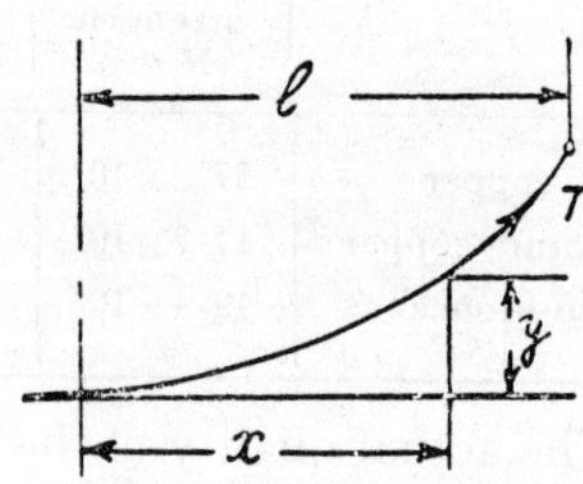

FIG. 85.

It is sometimes convenient to express the equation in terms of the sag instead of the conductor weight:

$$\text{Putting } mg = \frac{2\text{T}d}{l^2}$$

$$\text{gives } y = d \cdot \frac{x^2}{l^2}$$

The values of the sag and tension which the wire must have under normal temperature and load conditions are fixed by the designer, and the construction engineers require to know the tension or sag to which to string the conductor for the particular temperature at which it is being erected. Also it will be necessary to calculate the tension in the wire when it is coated with a layer of ice, since the tension will be a maximum under these conditions and the stress must not exceed the safe value. To make the above calculations the effect of a change of load and temperature on the sag and tension must be investigated, and this may be done as follows :

A change in stress in the conductor or a change in temperature will produce a change in the length of the wire, and an expression for the length must therefore be found from :

$(ds)^2 = (dx)^2 + (dy)^2$ where s = conductor length in half-span

$$\frac{dy}{dx} = \sqrt{\left(\frac{ds}{dx}\right)^2 - 1} = \frac{w}{\text{T}} \cdot x$$

$$\left(\frac{ds}{dx}\right)^2 = 1 + \frac{w^2}{\text{T}^2}x^2$$

$$\therefore s = \int\sqrt{1 + \frac{w^2x^2}{\text{T}^2}}\,dx$$

Expanding by the Binomial Theorem :

$$= \int\left(1 + \frac{1}{2}\frac{w^2\,x^2}{\text{T}^2} - \frac{1\times 3}{2\times 4}\cdot\frac{w^4x^4}{3\text{T}^4} + \cdots\right)dx$$

$$= x + \frac{w^2x^3}{6\text{T}^2} + \cdots$$

Thus total conductor length in a half-span (putting $x = l$ and neglecting terms beyond the second) :

$$s = l + \frac{w^2l^2}{6\text{T}^2} \quad . \quad . \quad . \quad . \qquad (30a)$$

or in terms of sag instead of conductor weight :

$$s = l + \frac{2d^2}{3l} \quad . \quad . \quad . \quad . \qquad (30b)$$

Now, suppose the load changes from w_1 to w_2 and the temperature changes from θ_1 to θ_2 ; the latter will cause an increase in length of $(\theta_2 - \theta_1)\alpha s = (\theta_2 - \theta_1)\alpha l$ to a close approximation, α being the coefficient of expansion; while if E is the modulus of elasticity there will also be an increase in length of $\frac{f_2-f_1}{E}l$, due to the change of stress in the wire, caused partly by the change in load and partly by the change in length due to the temperature change.

The new length of conductor is therefore:

$$s_2 = s_1 + \frac{f_2-f_1}{E}l + (\theta_2-\theta_1)\alpha l$$

$$= l + \frac{2}{3}\frac{d_1^2}{l} + \frac{f_2-f_1}{E}l + (\theta_2-\theta_1)\alpha l$$

But we may also write s_2 in terms of d_2, the sag under the new conditions, viz.:

$$s_2 = l + \frac{2}{3}\frac{d_2^2}{l}$$

Equating these:

$$l + \frac{2}{3}\frac{d_2^2}{l} = l + \frac{2}{3}\frac{d_1^2}{l} + \frac{f_2-f_1}{E}l + (\theta_2-\theta_1)\alpha l \quad . \quad . \quad (31a)$$

Substituting for f_2 and f_1 from Equation (29) and rearranging:

$$\frac{2}{3l}(d_2^2 - d_1^2) = \frac{l^3}{2aE}\left(\frac{w_2}{d_2} - \frac{w_1}{d_1}\right) + (\theta_2 - \theta_1)\alpha l \quad . \quad . \quad (31b)$$

Thus if we know the sag d_1 under one set of conditions (suffix 1), we can calculate what the sag will be for another load and temperature (suffix 2). If the sag is known the tension can be found directly from Equation (29). For stringing the conductor a curve showing the relation between temperature and sag or temperature tension, and known as a stringing chart, is employed. The construction engineer has simply to observe the temperature at the time of stringing, read off the sag or tension, depending on the method of construction employed, and string the wire to this value, knowing that it will then assume the correct sag and tension under the normal specified temperature. For a single wire the load at the time of stringing will be the same as that under normal conditions, so that a change of load does not have to be considered. It must be considered, however, when finding the sag and tension under ice-load conditions.

Catenary Construction.— For railway work, where higher speeds are encountered than on tramways, greater difficulty is experienced in keeping an even pressure between the trolley and the contact wire. The sags which are permissible for tramway work are quite inadmissible for railways, and a catenary construction, as shown in Figs. 86 and 87, is generally employed. This construction also avoids the hard, inflexible spots which occur at each of the supports with the single-wire suspension.

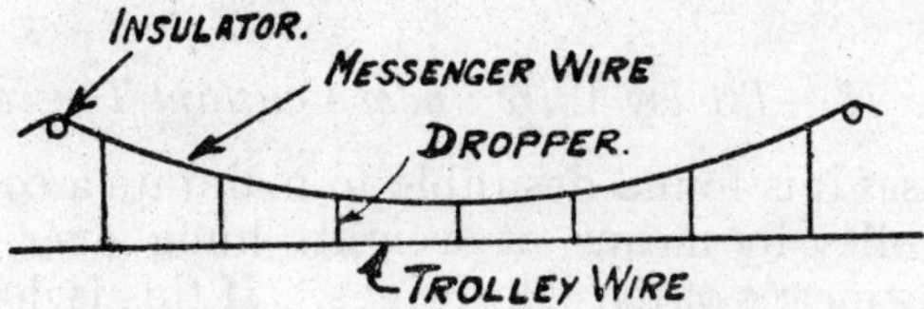

Fig. 86.—Single Catenary Construction.

The contact wire is suppported from a messenger wire at intervals of 3 to 4.5 metres in order that it shall be held very nearly level. To reduce the change in sag with temperature, the messenger wire is given a fairly high sag (2 to 3 per cent. of the span). To avoid the use of insulated droppers the whole of the messenger wire is usually insulated, and it may therefore be used if required for carrying current. On some d.c. systems where very heavy currents are encountered it is necessary to employ an auxiliary messenger wire in addition, as shown in Fig. 87, to give a greater cross-sectional area of conductor without making the whole structure too rigid. The messenger wire is suspended from bracket poles or light gantries spanning the track at intervals of about 60 to 90 metres.

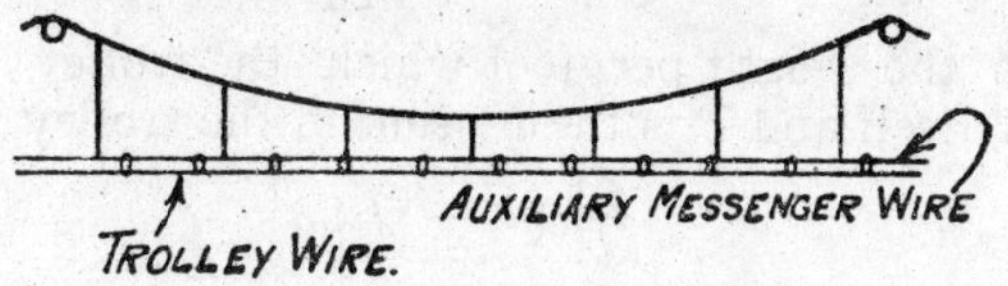

Fig 87.—Catenary with Auxiliary Messenger Wire.

Calculation of Sags and Tensions with Catenary Construction.—Three methods of construction are possible :

(i) The trolley wire completely free at each end and not under tension.

(ii) The trolley wire held under a constant tension by means of springs or counterweights.

(iii) The trolley wire rigidly fixed at each end so that the tension in it will vary with temperature.

Case I.—Trolley Wire Free

As the trolley wire is not under tension its whole weight is taken by the messenger wire. For calculation purposes it is reasonably accurate to assume that it is uniformly distributed and can therefore simply be added to the weight per unit length of the messenger and the problem treated exactly as that for a single wire.

Case II.—Trolley Wire under Constant Tension

In some cases it is found desirable to maintain a constant tension in the trolley by means of weights hung over pulleys at the end, or by means of tension springs. If this is done, some of the weight of the trolley wire will be taken by the wire itself, thus relieving the messenger of this amount. It must be noted, however, that if the trolley wire be level (i.e. with no sag) it cannot take any of its own weight, which is then all taken by the messenger, as in Case I; if the trolley wire is allowed to bow upwards instead of sagging, the effective weight on the messenger will be increased.

Let d_1 be the sag of the messenger wire with a level trolley wire.

Let d_2 be the sag of the messenger wire under any other condition.

From the expression for the sag of a wire we have for the trolley wire:

$$\text{sag} = d_2 - d_1 = \frac{w'l^2}{2T}$$

where w' is the weight per foot which the trolley wire is supporting for itself and T is the tension in the trolley wire.

Thus
$$w' = \frac{2T}{l^2}(d_2 - d_1)$$

If w_1 is the total weight per metre of the trolley wire and messenger combined, the weight which the messenger wire actually has to support is:

$$w_2 = w_1 - w' = w_1 - \frac{2T}{l^2}(d_2 - d_1) \quad . \quad . \quad (32)$$

A change in temperature will thus produce a change in sag and tension due to the expansion of the trolley and messenger wires, and this in turn will produce a further change in sag due to the fact that the effective load per metre on the messenger wire changes.

The effect of a change in load and temperature is given by Equation (31*b*). Now, the equipment will be so designed that the trolley wire is level at some particular temperature, say θ_1. The load at this temperature w_1 will thus be the total weight of both trolley and messenger wires, and the sag d_1 can easily be calculated. We thus have all the initial conditions of Equation (31*b*): if now the temperature increases to θ_2 the system will sag to some new value d_2 and the effective weight w_2 on the messenger wire will become, in accordance with Equation (32):

$$w_2 = w_1 - \frac{2T}{l_2}(d_2 - d_1)$$

T being the constant tension of the trolley wire.

Putting this new value of w in Equation (31*b*) gives:

$$\frac{2}{3l}(d_2^2 - d_1^2) = \frac{l^3}{2aE}\left\{\frac{1}{d_2}\left[w_1 - \frac{2T}{l^2}(d_2 - d_1)\right] - \frac{w_1}{d_1}\right\} + (\theta_2 - \theta_1)\alpha l \quad . \quad . \quad . \quad . \quad (33)$$

from which the relation between θ_2 and d_2 can be found, i.e. the change in sag produced by a given change in temperature. For any sag also, the effective weight per foot acting on the messenger wire can be found and the messenger tension calculated so that the behaviour under changing temperature conditions can be determined.

Case III.—Trolley Wire Fixed at Each End

The trolley-wire tension will be fixed at some value T_0 when the trolley wire is level, and will then vary in accordance with changes in temperature. Equation (33) above still holds, but the value of T is now a variable dependent on θ_2.

Consider the trolley wire level and strung to a tension T_1. If the tension changes to T_2 the length of conductor between supports will change by an amount $\frac{f_2 - f_1}{E} s = \frac{f_2 - f_1}{E} l$, while if the temperature changes from θ_1 to θ_2 the length will also increase by an amount $(\theta_2 - \theta_1)\alpha l$, α being the temperature coefficient of expansion of the trolley-wire material.

The total increase in length is thus:

$$\frac{1}{Ea}(T_2 - T_1) l + (\theta_2 - \theta_1)\alpha l$$

The total increase in length of trolley wire in terms of sag, is, however:

$$\frac{2}{3}\frac{(d_2 - d_1)^2}{l}$$

so that:

$$\frac{2}{3}\frac{(d_2 - d_1)^2}{l} = \frac{1}{\mathrm{E}a}(\mathrm{T}_2 - \mathrm{T}_1)\,l + (\theta_2 - \theta_1)\,\alpha l$$

$$\therefore \mathrm{T}_2 = \mathrm{T}_1 + \frac{2}{3}\frac{(d_2 - d_1)^2}{l^2}\,\mathrm{E}a - (\theta_2 - \theta_1)\,\mathrm{E}a\alpha \quad . \quad . (34)$$

This value of T_2 can be substituted for T in Equation (33), and we then have the relation between sag and temperature constructed in accordance with Case III. Having found the sag for any temperature, the tension in trolley wire or messenger can be calculated.

To illustrate the methods of calculating sags and tensions outlined above, the following numerical example has been worked out.

Example 13:—Calculate the sags and tensions for a catenary system, having the particulars given below, when subjected to temperatures of between—20°C and 60°C.

Single catenary construction, span . .		*64 m*
cross-sectional area of messenger wire (copper)	:	*2·42 cm²*
cross-sectional area of trolley wire (copper)	:	*1·61 cm²*
sag at normal temperature (15°C) at which trolley wire is level	:	*1·83 m*

Solution:

For copper $\mathrm{E} = 1{\cdot}2 \times 10^{11}\ \mathrm{N/m^2}$

$\alpha = 1{\cdot}66 \times 10^{-7}$ per °C

$l = 32$ m ($\frac{1}{2}$ span)

Mass (per metre) of messenger wire

$= 2{\cdot}42 \times 10^{-4} \times 1 \times 0{\cdot}885 \times 10^4$ kg $= 2{\cdot}140$ kg

Mass (per metre) of trolley wire

$= 1{\cdot}61 \times 10^{-4} \times 1 \times 0{\cdot}885 \times 10^4 = 1{\cdot}425$ kg

Mass (per metre) of droppers . . . . $= 0{\cdot}14$ kg

Total mass . . $= 3{\cdot}70$ kg

Tension in messenger at normal temperature (level trolley)

$$= \frac{3{\cdot}71 \times 9{\cdot}81 \times 32^2}{2 \times 1{\cdot}83} = 10150\ \mathrm{N}$$

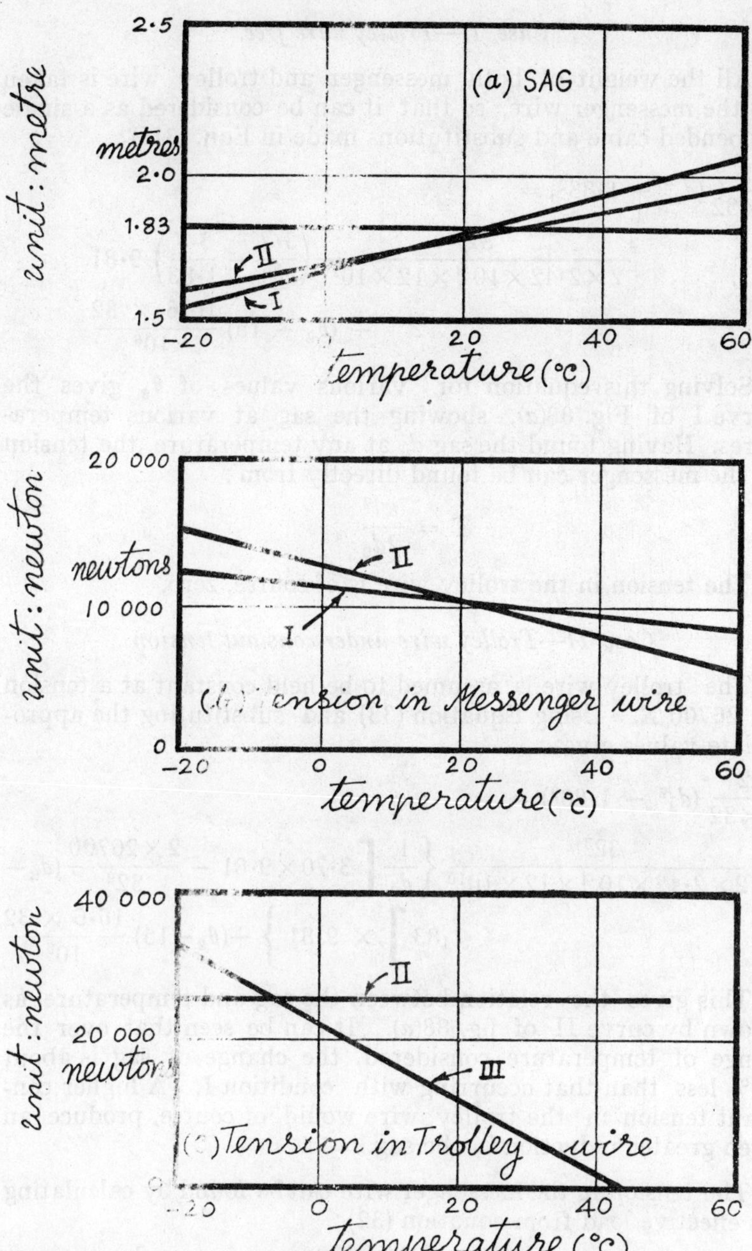

FIG. 83.—SAG AND TENSION CURVES. (EXAMPLE 13).

Case I.—Trolley wire free.

All the weight of both messenger and trolley wire is taken by the messenger wire, so that it can be considered as a single suspended cable and substitutions made in Eqn. (31*b*):

$$\frac{2}{3\times 32}(d_2^2 - 1{\cdot}83^2) = \frac{32^3}{2\times 2{\cdot}42\times 10^{-4}\times 12\times 10^{10}}\left(\frac{3{\cdot}7}{d^2} - \frac{3{\cdot}7}{1{\cdot}83}\right)9{\cdot}81 + (\theta_2 - 15)\frac{16{\cdot}6\times 32}{10^6}$$

Solving this equation for various values of θ_2 gives the curve I of Fig. 88(*a*), showing the sag at various temperatures. Having found the sag d_2 at any temperature, the tension in the messenger can be found directly from :

$$T = \frac{wl^2}{2d_2}$$

The tension in the trolley wire is of course, zero.

Case II—Trolley wire under constaut tension

The trolley wire is assumed to be held constant at a tension of 26700 N. Using Equation (33) and substituting the appropriate values gives :

$$\frac{2}{3\times 32}(d_2^2 - 1{\cdot}83^2) = \frac{32^3}{2\times 2{\cdot}42\times 10^{-4}\times 12\times 10^{10}}\left\{\frac{1}{d_2}\left[3{\cdot}70\times 9{\cdot}81 - \frac{2\times 26700}{32^2}(d_2 - 1{\cdot}83\right]\times 9{\cdot}81\right\} + (\theta_2 - 15)\frac{16{\cdot}6\times 32}{10^6}$$

This gives the relation between the sag and temperature, as shown by curve II of fig. 88(*a*). It can be seen that over the range of temperature considered, the change of sag is about 25% less than that occurring with condition I. A higher constant tension in the trolley wire would, of course, produce an even greater reduction in the sag.

The tension in the messenger wire can be found by calculating its effective load from equation (32):

$$w_2 = \left[3{\cdot}70\times 9{\cdot}81 - \frac{2\times 26700}{32^2}(d^2 - 1{\cdot}83)\right]$$

This is shown by Curve II in Fig. 81(*b*). The range of tension is greater than in case I, but this is frequently not of importance, since the section may be fixed by the current-carrying capacity and voltage-drop, so that tensions are well below the limiting values, and further more, as previously stated, the tensions kept low in order to reduce changes of sag with temperature.

Case III—Trolley wire fixed at Each End

The value of the tension in the trolley wire, which was kept constant at 26,700 N in *case II* now varies with change in temperature. In this case, it is assumed to be so constructed as to have a value of 13,350 N at normal temperature.

The tension in the trolley wire at any temperature is thus given by substituting in equation (34) :

$$T_2 = 13{,}350 + \frac{2}{3}\frac{(d_2-1{\cdot}83)^2}{(32)^2} \times 12 \times 10^{10} \times 2{\cdot}42 \times 10^{-4}$$
$$- 12\times10^{10}\,(\theta_2-15)\;16{\cdot}6\times10^{-6} \times 2{\cdot}42\times10^{-4}$$

Putting this instead of the figure 26,700 in the expression for case II gives the expression for the relation between sag and temperature for *Case III.*

Solving this expression gives the relation between sag and temperature—the curve lies between those of *Cases I and II* in Fig. 88(*a*).

The tension in the trolley wire can be found by putting the appropriate values of d_2 and θ_2 in the above expression for T_2. This is shown by curve III on Fig. 88(*c*). It can be seen that if falls to zero at about 42°C; at temperatures above this, the system would behave as in case I, since the whole of the weight of the trolley wire would then be taken by the messenger wire.

The tension in the messenger wire can be found by calculating the effective weight on the messenger wire as for case II. The curve obtained lies between those of Cases I and II in Fig. 88(*b*) upto 42°C after which it coincides with that of Case I.

Collector Gear for Overhead Equipment

In order that the collector gear shall pick up the current sparklessly, it must be so designed that it will maintain an even pressure against the trolley wire at all speeds. Three types of gear are in common use, namely, the trolley, the bow, and the pantograph types of collector. To ensure an even pressure the equipment must be flexible in order that it shall follow the variations in sag of the contact wire, and either a spring or compressed air is used to maintain the pressure. When the contact wire rises the collector has to move upwards in order to maintain contact, and the pressure exerted on the contact wire is the pressure of the spring or compressed-air piston minus the force required to accelerate the collector to its new position and minus any force necessary to overcome frictional resistance. To design a satisfactory collector therefore, particularly for high-speed work, the frictional resistance must be reduced to a minimum and the moment of inertia must be kept low. Furthermore, means must be provided for lowering when not in use and reasonable precautions taken to prevent the collector leaving the wire at points and crossings.

The Trolley Collector.—The trolley collector is familiar as being the usual type adopted on tramways in this country. Current is collected by means of a grooved wheel or a sliding shoe, supported at the end of a long trolley pole attached to the top of the car and held in contact with the wire by a spring. The pole is made to swivel about its support so that it can be reversed for reverse running, and rendering it unnecessary for the trolley wire to be accurately maintained above the centre of the track: this latter feature has led to the universal adoption of the trolley collector for trolleybuses, as it enables them to manoeuvre in traffic up to a distance of 3.5 to 4.5 *m* on either side of the contact wire. Although the wheel has a fairly deep groove there is a danger of its jumping off the wire, particularly at points and crossings, if used at speeds of more than 24 or 32 km/h.

The Bow Collector.—Instead of a trolley wheel the current may be collected by means of a light metal strip or bow 0.6 or 0.9 metre. wide attached to a framework mounted on the roof of the car, as shown diagrammatically in Fig. 89. This type of collector has been commonly used on the Continent for tramways and is coming into use in this country for this purpose, as it enables higher speeds to be run without danger of jumping off the wire. It is necessary, however, that the wire be accurately located above the track and staggered about six inches to each side of the centre line to avoid the wearing of a groove in the contact strip; also separate collectors must be used for forward and reverse running. The actual contact strip is usually of aluminium or copper and is of relatively soft metal, so that most of the wear which occurs will be on the easily renewable strip and not on the contact wire. Carbon is also used.

The Pantograph Collector.—For railway work, where speeds of up to 110 or 130 km. and currents of up to 2,000 or 3,000 A are encountered, the inertia of the bow collector is too high to ensure satisfactory current collection, and a light pantograph construction, as shown on the locomotive in Fig. 66, is used. Tubing of high-tensile alloy steel is generally employed to ensure lightness as well as adequate strength. The raising and lowering must be carried out from the driver's cab, and one of the following methods or some modification of it is usually adopted:

(i) Air raised, gravity lowered.
(ii) Air raised, spring lowered.
(iii) Spring raised, air lowered.

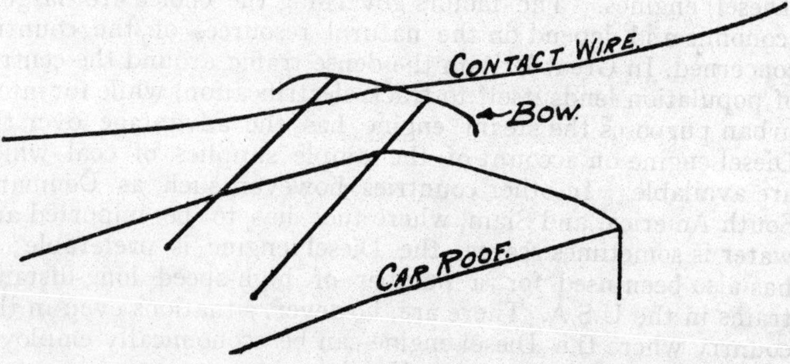

FIG. 89.—BOW COLLECTOR.

Where the upward pressure is supplied by compressed air, any failure of the air supply will render the locomotive inoperative, and any leakage will cause a continuous loss of air and possible reduction of contact pressure, otherwise there is little to choose between the various methods. A catch is usually employed to hold the pantograph in the lowered position to prevent bouncing and also, in the case of the air-lowered type, to avoid the necessity for a continuous supply of air when the vehicle is out of service.

The contact strips are of copper, steel, or carbon, and are mounted on a light metal shoe. A single contact strip can collect a current of several hundred amperes, which is quite adequate for high-voltage single-phase electrifications, but for d.c.

1,500-V. or 3,000-V. systems, which may require 500 to 1,000A at full speed and 2,000 to 3000A. at starting, a double-shoe construction must be adopted.

The upward pressure of the collector on the contact wire is usually between about 65 and 90 N for a single-shoe construction and 130 and 180N. for a double-shoe construction.

7. DIESEL-ELECTRIC EQUIPMENT

The high initial cost of any system of track electrification renders it uneconomic except where the traffic density is high or where heavy grades and loads preclude any other form of traction; under other conditions self-contained motive-power units are required, and these may employ either steam or internal-combustion engines as the prime movers. So far as road traction is concerned the internal-combustion engine is supreme, but for railway work the choice lies between steam and heavy-oil (Diesel) engines. The factors governing the choice are largely economic and depend on the natural resources of the country concerned. In Great Britain the dense traffic around the centres of population lends itself to track electrification, while for inter-urban purposes the steam engine has the advantage over the Diesel engine on account of the ample supplies of coal which are available. In other countries, however, such as Denmark, South America, and Siam, where fuel has to be imported and water is sometimes scarce, the Diesel engine is preferable; it has also been used for a number of high-speed long-distance trains in the U.S.A. There are, however, situations even in this country where the Diesel engine can be economically employed for light railcar work or for shunting.

Characteristics of the Diesel Engine

Of the different types of internal-combustion engine available, the compression-ignition heavy-oil engine is almost universally used for railway work and is coming into use for heavy road transport. The four-stroke cycle has been more commonly used, but the two-stroke engine, with its smaller weight per horse-power, is likely to be developed further as increased outputs are required.

For normal passenger services light weight is desirable, and engines of mass only 9 to 12 kg/kW. have been developed; but for shunting purposes, where a high adhesive weight is required, heavier engines can be used. Supercharging, although it enables a greater output for a given weight to be obtained, adds to the complication and has so far not been widely adopted.

Typical characteristics of a Diesel engine suitable for traction service are shown in Fig. 90. It can be seen that the torque obtainable is approximately constant and independent of the speed. In common with all internal-combustion engines, it has no starting torque and must be started by some auxiliary means such as compressed air or electrically, as in the ordinary motor car ; furthermore, it has only a very small overload capacity, and any attempt to obtain more than about 10 per cent. overload results in stalling of the engine.

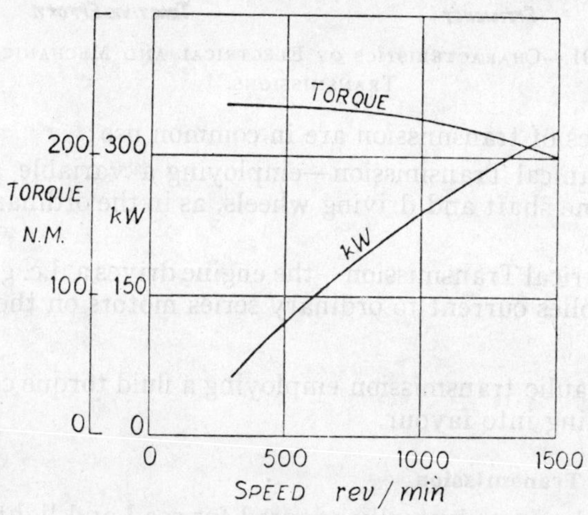

Fig. 90.—Diesel-engine Characteristics.

Transmission of Drive

The torque required in traction work is roughly inversely proportional to speed, being a maximum at starting and low speeds, so that the constant-torque characteristic of a Diesel engine is not entirely suitable ; if such an engine is directly coupled to the driving wheels and made of such a size as to give the required torque at very low speeds, then at full speed it would only be loaded up to one-quarter or one-fifth of its full load.

Some form of torque convertor must, therefore, be included in the transmission between the engine shaft and the driving axles in order to convert the constant torque at full engine speed into a torque which falls as the speed rises, maintaining the kilowatts (proportional to the product of torque and speed) approximately constant and therefore enabling the available output of the Diesel engine to be used to the full at all speeds.

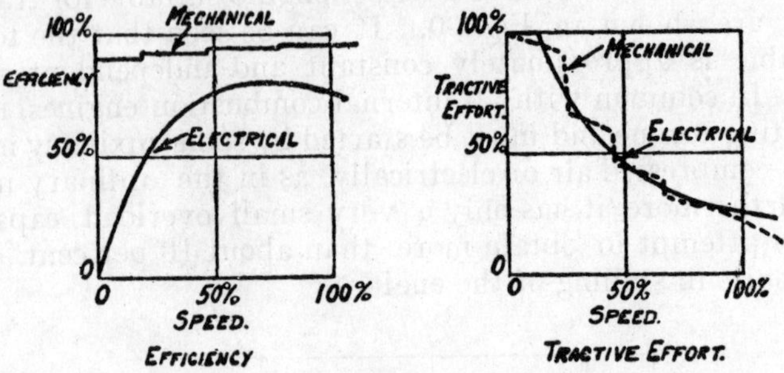

FIG. 91.—CHARACTERISTICS OF ELECTRICAL AND MECHANICAL TRANSMISSIONS.

Two types of transmission are in common use:

(i) Mechanical Transmission—employing a variable gear between engine shaft and driving wheels, as in the ordinary motor car.

(ii) Electrical Transmission—the engine drives a d.c. generator which supplies current to ordinary series motors on the driving axles.

An hydraulic transmission employing a fluid torque convertor is also coming into favour.

Mechanical Transmission

This is almost universally adopted for road and light railway vehicle, but has not been generally adopted for railway work where outputs of more than about 300 kW. are required, on account of the mechanical difficulties with the gears and gear-changing equipment. The mechanical transmission is, however, lighter and more efficient than the alternative electrical equipment, but it does not give such a flexible control. Comparative speed-torque curves and efficiency curves of a 5-speed geared equipment and an electrical equipment are given in Fig. 91.

Electrical Transmission Systems

The electrical transmission system, with which we are more particularly concerned, makes use of the simple speed-control properties and desirable speed-torque characteristics of the d.c. series motor. All electric transmission systems employ a d.c.

generator directly coupled to the Diesel engine and supplying d.c. series motors; although locomotives for outputs of up to 2250 kW. have been built, these have not been for exceptionally high speeds and nose suspension for the traction motors has been found satisfactory.

Assuming that the Diesel engine is governed to run at a constant speed and that the generator is giving a constant voltage, any increase in the tractive effort required by the train, due, say, to its meeting a gradient, will result in a reduction of speed of the traction motors due to the shape of their speed-torque characteristic. This reduction in speed will not, however, be sufficient to compensate for the increased tractive effort, and the kilowatts required will increase. It is shown in equation (28) that kW. is proportional to $\sqrt{T}$ for a series motor operating at constant voltage.

In order that the kilowatts delivered by the Diesel engine shall be held constant to prevent overloading it and at the same time to ensure that it will be used to its maximum capacity, various more or less complicated schemes of control have been developed.

The simplest way of doing this is by manual control of the generator field, as illustrated by the curves of Fig. 92. The full curves V_1, V_2 etc., are speed-tractive effort curves at various voltages. Suppose it is desired to hold the output constant at 220 kW. At a speed of 8 km/h, since

$$kW = \frac{T_E(N) \times \text{speed (m/s)}}{1000},$$

the tractive effort will be:

$$T_E = \frac{220 \times 1000 \times 60 \times 60}{8000} = \mathbf{99\ kN}.$$

The tractive effort at this kilowatts and other speeds can be found in a similar way and the dotted constant kilowatts curve plotted as shown.

Suppose the train is operating at point A, the generator field rheostat being adjusted so that a voltage V_2 is applied to the motors. If the train now meets an upward gradient the tractive effort required will be increased and the speed will drop, the operating point travelling along the speed-tractive effort curve V_2 to the left. It can be seen that this causes the kilowatts delivered to be increased and exceed the value of 300, so that the Diesel engine will be overloaded. To avoid this the driver must move his regulator to the next step so that operation is carried out on the lower speed-tractive effort curve V_3. Similarly had the train met a down gradient, the operating point would have moved along curve V_2 to the right and the kilowatts delivered would have been reduced, so that the Diesel engine would not have been delivering its maximum kilowatts. If the speed falls to 21.6 km/h (point C) the driver must, therefore, increase his generator field excitation so that operation takes place along curve V_1. By careful watching of his

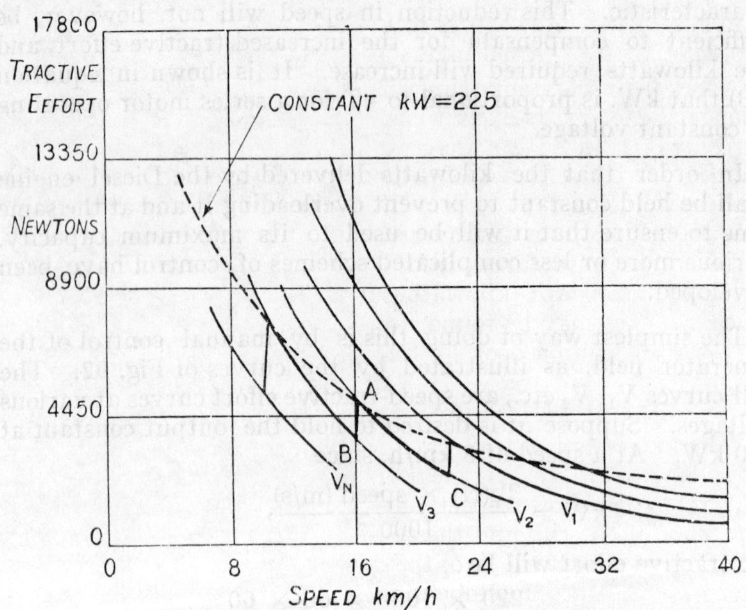

FIG 92.—CONSTANT KW. CONTROL OF DIESEL-ELECTRIC LOCOMOTIVE.

instruments, the driver can ensure that operation takes place along the heavy line, thus keeping the kilowatts approximately constant. Such vigilance, however, is not allowable, since the driver must have his whole attention available for watching the track and signals, and the above control must be carried out automatically.

The ideal requirements of such a control system can be determined as follows:

It is required to maintain a constant kilowatt, i.e. :

$T_E \times n$ must be constant, where T_E is the tractive effort and n is the speed.

Hence $\quad n \propto \frac{1}{T_E}$

But also, if $\Phi \propto I$, $\quad n \propto \frac{V}{I}$ and $T_E \propto I^2$

$$\therefore \text{ for constant kw. } \frac{V}{I} \propto n \propto \frac{1}{T_E} \propto \frac{1}{I^2}$$

$$\therefore \quad V \propto \frac{1}{I}$$

Thus, if the kilowatts is to be kept constant, the generator voltage must be varied inversely as the current.

The simplest way of doing this is to employ a series winding on the generator or its exciter connected in the traction-motor circuit and arranged so that an increase in the traction-motor current demagnetises the field. It is not possible to fulfil the above condition very closely by this method, and a large number of modifications and additions to it have been developed by different manufacturers in order to secure a closer agreement with the constant kilowatt curve. Detailed descriptions of such schemes may be found from time to time in the technical Press and also in a book by Reed (see Bibliography).

8. TRAIN MOVEMENT AND ENERGY CONSUMPTION

The movement of trains and their energy consumption is most conveniently studied by means of speed-time and speed-distance curves, which show respectively the speed at various times after the start of the run and the speed at various distances from the starting-point. Of the two, the speed-time curve is generally the more useful, since the slope of the curve represents the acceleration and the area under the curve ($\int vdt$) represents the distance travelled.

Typical Speed-Time Curve.—A typical speed-time curve for a suburban service with a short distance between stops in shown in Fig. 93. It can be seen that this curve may be divided into five parts:

(i) *Acceleration during Notching-up Period* (O *to* t_1).—Starting resistance is being cut out during this period, so that the current, and therefore the tractive effort, are approximately constant, producing a constant acceleration. Accelerations up to 0.6 or even 0.9 ms^{-2} are used.

(ii) *Acceleration on Speed Curve* (t_1 *to* t_2).—After the starting resistance has all been cut out (at point t_1) the train continues to accelerate, the torque gradually falling as the speed increases in accordance with the torque-speed characteristics of the motors, until a speed is attained at which the tractive effort exactly balances the resistance to motion of the train.

(iii) *Free-running Period* (t_2 *to* t_3).—The train continues to run at the speed reached at point t_2.

(iv) *Coasting* (t_3 *to* t_4).—Power is shut off and the train allowed to run under its own momentum, the speed gradually falling due to friction, windage, etc.

(v) *Braking* (t_4 *to* t_5).—The brakes are applied and the train brought to rest at the end of the run. The braking decelera-

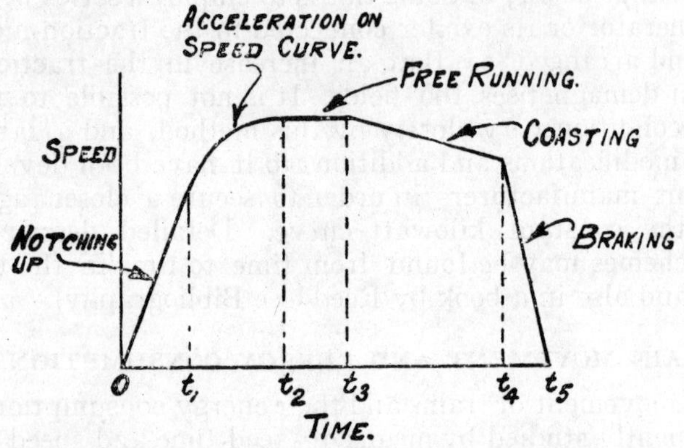

FIG. 93—TYPICAL SPEED-TIME CURVE—SUBURBAN RUN.

tion is usually between 0.6 and 0.9 *m* per sec. per sec. for suburban services, where rapid braking is essential.

The acceleration and free-running periods are governed by the speed-torque characteristics of the motor, and these must be available before this part of the curve can be determined. Coasting and braking are governed by the train resistance and the allowable braking retardation respectively. The actual shape of any particular speed-time curve will differ from the above on account of the existence of gradients and with different lengths of run. On a very short run, for instance, there may be no free-running period, while on a long run such as occurs with main-line services the majority of the run will be free running and the starting and braking periods negligible.

The drawing of these speed-time curves is an essential preliminary to any electrification scheme in order to find what schedule speeds can be maintained and what will be the energy consumption.

Construction of Speed-time and Speed-distance Curves

Speed-tractive Effort Curve.—The speed-torque characteristic of the motors must be converted to a speed-tractive effort curve, as described on page 71, the speed in this case being measured in kilometers per hour or meters per second. The method of constructing speed-time and speed-distance curves is described in Chapter I. A train driven by series motors affords an example of the case when the tractive effort is not a simple function of the

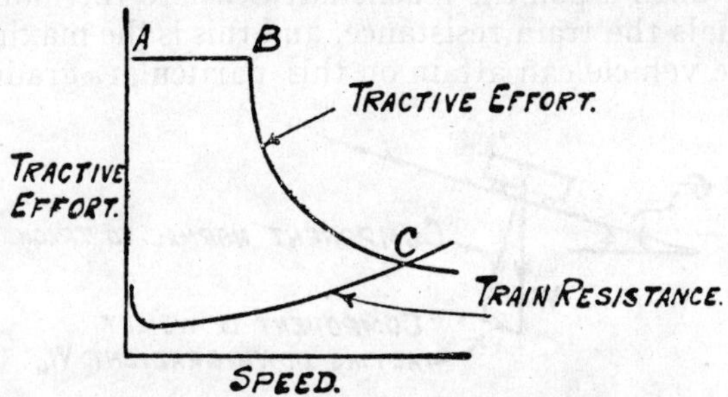

FIG. 94.—TYPICAL TRACTIVE-EFFORT AND TRAIN-RESISTANCE CURVES.

speed, and the integrations must therefore be performed graphically. The tractive-effort/speed curve can be plotted as shown in Fig. 94. The current during the notching-up period will be limited to an approximately constant value of about $1\frac{1}{2}$ to 2 times full-load current, so that for low speeds the tractive effort will be approximately constant, as shown by the portion of the curve AB.

Train Resistance.—The tractive effort available for accelerating a vehicle is equal to the tractive effort available at the rim of the driving wheel minus that required to overcome the friction and wind resistance of the train and the component of the train weight acting down a gradient when the vehicle is ascending the gradient; when running down a gradient the latter, of course, assists the motion. The component of the weight up or down the gradient is easily obtained by reference to Fig. 95. The friction and wind resistance of the train cannot, however, be calculated from first principles and empirical data obtained from tests on actual trains must be relied upon.

A typical curve of train resistance is shown in Fig. 94 ; it may be noted that the curve rises very steeply at low speeds, due to static friction—this is not taken into account in the above or any of the other usual formulæ. For tramway work, where there is not such a great range of speed, a constant figure of between 100 and 150 N per tonne is generally chosen.

Acceleration.—As mentioned above, the tractive effort available for producing acceleration is the difference between the tractive effort of the motors and the train resistance due to wind and friction and to gradients, and this value can be read from the curve on Fig. 94 for any speed. It can be seen that the value decreases until a point is reached at C where the motor tractive effort equals the train resistance, and this is the maximum speed which the vehicle can attain on this particular gradient. The

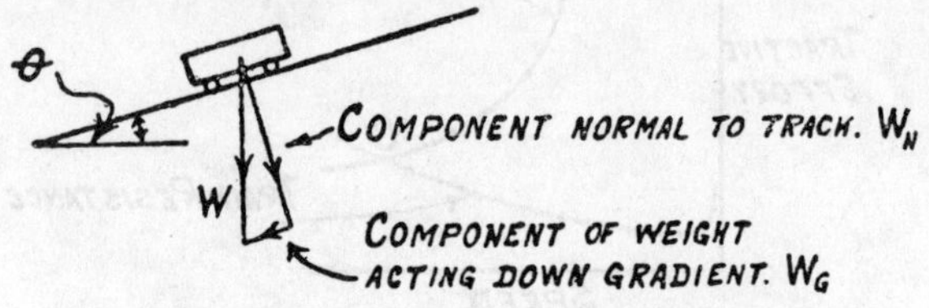

FIG. 95.—WEIGHT ACTING DOWN GRADIENT.

acceleration at any particular speed may be calculated from the formula (Equation (20*a*)) :

$$f = \frac{T_E}{m} ms^{-2}$$

(T_E in N and *m* in kg)

where T_E is the net tractive effort at that speed, and m the train mass. It may be mentioned here that in addition to accelerating the vehicle along the track, the motors have to produce a rotational acceleration of the rotating parts (armatures, gears, driving wheels, etc.), so that the acceleration will therefore be less than the value calculated above. This is usually taken into account by adding 8 or 10 per cent. to the train weight in the above expression.

Speed-time Curve during Acceleration.—Acceleration is proportional to rate of change of speed, i.e. :

$$f = \frac{dv}{dt}$$

so that
$$t = \int \frac{1}{f} dv + C$$

C being the constant of integration (C = 0 if the train starts from rest).

In the majority of traction problems, however, the acceleration does not follow any definite law and the integration must be performed graphically. This can be done by plotting, to a base of speed, the values of $\frac{1}{f}$. If $\frac{1}{f}$ is in SI units and the speed is in metres per second, any area under this curve represents "time" in seconds. Such a curve is plotted in Fig. 96, and by finding the area up to a certain speed (e.g. the area OABC), the time taken to reach that speed can be found and this value plotted as an ordinate at that speed. A number of such points can be found and a curve plotted between speed and the time taken to attain that speed, i.e. the speed-time curve.

Speed-distance Curve during Acceleration.—Speed is equal to the rate of change of distance travelled, i.e. $v = \frac{ds}{dt}$, so that $s = \int v dt$. In general the integration will have to be performed graphically as before. The speed-time curve may be replotted with speed in metre per second as the ordinates and time in seconds as abscissæ. Areas under the curve, therefore, represent distance travelled in metres so that the distance travelled in a certain time may be obtained by finding the area under the curve up to the ordinate at this time. Plotting the points so obtained on a base of speed gives the distance-time curve. For any given time, therefore, we have from these curves a value of distance travelled and speed attained, so that a speed-distance curve can be plotted if desired.

In practice these curves can conveniently be drawn on a single sheet, as shown in Fig. 96, thus eliminating the replotting of any curves. The procedure is illustrated by a numerical calculation in Example 14.

Full information regarding the movement of the train up to the end of the accelerating period is thus obtained.

Free Running.—After the end of the accelerating period, provided there is no change in gradient, the train will continue to run at a constant speed until power is shut off. If the gradient or any other of the variables changes there will, of course, be acceleration or retardation until a new constant speed is reached, and conditions during this period can be obtained by applying the same principles as above, the only difference being that the initial speed is not now zero.

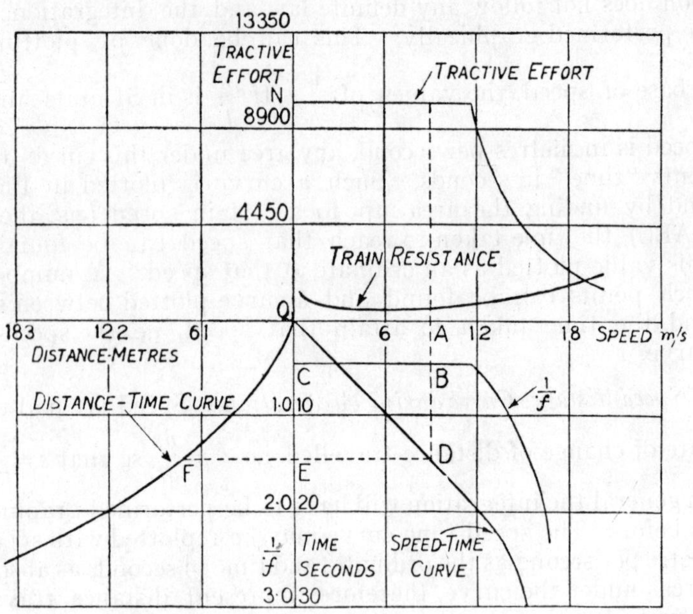

FIG. 96.—DETERMINATION OF SPEED-TIME AND DISTANCE-TIME CURVES. (EXAMPLE 14.)

Coasting.—During this period the train resistance produces a retarding force, causing a gradual deceleration. For the speed range over which coasting usually takes place the train resistance may be regarded as constant, and the retardation will therefore be obtained from $\frac{R}{M}$ where R is the train resistance. The inertia of the rotating parts will help to keep the train going, and therefore reduce the retardation, and the train mass must be increased by the 8 or 10 per cent. previously mentioned to allow for this. Another point which should be allowed for is the friction of the motors and gearing. During the accelerating period this was taken into account in calculating the available tractive effort, but now these produce an additional retarding force of 10 or 12 per cent., tending to reduce the speed.

Braking.—The braking retardation is usually constant and is governed by the comfort of the passengers or by the braking equipment available. Assuming constant retardation, the speed-time and speed-distance relations can easily be calculated.

Speed-time and Speed-distance Curves for Complete Run.—The problem usually presented is to find at what point power should be cut off and at what point the brakes should be applied in order to maintain a satisfactory average speed with a reasonable economy in energy consumption. The simplest method of procedure is to select what appears to be a reasonable value of average speed for the particular run under consideration; the time for the run may then be calculated and the base of the speed-time curve drawn. The speed-time curves for the acceleration and braking periods can then be drawn from each end of this base, as shown in Fig. 97. The slope of the coasting-period curve can be calculated and a number of possible coasting curves drawn in, giving a line such as AB. It has already been pointed out that the area under the speed-time curve represents distance, so that the correct coasting curve for this case will be that which makes the area under the curve equal to the length of the run under consideration. The maximum speed can be observed and the energy consumption calculated by a method to be described later. If these are satisfactory the speed-time curve so drawn may be regarded as suitable for the run, but if not, then the process must be repeated with another value of average speed. Having fixed the speed-time curve, the speed-distance curve can be easily found; using the length of run as base, the speed-distance curves for accelerating and braking can be plotted from the two ends. Knowing the maximum speed from the speed-time curve, the point at which coasting starts can be immediately found and the coasting curve drawn in. Where this cuts the braking curve is the point at which braking must begin.

Energy Consumption

The value of the current per motor at any speed can be obtained from the motor characteristic curves, so that the total current taken by the vehicle can be found and plotted on the speed-time curve. During the notching-up period the current per motor will be approximately constant ; when series-parallel control is used the current will be doubled at the instant of switching into parallel, as shown in Fig. 97. The area under the current-time curve represents quantity of electricity in ampere-seconds, and if the supply voltage is assumed constant the energy consumption can be calculated from :

$$\text{Energy} = \frac{\text{amp.-sec.} \times \text{voltage}}{3600} \text{ watt-hours.}$$

For purposes of comparison it is usual to express the energy consumption in watt-hours per tonne-km. this figure being called the *specific energy consumption.*

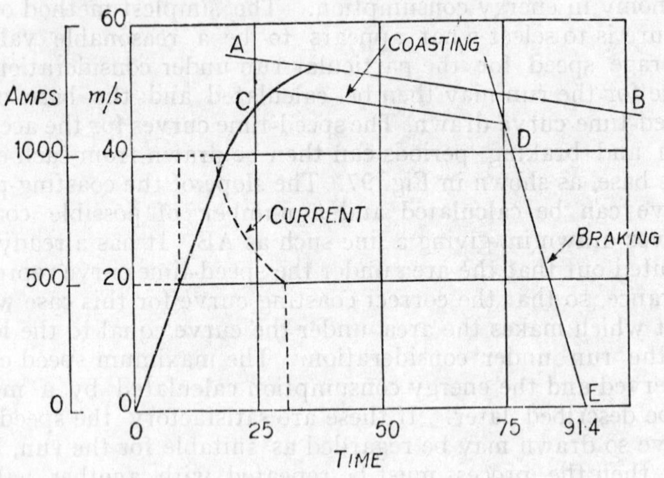

FIG. 97.—SPEED-TIME CURVE FOR COMPLETE RUN. (EXAMPLE 14)

Typical values of specific energy consumption are :
Suburban service with frequent stops 50 to 75 Wh. per tonne-km.
Main-line express services . . 20 to 30 Wh. per tonne-km.

The actual value of energy consumption in any particular case depends, of course, on gradient, distance between stops, average speed, and various other factors ; the effects of some of these variables are illustrated in Figs. 100 and 101.

Example 14 : Determine the speed-time and speed-distance curves and the energy consumption of a motor-coach train when operating between stops on a section of line 1 005 m long and having an

up-gradient of 1:in 660. The average speed is to be 39.7 km/h·
Particulars of train:—

Three-coach train with four 750-V motors, connected in two pairs to make 1 500 V mains; Motor characteristics see Fig. 98. Maximum current during notching up period per motor=500 A. Mass of train 136 000 kg (loaded). Train resistance due to friction and windage, see Fig. 96.

Solution:

The tractive-effort/speed curves for the whole train (four motors) is plotted in the first quadrant of fig. 96. The horizontal

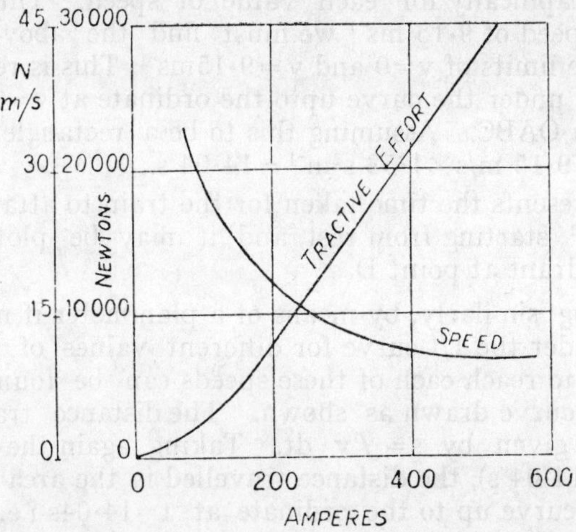

Fig. 98.—Motor Characteristics. (Example 14.)

portion of this represents the notching up period during which the current, and, therefore, the tractive effort is held approximately constant by the starting resistance.

The train resistance due to friction and windage is plotted from experimental data as shown and to obtain the total train resistance there must be added to this the component of the train weight acting down the grade, in this case:—

$$\text{Component of train weight} = 136{,}000 \times 9{\cdot}81 \times \frac{1}{660} = 2050 \text{ N}$$

The net tractive effort available for accelerating the train is the difference between these two, i.e. at a speed of 9.15 ms^{-1} net tractive effort=(104 500N-6 675 N)=97 825 N.

The acceleration which this will produce, allowing 10% for the inertia of the rotating parts, is :

$$f = \frac{97825}{1 \cdot 1 \times 136000} = 0 \cdot 653 \ ms^{-2}$$

The quantity required for the integration, however, is not f but $\frac{1}{f}$ which in this case is $1/0 \cdot 653 = 1 \cdot 53 \ s^2 m^{-1}$.

Performing a similar calculation for various values of speed and plotting the result against speed gives the curve shown in the second quadrant of fig. 96. The integral $t = \int (1/f) \, dv$ must be found graphically for each value of speed. Thus, taking again the speed of $9 \cdot 15 \ ms^{-1}$ we must find the above integral between the limits of $v=0$ and $v=9 \cdot 15 ms^{-1}$. This is represented by the area under the curve upto the ordinate at $v=9 \cdot 15 \ ms^{-1}$; i.e. the area OABC. Assuming this to be a rectangle, the area is given by $9 \cdot 15 \ m/s \times 1 \cdot 53 \ s^2 m^{-1} = 14 \cdot 04$ s.

This represents the time taken for the train to attain a speed of $9 \cdot 15 \ ms^{-1}$, starting from rest, and it may be plotted in the second quadrant at point D.

By finding similarly, by means of a planimeter if necesssary, the area under the 1/f curve for different values of speed, the time taken to reach each of these speeds can be found and the speed-time curve drawn as shown. The distance travelled in any time is given by $s = \int v \ dt$. Taking again the speed of $9 \cdot 15 \ ms^{-1}$ ($14 \cdot 04$ s), the distance travelled is the area under the speed-time curve up to the ordinate at $t=14 \cdot 04$s i.e. the area OED.

This area equals $\frac{1}{2} \times 14 \cdot 04 s \times 9 \cdot 15 \ ms^{-1} = 64 \cdot 3$ m.

This is plotted in the third quadrant, at the point F. Finding the area up to other speeds gives the complete time-distance curve as shown, and a speed-distance curve can be plotted if required.

To find now the speed-time curve for the complete run, the speed-time curve for the acceleration period calculated above is replotted as shown in Fig. 97 with speed as ordinate.

The average speed for the whole run is to be

$$39 \cdot 7 \ km/h = 11 \cdot 05 \ ms^{-1}.$$

The total time taken for the journey is $1005/11 \cdot 05 = 91$ s.

This fixes the length of the base of the curve. Braking is at a constant retardation of $0 \cdot 891 \ ms^{-2}$ so that the braking portion of the curve can be drawn. The time to brake from 12·2 ms^{-1} to stand still is (12·2/0·89)=13·65 s.

The retarding force during coasting can be assumed constant for the speed range over which it takes place, and can be found from the total train resistance curve, say, a speed of 12·2 ms^{-1} and is thus 4448 N.

$$\text{Retardation during coasting } \frac{4448}{1\cdot1\times1{,}36{,}000} = 0\cdot297\ ms^{-2}$$

The slope of the speed time curve during coasting is thus given by the line AB. It now remains to fit a line of this slope into the diagram in such a position that the area under the complete curve is equal to the total distance travelled (1005 m). This can be done only by a process of trial and error. It will be found that the position CD fulfills the required condition and the curve OCDE therefore represents the speed time curve for the whole run.

If desired, the speed-distance curve for the whole run can also be plotted by reproducing the speed-distance curve for the accelarating period from Fig. 96 as far as the maximum speed, in this case 15·85 ms^{-1} and then calculating the remainder by ordinary formulae of dynamics from the known constant retardations during coasting and braking.

To find the energy consumption it is necessary to plot a curve of current to a base of time which gives ampere-seconds. If a constant voltage is assumed this can be converted to watt-hours. The current at any speed can be found from the characteristic curves of the motors (Fig. 98). Series parallel control is employed, so that during the first part of the notching up period the motors are in series, and the total current will be 500 amps ; at about half-speed the connections are changed to parallel and the total line current, therefore, doubles to 1000 amps.

The area under the current curve is found to be 21 300 ampere-second.

$$= \frac{21\ 300 \times 1\ 500}{3\ 600} = 8\ 900 \text{ Wh.}$$

Therefore, the specific energy consumption

$$= \frac{8\ 900}{1\ 36\ 000 \times 1\ 005} = 6\cdot5\times10^{-5} \text{ Wh/kg-m.}$$

Simplified Speed-time Curves

For preliminary work and for observing the effect of different values of acceleration, average speed, etc., on energy consumption, approximate shapes for the speed-time curves can be assumed, thus saving labour in repeating the calculations described above a very large number of times; furthermore, such calculations can be made without any knowledge of the motor characteristics.

Quadrilateral Speed-time Curve.—The quadrilateral speed-time curve is illustrated in Fig. 99. The accelerating period is assumed to be a straight line up to the point at which power is shut off, after which coasting continues up to the end of the run, the braking being neglected.

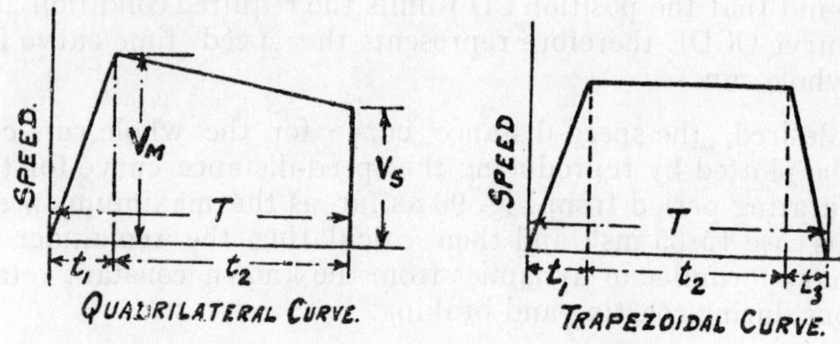

FIG. 99.—SIMPLIFIED SPEED-TIME CURVES.

Let α be the acceleration during the accelerating period

β be the acceleration during the coasting period (usually negative unless on a down gradient)

I be the total length of the run

T be the total time.

The other quantities being as shown on the diagram.

$$t_1 = \frac{V_m}{\alpha};\ t_2 = T - t_1$$

$$V_s = V_m + \beta t_2 = V_m + \beta(T - t_1)$$

$$\text{Area under curve} = L = \tfrac{1}{2} V_m t_1 + \tfrac{1}{2} V_m t_2 + \tfrac{1}{2} V_s t_2.$$

$$\therefore\ 2L = V_m t_1 + V_m (T - t_1) + [V_m + \beta(T - t_1)]\,(T - t_1)$$

Substituting for t_1 and simplifying gives:

$$V_m^2 \left(\frac{\alpha - \beta}{\alpha^2}\right) - 2TV_m \left(\frac{\alpha - \beta}{\alpha}\right) + (2L - \beta T^2) = 0 \qquad (36)$$

Solving this equation for one of the quantities V_m or T in terms of the others enables the influence of these quantities to be observed. The energy consumption may also be estimated by finding the work done in accelerating the train to a speed V_m.

The stored energy is $\frac{1}{2}mV_m^2$ J, where m is the vehicle mass (including allowance for rotating parts). The work done against the vehicle resistance, F, is $F \times d$ N.*m*., where d is the distance travelled during the accelerating period. The sum of these two quantities represents the energy received by the vehicles, i.e. the output of the motors. The input will, of course, be greater than this by the losses in the motors, and, with d.c. motors, the losses in the starting resistance; in the latter case an efficiency of 50 or 60 per cent. may be taken, while with a.c. motors it will be between 80 and 90 per cent.

Trapezoidal Speed-time Curve.—Another shape of curve which may be used is also illustrated in Fig. 99. In this case a horizontal portion is used to represent a free running or coasting period and braking is taken into account.

Let γ in this case represent the retardation during braking (it will, therefore, always be positive), the other symbols being as before.

$$t_1 = \frac{V_m}{\alpha} \qquad t_3 = \frac{V_m}{\gamma}$$

$$t_2 = T - (t_1 + t_3)$$

$$\text{Area} = L = \tfrac{1}{2} V_m t_1 + \tfrac{1}{2} V_m t_3 + V_m t_2$$

Substituting for t_1, t_2, and t_3 gives:

$$V_m^2\left[\tfrac{1}{2}\left(\frac{1}{\alpha}+\frac{1}{\gamma}\right)\right] - V_m T + L = 0 \quad . \quad . \quad (37)$$

This equation may be solved as before and the relation between the various quantities found.

An example illustrating the method of using these simplified speed-time curves is illustrated below.

Example 15: It is desired to find the effect of average speed on energy consumption for a given run (1525 m) and for a given value of acceleration, namely 0.366 ms^{-2}. Train resistance during acceleration is 52.6 N per 1000 kg and during coasting is 61.2 N per 1000 kg, 10% being allowed for rotational inertia. The efficiency of the equipment during the accelerating period is 50%.

TABLE V

V_m m/s.	Equation	T (Sec.)	Average Speed (m/s)	Stored energy (J/1000kg)	Distance travelled during accelera-tion (m)	Frictional energy (J/kg)	Total energy con-sumption (J/kg)	Specific energy con-sumption Wh/1000 kg/km
33·4	$0{\cdot}0555T^2 - 77{\cdot}5T + 6580 = 0$	88·0	17·40	617 000	1525	80·2	697·2	254·00
27·45	$0{\cdot}0555T^2 - 63{\cdot}4T + 5425 = 0$	93·5	16·35	415 000	1028	54·1	469·1	170·5
21·35	$0{\cdot}0555T^2 - 49{\cdot}4T + 4490 = 0$	102·0	14·95	251 000	619	32·6	283·6	103·4
15·25	$0{\cdot}0555T^2 - 35{\cdot}2T + 3780 = 0$	135·0	11·30	128 400	317	16·7	145·1	52·7
12·20	$0{\cdot}0555T^2 - 28{\cdot}2T + 3520 = 0$	221·0	6·90	81 500	203	10·7	92·2	36·7

$$\text{Stored energy} = \tfrac{1}{2}m\,V_m^2 = \tfrac{1}{2}\times 1 \times 1{\cdot}1\,V_m^2 = 0{\cdot}55\,V_m^2 \text{ Joules/kg}$$

$$\text{Distance travelled during acceleration} = V_m^2/2 = \frac{V_m^2}{0{\cdot}732}\text{ m}$$

$$\text{Frictional energy} = 0{\cdot}526 \times s \text{ J/kg}$$

$$\text{Specific energy consumption} = \text{Total energy in J/kg} \times 10^6 \times \frac{1}{1525} \times \frac{1}{3600} \times \frac{100}{50}$$

$$= \frac{\text{Total energy in J/kg}}{2{\cdot}74}\text{ wh/1000 kg/km}$$

Solution :

The quadrilateral speed-time curve is used.

Coasting acceleration

$$\beta = -\frac{61{\cdot}2}{1\,001 \times 1{\cdot}1} = -\ 0{\cdot}055\ 7\ ms^{-2}$$

$$\alpha - \beta = 0{\cdot}422\,;\quad \frac{\alpha-\beta}{\alpha} = 1{\cdot}152\,;\quad \frac{\alpha-\beta}{\alpha^2} = 3{\cdot}145.$$

Equation (36), thus becomes :

$$3{\cdot}145\ V_m^2 - TV_m\ 2{\cdot}31 + 3050 + 0{\cdot}0557\ T^2 = 0.$$

Various values of V_m may be chosen and the corresponding values of T calculated as shown in Table V. The quantities shown in the succeeding columns can then be calculated arriving finally at the energy consumption.

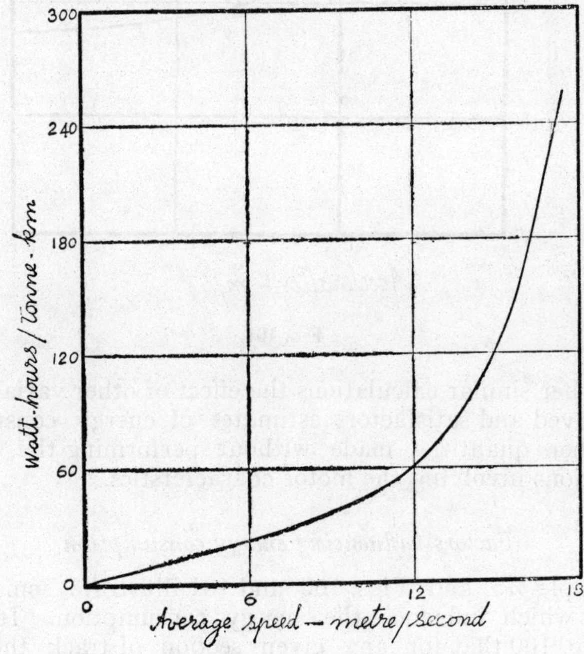

Fig. 100.

The relation between energy consumption and average speed is plotted in Fig. 100.

Another useful curve, calculated in a similar manner, is shown in Fig. 101 and illustrates the effect of the rate of acceleration on energy consumption, when the average speed is fixed at 12.2 ms^{-2} the other conditions remaining as above.

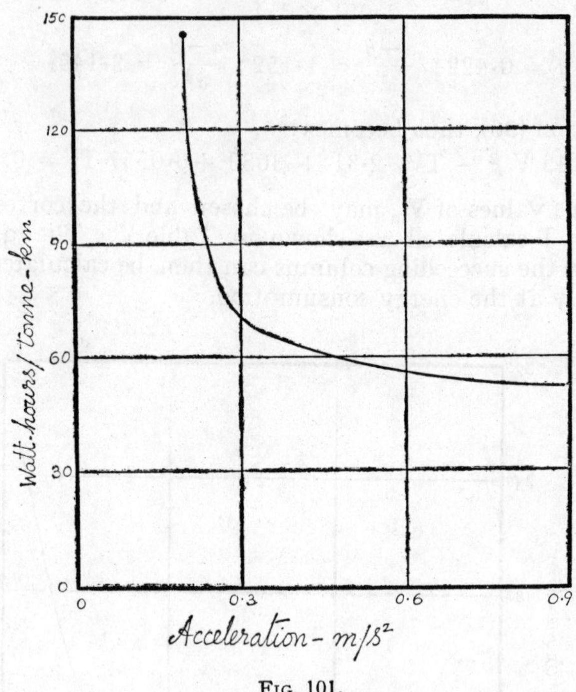

FIG. 101.

By other similar calculations the effect of other variables can be observed and satisfactory estimates of energy consumption and other quantities made without performing the detailed calculations involving the motor characterstics.

Factors influencing energy consumption

Example 15 and Figs. 100 and 101 illustrate some of the factors which influence the energy consumption. It is seen from Fig. 100 that for any given section of track there is a value of average speed above which the energy consumption begins to increase very rapidly; for the track in question (1525 m long and level) and with equipment giving an acceleration of 0.336 ms^{-2} it would not be economical to exceed an average speed of above 13.72 ms^{-1}. The curve of Fig. 101 shows the effect of different accelerations and indicates that any value below about 0.3048 ms^{-2} results in high energy consumption; provision of higher accelerations than this reduces the energy consumption, but involves the use of larger motors and requires heavier peaks of current from the supply, so that in any particular case a balance must be struck between the saving in energy costs and the higher costs of the equipment.

CHAPTER II

QUESTIONS

1. Certain locomotives (for the Montreux-Bernese Oberland Railway) have to be capable of accelerating a train of mass 152·4 metric tons (excluding loco) up a gradient of 1 in 16, with an acceleration of 0.08 ms^{-2}. The maximum allowable axle load is 11.2 metric tons. If the coefficient of adhesion is 24%, estimate a suitable value for the weight of the locomotive and the number of driving axles required.

2. A locomotive is hauling a train along a level track at a steady speed of 64.36 km/h and is exerting a tractive effort of 45 000 N. What power is the locomotive exerting? If the train meets a gradient necessitating an increase in tractive effort to 67 500 N, what will be the power required from the locomotive, if it is driven by:

(*a*) d.c. series motor ($n \propto \frac{1}{I}$)?

(*b*) induction motor (n approximately constant)?

3. In an emergency, two 3-phase locomotives are coupled to haul a heavy train. The motors of both locos have a slip of 5%, when the loco is delivering its full load tractive effort of 53 400 N, but loco A has driving wheels of 1.27 m diameter, while the wheels of loco B are worn down to 1.245 m. How will the two locomotives share a tractive effort of: (a) 115 700 N, (b) 13 350 N? How would the above tractive efforts been shared if, in addition to the inequality of the driving-wheel diameters, the loco B had had a slip of 4% instead of 5%.

4. Rheostatic braking is employed on a tram car driven by two series motors. The magnetisation curve of the motors when driven at a speed corresponding to 24 km/h is given by the following figures:

Current (A)	20	40	60	80
Voltage (V)	280	500	630	700

The total resistance of each motor is 0.2Ω. What resistance must be put in series with each motor in order to limit the speed to 16 km/h, when the net driving force on the car is 4 500 N? The gear efficiency is 85%. Assume motors to be in parallel during braking. If a resistance of 5Ω were put in series with each motor, what would be the speed attained by the car, the driving force still being 4 500 N?

5. The following figures give the characteristics of a 220-kW railway motor when operating with its full field excitation:

Current (A)	100	200	300	400	500
Speed (km/h)	104.7	58.8	48	42.7	39.8
Tractive effort (N)	1 480	4 500	12 300	18 400	24 450

Draw the characteristic curves for the motor when it is operating on a weak field tapping which cuts out 25% of the total number of field turns.

6. If the characteristics given in Question 5 are obtained with the motor driving, through a gear ratio of 20 : 70, and a wheel of 0.9m in diameter, plot the characteristics which would be obtained if the gear ratio were changed to 20 : 80 and the wheel diameter to 1.0m.

7. The trolley wire for a tramway system having poles spaced 36.6m apart is 4/0 hard drawn copper wire (cross sectional area = 81.3 mm^2). The sag is not to exceed 1% of the span at the maximum temperature likely to be encountered, namely, 49°C?. What will be the tension in the wire:

(*a*) at the above temperature?
(*b*) at normal temperature (15.5°C)?
(*c*) at −5.55°C?
(*d*) at −5.550°C and with a 10mm radial thickness of ice adhering to the wire?

What will be the sag in the three latter cases?

8. The following particulars refer to the overhead equipment of a section of the GIP Railway, India. Span = 67 m; Cross-sectional area of standard-copper of catenary wire = 240mm^2; cross sectional area of contact wire = 160mm^2; Number of droppers per span = 12. If the contact wire is level

at 20°C, the sag of the catenary is then 1.83 m and the tension in the contact wire is 13.35 kN determine what will be the sag of the contact wire and the tensions in the catenary and contact wires at 55°C. Neglect the weight of the droppers and assume the contact wires to be fixed at the ends.

9. A surburban electric train having an acceleration of 2.25km/h per second and a braking retardation 4km/h per second has to maintain an average speed between stops of 41.8km/h on a run of 0.965 km. The train resistance is 52.6 N/metric ton and the efficiency of motor and gears during starting is 60%. Estimate, using : (a) a trapezoidal speed-time curve, (b) a quadrilateral speed-time curve, the maximum speed which the train must reach and the energy consumption in watt-hours per tonne-km series parallel control may be assumed.

10. Repeat Worked Example No. 15 (in the text) using a trapezoidal speed-time curve and assuming a train resistance of 60 N/metric ton. Compare the results obtained by the two methods.

11. The figures below give the tractive effort and current of a 600-V motor coach train weighing 168 metric tons.

speed (km/h)	79.6	63.5	57.5	45 8	41.7
tractive effort (N)	12 100	23 600	35 600	53 000	65 000
current (A)	570	880	1 160	1 430	1 600

During starting, the current is limited to 1 600 A, giving a constant tractive effort of 65 000 N. The train resistance is given by the Eqn. 35. Draw the speed-time and time-distance curves for the train during acceleration upto a speed of 80.° km/h when the train is ascending a gradient of 1 in 270.

Draw speed-time and speed-distance curves for the train on a complete run over a section of 1 158m between stops and with an upward gradient of 1 in 270. Power is shut off at 548m from the start and braking is at 3.22-km/h per second.

Find the maximum speed attained, the average speed, and the energy consumption for the run, assuming series-parallel control during starting and a constant supply voltage of 600 V.

CHAPTER III

HEATING AND WELDING

1. ADVANTAGES AND METHODS OF ELECTRIC HEATING

PRACTICALLY all heating requirements, whether domestic or industrial, can be met by some form of electric heating equipment, and the present low price of electrical energy, together with its other advantages, render this method of producing heat an economic proposition in a great many cases.

Relative costs of methods of producing Heat :

The consumer interested in the cost of heating needs the following information:

(i) Output rating of the appliance ;

(ii) the efficiency of the appliance ;

(iii) the cost of fuel used.

There are certain difficulties in making the calculations with the existing units (FPS) e.g. that it demands the calorific value of fuel expressed as 'Btu per lb'. In SI, the calorific value of a fuel is given as MJ/kg. Also, even in SI, there are two energy units: (i) joule and (ii) kilowatt hour. The choice of energy units for (everyday use is thus not so simple as the choice of units for) power or heat output (Watt or kilowatt or megawatt). The SI Unit of energy is the joule and its multiples and sub-multiples. The kilowatt hour is recorded by the International Standards Organisation (ISO) as a unit that may be used for 'energy' and 'work' but is not stated as a unit for 'quantity of heat'. For the ordinary domestic consumer, the relationship between the kilowatt and kilowatt-hour is easy to understand. The kilowatt-hour is also used internationally, and is therefore widely understood. It is also widely known as the 'unit of energy'; only one has to remember that 1 kwh = 3.6 MJ.

This is a simpler relationship than those relating the Btu to kwh and the kcal to kwh, currently in use. The factor 3.6 comes from the fact that 1 hour = 60 minutes and 1 minute = 60 seconds. However, it is useful to remember that: 1 Btu = 1.055 kJ. The exclusive use of the joule and its multiples for public and commercial purposes would require a change of practice by the world's electrical industries to the use of megajoule (MJ) and gigajoule (GJ). The easier alternative would be to use the kWh for all public and commercial purposes, reserving the joule and its multiples for all technical and engineering purposes.

The relative cost of producing heat from electricity and other fuels can be easily calculated on two criteria : (*a*) joule-oriented ; (*b*) kilowatt-hour-oriented—see Tables VI(a) and VI(b). These tables have taken into account the efficiency of utilisation of the apparatus for converting the energy into heat, as it varies in each case (see column 3 of both tables). Therefore, cost (in paise) per useful MJ is shown in the last column of Table (a) and correspondingly the cost (in paise) per useful kWh in the last column of Table (b). For easy calculation purposes, the cost of 1 kWh has been assumed at 19.5 paise taking 1 penny = 10 paise. (This table was adopted from a British Paper Energy Units and the Consumer'—See Sec. 8 : 1 of item No. 13 in the Bibliography—under B. Foreign, at the end of this book). The last column gives the relative costs of heating by five different energy sources.

TABLE VI

(*a*) COMPARATIVE HEATING COSTS : JOULE-ORIENTED :

Type of fuel	Gross heat value	Apparatus efficiency	Net heat value	Cost	Cost (in paise) per useful MJ
1. Electricity	1 kwh/unit	100%	1 kwh/unit	19·5 p/unit	5·41
2. Oil . .	36·0 MJ/l	75%	27·0 MJ/l	45 p/l	1·67
3. Coke . .	28·0 MJ/kg	65%	18·2 MJ/kg	38·2 p/kg	2·10
4. Anthracite	33·8 MJ/kg	76%	25·7 MJ/kg	45 p/kg	1·75
5. Gas . .	18·6 MJ/m³	75%	13·9 MJ/m³	30·1 p/m³	2·16

(b) COMPARATIVE HEATING COSTS : KILOWATT HOUR-ORIENTED :

Type of fuel	Gross heat value	Apparatus efficiency	Net heat value	Cost	Cost (in paise) per useful kWh
1. Electricity	1 kwh/unit	100%	1 kwh/unit	19 5 p/unit	19·5 p
2. Oil . .	10·0 kwh/l	75%	7.50 kwh/l	45 p/l	6·0 p
3: Coke . .	7·76 kwh/kg	65%	5·04 kwh/kg	38.2 p/kg	7·57 p
4. Anthracite	9·38 kwh/kg	76%	7·13 kwh/kg	45 p/kg	6·30 p
5. Gas . .	5·17kwh/m³	75%	3.88 kwh/m³	30·1 p/m³	7·76 p

It is thus seen that electrically produced heat, although appearing at first sight to be considerably more expensive than that produced from other sources, is not very much so when the efficiency of utilisation is taken into account. When the various other indirect savings enumerated in the next paragraph are also taken into account it may frequently become considerably cheaper. Referring again to the Tables VI(a) and (b), it may be noted that while electricity for heating purposes can in many urban districts be obtained considerably cheaper especially for bulk H. T. Supply (industrial tariff) than what was assumed in the tables ; there may be wide variations in the cost of other types of fuels (especially coke), as well as in their calorific value. Suitable adjustments can, however, be made to the above figure, to suit any particular case.

Advantages of electrically produced Heat

For nearly all purposes electrically produced heat possesses advantages over other forms of heat, the most important of which are as follows:

(i) *Cleanliness.*—The complete elimination of dust and ash keeps cleaning costs down to a minimum.

(ii) *Absence of Flue Gases.*—No space has to be used in providing flues and there is no risk of contamination of the atmosphere or of the objects being heated.

(iii) *Ease of Control.*—Simple and accurate control of temperature can be provided either by hand or by fully automatic devices, so that temperature can be maintained constant or made to vary in accordance with a predetermined plan ; furthermore, any particular temperature or temperature cycle can be accurately repeated at any time.

(iv) *Low Attention and Maintenance Costs.*—Electric heating equipment in general requires no attention, while maintenance costs are negligibly small, thus resulting in a very considerable saving in labour costs over alternative heating systems.

Types and Applications of Electric Heating Equipment

The various methods of producing heat for general industrial work, heating of buildings, and for welding may conveniently be classified as follows :

(i) *Direct-resistance Heating.*—Current is passed through the body to be heated. A few industrial processes, including resistance welding, employ this method, and it is also used in the electrode boiler for heating water.

(ii) *Indirect-resistance Heating.*—Current is passed through a wire or other high-resistance material forming a heating element; the heat (I^2R loss) so produced is transmitted by radiation or convection to the body to be heated. This method is used in the ordinary domestic radiator, the immersion water heater, and in the various types of resistance ovens used for domestic and commercial cooking, heat treatment of metals, and other purposes.

(iii) *Indirect-induction Heating.*—Eddy currents are induced in the heating element by electro-magnetic action, the heat so produced being transmitted to the body to be heated by radiation and convection, as in the indirect-resistance method. Certain types of induction oven used for the heat treatment of metals operate on this principle.

(iv) *Direct-induction Heating.*—Currents are induced by electromagnetic action in the body to be heated, and, in the case of steel and other metals, produce a sufficiently high temperature to melt the metal. The equipment used for melting is known as the induction furnace, whilst the process used for general heat treatment of metals is referred to as eddy-current heating.

(v) *Dielectric Heating.*—Use is made of the dielectric losses set up in non-metallic materials when subjected to an alternating electric field.

(vi) *The Electric Arc.*—An arc drawn between two electrodes has a temperature of between 3,000 and 3,500°C., depending on the electrode material, and is therefore valuable for producing very high temperatures; it is employed in the arc furnance nor the melting of metals and also for arc welding.

Transfer of Heat

Before discussing in detail the various methods and apparatus for producing heat electrically, it will be desirable to consider the methods whereby heat is transferred from a hot to a cooler body, e.g. from the heating element to the body to be heated. This may occur as a result of conduction, convection, radiation, or by a combination of these methods.

Conduction.—The rate at which heat is conducted through a substance depends on the temperature gradient, i.e. on the difference between the temperatures of the surfaces on each side of the body; it may be expressed in MJ per hour per square metre per metre or preferably, when dealing with electric heating, in watts per square centimetre per centimetre.

Values of the thermal conductivity and also specific heats for various substances are given in Table VII (a) & (b).

Conduction of heat is important chiefly in connection with refractory and heat-insulating materials when these are used for preventing the escape of heat in directions in which it is not required.

TABLE VII (*a*)

MASS DENSITY AND SPECIFIC HEAT OF VARIOUS SUBSTANCES:

S. No.	Substance	Mass density (kg m^{-3} or kg/m^3)	Specific heat capacity or specific heat (at ordinary temps.) J kg^{-1} K^{-1} or J kg^{-1} °C^{-1}
1.	Still air (16°C)	1·21752	1000
2.	Water (16°C)	998	4200
3.	Iron: pure	7870	438
	wrought	7850	440
	cast	7600	
	mild steel	7800	444
4.	Copper	8960	386
5.	Brass	8500	365 to 395
6.	Zinc	7130	390
7.	Aluminium	2710	875
8.	Porcelain	2307	924
9.	Fire brick	2085	840
10.	Magnesite brick	2085	1050
11.	Wood	801	1345 to 1465
12.	Asbestos	3044	840
13.	Mercury	13546	140

TABLE VII (*b*)

THERMAL CONDUCTIVITIES

	Material		SI Unit (W/m deg C)
1.	Aluminium	18°C 100°C	209 205
2.	Copper	18°C 100°C	386 382
3.	Iron	18°C 100°C	67 62·9
4.	Steel	18°C 100°C	45·3 44·8
5.	Mercury	0°C 50°C	6·2 7·92
6.	Glass	20°C 100°C	0·713 0·754
7.	Wood		0·17
8.	Asbestos	0°C 100°C	0·155 0·193
9.	Cork		0·046

TABLE VII (*c*)

COMPARATIVE HEAT CONDUCTIVITIES (with air = 1)

Substance	Relative heat conductivity
Air	1
Cotton wool	1
Cork	2
Water	3
Wood	10
Asbestos	12
Glass	30
Mercury	400
Lead	1 700
Iron	2 400
Brass	4 500
Aluminium	10 000
Copper	18 000
Silver	20 000

The figures given above for refractory materials (firebrick and magnetic brick) are only very approximate, since the actual figure may vary as much as 50 to 100 per cent. with the composition of the material and also with its temperature.

Contact.—In certain cases material must be heated by contact with heated rollers or other surfaces. With good contact it is found that it is possible to transfer to a surface at 95°C—150°C as much as 110 KW/m² by this method.

Convection.—Heat is transmitted by convection in immersion-type water heaters and in certain low-temperature heating equipments for buildings, but not to any great extent in oven or furnace work except in the heat dissipation from the outside walls. For vertical heating surfaces in air, natural convection takes place according to the law :

$$\text{Heat dissipation (H)} = 3{\cdot}875\,(T_1 - T_2)\,1{\cdot}25 \text{ W/m}^2 \qquad (38)$$

where T_1 and T^2 are the temperatures (in kelvins) of the heating surface and the air respectively. This indicates the general law of convection, but the constants may require considerable modification, depending on the circumstances, e.g. the shape of the heating surfaces, facilities for air circulation, etc.

Radiation : The stefan law of radian may be written :

$$\text{Heat dissipation (H)} = 5{\cdot}72 \times 10^4\,\eta\epsilon \left[\left(\frac{T_1}{1000}\right)^4 - \left(\frac{T_2}{1000}\right)^4\right] \text{W/m}^2 \quad . \quad . \quad (39)$$

where T_1 = Absolute temperature (K) of radiating surface

T_2 = Absolute temperature (K) of absorbing surface

η = constant, commonly called the radiating efficiency, depending on disposition of heating elements and

= 1 for single element

= 0·5 to 0·8 for several elements side by side

ϵ = emissivity

= 1 for black body

= 0·9 for resistance heating element

It can be seen that since radiation is proportional to the difference of fourth powers of the temperatures, it will have a preponderating effect in high-temperature heating.

2. RESISTANCE OVENS

Electrically heated ovens are used for a wide variety of purposes, including the heat treatment of metals (annealing, hardening, etc.), stoving of enamelled ware, drying and baking of pottery, and commercial and domestic cooking. Ovens using wire resistance elements can be made to produce temperatures of up to about 1,000 °C., while if special elements of graphite are employed temperatures of up to 3,000 ° C. can be obtained, although, in general, such high temperatures are more conveniently obtained by other means.

FIG 102—ELECTRIC RESISTANCE OVEN.
(*Electric Furnace Co.*)

General Construction

A typical resistance oven for heat treatment of metals is illustrated in Fig. 102, and ovens for other purposes are generally similar in construction. The oven itself is constructed of fire-brick or other heat-insulating material supported on a metal framework. The heating elements are mounted on the top, sides, or bottom of the oven, according to circumstances.

The type illustrated is known as a " batch " type of oven to distinguish it from a " continuous " oven, in which the charge travels continuously through on a moving platform.

Heating-element Material.—A material for use as a heating element should have the following properties:

High specific resistance, so that only a small quantity of wire is required to produce a given amount of heat.

High melting-point, so that high temperatures can be produced.

Freedom from oxidation at high temperatures to ensure a long life.

Small temperature coefficient, so that the resistance does not change with temperature.

The materials which most satisfactorily fulfil these requirements at a reasonable cost are either alloys of nickel and chromium containing about 80 per cent. nickel, or alloys of nickel (65 per cent.), chromium (15 per cent.), and iron (20 per cent.). Details regarding these are given in Table VIII.

The introduction of the iron into the alloy cheapens the product but reduces the temperature at which oxidation takes place. Wires having a still higher iron content are sometimes used, but oxidation then takes place at much lower temperatures. A more recent range of alloys containing iron, chromium, cobalt, and aluminium can withstand temperatures up to 1,300°C.

Design of Heating Elements.—Both circular and ribbon resistance wires are in common use, and the size and length of wire to be used to produce a given temperature can be found if the electrical input to the oven and the voltage are known.

TABLE VIII

PROPERTIES OF NICKEL-IRON HEATING ELEMENTS

Property	Nickel-chrome	Nickel-chrome iron
1. Resistance (ohm-m)	$1{\cdot}03 \times 10^{-6}$	$1{\cdot}06 \times 10^{-6}$
2. Melting point	1375°C	1400°C
3. Limiting temperature	1000°C	850°C
4. Temperature coefficient (upto 500°C) per °C	0·000098	0·000202
5. Temperature coefficient (upto 500°C) per °C	0·0000981	0·0002016
6. Mass density (kg/m³)	8350	8270
7. Specific heat (J/kg deg C)	441	467

When the wire of the heating element has reached a steady temperature, the electrical input will be equal to the heat dissipated from its surface—in almost all cases the temperature will be sufficiently high to assume that heat is dissipated by radiation and Equation (39) may be used.

Heat dissipated per m^2

$$= H = 5{\cdot}72\,\eta\epsilon\left[\left(\frac{T_1}{1000}\right)^4 - \left(\frac{T_2}{1000}\right)^4\right] \text{ watts.}$$

If the electrical input is P watts and the voltage is V, then we have for a circular wire:

$$\text{Heat input} = P = \frac{V^2}{R} = \frac{V^2 a}{\rho l}$$

$$= \frac{V^2 \pi D^2}{\rho l 4}$$

where R = resistance of the wire (Ω)
l = length of the wire (m)
a = cross-sectional area of the wire (m^2)
d = diameter of the wire (m)
ρ = specific resistance of wire material ($\Omega\cdot m$)
surface area = πDl (m^2)

$$\therefore \text{ Heat input per } m^2 \text{ of surface area} = \frac{V^2\pi D^2}{\rho l 4}\cdot\frac{1}{\pi Dl} = \frac{V^2 D}{4\rho l^2}$$

Equating this to the heat radiated per m^2 gives a value for $\frac{D}{l^2}$, i.e.

$$\therefore \frac{D}{l^2} = \frac{H.4\rho}{V^2}$$

But we also have

$$R = \frac{V^2}{P}$$

$$\therefore \frac{V^2}{P} = \frac{\rho l 4}{\pi D^2}$$

$$\therefore \frac{l}{D^2} = \frac{V^2}{P}\cdot\frac{\pi}{4\rho}$$

The by solving these expressions for $\frac{l}{D^2}$ and $\frac{D}{l^2}$, the diameter and length of wire can be found. Ribbon resistance wires can be treated in an exactly similar way, a typical calculation being given in Example 16.

Example 16 : A 30-kW, 3-phase, 400-V resistance oven is to employ nickel-chrome strip 0.254 mm thick for the three, star-connected heating elements. If the wire temperature is to be 1100°C and that of the charge is to be 700°C, estimate a suitable width for the strip.

Assume: Emissivity (ϵ) = 0·9
radiating efficiency (η) = 0·5

What would be the temperature of the wire, when the charge is cold ?

Solution:

$$\text{Power per phase} = 10{,}000 \text{ W} = \frac{V_{ph}^2}{R}$$

$$\therefore\ R = \left(\frac{400}{\sqrt{3}}\right)^2 \times \frac{1}{10{,}000} = 5{\cdot}34\ \Omega$$

But,
$$R = 1{\cdot}016 \times 10^{-6}\ \frac{l}{a}$$

$$= 1{\cdot}016 \times 10^{-6}\ \frac{l}{0{\cdot}254 \times 10^{3} w}$$

where w is the width of the strip.

$$\therefore\ \frac{l}{w} = \frac{5{\cdot}34 \times 1000 \times 0{\cdot}254}{1{\cdot}016} = 1335 \qquad . \quad . \quad (a)$$

Heat dissipated from surface, from equation (39)

$$= 5{\cdot}72 \times 10^{4} \times 0{\cdot}9 \times 0{\cdot}5 \left[\left(\frac{1373}{1000}\right)^4 - \left(\frac{973}{1000}\right)^4\right]$$

$$= 6{\cdot}86 \times 10^{4}\ W/m^2$$

Area available for heat radiation, neglecting edges of the strip,

$$= 2\,wl\ m^2.$$

$$\therefore\ 6{\cdot}86 \times 10^{4} \times 2\ wl = 10{,}000$$

$$\therefore\ wl = 0{\cdot}0728 \qquad . \quad . \quad . \quad . \quad (b)$$

Solving Equations (a) and (b) gives :

$$w = \frac{0{\cdot}0728}{l}$$

$$\therefore\ \frac{l}{0{\cdot}0728/l} = 1335$$

$$\therefore\ l^2 = 97{\cdot}1$$

$$\therefore\ l = 9{\cdot}86 \text{ m. per phase}$$

$$w = \frac{0{\cdot}0728}{9{\cdot}86} = \mathbf{7{\cdot}37\ mm}$$

When the charge is cold (20°C),

$$\text{Heat radiated} = 6{\cdot}86\times10^4$$

$$= 5{\cdot}72\times10^4\times0{\cdot}9\times0{\cdot}5\left[\left(\frac{T_1}{1000}\right)^4-\left(\frac{293}{1000}\right)^4\right]$$

$$= 2{\cdot}56\times10^4\left[\left(\frac{T_1}{1000}\right)^4-0{\cdot}0074\right]$$

$$\therefore\left(\frac{T_1}{1000}\right)^4=\frac{6{\cdot}86\times10^4}{2{\cdot}56\times10^4}+0{\cdot}0074=2{\cdot}6874$$

$$\therefore T_1 = 1280°\text{K}$$

$$\text{or}\quad T_1 = 1003°\text{C}$$

Efficiency and Losses

Loss of heat in a resistance oven occurs due to:

A—Heat used in raising temperature of oven

B—Heat used in raising temperature of containers or carriers.

C—Conduction of heat through walls

D—Escape of heat due to opening door

If W is the heat required to raise the charge to the required temperature, then the efficiency of the oven is given by:

$$\text{Efficiency} = \frac{W}{W+A+B+C+D}\quad . \quad . \quad (40)$$

Heat transferred to Charge.—The heat required to raise the charge to the required temperature can be found from the mass of charge and its specific heat:

$$W = G\times s\times {}^\circ\text{C. J}\quad . \quad . \quad . \quad (41)$$

where G is the mass of charge in kg and s is its specific heat (J/kg deg C).

Heat used in raising Temperature of Oven.—This is calculated in the same way as for the charge, typical values of specific heat and weight of different refractory materials being shown in Table VII(a). It must be noted, however, that this loss occurs only when the oven is cooled down, and if the heat-treatment process can be carried out continuously for a week or more it becomes a negligible factor.

Heat used in raising Temperature of Containers.—This is calculated in exactly the same way as for the oven. The container usually has to be heated up afresh for each charge.

Heat lost by Conduction through Oven Walls.—This is the most important source of loss, since it occurs continuously; it can, however, be calculated fairly accurately if the thermal conductivity, K, of the walls is known.

If t = thickness of wall in metres
A = area of wall in square metres (mean value of inside and outside surface areas)
θ_1 and θ_2 = inside and outside temperatures respectively
K = thermal conductivity in (°c) (W/m² deg C)

The rate of heat loss through the walls is then:

$$\text{Heat loss} = \frac{KA}{t}(\theta_1 - \theta_2) \text{ W. per hour} \quad . \quad . \quad (42)$$

Open-door Loss.—No formulæ can be laid down to determine the loss occurring when the door is opened for inspection of the charge or for the insertion of a new charge. Experience indicates, however, that a loss of the order of 0.16 to 0.32 kWh. per square metre of door area is likely to occur every time the door is opened for a period of 20 to 30 seconds.

Typical Values of Efficiency.—Efficiencies defined in the above manner usually lie between about 60 and 80 per cent. A more convenient figure for expressing the behaviour of an oven, however, is the energy required per tonne of charge treated. Typical figures for various processes are given in Table IX.

TABLE IX

ENERGY CONSUMPTION OF RESISTANCE OVEN PROCESSES (APPROX)

	kWh. per tonne
Annealing steel	200-250
Annealing copper	100-200
Vitreous enamelling of sheet steel	400-700
Carburising	250-500
Baking of bread	50-100

Resistance Ovens for Special Purposes

Control of Oven Atmosphere (Bright Annealing).—The usual process of annealing metals (heating followed by slow cooling to eliminate brittleness and remove stains) leaves the charge covered with a scale of oxide which has to be subsequently removed if a bright finish is required. The formation of this scale can be prevented by carrying out the annealing process in an atmosphere free from oxygen, carbon dioxide, or water vapour. Such conditions can be ensured with fuel-fired furnaces, but only at a considerable loss of efficiency and convenience, whereas the electric furnace is admirably suited to such a process. The Grunewald system, which is commonly used, is based on the fact that it is only necessary to protect the charge against oxidation during the cooling period ; during heating the air is expelled, through a non-return valve in an otherwise sealed oven, due to its own expansion and also that of occluded oil and other vapours. On cooling, the non-return valve closes, thereby preventing access of oxygen or other gases to the charge and ensuring the retention of its bright surface.

Air-circulation Ovens.—With ordinary resistance ovens, in which the heat is transferred to the charge almost entirely by radiation, there is the possibility of considerable temperature differences in various parts of the charge. With processes where a uniform temperature is essential and where this temperature does not exceed about 600°C. an air-circulation oven can be employed. Air is passed over the heating elements, which are screened to prevent direct radiation to the charge, and then flows through the oven proper and imparts its heat uniformly to all parts of the charge. If the air flow is, say, from the bottom to the top of the oven, those parts of the charge at the bottom will heat to a slightly higher temperature than those at the top, since heat will be given up by the air as it travels upwards ; if, however, a sufficiently large volume of air is used, this difference can be made very small, while in special cases an even more uniform distribution can be obtained by periodically reversing the direction of flow. An important item in the design of an oven of this type is the characteristic of the fan. A centrifugal fan is employed, but it must be designed so that a change in the resistance of the air path due to charges of different size and shape does not appreciably affect the volume of air delivered or the kilowatt required by the motor.

Control Equipment

To control the temperature of a resistance oven some means of varying the current in the resistance elements is necessary. Such control may be required in order to hold the temperature constant or to vary it in accordance with a predetermined cycle, and in either case it can be carried out by hand or automatically.

Supply Voltage.—Resistance ovens are almost invariably supplied from the ordinary low-voltage network at 240 or 415 V. and may be either for d.c., 1-phase, or 3-phase operation. The additional cost of high-voltage units is not warranted for the outputs normally required for this type of oven, which is not usually more than 50 or 60 kW., although in certain cases continuous-type ovens up to 300 kW. are employed.

Methods of Control.—The methods in use for varying the current in the heating elements are as follows :

(i) Use of a Variable Number of Elements.—This tends to give uneven heating unless the elements not in use at any particular instant are well distributed over the oven surface : to secure such a condition means complicated wiring.

(ii) Series-paralled or Star-delta Connection of the Elements. —This is the simplest and most widely used method of control, and when combined with (i) gives a sufficient variation for most practical purposes.

(iii) External Series Resistance.—Not economical, but sometimes used for small furnaces on account of its simplicity and cheapness.

(iv) Transformer Tappings.—Economical and satisfactory in operation if a transformer is to be used in any case to step down the voltage for supply to the oven ; such conditions, however, only rarely arise.

Automatic Control.—When it is desired to control the temperature automatically some form of thermostat must be employed which, when the temperature exceeds or falls below certain predetermined values, operates a relay which varies the current in the elements by one of the above-mentioned methods or by completely switching the oven in and out of service, the actual switching being carried out by contactors.

Protective Equipment.—Protection should be provided against overloads, excess temperatures, and, in some cases, against the possibility of workmen loading or unloading the furnance with the power on.

The only possibility of overload is due to a part of a metallic charge falling against and short-circuiting the elements. An instantaneous overload relay set to trip the circuit at 10 or 15 per cent. above normal current adequately guards against damage due to such a contingency.

Failure of the automatic temperature-control equipment would result in an excessive temperature, which might impair the life of the elements or damage the charge ; protection can be effected by the use of a fuse situated inside and connected either in the main oven circuit or in the hold-on coil of the energising contactors. For the protection of nickel-chrome wire in this way a gold fuse is used, as it has a sharp melting-point of 1,060°C., and does not oxidise. Fuses melting at a lower temperature can be obtained, but although of some service are not completely reliable.

Radiant Heating

The resistance ovens previously described transfer their heat from the elements to the charge partly by radiation and partly by convection, the latter predominating at low and medium temperatures. An alternative process, suitable for circumstances where these low and medium temperatures are required uses purely radiant or infra-red heating, the heating elements consisting of special tungsten filament lamps with their filaments operating at about 2,300°C. instead of nearly 3,000°C. as in the ordinary tungsten lamp; this lower temperature results in the emission of a greater proportion of infra-red radiation (see Chapter V) and a longer life. The high temperature of this heating element as compared to the ordinary resistance element enables a greater amount of heat to be emitted for a given size of heater and facilitates the use of a reflector to direct the whole of the heat emitted on to the charge.

In using this process the lamps with their reflectors are grouped close together to form the walls and possibly the top of a heating chamber; the lamps are mounted on a light angle-iron framework, no heat insulation being necessary since all heat is directed inwards. Individual reflectors for each lamp or trough reflectors may be used, the latter enabling a greater number of lamps to be installed in a given area; the reflecting surface was originally plated with gold which is highly reflective to the wavelengths employed, but more recently rhodium has been used which, being harder, has a longer life and is easier to maintain. The precise shape of the chamber depends on the size and shape of the charge to be heated and the framework can easily be made adjustable; continuous processes can be arranged, the articles to be heated being carried through the chamber on a conveyor belt.

Charge temperatures of 200° to 300°C. can be obtained. Heat emission intensities up to 7150 or 7700 W. per sq. m. of chamber surface can be obtained leading to heat absorptions at the charge surface of up to 4400 W. per m^2. This is much higher than that obtained with ordinary resistance ovens (550 to 1650 W. per m^2 when the charge is cold), and is due to the fact that the heating element runs at a much higher temperature, this being brought about by the element being enclosed in a bulb containing inert gas which prevents oxidation and also reduces convection losses. A further advantage of radiant heating is that the heat absorption remains approximately constant whatever the charge temperature (since T_2 in Equation (39) is small relative to T_1), whereas with the ordinary oven the heat absorption falls off very considerably as the temperature of the charge rises. The time taken for various drying processes can thus be reduced from hours with an ordinary oven to minutes with radiant heating.

The lamp ratings used are usually between 250 and 1,000 W., and are frequently arranged for 115-V. operation in order to ensure a robust filament. Plant sizes range from a single lamp to chambers containing several hundred kW. of lamps.

Paint drying is the most common application of this method, and great savings in time can be effected as compared to convection heating ovens; other uses are for drying foundry moulds, low-temperature heating of plastics, and for various dehydration and other processes.

Salt-bath Heating

In order to prevent oxidation during hardening, a process applied to tool steels employs a method in which they are heated by immersion in molten sodium chloride or some other suitable salt. Such salts have a fusing-point of about 1,000°C. and can be heated to temperatures of ,500°C. or more by passage of current between electrodes immersed in the salt, such an arrangement being known as a salt-bath furnace.

Care must be taken with the arrangement of the electrodes to ensure that the current flows through the salt and not through the metal being heated. Alternating current is used (since d. c. would cause electrolysis) at voltages up to 20 V. and with currents between a few amperes and about 3,000 A., depending on the type of furnace.

A step-down transformer is thus needed for the supply to such a furnace, and means must be provided for varying the voltage, by tappings or an induction regulator, so that a constant power input can be maintained during the heating process when the resistance of the salt is continuously decreasing.

3. INDUCTION HEATING

Induction heating processes make use of currents induced by electro-magnetic action in the material to be heated. It is, however, only in materials of low resistivity, such as metals, that sufficient currents to cause effective heating can be produced, and even then it is often necessary to use a magnetic

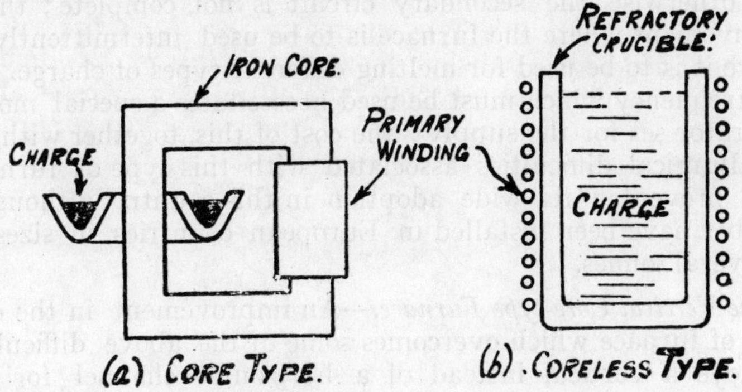

Fig. 103.—Induction Furnaces

field of very high frequency. Magnetic materials are easier to treat in this way than non-magnetic materials, since a given magnetising force gives rise to a greater flux on account of the high permeability.

For melting or refining metals various types of induction furnace are available, while for other purposes, such as case-hardening and soldering, the necessary currents are induced in the article at the appropriate stage of its manufacture; the latter process always requires a high frequency, and is commonly referred to as high-frequency eddy-current heating.

Core-type Furnaces

The core-type furnace is essentially a transformer in which the charge to be heated forms the secondary circuit, and is magnetically coupled to the primary by an iron core as shown diagrammatically in Fig. 103 (*a*). It can be seen from the diagram that the magnetic coupling between the primary and secondary is very poor, resulting in a high leakage reactance and a low power factor. To overcome this difficulty the furnance can be designed for a low frequency, and such furnaces have been built to operate at frequencies as low as 10Hz. The electro-magnetic forces cause turbulence of the molten metal which, although useful up to a point, is liable to become too severe unless the frequency is kept low. If the current density is allowed to exceed about 5A/mm^2 the "pinch" effect due to these forces may cause a complete interruption of the secondary circuit. Other disadvantages are that a crucible of inconvenient shape from the metallurgical point of view must be used and also that, in order to start the furnace, a complete ring of metal must be present in the crucible, otherwise the secondary circuit is not complete; this is inconvenient where the furnace is to be used intermittently or where it is to be used for melting different types of charge. The low frequency which must be used necessitates a special motor-generator set for the supply; the cost of this, together with the metallurgical difficulties associated with this type of furnace, have prevented its wide adoption in this country, although a number have been installed in European countries in sizes up to several tonnes.

The Vertical Core-type Furnace.—An improvement in the core type of furnace which overcomes some of the above difficulties employs a vertical instead of a horizontal channel for the charge: the modern form of such a furnace, known as the Ajax-Wyatt furnace, is shown diagrammatically in Fig. 104. The tendency of the circuit to rupture due to the pinch effect is counteracted by the weight of the charge in the main body of the crucible, while circulation of the molten metal is kept up round the Vee portion by convection currents, as indicated, and by the electro-magnetic forces between the currents in the two halves of the Vee. It is, of course, necessary to keep the Vee full of metal in order to maintain continuity of the secondary circuit, so that this type of furnace is suitable only for continuous operation; the power factor, however, is relatively high, and it can be operated from a normal frequency supply with power factors of between about 0.8 and 0.85 in sizes up to about 1 tonne. Under these conditions it is very widely used in foundries for melting and refining brass and other non-ferrous metals.

Typical figures for energy consumption for the melting and refining of non-ferrous metals are:

	kWh. per tonne
Copper and bronze	300-500
Brass	200-300
Zinc	100-150

The power required for the furnace in order to complete the melt in a reasonable time is about 200kW. her tonne. An idea of the power and energy requirements can be obtained by calculations, as in Example 17.

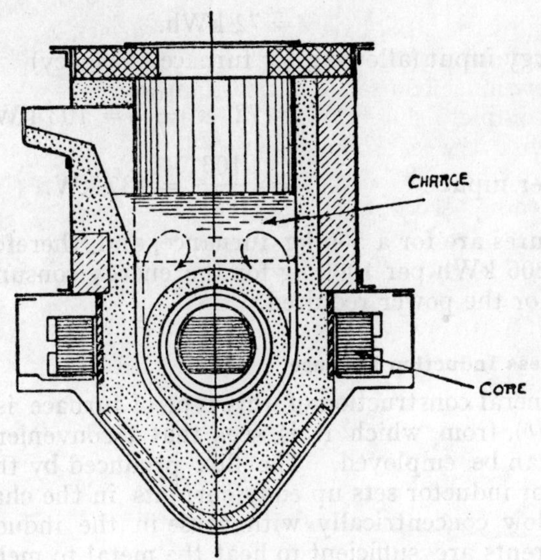

FIG. 104.—AJAX-WYATT VERTICAL CORE-TYPE FURNACE.

Example 17 :—Estimate the energy required to melt 500 kg of brass in a 1-phase Ajax-Wyatt furnace. If the melt is to be carried out in $\frac{3}{4}$ hour, what must be the average power input to the furnace?

Given :

Specific heat of brass = $393{\cdot}6$ J kg^{-1} °C^{-1}

Latent heat of fusion of brass = 163×10^3 J/kg

Melting point of brass = 920°C

Assume a furnace efficiency of 70%.

Solution :

Mass of charge = 500 kg

Heat required to raise temperature to 920°C from cold (20°C)

$$= 500 \times 393{\cdot}6 \times (920\text{-}20) \text{ J}$$
$$= 177\,000 \times 10^3 \text{ J}$$
$$= 177\,000 \times 10^3 \text{ J}$$

Heart required to melt charge

$$= 500 \times 163 \times 10^3 = 81\,500 \times 10^3 \text{ J}$$

Total Joules required $= 258\,000 \times 10^3$ J
$= 258\,000 \times 10^3 \text{J} \times 2{\cdot}78 \times 10^{-7}$kWh
$= 72$ kWh.

Energy input (allowing for furnace efficiency)

$$= 72 \times \frac{100}{70} = 103 \text{ kWh.}$$

Power input $= \dfrac{103}{0{\cdot}75} = 137$ kW.

These figures are for a 500 kg furnance, and, therefore, correspond to 206 kWh per 1000 kg for the energy consumption and 274 kW for the power required.

The Coreless Induction Furnace

The general construction of this type of furnace is shown in Fig. 103 (*b*), from which it is seen that a convenient shape of crucible can be employed. The flux produced by the primary winding or inductor sets up eddy currents in the charge which tend to flow concentrically with those in the inductor; these eddy currents are sufficient to heat the metal to melting-point, and they also set up electro-magnetic forces which produce a stirring action.

Constructional Features.—Apart from the usual constructional details associated with the refractory lining of a furnace, there are certain special features which require careful attention in the coreless induction furnance. At the frequencies generally employed the skin effect in the inductor coil causes the copper losses in that coil to be high, and artificial cooling is necessary—the coil is generally made of copper tube, through which cooling water is circulated. Attention must also be paid to the stray magnetic fields on the outside of the inductor coil. Although the flux density here is by no means as great as that inside the coil, it is sufficient to cause serious eddy-current losses in metal supporting structures unless care is taken in the design.

In the Stobie furnace a laminated yoke is built on the outside of the induction coil to provide a definite path for the flux. This minimises the stray field and also reduces the exciting current necessary to produce the flux.

Choice of Frequency.—Even when the charge is molten, calculations of the effective resistance and reactance and the power consumption of the coreless furnace are very complicated and involve the use of Bessel functions. It can be shown, however, that when the frequency is above about 500Hz a fairly close approximation to the exact calculations can be made by the use of a penetration formula, in which the secondary current is assumed to be uniformly distributed over a cylindrical layer at the outside edge of the crucible and having a thickness

$$t = \frac{1}{2\pi}\sqrt{\frac{\rho \cdot 10^9}{\mu f}} \text{ cm.} \qquad (43)$$

where ρ = specific resistance of molten charge (200×10^{-6} ohm/cm. for steel)

f = frequency (Hz).

μ = permeability (1 for molten steel).

The exact theory also shows that for efficient operation the ratio $\frac{r}{t}$ should be greater than 3, r being the radius of the pieces of material in the charge.

Putting $\frac{r}{t} = 4$, say, we get an expression for the frequency at which efficient operation can be obtained:

$$f = \frac{1}{4\pi^2} \cdot \frac{\rho \cdot 10^9 \cdot 16}{\mu \cdot r^2}$$

As r is increased, therefore, efficient operation can be obtained with lower frequencies, and modern practice employs frequencies of 500 to 1,000 Hz for large furnaces of up to about 5 tonnes capacity, and frequencies up to 100,000 or even a million cycles for very small laboratory furnaces for melting small quantities of finely divided metal.

The power factor of the furnace is very low (of the order of 0·1), and in the larger sizes static capacitors are invariably used in parallel with the furnace in order that the converting apparatus necessary to produce the high frequency may be designed for unity power-factor operation, the choice of frequency is therefore affected also by the cost of these capacitors, which decreases with increase of frequency, and the cost of the converting apparatus, which increases with frequency.

Power Supply.—The high-frequency currents for the coreless furnace are usually obtained from the ordinary supply network through one or other of the following types of frequency-converting equipment:

Motor-generator Set with Salient-pole Alternator.—Suitable for frequencies up to about 1,000 Hz. and for any outputs so far required.

Motor-generator Set with Inductor Alternator.—Suitable for frequencies up to about 10,000 Hz and for furnace capacities up to about 1 tonne.

Valve Oscillator.—Applicable to very small furnaces such as are used for melting the rate metals and which require frequencies up to 1 million cycles.

The voltage applied to the furnace varies from 1,000 or 2,000 in the large sizes up to about 10,000 for the small valve-operated furnaces. Control is effected by tappings on an auto-transformer or on the inductor coil itself, or, where a motor-generator set supplies a single furnace, by variation of the generator field.

Energy Consumption and Applictions.—The chief application of the coreless induction furnace in industrial practice is for the manufacture of steel, and in this sphere it is in competition with the electric arc furnace described in Section 5 and also, of course, with the older non-electric types of furnace. The energy consumption varies between about 600 and 1,000 kWh. per tonne of steel, and does not differ widely from that of the arc furnace; the power requirements vary from about 350 kW. per tonne for a 4- or 5-tonne furnace up to about 600 kW. per tonne for a 250 kg furnace. The initial cost, however, is three or four times as great as that of other types of furnace, so that the coreless furnace has not been found economically practicable in sizes above 4 or 5 tonnes. As, however, there is practically no danger of the product being contaminated by impurities and the composition can be accurately controlled and reproduced at will, it is suitable for the production of the very highest grade of alloy steels, and it is in this sphere that it finds its chief application. In small sizes it is widely used for work on alloys and precious metals, an important point in this connection being that the furnace can easily be arranged for melting in a vacuum.

The Indirect-Induction Oven

In addition to its use for melting metals, as described earlier, the induction principle can also be used for general heat treatment of metallic and other charges if an inductively heated element is employed to transmit the heat to the charge by radiation. So far as the charge is concerned the conditions are then similar to those in the resistance oven. A diagram of an inductively heated oven is shown in Fig. 105; it can be seen that the iron core links the primary winding and also the secondary, which in this case consists of a metal container forming the walls of the oven proper. Currents are induced in and heat this metal container, and this transmits its heat to the charge by radiation, as previously mentioned. An oven of this type is in direct competition with the ordinary resistance oven, and in order to make up for the relatively poor power factor (0·8) and the more complicated construction, it must possess some special advantage if it is to be commercially successful. The particular advantage obtained is a simple and almost foolproof method of temperature control—the part AB of the magnetic circuit is situated in the oven chamber and consists of a special alloy which loses its magnetic properties at a particular temperature and regains them again when cooled to approximately the same temperature. As soon as the oven reaches this critical temperature, therefore, the reluctance of the

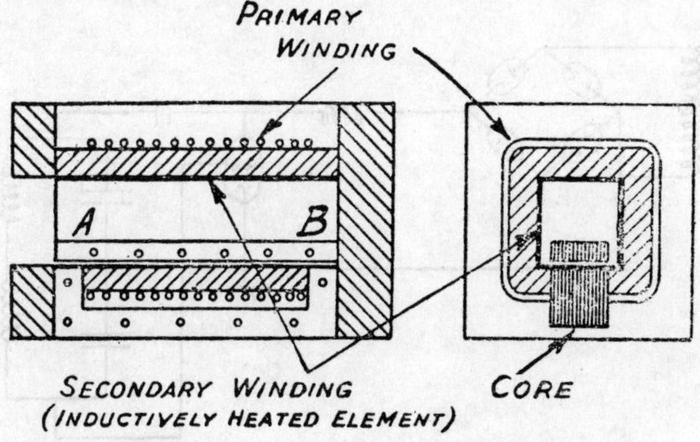

FIG. 105.—INDIRECT-INDUCTION OVEN.

magnetic circuit increases many times and the inductive effecs correspondingly decreases, thereby effectively cutting off the supply of heat. The oven temperature is thus limited to thit critical value without the use of external control equipment, such as that described already in connection with the resistance oven. The bar AB is made detachable, so that it can be replaced by other shaving different critical temperatures ranging between about 400° and 1000° C.

High-frequency Eddy-current Heating

The heating of partially manufactured articles is effected by placing them within a coil carrying high-frequency currents, these currents setting up a high-frequency alternating magnetic field which induces eddy currents in the article concerned. The frequencies employed are usually between 10,000 and 400,000 Hz. To be effective the coil must be shaped to give as tight a magnetic coupling as possible between itself and the work, the turns of the coil being parallel to the paths in which it is desired that the eddy currents shall flow. The depth of penetration of the eddy currents into the charge is inversely proportional to the square root of the frequency, as shown by Equation (43), so that this method of treatment is most suitable for circumstances where only a relatively thin surface layer requires to be heated. With the higher frequencies it is possible to obtain power inputs to the charge of 1.6 kW or more per square c.m. of surface.

A typical application is the tempering and surface-hardening of tool steels, crankshafts, bearing pins, etc. As only a small depth, about 1·25 mm. needs to be heated, a fairly high frequency can be used and the heating limited to this thickness.

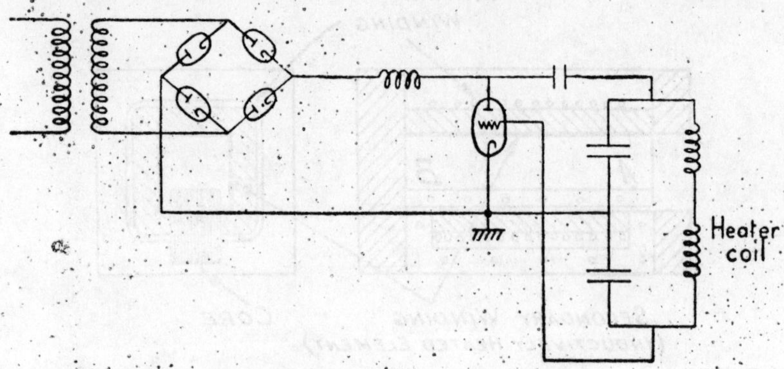

FIG. 106.—OSCILLATOR CIRCUIT FOR EDDY-CURRENT HEATING.

The time taken is consequently very small (about 1 second), so that after the operation the heat is rapidly conducted away to the rest of the metal, so that quenching in oil is unnecessary.

Other applications are the annealing of steel strip, which can be done on a continuous process, brightening of electrolytic tin plate, and various routine soldering processes.

Although for the lower frequencies, up to about 10,000 Hz, an inductor alternator can be used as the high-frequency source, an oscillator must be employed for the higher values. A typical simplified diagram for such an oscillator is shown in Fig. 106, the circuit being based on that of the Colpitts oscillator. The transformer steps the voltage up to about 10 kV.; it is then rectified and applied to the oscillator circuit. The heater coil forms part of the oscillator inductance as shown, this being tuned to resonance with the capacitance at the desired frequency.

4. DIELECTRIC HEATING

For the heating of non-metallic materials, such as wood, plastics, or ceramics, use can be made of the dielectric loss which occurs in such materials when subjected to an alternating electrostatic field. The material to be heated is placed between two metallic electrodes across which a voltage is applied. To ensure sufficient loss to give an adequate amount of heating, frequencies between about 10 and 30MHZ. must be used, and the voltage needed may be as high as 20kV.

The advantage of heating materials of poor thermal conductivity by this method results from the fact that the heat is produced within the material itself, whereas with oven heating it must be conducted to the inside, which takes a long time and also results in a non-uniform temperature distribution. Processes which would take hours with oven heating can be carried out in minutes by dielectric heating.

The necessary high-frequency supply is obtained from a valve oscillator as in the case of the high-frequency eddy-current heating. A typical calculation of the quantities involved is shown in the following example.

Example 18 :—A laminated wooden board 0.3 m long by 0.15 m wide and 0.025 m thick is to be heated to 160°C in 10 minutes by dielectric heating employing a frequency of 30 MHz. The wood has a specific heat of 1465 J kg^{-1} °C^{-1}, a weight of 575 kg m^{-3}, a permittivity of 5 and a power factor of 0.05. Determine the power required, the voltage across the work, and the current through it during the heating process.

Solution :

Volume of wood $= 0{\cdot}3 \times 0{\cdot}15 \times 0{\cdot}025 = 11{\cdot}25 \times 10^{-4}$ m^3

Weight of wood $= 11{\cdot}25 \times 10^{-4} \times 575 = 0{\cdot}647$ kg.

Heat required to raise temperature to 160°C from, say 10°C

$$= 0{\cdot}647 \times 1465 \times 150$$

$$= 142 \times 10^3 \text{ J}$$

$$= 39{\cdot}5 \text{ Wh} \quad (\because 1 \text{ kWh} = 3{\cdot}6 \times 10^6 \text{ J})$$

15

This is to be done in 10 minutes so that

$$\text{power required} = 39{\cdot}5 \times \frac{60}{10}$$
$$= 237{\cdot}0 \text{ W.}$$

Due to the heating up of the electrodes and slight loss of heat by convection and radiation, the efficiency of the process will be between 85 and 90%, so that the total power input required will be about 290W.

The material being heated may be regarded as the imperfect dielectric of a condenser and represented by a capacitance inparallel with a resistance, as shown in Fig. 107(a). The vector diagram of the circuit is shown in Fig. 107(b).

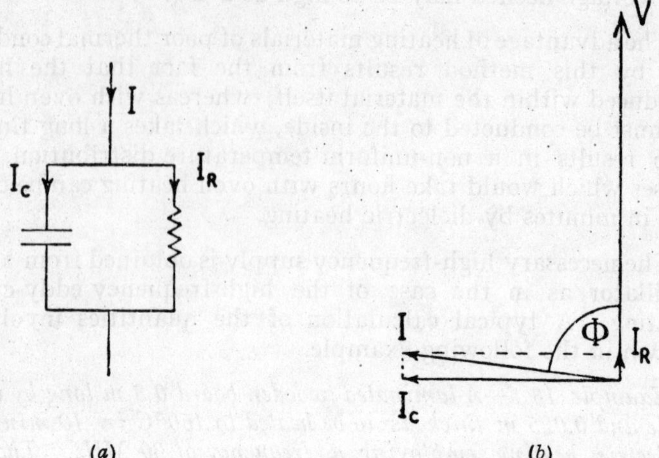

FIG. 107.—EQUIVALENT CIRCUIT FOR DIELECTRIC HEATING.

The capacitance can be calculated from the dimensions as follows.

$$C = \frac{A\,k\,k_0}{4\pi\,t}\ \text{F},$$

where A = surface area of electrodes (m^2)
t = thickness of dielectric (m)
k = relative permittivity (5 in this case)
k_0 = absolute permittivity = $1{\cdot}113 \times 10^{-10}$ Fm^{-1} (in SI units)

Hence, $C = \dfrac{0{\cdot}3 \times 0{\cdot}15 \times 5 \times 1{\cdot}113 \times 10^{-10}}{4\pi \times 0{\cdot}025}$

$= 0{\cdot}081 \times 10^{-9}$ F

Capacitive reactance $= \dfrac{1}{\omega c} = \dfrac{1 \times 10^{9}}{2\pi \times 30 \times 10^{6} \times 0{\cdot}081}$

$= 65{\cdot}5\ \Omega$

Power factor, $\cos\phi = 0{\cdot}05$

$\therefore \quad \tan\phi = 19{\cdot}74$

$\therefore \quad R = 65{\cdot}5 \tan\phi = 1290\ \Omega$

Power $= \dfrac{V^2}{R} = 290$ W

$\therefore \quad V = \sqrt{290 \times 1290}$

$= 612$ V

Total current in work $\simeq I_c = \dfrac{612}{65{\cdot}5} = 9{\cdot}34$ A.

This current flows in the resonant oscillatory circuit—(only the power component, i.e. $9{\cdot}34 \times 0{\cdot}05 = 0{\cdot}47$ A has to be dealt with by the values of the oscillator).

Choice of Frequency.—It can be seen from the previous calculation that in general terms the loss in a dielectric is proportional to $V^2 \cdot f \cdot K \cdot \cos\phi$ where V = voltage, f = frequency (Hz), K = permittivity, $\cos\phi$ = power factor; $K\cos\phi$ is known as the *loss factor* and, for a given material, does not vary greatly with frequency. To obtain a given amount of heat, therefore, it is possible to use a high voltage and medium frequency or vice versa. The voltage is limited, particularly for thin specimens of material to be heated, by the breakdown voltage and also by insulation and safety considerations. Although voltages up to 20kV. are sometimes used, more common figures are between 600 and 3,000 V. In order to obtain high rates of heat production and consequent short heating times, it is therefore necessary to use very high frequencies.

There are, however, certain limits to the frequency—firstly the value of the impedance of a resonant circuit comprising an inductance and the capacitance of the charge in parallel decreases with increasing frequency; to get the maximum power output from the supply oscillator its impedance should be matched to that of the load, and this may necessitate a special matching circuit at the higher frequencies. Another limit is imposed by the possibility of a standing wave being maintained across the electrode surface if its dimensions approach a quarter wavelength of the frequency being used ; such a standing wave would result in a variation of voltage over the surface of the electrode and consequent non-uniform heating. At 40MHz. an electrode length of about 305mm should not be exceeded with a material having a permittivity of 3 if more than 10 per cent. variation of voltage over the surface is not to be permitted.

A final consideration is the difficulty of constructing a tuning inductance to resonate with the capacitance of the charge at very high frequencies—thus at 40MHz. the maximum capacitance of charge which can be tuned is about 500pF., this requiring a tuning inductance of about 0·15 μH.

Taking these various factors into account, it is found that the frequencies commonly used range between 10 and 40 MHz.

Efficiency and Applications.—It was mentioned in the calculation that the efficiency of transfer of heat from the oscillator output to the charge is 85 per cent. or more ; the overall efficiency, however, including that of the oscillator, is usually about 50 per cent. The cost of the equipment is also high, so that dielectric heating is only employed where other methods are impracticable or too slow. Amongst such applications may

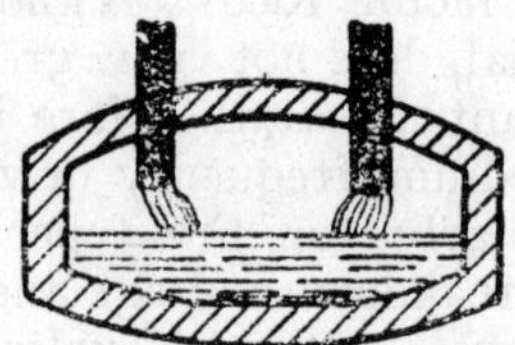

FIG. 108.—TYPES OF ARC FURNACE.

be mentioned the bonding of laminated wood and plastic materials, drying of textiles, dehydration of food and tobacco, and the sterilisation of cereals.

5. THE ARC FURNACE

Arc furnaces may be classified as direct-arc and indirect-arc furnaces. In the former, shown diagrammatically in Fig. 108(*a*), the arc is formed between the electrodes and the charge, while in the indirect type the arc is formed between the electrodes, as shown in Fig. 108 (*b*), and transmits its heat to the charge solely by radiation. Either carbon or graphite electrodes are used, which give an arc temperature of between 3,000° and 3,500°C., so that processes requiring temperatures of between 1,500° and 2,000°C. can easily be carried out.

With both types of furnace the arc chamber itself consists of a suitable acid or basic refractory lining supported on a metal framework ; the electrodes project through the top or sides of the chamber and are arranged for easy replacement and adjustment. Charging doors and a spout or tap-holes for pouring are also included, the whole furnace being frequently made to tilt for the latter purpose. The melting chamber is made as nearly spherical as practicable in order to give the minimum surface of refractory material for a given volume.

The Direct-arc Furnace

As the arc is in direct contact with the charge and heat is also produced by current flowing through the charge itself, the

FIG 109— 10-12 TONNE 3,500 KVA. ARC FURNACE.
(*Electric Furnace Co.*)

direct-arc furnace permits the highest temperatures to be attained. The most common application of this type of furnace is for the production of steel, and units capable of holding a charge of 50t and even 100t have been built, although 5 to 10t is a more common size. A 10 to 12t furnace is illustrated in Fig. 109.

Another type known as the submerged-arc furnace is used for ferro-alloy manufacture (e.g. ferro-chrome and ferro-manganese): the electrodes project down into the charge so that much of the heat generated is produced by the resistance offered to the flow of current through the charge.

To deal with the large powers usually required a 3-phase supply is generally employed, which is connected to three electrodes spaced at the corners of an equilateral triangle; the charge itself thus forms a star point. Control of the power is obtained by applying a variable voltage to the furnace and by raising or lowering the electrodes, thus varying the length of arc and the arc resistance.

An important feature arising from the fact that the current actually flows through the charge itself is the stirring action caused by the electro-magnetic forces thereby set up, which ensures a very uniform product.

Applications.—The chief application of the direct-arc furnace is for the production of steel, and its advantage over the cupola method lies in the purer product which is obtainable and the ease with which its exact composition can be controlled during the refining process. These advantages frequently outweigh the greater capital and operating costs as compared with the older types of furance. Although in many cases the arc furnace is used both for melting and refining, the practice of melting in a cupola and refining in an electric furnace is commonly adopted on grounds of economy particularly where electrical energy is expensive.

The Indirect-arc Furance

The temperature of the charge in the indirect-arc furnace is lower than in the direct-arc furnace, since heat is transmitted to it solely by radiation. As no current flows through the charge there is no inherent stirring action, and the furnace must be rocked mechanically; for this reason a cylindrical shape is adopted, with the electrodes projecting through the chamber at each end along the horizontal axis. This construction limits the number of electrodes to two and therefore necessitates a 1-phase supply; the size of furnace is thus limited by the amount of 1-phase load which may be taken—units dealing with charges up to 1t are, however, quite common.

Suitable guides and rollers are provided for the rocking action, which is imparted by an electric motor. At starting the rocking is carried through an angle of 15° to 20°, but when the charge is fully molten this is increased to about 200° at a frequency of about $\frac{1}{80}$ Hz. In addition to providing a thorough mixing of the charge, the rocking action adds to the efficiency and increases the life of the refractory lining, since every portion of it is at some time covered with metal, which abstracts its heat and prevents it from attaining an excessive temperature.

Applications.—The melting of non-ferrous metals is the chief field of application of the indirect-arc furnace, although it is also used to a considerable extent in iron foundries where relatively shall quantities of metal are required intermittently. Although it is less efficient than the Ajax-Wyatt induction furnace, which is its chief rival in the non-ferrous field, it is more suitable in situations where the charge has to be varied frequently or where heating is intermittent.

Electrodes

Carbon or graphite electrodes are used in both types of furnace, and in the very largest units these may be 300 to 450 mm. in diameter. The salient points of the two types are indicated below:

Resistance.—Graphite electrodes have lower specific resistance than carbon electrodes, and therefore need be only about half the size for a given current, thus facilitating replacement and allowing a lighter control mechanism to be used.

Evenness of Heating.—The larger area of carbon electrodes means a greater surface area of charge covered by the arc and consequently a more uniform distribution of heat; on the other hand, however, the arc is brought nearer to the side of the furnace, which tends to shorten the life of refractory lining.

Consumption.—The electrodes are consumed by oxidation at temperatures about above 600°C., and this consumption is 50 to 100 per cent. greater with carbon than with graphite electrodes.

Cost.—Graphite electrodes cost about twice as much per kg. as carbon electrodes, so that the savings due to their use are largely nullified, especially if the process is one in which the electrode consumption is large.

From the metallurgical point of view there is usually little to choose between the two types of electrode, so that the choice depends chiefly on the question of total cost. In general it may be stated that for processes requiring large quantities of electrode, the carbon electrode is used, but for other processes the choice depends on local conditions. Electrode consumption for steel-melting furnaces varies between about 4·5 and 9 kg of electrode per tonne of steel with carbon electrodes, and between about 2·27 and 6·8 kg. for graphite electrodes.

Power Supply and Control

The power requirements of an are furnace for steel melting and refining vary from about 500 kW per tonne for small $\frac{1}{2}$ tonne furnaces to about 200 kW per tonne for very large 50 or 100 t furnaces. The energy required is usually between 600 and 800 kWh per tonne. Where refining only is carried out electrically the consumption is about 100 to 120 kWh per tonne. The production of ferro-alloys in the submerged-arc furnace requires between 9,000 and 18,000 kWh per tonne of alloy.

The Furnace Transformer.—The arc voltage is usually somewhere between 50 and 150 V., so that to obtain the powers indicated, currents of several hundred or thousand amperes may be required ; this necessitates the use of a special furnace transformer with a low-voltage, heavy-current secondary winding. The transformer differs from the ordinary power tranfor-

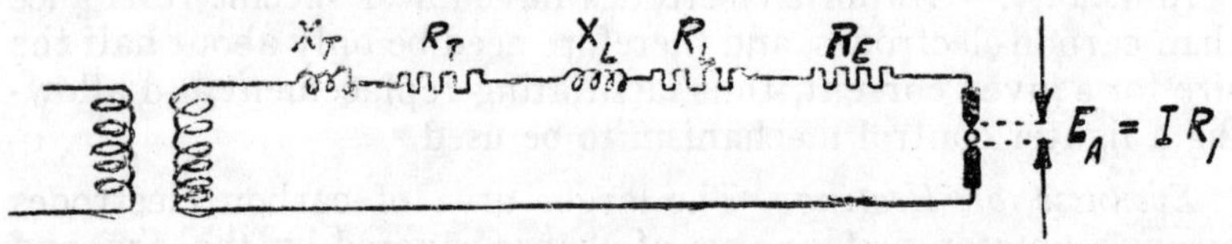

FIG. 110.—EQUIVALENT CIRCUIT OF ARC FURNACE.

mer only in the provision of this winding ; both shell and core types are used, although the former often facilitates the bringing out and bracing of the heavy current leads. Tappings for voltage regulation are provided on the primary side.

Furnace Leads.—The leads from the transformer to the furnace constitute a difficult problem on account of the heavy currents, and the transformer should be arranged as near to the furnace as possible so that their run may be short and straight. To reduce inductance the conductors must be placed as close together as possible, and they must be of such a shape as to reduce skin effect to a minimum. It has been found that rectangular copper strip spaced a few millimetres apart gives the most satisfactory results in most cases.

Characteristics and Control.—The current in the furnace circuit is limited by the resistance and reactance of the transformer (R_T and X_T), the resistance and reactance of the leads (R_L and X_L), the resistance of the electrodes (R_E), and the voltage drop in the arc (E_A) which behaves as a non-inductive resistance (R_A) ; one phase of the circuit can therefore be represented as in Fig. 110. Control of the power input is carried out by raising or lowering the electrodes, i.e. by varying the resistance of the arc, or by varying the applied voltage by means of tappings on the transformer ; to have complete control of furnace temperature and to ensure the best operating conditions for the particular charge being melted the operator must have both voltage and electrode control.

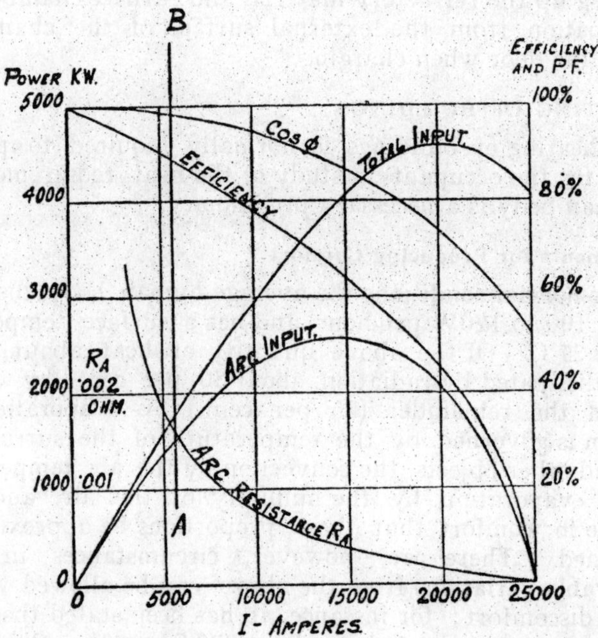

FIG. 111.—CHARACTERISTICS OF 5 TONNE 3-PHASE ARC FURNACE.

When the electrodes are touching the charge, i.e. zero arc resistance, the current is limited by the impedance of the furnace circuit and the power input to the furnace is almost zero. If the electrodes are raised so that the arc is extinguished, the input to the furnace is again zero; between these two limits there is some position of the electrodes for which the input to the furnace is a maximum. This is illustrated by the curves of Fig. 111, which have been calculated as shown in Table X for a 5 tonne 3-phase furnace.

It can be seen that when the power input to the furnace is a maximum the power factor is only about 0·87 and the efficiency is under 70 per cent. To obtain a reasonable efficiency and power factor, and at the same time to get a reasonable service from the furnace, it is normally operated at a point in the neighbourhood of the line AB.

The efficiency mentioned above is, of course, the electrical efficiency, allowing only for the ohmic losses in the furnace circuit. In practice, only 50 to 60 per cent. of the arc input is usefully employed in heating the charge; the remainder is used in heating up the refractory material and furnace chamber, and in dissipation from the external surface of the chamber or through the door when charging.

6. HEATING OF BUILDINGS

Since heating of buildings is normally required to provide comfort for the occupants, a study of the heat requirements of the human body is a necessary preliminary.

Requirements for Producing Comfort

Under normal conditions the average human body dissipates between 100 to 120W per hour, and has a surface temperature of about 27°C. Of the above quantity of heat about 45 per cent. is dissipated by radiation, about 30 per cent. by convection, and the remainder (25 per cent.) by evaporation; the radiation is governed by the temperature of the surrounding walls and other objects, the convection by the air temperature, and the evaporation by the humidity of the air, and it is desirable for comfort that these proportions be approximately maintained. There are, however, circumstances in which considerable variations from the above can be allowed without causing discomfort; for instance, it has been stated that if the walls of a room are heated to about 27° C., so that there is no radiation, and the air temperature maintained at about 15.5°C

TABLE X(*a*)

DATA FOR 5 TONNE, 3-PHASE ARC FURNACE
Supplied from 6,600/180-volt, λ/λ Transformer.

	Resistance. ohms	Reactance. ohms (equivalent values on L.T. side)
Transformer	·000374	·000767
Leads	·00123	·00278
Electrodes	·000536	—

TABLE X(*b*)

CHARACTERISTICS WITH A CONSTANT VOLTAGE OF 6,600 ON H.T. SIDE

I	$Z = \frac{V_{ph}}{I} = \frac{180}{\sqrt{3}\,.\,I}$	$R = R_T + R_L + R_E + R_A = \sqrt{Z^2 - (X_T + X_L)^2}$	$R_A = R - (R_T + R_L + R_E)$	$E_A = IR_A$	$P_A = \frac{3IE_A}{1000}$ kW.	$\cos\phi = \frac{R}{Z}$	Input $= \frac{\sqrt{3}\,.\,VI\cos\phi}{1000}$ kW.	Efficiency $= \frac{P_A}{\text{input}}$ Per cent.
5,000	·0208	·0205	·0184	92	1,380	·986	1,540	89·6
10,000	·0104	·00978	·0076	76	2,280	·94	2,930	77·7
15,000	·00693	·00598	·0038	57	2,565	·86	4,040	63·8
20,000	·0052	·00377	·0016	32	1,920	·725	4,520	44·4
25,000	·00415	·00210	·000	0	0	·516	4,030	0

the effect is decidedly invigorating. In addition to maintaining correct temperature and humidity, various psychological and decorative aspects must also be taken into account, such as the cheerful appearance of an open coal fire as compared, say, to a hot-water radiator.

As the exact conditions necessary for producing comfort are still largely a matter of controversy, the usual practice in designing a heating installation is to aim at maintaining an inside temperature of between 17·2° and 18·3°C. It is not desirable, however, to maintain more than a 8·3 to 11°C. difference between indoor and outdoor temperatures., or discomfort ensues when passing from one to the other.

Heating Systems Available

Numerous types of electric heating equipment have been developed, and those which have found application in practice may be classified as follows:

High-temperture Radiators.—The familiar domestic radiator employing a resistance element running at a red heat.

Low-temperature Convectors.—Open or enclosed resistance elements operating at 66° or 93 °C. designed and located to produce convection currents.

Panel Heating.—Large panels of fireclay or other suitable substance in which is incorporated resistance wire. Such panels are mounted on or built into the walls or ceiling and dissipate their heat chiefly by radiation.

Air Conditioning.—The air circulated through the building by the ventilating equipment is preheated and also, if desired, treated for control of humidity.

Thermal Storage.—Hot water is circulated through pipes and radiators, the water being heated electrically. The salient feature of this system is that sufficient heat can be stored in the water to allow the current to be switched off for periods of several hours, enabling use to be made of specially cheap off-peak tariffs for the electrical energy.

High-temperature Radiators

The ordinary domestic electric radiator or fire consisting of a resistance element operating at a red heat in a more or less ornamental frame is well known and needs no description. Between 50 and 70 per cent. of the heat from it is dissipated as radiant heat and the remainder by convection. This type of heater has the advantage of quickly attaining its full temperature, but the heat is strictly localised and, being mostly radiant, is apt to cast "shadows." Although admirably suited to domestic use, particularly when intermittent heating is required, they are applicable to large-scale heating only when used in conjunction with one of the other methods.

Low-temperature Convectors

The most common type of low-temperature convector takes the form of a metal tube about 50mm in diameter, inside which is mounted a spiral of resistance wire. Such tubes are made in lengths of between 0·6 and 4·57m, and are mounted around the skirting board of the room to be heated. The temperature of the external surface is about 93·3°C and about 60 watts per 0.3 m. length of tube is necessary to maintain this : about 90 per cent. of the heat is transferred by convection.

Alternative forms of convector consist of resistance wire operating at low temperatures and mounted inside an ornamental box provided with suitable holes to allow air to pass through the box over the elements.

Panel Heating

The mounting of the resistance elements in suitable heat-resisting material in the form of large panels which can be attached to or even incorporated in the walls or ceiling of a room has advantages from the decoratve point of view, and also tends to give a very uniform distribution of heat, the greater portion of which is radiated.

Non-embedded panels for attaching to the walls or ceiling, or even suspending from the ceiling in the same way as lamps, operate at temperatures between 37.8°C and 287.8°C and usually have an area between 0.09 and 0.28m^2. The loading varies between about 444 W/m^2 for the low temperature panels to about 6666 W/m^3 for the high temperature panels.

In the embedded type of panel, the resistance wire is mounted on a heat-resisting backboard or fabric, which is embedded in the plaster of the wall or ceiling. The loading is usually between 222 and 333 W/m^2 and the temperature between 27 and 37.8°C.

Certain types of building can be heated by means of heating cables embedded in the floor. The floor temperature should not exceed 21-24°C and a typical loading is 130-155 W/m^2.

Thermal Storage

A system of pipes is employed which circulates hot water to radiators or heating pipes situated throughout the building, the water being heated by an electrode boiler or an immersion heater in the storage tank. The pipe and radiator system does not differ from that of the well-known central-heating system employing a coal- or coke-fired boiler ; in fact, many such systems have been converted to electric operation by the immersion of an electric heater in the storage tank. It must be noted that when electric heating is employed the tank and piping must be lagged to prevent loss of heat, a feature which is usually omitted with fuel-fired systems, since with such systems the efficiency is so low that the additional loss due to lack of lagging is relatively unimportant.

Both oil and iron have been suggested as alternative media for the storage of heat instead of water, but have not so far found any wide application in practice for building heating installations ; in addition to its cheapness and satisfactory specific-heat value, the use of water has the advantage of enabling the heating equipment to perform the dual purpose of heating the building and providing a supply of hot water.

The water in the storage tank and circulating system stores sufficient heat to enable power to be switched off during the day, thus enabling specially low tariffs, between 2.5p and 5p per unit, to be obtained ; were it not for this, the thermal-storage system would not usually be an economic proposition.

The Immersion Heater.—The immersion heater used for heating the water in a storage tank consists of a spiral of resistance wire embedded in refractory insulating material and enclosed in a copper or steel tube ; the tube is provided with a flange at one end, so that it can be bolted to the vertical side of the tank with the heating element projecting horizontally into the water.

The loading of such a tube is generally between 16 and 24 kW/m^2 of face, so that a tube 305mm long and 51·0mm in diameter will be rated at about 1 kW. Single tubes having a loading up to 4 or 5 kW. can be built, while, by employing a group of such units, loadings of 100kW. or more can be obtained for large installations. Beyond this size the electrode boiler is preferable.

The Electrode Boiler.—In the electrode boiler current is passed between electrodes immersed in the water to be heated. A.c.

must be employed, since d.c. would electrolyse the water. Two electrodes are used for a 1-phase boiler, and three for a 3-phase unit, the tank then being at earth potential, so that the boiler is similar to a star-connected resistance with its neutral point earthed. In the sizes of installation for which an electrode boiler is used, a 3-phase unit is generally desirable.

The resistance of average cold tap-water varies between about 20 and 50 ohm-m., so that in order to get a reasonably low resistance it is necessary to add a salt, usually sodium carbonate (soda) in order to improve its conductivity. A further important point is the decrease in the resistance of the water as the temperature increases, the value at 100° C. being about one-third of that at 20° C.; if a constant input is required this necessitates some form of automatic control of the power supplied.

Control of the power input may be effected by varying the height of the electrodes in the water, by the use of a movable shield surrounding the electrodes, by moving one electrode relative to the other, or, in large units, by varying the water level by means of a pump.

When the power input required for heating is less than 100 to 200 kW. the immersion heater is more economical than the electrode boiler; for powers above this and up to 500 to 700 kW. a low-voltage boiler operating at 440 V. is commonly used, while for still larger sizes a high-voltage boiler operating at voltages up to 11,000 or even higher is applicable.

It may be noted that the electrode boiler is also used for producing steam in industrial establishments such as textile works, paper mills, dairies, etc.

Air Conditioning

Air conditioning in its fullest sense involves control of the humidity and purity of the air as well as its temperature; the latter involves cooling in summer and heating in winter. After conditioning, the air is circulated throughout the building either naturally or mechanically by means of a fan; the latter method is more usual, the fan being driven by an electric motor. Variation of air quantity is carried out by means of dampers or by a two-speed or variable-speed motor.

Heating is generally carried out by passing the air over a resistance heater, although a thermal-storage heater can be employed in certain cases where it is desired to make use of special tariffs.

To avoid cold draughts the air must be heated to the desired room temperature (about 18·3°C.), quite irrespective of whether or not there are any other sources of heat, such as electric radiators, in the building. To prevent excessive evaporation from the body and consequent discomfort, the relative humidity must be kept at about 60 per cent.

Heat requirements and Humidity : The heat required to raise the temperature of the air at normal humidity can easily be calculated from the specific heat of air and its density (1·21752 kg/m³ at 16° C).

Thus, the heat required to raise the temperature of 1 m³ of air through 1°C is :

$$1{\cdot}217 \times 1000\,\text{J or say, } \mathbf{1{\cdot}22 \times 10^3\ J}$$

This is a useful average figure, although, of course, it varies slightly with variations of temperature and humidity.

Therefore, 1220 J will raise the temperature of 1 cubic metre of air through 1°C.

As mentioned above, the required value of relative humidity is about 60 per cent ; this corresponds to a moisture content of about 9·3 grams per m³ at 18·3°C. Average figures for the state of the outdoor air in the U.K. are 5°C. and 75 per cent humidity, and under these conditions it has a moisture content of 4·9 grams per m³. If this air is heated to 18·3 °C, it must, therefore, also have added to it 4·843 grams of moisture per cubic metre, in order to bring its content upto the required figure of 9·3 gram per metre³. If the humidity is not controlled in this way by adding to the moisture content and the outdoor air merely heated to 18·3 °C, the relative humidity will drop to 31·6 per cent. and will give a decided sensation of stuffiness to the atmosphere.

Example 19 :—It is required to condition 3000 m³ of air, the original state being 4.5 °C and 75% humidity, the required final condition being 18.5 °C and 60% humidity. Estimate the heat requirements.

Solution :

Heat required to raise the temperature of the air (using the previously mentioned figure of $1{\cdot}22 \times 10^3$ J for heating 1 cm meter through 1°C) :

$$= 1{\cdot}22 \times 10^3 \times 3000 \times 14\ \text{J/h}$$
$$= 14{\cdot}15\ \text{kW}$$

Moisture to be evaporated $= 0{\cdot}004\ 40$ kgm^{-3}

Latent heat $= 2450 \times 10^3$ J/kg.

Weight of moisture to be evaporated $= 0{\cdot}004\ 4 \times 3\ 000$ kg/h

$= 13{\cdot}2$ kg/h

Heat required $= 2\ 450 \times 10^3 \times 13{\cdot}2$ J/h

$= 9$ kW.

Total heat requirements $= 14{\cdot}15 + 9 = 23{\cdot}15$ kW

$\simeq$ **23 kW.**

It is thus seen that the heat requirements when humidity control is carried out are about 60% greater than when only temperature is considered.

TABLE XI

AIR CHANGES REQUIRED PER HOUR

	Changes per hour.
Dwelling houses	2- 3
Offices	4- 6
Factories	6-10
Cinemas, theatres, kitchens	10-20
Works with noxious fumes	30-40

The Heat Pump.—Attention has recently been devoted to the " reversed refrigeration " process for producing heat employing the " heat pump. " In the ordinary refrigerator heat is abstracted from the cold storage chamber and, by means of a mechanically driven compressor, converted to heat at a higher temperature, which is dissipated to the surrounding atmosphere by a radiator. In the heat pump similar apparatus is used, but heat is abstracted from the outside atmosphere, which may be at quite a low temperature, and, by means of the compressor, converted to heat at a higher temperature, which is dissipated by means of radiators within the building to be heated. Neglecting losses, the heat which is available for distribution within the building is the heat abstracted from outside plus the equivalent of the mechanical work put into the compressor.

Since the temperatures produced are not very high, the most convenient way of dealing with the heat produced is to heat the air of an air-conditioning system ; furthermore the plant can quite easily be arranged to act as a refrigerator for cooling the the air during hot weather.

The process is important from the electrical point of view, because the only practicable way of driving the compressor is by means of an electric motor. The amount of heat produced is 2 to 3 times (depending on outside and inside temperature conditions) that corresponding to the electrical input, i.e. 2 to 3 times as much as would be produced by a resistance heater of the same input. Although very economical in running costs, the capital cost is high, and the scheme has so far found only a negligible application for domestic heating, although a number of commercial and industrial plants have been equipped in this way.

Factors affecting Choice of Heating System

It is not possible to lay down any hard-and-fast rule as to which of the above heating systems is preferable in any particular case as so many factors have to be taken into account and each case must be considered on its merits.

Influence of Construction of Building—With an electric heating system the whole of the heat produced is available for heating, the only losses being due to conduction through the walls, roof, and floor and the heat carried away by ventilating air. With other forms of heating, particularly the open coal fire, a large proportion of the heat is carried away up the chimney and the loss through the walls, etc., is negligible by comparison. With electric heating, therefore, the loss through the walls, etc., becomes of great importance, and to ensure satisfactory results particular attention should be paid to its reduction; the whole of the outside walls and roof should be heat-insulated with a layer of 25 to 50 mm of cork or other suitable insulating material. The additional cost of this will be saved very soon by the reduced cost of energy. It may be noted that *still* air forms one of the most satisfactory heat insulators available.

The elimination of flues for carrying away the products of combustion with coal or gas fires results in a saving in building cost and gives the architect a freer hand in the design of the building; it must be remembered, however, that the chimneys provide a useful and completely automatic means of ventilation, and some method of replacing this must be provided when electric heating is used.

Continuous and Intermittent Heating.—If a building is not in continuous use the problem arises as to whether it should be heated continuously or only at the times when it is occupied. Such conditions arise in schools, which are used only for about 7 hours per day, or in churches, which may be used only one day per week; it also occurs, of course, in domestic heating. Although at first sight it would appear to be cheaper to heat the building only when requried, a closer examination of the problem indicates that continuous heating is preferable in many cases. The chief cause of this apparent anomaly lies in the time taken to heat up the building from cold and the fact that the rating of the heating equipment which must be installed to do this in a reasonable time is 20 to 30 per cent. greater than that required to maintain a given temperature continuously; although there will be a saving in energy costs by adopting intermittent heating, this may be more than out weighed by additional capital costs. Furthermore if continuous heating with thermal storage is adopted, energy may be obtainable at a cheaper rate than if intermittent heating be employed.

In cases where it is found desirable to employ intermittent heating, a convection system is preferable, since it heats up a room more quickly than a low-temperature radiant-heat system, such as panel heating.

Calculation of Heat Loss

The capacity of the electric heating equipment which must be installed depends chiefly upon the rate of heat loss from the room or building under consideration and, if intermittent heating is being considered, upon the heat required to raise the temperature of the building.

Heat Loss from Walls, Roof, etc.—The heat conducted through the walls and roof can be calculated from a knowledge of the conductivity of these parts, thus:

$$\text{Heat loss} = K\,(\theta_1 - \theta_2)$$

where K is the heat conductivity in W/m deg C., and θ_1 and θ_2 are the temperature of the inside and outside surfaces of the wall respectively, in degrees celsius.

Typical values of K for various common types of construction used in building are shown in Table XII.

TABLE XII

Type of wall	*K*
230 mm brick, plastered inside	7·28
410 mm brick, cavity wall, plastered inside	4·00
410 mm concrete, plastered inside	8·53
Single window	33·50
Double window	10·81
12·5 mm wooden partition	8·32
Lath-and-plaster ceiling, tiled roof above and no floor to loft	12·48
Lath-and-plaster ceiling, with floor above	5·00
Reinforced concrete ceiling, wood floor above	2·00

The method of applying these coefficients to the calculation of the heat loss from a typical room is illustrated in Example 20.

Example 20 :—Calculate the heat required to maintain a temperature of 18°C in an office having the following particulars :

Floor area = 6×6 m^2 (rooms below heated to 18°C) ; Ceiling area = (6×6) m^2, lath and plaster, with loft and tiled roof above.

Walls A and B :—each (6×3) m^2 outside 0·4 m cavity walls, containing a 1·2 m by 1·8 m single window.

Wall C :—6 × 3 metre wodden partition on to corridor maintained at 12 °C.

Wall D :—on to room maintained at 18°C.

External air temperature = 1·5° C.

Heat losses from walls, etc :

Floor—No heat loss.

Ceiling—area = 36 sq. m.

Loss $= 36 \times 12{\cdot}288 \times 10^3 \times (18-1{\cdot}5)$

$= 7300 \times 10^3$ J/h

Walls A and B area $= 2(18-2{\cdot}16) = 31{\cdot}68$ m^2

Loss $= 31{\cdot}68 \times 3{\cdot}885 \times 10^3 \times (18-1{\cdot}5)$

$= 2030 \times 10^3$ J/h

Window-area $= 2 \times 2{\cdot}16 = 4{\cdot}32$ m^2

Loss $= 23{\cdot}1 \times 10^3 \times 4{\cdot}32\ (18-1{\cdot}5)$

$= 1650 \times 10^3$ J/h

Wall C :— area = 18 m^2

Loss $= 18 \times 8{\cdot}18 \times 10^3 (18-12) = 885 \times 10^3$ J/h

Wall D :—No heat loss

Total heat loss by conduction through walls $= 11\ 865 \times 10^3$ J/h

With natural ventilation, a complete change of air $1\frac{1}{2}$ times per hour may be assumed. Using the previously mentioned figure of $1{\cdot}22 \times 10^3$ J for heating 1 m^3 through 1°C we obtain :

Volume of air per hour $= 6 \times 6 \times 3 \times 1{\cdot}5$

$= 162$ m^3

Heat loss per hour $= 1{\cdot}22 \times 10^3 \times 162 \times (18-1{\cdot}5)$

$= 3260 \times 10^3$ J/h $= 4{\cdot}2$ kW

Total volume of room = 108 m^3

Heat per metre^3 $= \dfrac{4200}{108} = 38{\cdot}8$ W/m^3

Typical Figures for Heat Requirements.—For rough or preliminary calculations, typical values for the watts per cubicmetre may be said to lie between about 2.0 for a room with one exposed wall of 360 mm. brickwork and 53 for a room with four exposed walls of 230 mm. brickwork, a temperature difference of 16.1°C being assumed between inside and outside temperatures in each case.

Heat required to raise Temperature of the Building.—When dealing with intermittent heating, the heat required to raise the temperature of the building becomes important: this can be calculated from the specific heat and density of the masonry employed for the building.

An average figure for the specific heat of masonry is 840 and the density may be taken as 2380 Kg./m^3, so that the heat required to raise its temperature is:

$$2\ 380 \times 840 = 2\ 000\ \text{kJ/m}^3$$

7. ELECTRIC WELDING

The welding together of metal parts by heating them to melting-point is one in which considerable progress has recently been made, this being largely due to the advent of electrical methods of welding, which enable accurately controlled local heating to be obtained. Electrically welded joints are being used to replace riveted or bolted joints in the construction of ships, bridges, steel-frame buildings, tanks, pipe-lines, and for many other applications; machine parts formerly made of castings are now frequently made of welded steel plates, and the repair of castings, hitherto considered impracticable, is rendered comparatively simple.

Two general methods of electric welding are employed, namely, resistance welding and arc welding. In the former a current is passed through the joint to be welded and the heat caused by the resistance of the joint is sufficient to cause fusion of the metals; in arc welding the heat is produced from an arc struck between an electrode and the metal to be welded.

Resistance Welding

The essentials of resistance welding are a heavy current, sufficient to cause melting of the metals at the point of contact, together with the application of sufficient mechanical pressure to ensure fusion of the parts. Three different types of resistance welding are employed.

(i) *Butt Welding.*—Used for welding of rods, wires, or small pipes; the two ends are pressed together mechanically to form a butt joint, as shown in Fig. 112(*a*), while current is passed across the joint.

(ii) *Spot Welding.*—For joining two or even three sheets of metal by means of an overlapping joint, as shown in Fig. 112(*b*). The sheets are held between two electrodes and current is passed between these electrodes, causing fusion at a single spot.

(iii) *Seam Welding.*—Where a continuous joint is required between two overlapping sheets of metal, as in constructing a tank, the two electrodes used in spot welding are replaced by two wheels, between which the work travels. In practice it is not satisfactory to make a continuous weld, that is, to have the current flowing continuously, as there is then a tendency for the heat

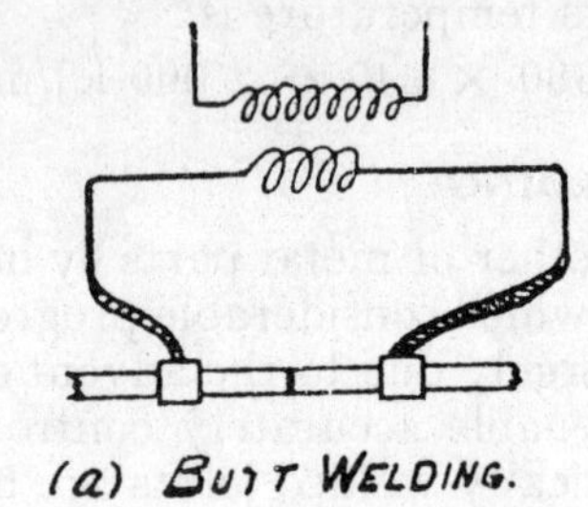

(a) BUTT WELDING.

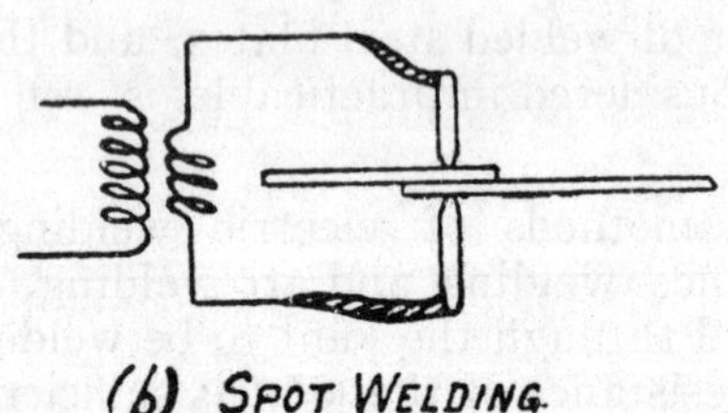

(b) SPOT WELDING.

FIG. 112.—METHODS OF RESISTANCE WELDING.

gradually to build up as the weld progresses and cause burning and warping. It is usual to employ, therefore, an intermittent current, so that a seam weld is actually a series of overlapping spot welds. The number of such spots varies between about 24 and 40 per 100 mm, so that if the work is travelling at a speed of, say, 4.6 m/min, the number of current interruptions will have to be between 1000 and 1800 per minute.

Resistance welding can be applied to iron and steel, brass, copper, aluminium, and certain other metals with eminently satisfactory results.

Resistance-welding Machines.—Alternating current is used for resistance welding on account of the ease with which the necessary heavy current at a low voltage can be obtained by means of a transformer. A welding machine for all three types of resistance

FIG. 113.—SPOT-WELDING MACHINE.
(British Insulated Cables, Ltd.)

welding is similar in principle and incorporates a transformer, suitable electrodes for supplying the current to the weld, apparatus for applying and controlling the necessary mechanical pressure, and, finally, means for controlling the duration of flow of the current. A typical spot-welding machine is illustrated in Fig. 113 and a seam-welding machine in Fig. 114.

The power for supplying the mechanical pressure may be obtained from a continuously running electric motor operating through a series of levers and clutch, or, in some cases, more particularly in France, pressure may be applied by compressed air. The magnitude of the pressure required varies from a few kg. for welding thin sheets or wires up to a tonne or more for heavy work.

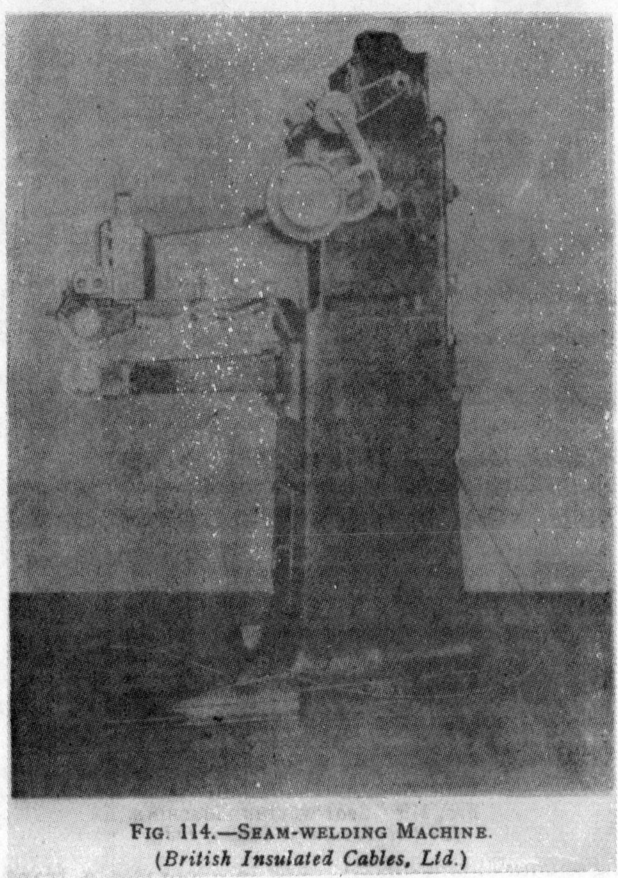

FIG. 114.—SEAM-WELDING MACHINE.
(*British Insulated Cables, Ltd.*)

Control Equipment.—In the earlier types of welding machine the electrodes were brought on to the work and the electrical circuit closed by the operation of a pedal, so that the duration of the current flow and also, in some cases, the mechanical pressure were entirely under the control of the operator; considerable skill is required to produce consistently satisfactory welds under these conditions. The modern tendency is to increase the speed of production by employing heavier currents and shorter times, particularly for spot and seam welding. Times of between $\frac{1}{10}$ and $\frac{1}{100}$ second are in use, and with these some form of automatic control is essential.

The particular type of equipment used may be of the constant-time, current-actuated, or energy-actuated types.

The constant-time equipment allows the welding current to flow for a certain fixed time quite independent of the magnitude of the current and resistance of the joint; when the work is uniform and has a consistently clean surface, which covers the majority of cases where high-speed production is required, this system of control is entirely satisfactory.

Mechanical Control for Constant-time Equipment.—A cam-operated switch connected in the primary circuit of the welding transformer and driven from the welding machine provides a simple and widely used device; it can be made to give up to 300 welds per minute. For high-speed work requiring very short intervals of current flow it is difficult to obtain consistently acurate timing, due to wear of the cam and operating mechanism, arcing and burning of the contacts, and irregularities caused by closing the switch at different instants in the cycle.

Valve-operated Control for Constant-time Devices.—To overcome the difficulties with mechanically operated gear at high speeds various valve-operated devices have been developed. The mercury-vapour valve is employed, either of the grid-controlled or the ignitron type. In both cases means are provided for starting the flow of current through the tube at any desired point in the cycle and stopping it at the end of any half-cycle; this is carried out by controlling the potential of the grid in the grid-controlled valve and of the auxiliary electrode in the ignitron. The valve may be used purely as an accurate timing device for controlling the operation of a contactor, but it is better employed to control the supply to the welding transformer.

The control of the transformer primary current in this way is illustrated in Fig. 115(*a*): the valves, two of which are used so that both half-waves of current can be carried, are connected in the primary circuit of the transformer as shown and will interrupt the circuit at the first current zero after the grids or auxiliary electrodes have been made negative. In practice, particularly with grid-controlled valves, it is easier to build tubes for a high voltage and small current than with a low voltage and high current and an alternative method of connecting the tubes to make use of this is shown in Fig. 115(*b*). When the tubes are conducting, the series transformer, which has a relatively high secondary voltage, is short-circuited and full voltage appled to the welding transformer, but when the

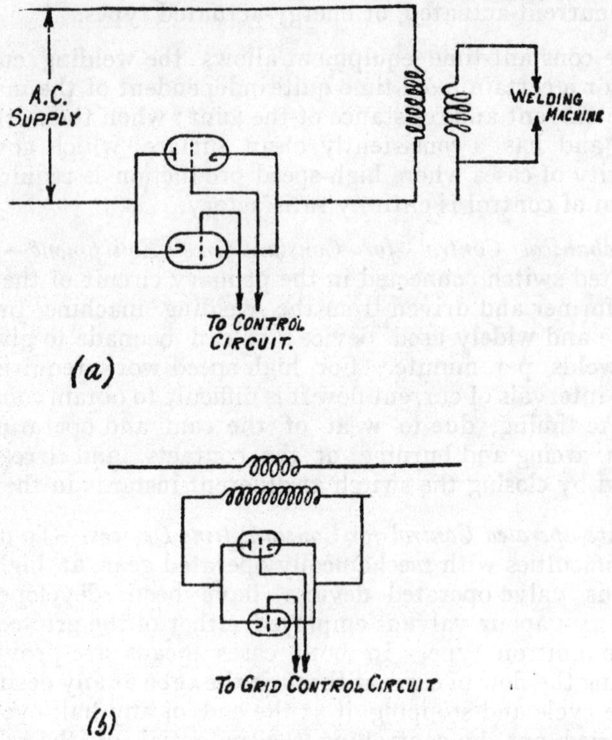

FIG 115—CIRCUITS FOR VALVE-CONTROLLED RESISTANCE-WELDING MACHINES

tubes are not conducting, the impedance of the series transformer so reduces the applied voltage to the welding transformer that the current is negligible. In both cases auxiliary valves are used to control the timing of the negative potential applied to the grids of the main valves.

Current and Energy-actuated Control.—When there may be variations in the conditions under which successive welds are made, due to variable supply voltage or mechanical pressure, wearing of electrodes, surface irregularities, or other causes, the constant-time method of control does not always give consistently good results, and a method may be employed in which the time of application of the current is dependent on the change in current which occurs at the instant of fusion or in which the total energy supplied to the weld is kept contant. The former method has not met with complete success, particularly with modern high-speed welding; energy control, however which allows the current to flow until a predetermined amount of energy has been supplied to the weld, is theoretically an ideal method, and, when the additional complication of the control equipment is warranted, it has been used with success.

Power Supply for Resistance Welding.—The kVA. taken from the supply when actually making a weld may be between a few kVA. and as much as 1,000 kVA., and the power factor will be about 0·25 or 0·3 lagging ; this low power factor is due chiefly to the high ratio of reactance to resistance of the loop formed by the jaws of the welding machine. Such heavy intermittent single-phase loads may cause serious voltage drop difficulties in the supply net work, and often result in flickering of lamps if these are supplied over the same feeders. Capacitors can be used to improve matters ; they can be connected in parallel with the welding transformers in order to improve the power factor in the usual way, but this means that the power factor will lead when welding current is not being taken; alternatively they may be connected in series with the welding transformer and arranged to neutralise the reactance drop in the supply circuit.

Arc Welding

The heat in this type of welding is obtained from an arc struck between an electrode and the metal to be welded, as shown

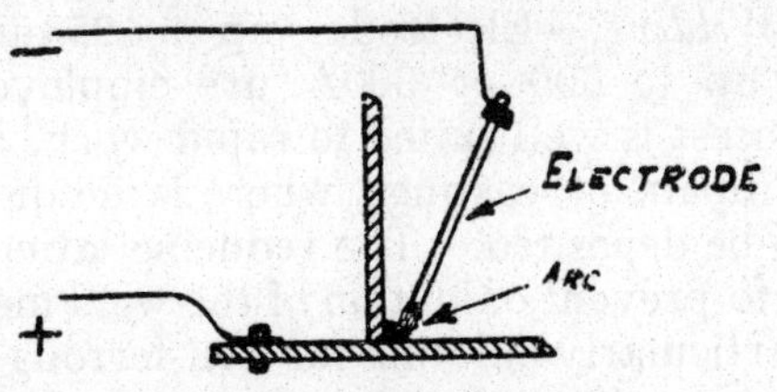

FIG. 116.—ARC WELDING.

116.—ARC WELDING.

in Fig. 116. In addition to the fusion of the metals at the joint the process involves the provision of a filler metal, that is, additional metal necessary to fill in and complete the joint. The arc-welding process is widely used for the joining of metal parts instead of riveting or bolting, the repair of fractured castings, and the filling in, by the deposition of new metal, of worn parts.

The electrode employed may be either of carbon or of metal, giving rise to the carbon-arc and the metallic-arc processes. In the former the current supplied must be d.c., but in the latter it may be either d.c. or a.c. The length of the arc is generally between one and two times the diameter of the electrodes, i.e. anything up to 25 to 50 mm. The voltage across the arc to produce a good weld should be between 20 and 30.

Characteristics of the Arc.—The temperature of the electric arc is about 3,500°C., so that it is adequate for the melting and welding of any of the normally used metals. Its most important feature is the negative resistance characteristic, meaning that the resistance decreases as the current increases, so that any slight increase in the current causes a decrease in the resistance and a consequent further increase in the current, making the maintenance of a steady arc impossible. To overcome this the supply to the arc must be such that the voltage falls off rapidly as the current rises, thus counteracting the rise in current ; this drooping characteristic also helps to prevent the arc from going out inadvertently, since any tendency to go out results in a decrease in current, and a consequent rise in voltage which will tend to maintain it. On open circuit, the supply to the arc should not exceed about 60V. for a d.c. arc or 100/V. for an a.c. arc, or a flaming arc is liable to result as well as danger of shock to the operator.

Carbon Arc Welding.—Electrodes up to 25 mm. in diameter with currents up to 600 or 800A. are employed, so that the carbon arc process is well suited to rapid work, or cases such as arise in the repair of castings, where large quantities of filler metal have to be deposited. The reducing atmosphere around the arc tends to prevent oxidation of the weld metal and renders the process particularly suitable for non-ferrous metals. Unless the electrode is negative relative to the work, there is a tendency for particles of carbon to be carried across the arc into the weld, causing brittleness ; a d.c. supply must therefore be used, with the positive terminal connected to the work.

Metallic Arc Welding.—The electrode itself forms the filler metal in metallic arc welding, and it must therefore be of suitable composition for giving a satisfactory weld. The means whereby the metal is carried across from the electrode to the weld, even if the latter is vertically above the electrode, as in overhead welding, is a matter of controversy; the latest researches appear to indicate that it is transferred chiefly in the form of small globules of metal expelled with considerable force from the electrode, but transfer as a vapour and as a fine mist also takes place.

The transfer process limits the size of electrode and the current which can be used to about 11 mm. and 200 to 300A.

Electrodes for Metallic Arc Welding.—The chief application of metallic arc welding is for the welding of iron and steel, for which an electrode of low carbon content (not more than 0·2 per cent.) is generally suitable; certain high-carbon steels, however, require electrodes containing up to 1 per cent. carbon.

Bare or covered electrodes may be used: the latter have a layer of a compound containing salts of silicon, calcium, magnesium, or other basic substance, which forms a slag on the metal and prevents oxidation and also chilling of the metal. Modern practice tends towards the general use of covered electrodes.

D.C. or A.C. for Metallic Arc Welding.—From the metallurgical standpoint there is little to choose between the use of a.c. and d.c. in metallic arc welding, provided suitable equipment is used in each case; the choice is therefore governed largely by considerations affecting the supply of current to the arc.

Some of the salient features of the two systems are as follows:

With an a.c. arc there is a tendency for it to cool at the current zero in each cycle, and, in order to assist in maintaining an even temperature, covered electrodes are essential.

The open-circuit voltage necessary to strike the arc is between 50 and 60 V. for d.c. and between 70 and 100 V. for a.c. The former is therefore considered to be safer, particularly when welding structural work, when a shock may cause an operator to lose his balance and fall.

Most power supplies are now a.c., so that if d.c. welding is used a motor-generator set must be provided, whereas only a transformer is required for a.c. welding; the latter has a greater overall efficiency, since it consumes no power when a weld is not actually being made, whereas a motor-generator set must be kept running continuously.

The single-phase transformer of the a.c. equipment produces unbalancing when connected to an ordinary 3-phase network, and the power factor at full load will be somewhat less than that of an induction motor driving a motor-generator set.

Early welding plants invariably adopted d.c., but improvements in the technique of a.c. welding are leading to its more general adoption in cases where an a.c. supply is available. For field work, where the supply is obtained from a generator driven by a petrol or Diesel engine, d.c. is universal.

D. C. Welding Equipment.—As previously explained, the actual supply to the arc must have a drooping characteristic ; this may be obtained from a special generator designed to give such a characteristic or from a constant-potential supply with a resistance inserted in series with the arc. The drooping characteristic of the generator is generally obtained by the use of shunt and series fields in opposition, control of the welding current being obtained by variation of the shunt, or sometimes both fields. With a constant-potential supply control is effected by variation of the series resistance. In both cases a reactance is often included in the circuit to prevent too rapid changes of current.

For supplying current to two or more operators a multi-operator equipment is used. This must be of the constant-potential type so that there is no interference between operators ; each operator then has a series resistance to control and stabilise his particular arc.

A. C. Welding Equipment.—A transformer reduces the voltage from that of the supply down to about 100. To regulate the current and produce the drooping characteristic required a resistance or reactance may be used. The resistance reduces the efficiency, while the reactance reduces the power factor, and is, at the same time, more expensive in first cost. When a reactance is used it must be designed to operate well below the saturation-point of its magnetic circuit to prevent the introduction of harmonics, which tend to lengthen the zero-current period in each half-cycle and allow cooling of the arc : a reactance with an air gap in the magnetic circuit is generally employed.

Automatic Arc Welding.—Both carbon and metallic arc welding can be carried out by an automatic welding machine where-repetition work is to be done. The electrode is carried in a welding head which is moved at a constant speed along the joint to be welded. The electrode is fed into the arc at a speed which is controlled by the voltage of the arc—a lengthening of the arc which causes a rise in the arc voltage increases the rate of feed until the correct length has been regained. Welds joining two plates can be made at a speed of about 30.5m. per hour with 1.6mm plate and about 1.8 or 2.1m per hour with 19mm plate.

Atomic Hydrogen Welding

In this process an arc is struck between a pair of tungsten electrodes; hydrogen is fed into the arc which causes it to be atomised. The recombination of these atoms outside the arc is accompanied by an intense heat, and it is this, not the heat of the arc, which produces the weld. Arc currents up to 150A. can be used, and the power supply arrangements are similar to those for ordinary a.c. arc welding, except that the transformer voltages are higher, being abut 300 V. on open circuit for striking the arc and between 80 and 100 V. when operating; an automatically operated valve cuts off the hydrogen supply when there is no current flowing.

CHAPTER III

QUESTIONS

1. A 20-kW, single-phase, 220-V resistance-oven employs circular nickel-chrome wire for heating element. If the wire temperature is not to exceed 1 170°C and the temperature of the charge is to be 500°C, calculate the size and length of wire required. Rediating efficiency=60%

2. The resistance elements of each phase of a 3-phase, delta-connected resistance-oven consists of two groups of elements in parallel. If the operating temperature of the elements when supplied at normal voltage under these conditions is 1000°C, what other possible temperatures could be obtained by reconnecting the elements, the supply voltage remaining the same ?

3. A resistance-oven having internal dimensions of 0·60×0·60×1·20 m, has walls of refractory material (firebrick) 0·23 m thick. The internal temperature of the oven is 482°C and the heat dissipation from the external surface is such that its temperature is 38°C. Estimate the heat loss in joules/hour and the heat required to raise the temperature of the oven from cold (10°C) to its operating temperature. A charge consisting

of 1 tonne of steel is to be heated and maintained at 482°C for 3 hours ; estimate the energy (in kWh) required to do thus :—

(a) if only a single charge has to be treated,

(b) if a series of such charges has to be treated so that the heat required to raise the temperature of the oven becomes negligible.

4. It is desired to employ an induction furnace for melting 1 tonne of zinc at each charge, the time taken for each melt being about 1 hour. What must be the approximate kW input to the furnace, assuming it to have an efficiency of 65% ?

Specific heat of zinc	$=390$ J kg^{-1} °C^{-1}
Latent heat of fusion of zinc	$=111{\cdot}65$ kJ/kg
Melting point	$=455$°C

5. A low-frequency induction furnace operating at 10V in the secondary circuit, takes 400 kW at 0·6 power factor when the hearth is full. If the secondary voltage be maintained at 10 V, estimate the power absorbed and the power factor when the hearth is half-full. Assume the resistance of the secondary circuit to be thereby doubled and the reactance to remain the same.

6. The power input to the charge in a 500 kg, 960 Hz induction furnace having 20 turns on the primary winding is 325 kW. The cylindrical crucible has an internal diameter of 0·45 m and the depth of the charge in it is 0·5 m. Estimate the equivalent resistance of the charge and the current in the primary winding which is necessary to counterbalance the mmf due to the secondary currents.

7. A 3-phase arc-furnace to melt 10 tonne of steel in 2 hours ; estimate the average kW input to the furnace, if its overall efficiency is 50%. If the current input is 9000A with the above kW input and the resistance and reactance of the furnace leads (including transformer) are 0·003 Ω and 0·005 Ω respectively, estimate the arc voltage and the total kVA taken from the supply.

Specific heat of steel	$=444$ J kg^{-1} °C^{-1}
Latent heat of Fusion of steel	$=37{\cdot}25$ kJ/kg
Melting point of steel	$=1370$°C

8. What would be the loading of the heating elements to be placed in a 180-litre water tank in order to raise the temperature of the water from 10°C to 93·3°C in 6 hours?

Assume: (a) that the heat loss is negligible; (b) that the heat loss is constant at 2 110 kJ/h; (c) that the heat loss is 38 kJ/h per °C rise.

9. Estimate the efficiency of a high-frequency induction-furnace which takes 10 min. to melt 1·8 kg of aluminium, the input to the furance being 5 kW and the initial temperature 15°C. [Sp. heat of aluminium = 880 J kg^{-1} $°C^{-1}$; melting point = 660°C; Latent heat of fusion of aluminium = 32 kJ/kg.]

10. An office measuring 7·5 × 3·5 × 4·0 m, has to have two changes of air per hour, the incoming air being at 5°C. Estimate the kW rating of heating elements which should be provided to maintain the internal air temperature at 15°C. Neglect any loss of heat by radiation from outside walls.

11. The 500-kW electrode boiler of the thermal storage system for heating an office building takes energy from the supply only during the hours between 8 p.m. and 6 a.m. The total storage capacity of the system is 4·55 m^3 and the the temperature at 6 a.m. is 95°C, during the day 3·64 m^3 per hour are circulated through the building with an outgoing temperature of 75°C and a return temperature of 50°C. In addition, 1·82 m^3 per day are drawn off for washing and replaced by cold water at 15°C. Assuming the efficiency of the boiler to be 95%, estimate:

(a) the time taken to heat the water initially to a temperature of 95°C;

(b) the temperature of the water in the storage tank at the end of a day (8 a.m.);

(c) the time taken to restore the temperature to 95°C, assuming no water circulated or drawn off during this period;

(d) the cost per day of running the equipment if energy costs 3.5 paise per unit.

12. Dielectric heating is to be employed to heat a slab of insulating material 20 mm thick and 1 500 mm^2 in area. The power required is 200 W and a freguency of 30 MHz is to be used. The material has a permittivity of 5 and a power factor 0·05. Determine the voltage necessary and the current which will flow through the material. If the voltage were to be limited to 600, to what value would the frequency have to be raised?

CHAPTER IV

ELECTROLYTIC PROCESSES

THE fact that metals can be deposited in a very pure form from solutions of their salts by passing a current through them (electrolysis) has been known since about 1800, and processes based on this are widely used for the extraction of metals from their ores, for the refining of metals, and for the electro-deposition of metals, including electroplating, electrotyping, and the building up of worn parts. Similar electrolytic processes are also used in the manufacture of various chemicals.

1. FUNDAMENTAL PRINCIPLES

Although the processes mentioned above differ widely in detail, the underlying principles are the same in each and consist simply of the passing of a direct current through a solution of a chemical compound in order to dissociate the solution into its constituent parts.

Ionic Dissociation

Solutions with which the above process can be carried out are known as electrolytes, and in such solutions each molecule of the substance dissolved dissociates into two *ions*, one of which is negatively charged and the other positively charged. Thus when copper sulphate is dissolved in water it dissociates into positively charged copper ions and negatively charged sulphions (SO_4). If now two electrodes are placed in the solution and a potential difference maintained between them, the negative ions (sulphions) will be attracted to the positive electrode (anode) and the positive copper ions to the negative electrode (cathode). As soon as the ions reach the electrodes they give up their charges and become ordinary molecules. Thus in the above case the copper ions become ordinary molecules of copper, which are deposited on the cathode, while the sulphions, on reaching the anode, become ordinary SO_4 molecules. With the latter a secondary reaction takes place, as they react with the water to produce oxygen, which is liberated as a gas, and sulphuric acid, which dissolves in the water or, if the anode is of copper, attacks the anode and produces more copper sulphate. In this case, therefore, the effect is that copper is dissolved from the anode and deposited on the cathode.

Applications.—The commercial applications of the above principle are as follows :

Extraction of Metals from their Ores.—The ore is either melted or treated with strong acid and current passed through the resulting solution ; the solution is dissociated and pure metal deposited on the cathode.

Refining of Metals.—Anodes of impure metal are placed in a suitable electrolyte and, on passing a current through the bath, pure metal is deposited on the cathode.

Electroplating and Electrotyping.—The article to be plated is made the cathode in a suitable electrolyte together with an anode of the metal to be deposited.

Manufacture of Chemicals.—Current is passed through a solution of some compound, causing it to dissociate into its constituent parts, which are liberated at the anode and cathode, and which can be collected or allowed to take part in a secondary reaction with the original solution to obtain the desired product.

Faraday's Laws

The laws which govern the above electrolytic processes were formulated by Faraday and may be stated as follows :

(i) The weight of a substance deposited from an electrolyte is proportional to the quantity of electricity (coulombs) which has passed through it.

(ii) If the same current is passed through different electrolytes the weights of the substances deposited from each will be proportional to the chemical equivalents of those substances.

To understand electrolysis, the reader must have a clear concept of the following terms and definitions :

1. *The electrochemical equivalent* of a substance is the mass of it liberated in a process of electrolysis by this passage of unit quantity of electricity, i.e. by unit current (ampere) for unit time (second). The SI Unit of electrochemical equivalent Z, is the kilogram per coulomb. (kg/C).

2. *The atomic weight* of an element is a number, which is the average of the masses of its various isotopes, weighed

according to their relative abundance, on a scale in which 12_6C nuclide of carbon is designated exactly, e.g. on this scale the atomic weight of chlorine is 35.543 because this is the average of the masses of the various isotopes having regard to their relative percentage occurrence.

3. *The formulae weight* of a chemical entity (atom, radicle, molecule, ion, etc.) is the sum of the atomic weights of its constituents. Under ordinary conditions, an oxygen molecule consists of two oxygen atoms (at. wt. of oxygen=15·999 4), the formula weight of molecular oxygen is 2×15.999 4=31.998 8. Sulphuric acid (formula : H_2SO_4), has a formula weight= 98.063 59 calculated as follows :

$$\text{formula weight} = 2 \times \text{atomic weight of hydrogen} + \text{formula wt. of sulphate radicle}$$
$$= 2 \times 1{\cdot}000\ 797 + 96{\cdot}062 = 98{\cdot}063\ 594$$

A mass of a chemical entity numerically equal to its formula weight is termed a kilogram weight in SI Units. Thus, 31.988 8 kg is the 'kilogram formula weight' of oxygen.

4. *Valency* : The valency of an atom or radicle (i.e. a group of atoms) is the number of hydrogen atoms with which it will react chemically ; valency is always an integer (1, 2, 3, etc.) but for a given atom or radicle, it can have different values in different chemical reactions.

5. *Equivalent Weight* : The equivalent weight of a substance is the quotient of its formula weight divided by its valency, i.e.

$$\text{equivalent weight} = \frac{\text{formula weight}}{\text{valency}}$$

In the case of hydrogen, the electrochemical equivalent is $1{\cdot}045 \times 10^{-8}$ kg. per coulomb, so that for copper displaced from a cupric salt it is, according to Faraday's second law, $1.045 \times (63.54/2) = 32.927 \times 10^{-8}$ kg./C. Values of the atomic or formula weight, valency and electrochemical equivalents of the various substances concerned in commercial electrochemical processes are given in Table XIII.

TABLE XIII

CHEMICAL AND ELECTRO-CHEMICAL EQUIVALENTS

Element (atom or radicle)	At. wt. or form. wt.	valency	Chemical equivalent	Electro-chemical equivalent kg/coulomb
Aluminium ..	26·9815	3	9·1	$9{\cdot}321 \times 10^{-8}$
Cadmium ..	112·41	2	56·2	58·20
Calcium ..	40·08	2	20·04	20·75
Chlorine ..	35·453	1	35·37	36·740
Copper (cupric) ..	63·54	2	31·8	32·937
Gold ..	197·2	3	65·4	67·68
Hydrogen ..	1·008	1	1	1·045
Iron (ferrous) ..	55·85	2	27·9	28·90
Lead ..	207·21	2	103·2	107·16
Magnesium ..	24·32	2	11·97	12·43
Nickel ..	58·69	2	29·3	30·349
Nitrogen ..	14·008	3	4·67	4·85
Oxygen ..	15·9994	2	7·98	8·29
Potassium ..	39·100	1	39·04	40·54
Silver ..	107·880	1	107·67	111·80
Sodium ..	22·991	1	22·99	23·87
Tin (stannous) ..	118·70	2	59·3	61·40
Zinc ..	65·38	2	32·45	33·88

Calculation of Current required :—From the electro-chemical equivalent it is possible to calculate the theoretical value of current required to deposit any given quantity of metal or alternatively the amount of metal which should theoretically be desposited by a given current.

Example 21 :—A sheet of iron having a total surface area of 0.36 m² is to be electroplated with copper to a thickness of 0.0254 mm. What quantity of electricity will be required ? The iron will be made the cathode and immersed, together with an anode of pure copper, in a solution of copper sulphate.

Given :

Mass density of copper as $8{\cdot}96 \times 10^3$ kg. m^{-3} ;

e. c. e. of copper as $32{\cdot}9\ 10^{-8}$ kg. C^{-1}

Solution :

Mass of copper to be deposited $= 0{\cdot}36 \times 0{\cdot}0254 \times 10^{-3} \times 8{\cdot}96 \times 10^3$ kg $= 0{\cdot}082$ kg.

The e. c. e. of copper $= 32{\cdot}9$ kg per coulomb

$\therefore\ 32{\cdot}9 \times 10^{-8} \times 3600 \times 1000$ kg per 1000 Ah.

$= 1{\cdot}184$ kg per 1000 Ah.

$$\therefore \text{ Ampere hours required } = \frac{0\cdot082}{1\cdot184}$$

$$= 69\cdot24 \text{ or say } 69\cdot5 \text{ amp-hours.}$$

The current density normally used in copper-plating bath is about 330 Am^{-2}, so that in the above case, a current of 15 A would be required. The time taken to perform the plating process would, therefore, be :

$$\frac{69\cdot5}{115} = 0\cdot604 \text{ hour.}$$

In practice certain losses occur, so that the above theoretical quantities would not be obtained and the current required or the time taken would have to be increased by about 10 per cent.

Current Efficiency.—The quantity of a substance or substances liberated is usually slightly less than the quantities calculated from Faraday's laws as above on account of impurities, which cause secondary reactions to occur. This is taken into account by employing a factor, known as the current efficiency. which is defined as the ratio of the actual quantity of substances liberated to the theoretical quantity. In practice it is usually between 90 and 98 per cent. Certain processes have an apparently low current efficiency on account of the fact that there is the unavoidable production of substances other than that which is required : thus, in chromium plating, in which the electrolyte is a solution of chromic acid, only about 12 to 15 per cent. of the current passed is actually used in depositing chromium from the solution, the remainder being used in producing hydrogen and oxygen which, for the purpose in hand, are useless.

Voltage.—The voltage necessary to pass current through any electrolytic cell is made up of the drop due to the resistance of the electrolyte and the drops at the anode and the cathode. The resistance of the electrolyte can easily be calculated from its specific resistance and the cross-sectional area and length of the current path. To economise power this resistance should obviously be kept as low as possible, and in many cases special *conducting agents* are added to the solution to reduce its resistance. Thus, in copper plating or refining, sulphuric acid is added to the copper-sulphate bath.

At the anode and cathode there is a potential difference between the electrode and the electrolyte, which is a measure of the tendency of the metal to go into solution. This is known as the electrode potential, and its value depends on the exact conditions (e.g. temperature and concentration), and also upon the nature of the metal and the electrolyte. For most substances the value as measured under ideal conditions lies between 0·5 and 1·0 V. The total voltage required to pass current through an electrolytic cell is thus not more than about 1 or 2 V.

Energy Efficiency.—The theoretical value of the metal deposited by a given current can be calculated from Faraday's laws, the voltage from the electrode potentials of the metal and solution concerned, and the specific resistance of the solution, so that the theoretical amount of energy required can be found. Due to various secondary effects and reactions, the metal deposited by a given current is less than the theoretical value and the voltage will be higher, so that the energy consumption will also be higher than the theoretical value. The ratio $\left[\frac{\text{theoretical energy required}}{\text{actual energy required}}\right]$ is known as the energy efficiency (η)

2. EXTRACTION AND REFINING OF METALS

Electrolytic methods of extraction and refining result in a purer product than most of the metallurgical processes and, as a result of the tendency of electric power costs to be reduced, are becoming widely used. In some cases, e.g. aluminium and some of the rarer metals, electrolytic extraction is the only available method. Large quantities of energy are required, and as the process is usually continuous the load factor approaches 100 per cent., so that it forms a desirable load for any power-supply company, and can generally be supplied at a fairly cheap rate.

Extraction of Metals

Processes for the extraction of metals may be divided into two classes according to whether the electrolyte is a solution of a salt of the metal obtained by treatment of the ore with strong acid or whether it consists of the ore in a molten state. Summaries of the chief processes in commercial use are shown in Table XIV.

TABLE XIV
EXTRACTION OF METALS

Metal	Treatment of ore	Solution	Consumption, kWh. per tonne (approx.)
Aluminium ..	—	Fused cryolite	20,000 — 25,000
Copper ..	Roasted and leached with sulphuric acid	Copper sulphate	2,000 — 2,500
Magnesium ..	—	Fused magnesium chloride or carnallite	17,000 — 20,000
Sodium ..	—	Fused sodium hydrate or sodium nitrate and sodium chloride	10,000 — 20,000
Zinc ..	Leached with sulphuric acid	Zinc chloride and zinc sulphate	3,000 — 5,000

Extraction of Zinc.—As an example of the processes employing an aqueous solution as electrolyte; the extraction of zinc from zinc ore may be cited. The ore, consisting largely of zinc oxide, is treated with strong sulphuric acid, roasted, and passed through various chemical processes to precipitate cadmium, copper, and any other impurities; the resulting zinc sulphate solution is passed to the electrolytic cells. These consist of large lead-lined wooden boxes, each containing a number of aluminium cathodes and lead anodes and carrying a current of several hundred or thousand amperes, according to the size. The current density on the cathodes is about 1100A/m². The potential drop in each cell is about 3·5V., so that with 100 or 150 of them in series a pressure of about 500V., is required. The zinc is deposited on the cathodes, which are removed once or twice a day for stripping.

Extraction of Aluminium.—An example of the fused-electrolyte process occurs in the extraction of aluminium from its ores, bauxite and cryolite. The bauxite is first treated chemically to reduce it to aluminium oxide and this is then dissolved in fused cryolite and electrolysed. The furance in which the fusion and electrolysis take place consists of a shallow rectangular bath lined with carbon; carbon anodes project downwards into the bath and the bottom of the bath forms the cathode. The high temperature (1,000°C.) necessary to keep the ores in a fused state is maintained by the ohmic losses of the current passing through the electrodes and the electrolyte. Aluminium is deposited at the cathode and settles at the bottom of the bath, from whence it is tapped off as required. A furnace having an area of 13.6 m^2 will require a pressure of 5 or 6 V. and a current of about 40,000A. It may be noted that the whole of the rapidly increasing world consumption of aluminium is produced electrolytically.

Refining of Metals

The metal obtained by electrolytic extraction is 98 to 99 per cent. pure, and this forms one of the chief advantages of that method of production. Sometimes, however, extraction cannot be economically carried out, and in such cases only the refining process is done electrolytically. Anodes of the impure metal obtained from metallurgical reduction furnaces are placed in an electrolytic cell containing a suitable electrolyte and the pure metal is deposited at the cathode. A summary of the more important refining processes is given in Table XV. Although both metallurgical and electrolytic processes are used for the extraction of copper, the whole of the very pure metal required by the electrical industry is refined electrolytically.

TABLE XV

REFINING OF METALS

Metal	Solution	Consumption kWh. per tonne (approx.)
Copper	Copper sulphate	150 — 300
Gold	Chloride of gold	300 — 350
Iron	Iron ammonium sulphate	1,000 — 1,500
Lead	Lead fluosilicate	100 — 120
Nickel	Nickel chloride and sulphate	2,500 — 4,000
Silver	Nitric acid and silver nitrate	400 — 420

3. ELECTRO-DEPOSITION

The term electro-deposition is usually regarded as covering the various processes whereby a coating of metal is electrically deposited on some other metal or non-metal. It includes electroplating, where a layer of metal is added for decorative or protective purposes, electrotyping for the production of printing-blocks, electro-forming for the production of thin sheet or foil, the making of gramophone records, and for the building up of worn parts to their original thickness.

Factors governing Deposition Processes

Although electro-deposition processes, where such are technically possible, can usually compete economically with any alternative process, there are various pactical difficulties which limit the number of metals which can actually be used to give a satisfactory deposit. A summary of the processes which have been found commercially practicable is shown in Table XVI.

Throwing Power.—One of the most important properties of a plating or deposition bath is its throwing power, that is, its ability to produce an even deposit on an article of irregular shape. Consider a bath as shown in Fig. 117. The potential difference

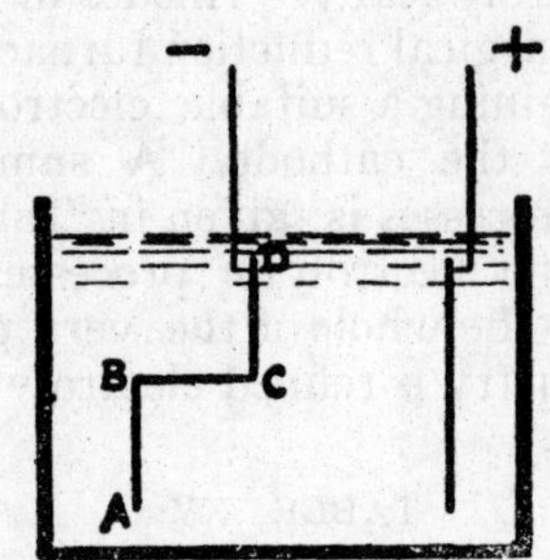

Fig. 117.—Electroplating Bath.

between the anode and any point on the article to be plated (cathode) is, of course, the same; the surface AB is however, twice as far from the anode as the surface CD, so that the resistance of the current path through the electrolyte to the former will be approximately twice as great; the current density and therefore the thickness of the deposit, will thus be smaller on this part of the surface. The difficulty can be overcome to some exent by placing the anode and cathode farther apart, so that the relative variation in resistance between the anode and different parts of the cathode is less. The voltage drop at the cathode surface also has an effect. In some cases decrease of current density causes a decrease in cathode drop, leaving more voltage available for overcoming the resistance of the electrolyte, thus tending to counteract any change in current density. For this reason solutions of the cyanides of metals usually give a greater throwing power than solutions of the sulphates.

TABLE XVI

Metal deposited	Chemical equivalent	Electro-chemical equivalent		Solution	Current density amps. per m^2	Temperature of solution
		mg. per coulomb	kg. per 1,000 Ah			
Cadmium ..	56·0	0·58	2·09	Cadmium oxide and sodium cyanide	110—165	Cold or warm
Chromium ..	8·75	0·91	0·33	Chromic acid	1650—2200	35° C.
Copper (from sulphate solution) ..	31·8	0·329	1·18	Copper sulphate	275—330	Cold or warm
Copper (from cyanide solution) ..	63·6	0·658	2·37	Cuprous cyanide and sodium cyanide	33—44	50° C.
Gold ..	197·0	2·03	7·35	Double cyanide of potassium and gold	110—330	60—80° C.
Iron ..	27·9	0·29	1·04	Ferrous sulphate	110—220	90° C.
Lead ..	103·6	1·07	3·86	Lead borate or fluosilicate	110—220	Cold
Nickel ..	29·3	0·305	1·10	Nickel sulphate	110—220	50—60° C.
Silver ..	108·0	1·118	4·04	Double cyanide of silver and sodium	33—66	Cold
Tin ..	59·3	0·615	2·22	Sodium stannate or stannous stannate	110—220	70° C.
Zinc ..	32·7	0·34	1·22	Zinc sulphate	220—330	Cold
Brass ..	—	—	—	Double cyanides of zinc and potassium and of copper and potassium	27·5—44	Cold or warm

Addition Agents.—The addition of acids or other substances to the electrolyte for reducing its resistance has previously been mentioned. There is another class of addition agent which takes little or no direct part in the chemical reactions, but which, in some way, influences the nature of the deposit, sometimes even making an otherwise unworkable process into one of practical importance. A typical example occurs in the deposition of zinc from zinc sulphate solution, when the addition of glucose or certain types of sugar is essential to the production of a satisfactory deposit.

Heating of the Bath.—Reference to Table XVI shows that many of the processes require the bath to be heated to fairly high temperature. Steam, gas, or electric heating may be employed for this purpose, the heating pipes or cables being placed in the bottom of the bath ; care must, of course, be taken to ensure that they are of materials which are not attacked by the chemicals in the bath. Steam is often required for other processes in the works. and in such cases provides the most economical method of heating, otherwise gas or electricity may be preferable.

Deposition of Alloys

Provided the electrode potentials of the constituent metals are approximately similar, it is possible to deposit alloys. Anodes of the alloy are used in an electrolyte consisting of a mixture of the electrolytes which would be used for the separate deposition of the metals concerned. Brass and bronze are widely plated in this way, and recent researches indicate that the deposition of various copper and nickel alloys will soon be commercially practicable.

Miscellaneous Deposition Processes

Other processes involving the principles of electro-deposition have been developed, the most important of which are the deposition of rubber and the anodic oxidation of aluminium. Both these processes involve reactions occurring at the anode instead of the cathode, as with the ordinary deposition from metallic salts.

Electro-deposition of Rubber.—Rubber latex as obtained from the tree consists of very fine colloidal particles of rubber suspened in water. In common with other collodical solutions, the particles are electrically charged, in this case negatively ; if electrodes are put in the solution, therefore, and a potential difference applied between them, the rubber particles will migrate towards the anode and be deposited on it. Current densities of about 100 A per square metre are employed, and deposits up to about 10mm thick can be obtained.

Anodic Oxidation of Aluminium.—When aluminium is made the anode in a suitable electrolyte (usually chromic or sulphuric acid), a very hard and adherent oxide film is deposited on it which is resistant to nearly all corroding media. The coating can be made to absorb dyes, so that coloured finishes can be obtained and are becoming widely used for decorative purposes on shipboard and in other situations where a corroding atmosphere exists.

4. MANUFACTURE OF CHEMICALS

The most important processes for the production of chemicals involve the electrolysis of brine, although other processes are also in commercial operation and are summarised in Table XVII.

In the electrolysis of brine, chlorine is given off at one pole and hydrogen at the other, leaving caustic soda in the vat. In the first of the two processes listed in the table, the chlorine and the

TABLE XVII
PRODUCTION OF CHEMICALS

Product	Solution	Consumption (approx.)
Caustic soda . . .	Brine	3,000—4,000 kWh./tonne
Chlorine compounds of sodium (chlorates, perchlorates, hypochlorates)	Brine	3,000—7,000 kWh./tonne
Oxygen and hydrogen . .	Water	125—150 kWh. (for $28 \cdot 32\ m^3\ H + 14 \cdot 16\ m^3\ O$)
Potassium permanganate .	Potassium manganate	70—80 kWh./tonne
Ammonium persulphate . .	Ammonium sulphate	2,000—2,500 kWh./tonne

hydrogen are pumped off as quickly as they are produced and form valuable by-products; in the second process no attempt is made to separate the hydrogen from the chlorine, and they therefore combine to form hypochlorates, chlorates, or perchlorates, according to the exact method of carrying out the process.

Certain industrial effluents, notably those from the soap industry, contain appreciable quantities of common salt, and these, as well as others, can sometimes be treated electrolytically to yield valuable by-products.

5. POWER SUPPLY FOR ELECTROLYTIC PROCESSES

The salient features of the power supply for electrolytic processes are that it must be direct current and a relatively low voltage. For electro-deposition the amount of power usually required is small (up to 100 or 200 amps. at 10 or 12V.) and can be obtained without difficulty from the ordinary supply system through a suitable convertor. The majority of installations employ a motor-generator set consisting of a standard induction motor driving a heavy-current generator. The mercury-arc rectifier is ruled out on account of its low efficiency at the low voltages which are required, but the copper-oxide rectifier has been developed for this purpose and, being a static piece of apparatus, has a lower maintenance cost than a motor-generator set, and also a higher efficiency, especially at low loads.

Where only a single bath is supplied from a generator, the control of the current to the bath is carried out by variation of the generator excitation, but in other cases a variable resistance is connected in series with each bath, so that the supply to each can be controlled independently.

Extraction and refining of metals and large-scale manufacture of chemicals require very large amounts of power—the British Aluminium Co., Ltd., use 90,000 kW. at their Lochaber works. With most processes the cost of this power is a major expense, and special attention must be paid to the obtaining of it at the minimum possible cost. Fortunately this is assisted by the fact that most processes are continuous and therefore have a load factor which approaches 100 per cent. The usual procedure is to locate the works near to a source of hydro-electric power, even if this necessitates extra trans-shipment of the raw materials, since the advantage of a high load factor is greater with such stations than with steam stations, and also transmission costs are eliminated. Electro-chemical works are thus built or are being built around the power stations at Niagara, Dnieprostroi, Boulder Dam, and elsewhere.

Although the voltage per cell is only about 10, a number of such cells can be connected in series, so that the voltage required is 500 to 800 with currents of up to several thousand amperes. With privately owned plants the water turbines can be made to drive d.c. generators, as at the Lochaber works mentioned above, but where the generating station is also connected to a general supply network, a.c. generation must be employed, with special heavy-current motor-generators, rotary convertors, or even mercury-arc rectifiers to convert to d.c. at the required voltage.

CHAPTER IV

QUESTIONS

1. The worn out part of a circular shaft 0.15 m in diameter and 0.3 m. long is to be repaired by depositing on it 1.6 mm of nickel by an electro-deposition process. Estimate the quantity of electricity required and the time taken if the current is to be 215.0 A/m^2. The current efficiency of the process may be taken as 95%.

2. A group of 400 cells in a copper refining plant carries a current of 5,000 A. The voltage per cell is 0.25 V. If the plant works for 100 hours per week, estimate the annual output of refined copper from the cells and the energy consumption in kWh per tonne.

3. How much aluminium would be produced from aluminium oxide in a working week of 100 hours in a cell carrying an average current of 5,000 A ? The current efficiency is 70%. If the voltage of the cell is 6 V and energy costs 3 paise per unit, what would be the energy cost per tonne of aluminium produced ?

4. Calculate the amount of energy required to produce 2700 m^3 of hydrogen by the electrolysis of water in cells operating at 2 V per cell. The current efficiency is 97%.

CHAPTER V

ILLUMINATING ENGINEERING

ARTIFICIAL lighting is playing an increasingly important part in modern everyday life, and electrically produced light, on account of its cleanliness and ease of control, as well as its low cost, possesses overwhelming advantages over alternative sources wherever an electricity supply is available.

Apart from its æsthetic and decorative aspects, good lighting has a strictly utilitarian value in reducing accidents, increasing the output of factory and other workers, and improving the general health of the community due to reduction of eye-strain. The science of illuminating engineering is therefore becoming of major importance.

1. Nature of Light

For the proper appreciation of modern developments in lighting, a study of the nature of light and the fundamental principles underlying its production is essential.

Ether Waves.—The behaviour of light can, for practical purposes, be explained by regarding it as a succession of waves of radiant energy transmitted through the ether as a result of some initial disturbance in much the same way as a stone thrown into a pond produces waves on the surface of the water. The properties and behaviour of these ether waves depend upon their wave-length, i.e. the distance between the top of one wave and the top of the next, and the wave-lengths which have been detected and made use of range from those having a length of 10^6 m used in radio broadcasting down to those having a length of only 100 pm. such as X-rays and cosmic rays; the complete range of wave-lengths known, together with their applications, is shown in Fig. 118. Certain of these, namely, those having wave-lengths of between 0.4 μm. and 0.75 μm., produce, when they impinge on the eye, the sensation known as light, and it is this small band with which the illuminating engineer is concerned. It may be noted that all these waves travel at a speed of 3×10^{10} cm. per sec. or 3×10^8 m/s.

Units of Wave-length.—The centimetre is not always a very convenient unit in which to measure wave-length, and the micron (represented by the symbol μ and equal to 10^{-6}m) is often used. Another commonly employed unit is the Angstrom Unit (AU.),* which is equal to 10^{-8}cm. or 10^{-10}m. Light waves

Frequency (Hertz) Hz.	Wave-length (m)	
3×10^{22}	10^{-14}	Cosmic rays
3×10^{20}	10^{-12}	X-rays
3×10^{18}	10^{-10}	X-rays
3×10^{16}	10^{-8}	Ultra-violet rays
3×10^{14}	10^{-6}	←Light
3×10^{12}	10^{-4}	Infra-red rays (heat)
3×10^{10}	10^{-2}	Short-wave radio waves
3×10^{8}	1	
3×10^{6}	10^{2}	
		Long-wave radio waves
3×10^{4}	10^{4}	
3×10^{2}	10^{6}	

FIG. 118.—RANGE OF ETHER WAVES.

within the visible spectrum therefore lie between the wave-lengths $0{\cdot}4\mu$ and $0{\cdot}75\mu$, or 4,000 AU. and 7,500 AU. It is sometimes convenient to specify waves by their frequency f, rather than by their wave-length, λ :

* See note : 'In Defence of Angstrom' at the end of this chapter.

$$f = \frac{v}{\lambda} = \frac{3 \times 10^8}{\lambda(\text{m.})} \text{ Hz}$$

Colour of Light.—Different wave-lengths within the above visible spectrum give light of different colours, as shown in Fig. 119.

Units of Light

Before any quantitative investigations concerning lighting can be carried out it is necessary to have units in which it can be measured, the most important quantities which have to be speci-

Frequency Hz.	Wave-lengh A.U.	
		Ultra-violet.
$7{\cdot}5 \times 10^{14}$	4,000	
		Violet
		Blue
$6{\cdot}0 \times 10^{14}$	5,000	
		Green
		Yellow
$5{\cdot}0 \times 10^{14}$	6,000	
		Orange
$4{\cdot}3 \times 10^{14}$	7,000	Red
$3{\cdot}75 \times 14^{14}$	8,000	
		Infra-red (heat)

FIG. 119.—WAVE-LENGTH AND COLOUR.

fied being luminous intensity of a source of light, the total quantity of light emitted by a source, and the illumination on a given surface.

Luminous Intensity.—The luminous intensity of a source of light is specified by comparing it to that of a standard lamp. The original standard adopted by Great Britian, France and the U.S.A. was the *standard candle*, made up in accordance with a rigid specification in the same way as a standard cell for e.m.f. measurements: such a source of light, when viewed in a horizontal direction, was said to have a luminous intensity of one *candle-power*. The brightness of other lamps could then be expressed as multiples of this. The term "candle-power" is still used, but the standard is now maintained in terms of carbon-filament vacuum lamps kept at the national laboratories of the above three countries. An ordinary 60-watt lamp as used for domestic lighting will, when viewed from the floor, have a luminous intensity of about 70 candle-power, while a searchlight viewed from along the beam may have a luminous intensity of as much as a million candle-power.

Brightness.—When the source of light covers an appreciable area, as when it is contained in an opal glass bowl or when the observer sees only reflected light as in a cinema screen, the term "brightness" is employed, this being defined as the luminous intensity per unit area and expressed in candles per cm^2. (stilb).

Quantity of Light.—The total quantity of light or luminous flux emitted from a source is expressed in *lumens*, the lumen being defined by stating that the amount of light emitted from a source having a luminous intensity of one candle-power in all directions is 4π lumens. An ordinary 60-watt lamp will have an output of about 700 lumens.

Illumination.—The illumination on a surface is governed by the amount of light or luminous flux falling on that surface and it is therefore measured conveniently in lumens per square metre. Another name for this unit is the lux (lx)=lm m^{-2}.

Further explanations of the above definitions and their applications are given later in the section dealing with lighting calculations, and also see at the end of this chapter regarding all the photometric definitions and formulae.

The most important concepts in illumination engineering are the following :

1. luminous flux	..	unit :	lumen (lm)
2. luminous intensity	..	unit :	Candele (cd)
3. illumination	..	unit :	lux (lx) or lm/m^2
4. luminance	..	unit :	Candela per square meter (cd/m^2)

To make the first three concepts clear in a simple manner, the light source can be compared to a water nozzle.

Then the following analogies will be helpful.

Water analogy		Light unit	Definition
1. Stream of water = quantity of water per second	—>	LUMINOUS FLUX	= quantity of light per second.
2. Jet intensity = intensity of water jet in a particular direction	—>	LUMINOUS INTENSITY	= intensity of luminous flux in a certain direction.
3. Irrigation intensity = quantity of water per square unit of area	—>	ILLUMINATION	= luminous flux per square metre.

Practical Examples of 'Light' UNITS *

1. *Luminous flux-lumen (lm)*

No.	Example	Value
1.	Bicycle lamp (electric)	10 lm
2.	'Argenta' incandescent lamp of 150W	1940 lm
3.	Fluorescent lamp 40W	3 000 lm
4.	Sodium lamp 200W	30 000 lm
5.	Mercury-vapour lamp HPL 1 000W	52 000 lm

2. *Illumination - lm/m² or lux (lx)*

No.	Example	Value
1.	Summer midday, in the open cloudless sky †	100 000 lx
2.	Winter, midday, in the open cloudless sky †	10 000 lx
3.	Summer midday, under a balcony †	2 000 - 5 000 lx
4.	Summer behind a window †	1 000 - 3 000 lx
5.	Sunrise and sunset †	500 lx
6.	Fullmoon and bright sky†	0.25 lx
7.	Living room table under good artifical lighting	200 lx
8.	Office with good artificial lighting	1 000 lx

3. *Luminous Intensity-Candela (cd)*

No.	Example	Value
1.	Bicycle lamp, straight ahead (without reflector)	1 cd
2.	Bicycle lamp, straight ahead (with reflector)	250 cd
3.	Lighthouse light, centre beam	2 000 000 cd

4. *Luminance-cd/cm² or cd/m²*

No.	Example	Value
1.	Sun	165 000 cd/cm²
2.	Moon	0·25 cd/cm²

* From PHILIPS LIGHTING COURSE--Part I, Lesson 3.

† These figures are for Temperate Zones; in tropics the figures will be higher.

3. Filament of an incandescent lamp 700 cd/cm^2
4. Fluorescent lamp (lateral direction)
   0.8 cd/cm^2 or 8 000 cd/m^2
5. Fluorescent lamp (longitudinal direction)
   0.5 cd/cm^2 or 5 000 cd/m^2
6. White paper (reflection factor 80%)
   illumination (400 lux) 100 cd/m^2
7. Grey paper (reflection factor 40%)
   illumination (400 lux) 50 cd/m^2
8. Black paper (reflection factor 4%)
   illumination (400 lux) 5 cd/m^2

Luminous Efficiency and the Eye

So far as human beings are concerned, the existence of light becomes apparent only as a result of the radiant energy of wavelengths of between 4,000 and 7,500 AU. falling upon the eye, which in turn transmits the sensation to the brain. The efficiency of any light source or illumination scheme must therefore be considered in terms of its effect on the human eye.

Sensitivity of the Eye

A diagrammatic section through a human eye is shown in Fig. 120, It can be seen that the rays of light pass through a lens which focuses the image on the retina ; this consists of a

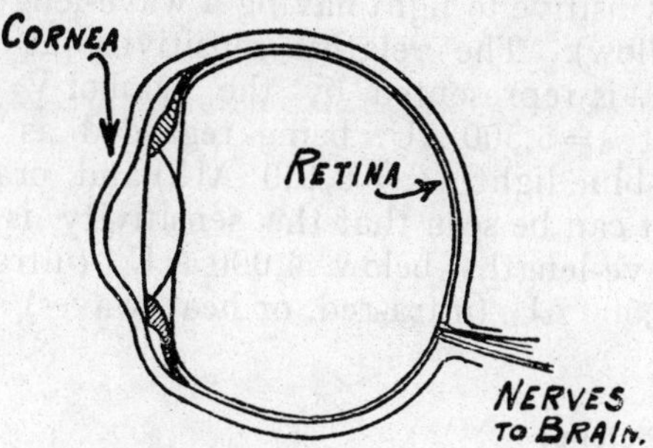

FIG. 120.—THE HUMAN EYE.

very large number of minute cells, each of which is connected by a nerve to the brain. These cells are sensitive to the quantity of light falling on them and to its colour, and transmit this information along the nerve to the brain, which, by combining all these scraps of "information," is enabled to build up complete picture of the view within the field of vision of the eye at any instant.

Sensitivity Curve.—The cells which make up the retina are of two types, the rod cells and the cone cell, the latter being

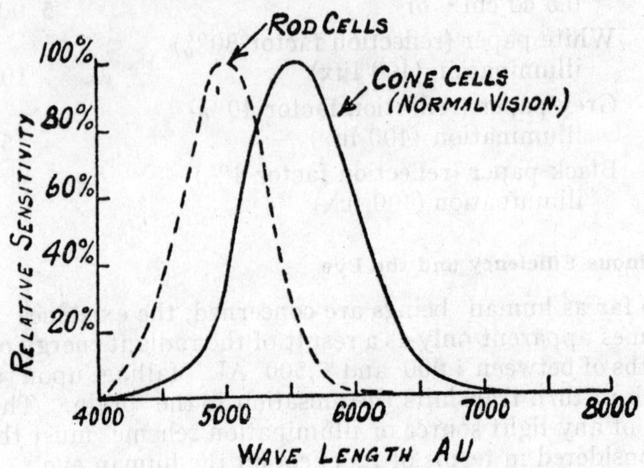

FIG. 121.—SENSITIVITY CURVES OF THE EYE

those in use for normal vision. The relative sensitivity of the cone cells in the average eye to light of various wave-lengths is shown by the full line in Fig. 121. This curve indicates that the eye is most sensitive to light having a wave-length of 5,500 AU. (greenish yellow). The relative sensitivity at any particular wave-length λ is represented by the symbol V_λ the maximum sensitivity at $\lambda = 5{,}500$ AU. being regarded as 100 per cent.; for greenish-blue light (λ = 8,100 AU.) and orange light (λ = 6,100 AU.) it can be seen that the sensitivity is 50 per cent., while for wave-lengths below 4,000 A.U. (ultra-violet waves) and above 7,500 AU. (infra-red, or heat waves) it is, of course, zero.

Luminous Efficiency

If an electric lamp were to transform the whole of its electrical input into radiant energy at a wave-length of 5,500 A.U. and this were observed under normal conditions of vision, it would produce 621 lumens per watt, and this is the maximum possible luminous efficiency which could be obtained from a light source. If the whole of the electrical input were converted into radiant energy of some other wave-length λ for which the eye has a sensitivity V_λ, the luminous efficiency would be $621 \times V_\lambda$ lumens per watt. Even if it were possible, however, to convert the whole of the electrical input into radiant energy of a wave-length of 5,500 AU., the light obtained would not be satisfactory on account of its colour.

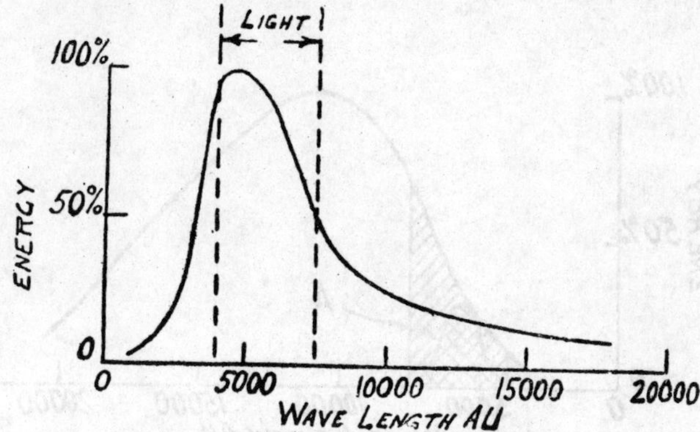

FIG. 122.—SPECIAL-DISTRIBUTION CURVE OF TYPICAL SUNLIGHT.

The ideal to be aimed at in the majority of lighting schemes is to produce a light which is similar to ordinary sunlight. This contains energy at all the wave-lengths within the visible spectrum and many beyond it, the relative amount of energy transmitted by each being shown by the curve in Fig. 122; such a curve is known as a spectral-distribution curve. The ultra-violet rays and heat rays shown on the diagram do not, however, directly concern the lighting engineer, who merely wishes to simulate those emitted between the wave-lengths of 4,000 and 7,500 A.U.

If E_λ is the energy radiated on a wave length λ and V_λ is the sensitivity of the eye to that wave-length (Fig. 121), then the light produced by this energy E_λ will be $621 V_\lambda E\lambda$ lumens. The total light emitted on all the wave-lengths between λ_1 and λ_2, the limits of the visible spectrum, will therefore be:

$$621 \int_{\lambda_1}^{\lambda_2} V_\lambda E_\lambda d\lambda \text{ lumens}$$

The total energy radiated will be the sum of the energy radiated on all wave-lengths, i.e.:

$$\int_0^\infty E_\lambda d\lambda \text{ watts}$$

so that the luminious efficiency will be :

$$\frac{621\int_{\lambda_1}^{\lambda_2} V_\lambda E_\lambda d\lambda}{\int_0^\infty E_\lambda d\lambda} \text{ lumens per watt} \quad . \quad . \quad (44)$$

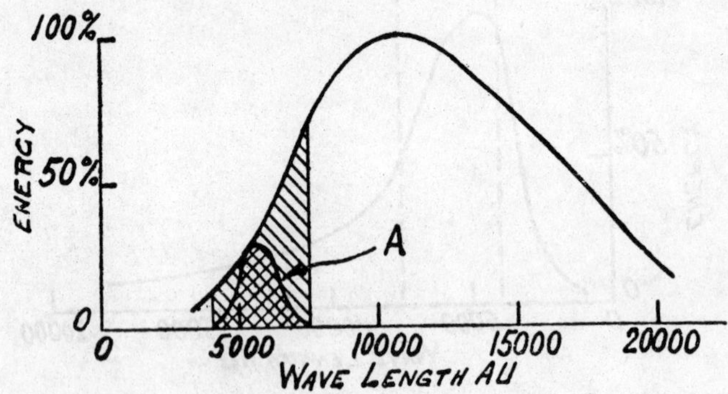

FIG. 123.—SPECTRAL-DISTRIBUTION CURVE OF TUNGSTEN-FILAMENT LAMP.

A curve showing the energy radiated at various wave-lengths by an ordinary metal-filament lamp is shown in Fig. 123. The singly hatched area represents the energy radiated within the visible spectrum, i.e. it is $\int_{\lambda_1}^{\lambda_2} E_\lambda d\lambda$ watts. Multiplying each ordinate by V_λ gives the curve A, which represents the effect of this energy on the eye, and the area under this curve (doubly hatched) represents the energy converted to light, i.e. $\int_{\lambda_1}^{\lambda_2} V_\lambda E_\lambda d\lambda$ watts. The total energy emitted, $\int_0^\infty E_\lambda d\lambda$, is the total area under the energy-radiated curve, and 621 times the ratio of the former to this represents the luminous efficiency. It can be seen to be very low, chiefly on account of the large amount of heat energy radiated; in this type of lamp it does not usually exceed 10 to 15 lumens per watt.

If it were possible to obtain a light source which emitted no energy outside the visible spectrum and which emitted, on each wave-length within that range an amount of energy proportional to that emitted by sunlight, then the luminous efficiency would be

$$\frac{621\int_{\lambda_1}^{\lambda_2} V_\lambda E_\lambda d\lambda}{\int_{\lambda_1}^{\lambda_2} E_\lambda d\lambda} \text{ lumens per watt} \quad . \quad . \quad (45)$$

Putting in the appropriate values of V_λ and E_λ from Figs. 121 and 122 and evaluating the integral gives a figure of 220 lumens per watt. This is the maximum possible efficiency which could be obtained from a lamp which gave a light similar to sunlight and at the same time emitted no energy at wave lengths outside the limits of the visible spectrum.

The Purkinge Effect

It was mentioned on page 278 that in normal circumstances vision takes place due to the action of the cone cells of the retina, and the visibility curve of these cells was given. In very poor lights, such as moonlight or street lighting, where the brightness of objects is below about 1·07 lux., vision takes place due to the action of the rod cells of the retina, and these have a sensitivity as shown by the dotted curve in Fig. 121. It is seen that under these conditions the eye has a maximum sensitivity at about 5,000 AU. and the visibility is zero above about 6,000 AU. This effect, known as the Purkinge effect, is of particular importance in connection with street-lighting schemes.

Glare

If the eye is exposed to a very bright source of light the pupil, or opening of the eye, contracts in order to reduce the amount of light admitted and prevent damage to the retina; this reduces the sensitivity, so that other objects within the field of vision can be only imperfectly seen. This phenomenon is known as glare and is familiar in connection with motor-car headlights.

It is not possible to lay down any hard-and-fast rules as to what constitutes a glaring source of light, as it depends on so many factors. For instance, a candle viewed at close range in a completely dark room may appear glaring, whereas a 100-watt lamp can be looked at in a brightly lighted restaurant without any discomfort. For normal interior decorations a light source having a luminous intensity of more than about 46 500 Cd/m^2 ($=4{\cdot}65$ candles/cm^2) candles per sq. *cm* generally produces glare. The actual measurement of reduction in visibility due to glare is also a matter of difficulty on account of the large number of variables; experiments indicate, however, that the reduction in visibility, or ability to perceive contrasts, is proportional to $\frac{I}{d^2\theta^{3/2}}$, the symbols referring to Fig. 124. It is considered that any source of artificial light less than 5m from the floor shall not have a brightness of more than 15 500 cd/m^2 if it is visible from any point within 30·0 m of it, except where the angle of elevation from the eye to the source exceeds 20°.

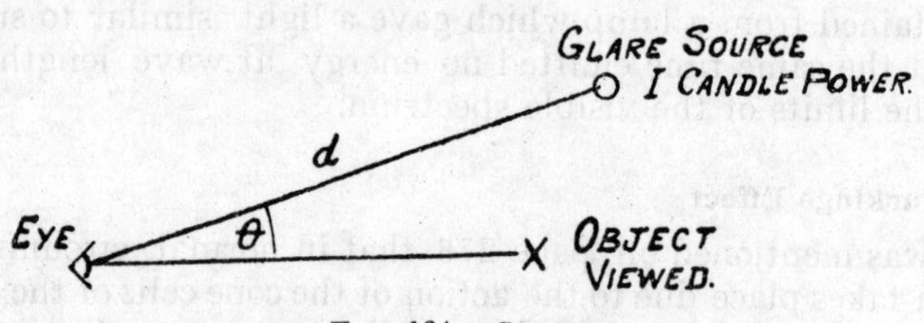

FIG. 124.—GLARE.

2. PRODUCTION OF LIGHT

The electro-magnetic ether waves having a long wave-length, and therefore a relatively low frequency, such as are used in radio broadcasting, are produced by the oscillation of electric charges in a transmitting aerial. The very high-frequency light waves can, however, be produced only by some disturbance or oscillation within the atoms themselves, so that the study of light production is closely bound up with that of the structure of the atom.

Excitation and Ionisation

All atoms consist of a positive nucleus with one or more electrons travelling round it in certain well-defined orbits. In any gas or solid, however, there are also a number of free electrons which are not attached to any atom. If, therefore, two electrodes are placed in a gas and a potential difference applied between them these free electrons will be attracted towards the positive electrode and will travel towards it with a velocity depending on the potential gradient; each electron will acquire a certain kinetic energy, which can be calculated by applying the ordinary laws of dynamics and electrostatics.

Thus we have:

$$\begin{aligned}\text{Electric field strength at any point} &= X \\ &= \text{potential gradient} \\ &= \frac{V}{x} \text{ volts per metre}\end{aligned}$$

where V is the difference in potential in volts, giving a uniform gradient over the distance x.

Force on an electron $= \frac{e \cdot V}{x}$ N, where $e =$ charge on an electron ($1 \cdot 601 \times 10^{-19}$ coulomb).

Work done in travelling through a distance x

$$= e \cdot V \text{ J}$$

$$= \text{kinetic energy acquired.}$$

If the electron travels between two points having a difference of potential of 1 volt, the kinetic energy acquired is therefore:

$$1 \times 1 \cdot 601 \times 10^{-19} \text{ J}$$

For convenience this quantity of energy is called the electron-volt, or sometimes simply a volt.

In travelling between the electrodes the electron will come into contact with the atoms of the gas, and on doing this one of three things may happen, depending on the kinetic energy of the colliding electron.

(i) *Elastic Collision.*—If the kinetic energy is small, the electron will simply bounce off the atom and travel on its way with practically no change in its velocity.

(ii) *Excitation.*—If the kinetic energy of the colliding electron is above a critical value caused by its falling through a certain potential, known as the excitation potential, the collision will be so violent as to cause one of the electrons of the atom to jump from its normal orbit into one of the other orbits. In the case of sodium vapour this will occur if the electron has a kinetic energy of 2·1 electron-volts. This amount of energy passes from the electron to the atom, and the latter is then said to be in an excited state. If the colliding electron had, say, 2·5 electron-volts of energy, 2·1 of these would be used in raising the atom to the excited state, while the electron would continue on its way with a velocity corresponding to an energy of 2·5—2·1 = 0·4 electron-volt. If, however, the colliding electron had a kinetic energy of 3·18 electron-volts, the whole of this would be used in raising the atom to its second excited state. Higher potentials will cause the atoms to be raised to third and fourth or higher excited states.

(iii) *Ionisation*—If the kinetic energy is sufficiently high it will cause an electron to be completely expelled from the atom. This new free electron will then move towards the positive electrode and produce more collisions and more free electrons, so that the process is cumulative, resulting in the passage of a heavy current, and in what is known as an electric arc. This process is known as ionisation, and the potential through which the electrons must fall in order to acquire the requisite amount of energy to produce ionisation is known as the ionisation potential. In the case of sodium vapour it is 5·12 volts.

Light Production by Excitation

When the atom is excited as described above, it normally remains in the excited state for about 10^{-8} s. After this time it returns to its normal state or to a lower excited state, and the difference in energy between the two states is given up and appears as radiation of a certain definite wave-length.

The frequency of the radiation is given by:

$$= \frac{\text{kinetic energy emitted (J)}}{h}$$

where h is a constant (Planck's constant), and is the same for all gases being equal to $6{\cdot}6256 \times 10^{-34}$ Js.

We have seen that the kinetic energy is:

$$k{\cdot}e = \text{V} \times 1{\cdot}6 \times 10^{-19}$$

$$\text{so that } f = \text{V} \times 2{\cdot}414 \times 10^{14} \text{ Hz.}$$

The wave-length λ is therefore:

$$\lambda = \frac{v}{f} = \frac{3 \times 10^8}{\text{V}.\ 2{\cdot}43 \times 10^{12}} = \frac{1{\cdot}2336}{\text{V}} 10^{-6}\text{m} = \frac{1{\cdot}2336}{\text{V}}\ 10^{-4} \text{ cm}$$

$$= \frac{12336}{\text{V}} \text{ AU.}$$

In the case of sodium in its first excited state, the energy given up in returning to normal corresponds to 2·1 electron-volts, and the wave-length emitted is $\frac{12336}{2{\cdot}1} = 5890$ AU.: this is a yellow light (actually two wave-lengths are emitted, namely, 5,890 and 5,896 AU.). When sodium is in its second excited state, corresponding to an excitation potential of 3·18 volt, the only change which can take place is to the first excited state, and the energy given up therefore corresponds to a potential of $3{\cdot}18 - 2{\cdot}1 = 1{\cdot}08$ volt, and the wave-length emitted is:

$$\frac{12336}{1{\cdot}08} = 11404 \text{ AU. or } 1140{\cdot}4 \text{ nm.}$$

(Actually, lines of wave-length 11,382 also are emitted.)

It may be noted that these are beyond the visible spectrum, and are therefore of no value so far as light production is concerned.

These transitions are illustrated in the diagram of Fig. 125,

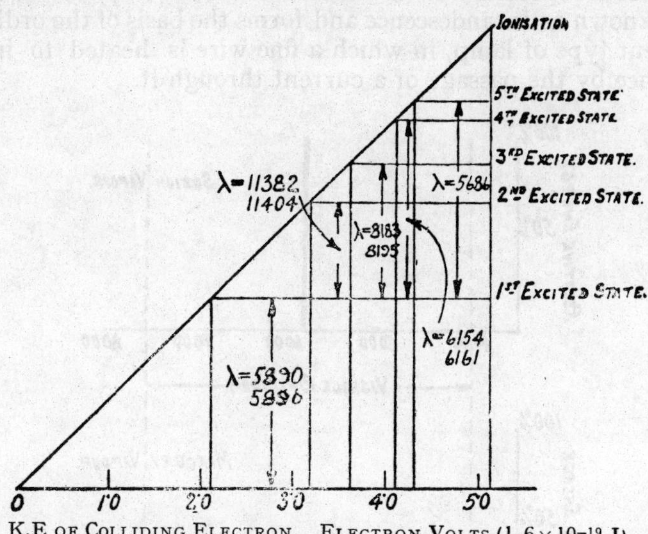

FIG. 125 —EXCITED STATES AND WAVE-LENGTHS EMITTED BY SODIUM VAPOUR.

which shows the chief excited states or energy levels in which a sodium atom may exist; the vertical lines with arrowheads represent the energy transferences which may occur and the wevelengths emitted. The relative amounts of energy emitted at the various wave-lengths depend on the potential between the electrodes and the temperature and pressure in the tube; for sodium vapour and mercury vapour under the conditions used in electric discharge lamps these are shown in Fig. 126.

Incandescence.—The above process occurs in gases and vapours at low pressures; as the pressure is increased the conditions become more complicated owing to the relative closeness of the atoms, which prevents the oscillations which take place during the various energy transfers from occurring freely. The law governing the wave-length of radiation emitted therefore ceases to hold accurately, and a band of wave-lengths is emitted instead of one single wave-length; as the pressure is increased further these bands tend to get wider, and they ultimately stretch over the entire spectrum, resulting in a continuous spectrum with, probably, the characteristic wave-lengths of the gas in question superimposed on it.

With solids, where the atoms are very closely spaced, a true continuous spectrum is always obtained; the phenomenon is then known as incandescence and forms the basis of the ordinary filament type of lamp, in which a fine wire is heated to incandescence by the passage of a current through it.

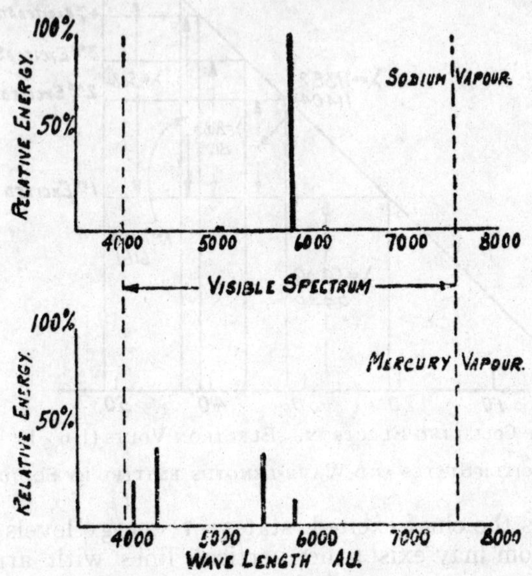

FIG. 126.—SPECTRAL-DISTRIBUTION CURVES OF SODIUM-VAPOUR AND MERCURY-VAPOUR LAMPS OF EQUAL WATTAGE.

Electric-discharge Lamps

Although the electric arc in air was the first type of electric lamp to be used, it possessed certain disadvantages and was almost entirely replaced by the metal-filament incandescent lamp; in recent years, however, as a result of rapid advances which have been made in the study of electron physics, attention has again been devoted to the production of light by excitation and ionisation processes, and new types of lamp have been developed based on these phenomena, which, for certain purposes, possess advantages over the filament lamp.

Gases and Vapours Available.—The discharge in sodium vapour has been described above as an illustration of the process of light production, but other gases and vapours can also be used. These will have different excitation potentials and energy levels in their excited states, and will therefore produce radiations of different wave-lengths, i.e. will give light of different colours. The number of such gases which are of practical use is limited, and some of the more important or more promising are listed in Table XVIII.

TABLE XVIII

Gas or vapour	Colour	Theoretical efficiency, lumens/watt.	Actual efficiency, lumens/watt.
Sodium vapour	Yellow	475	40 —50
Mercury vapour, low-pressure	Blue-green	248	15 —20
Mercury vapour, high-pressure	Blue-white	298	20 —30
Neon	Red	198	15 —40
Helium	Yellow-white	—	4 —10
Carbon dioxide	White	—	2 — 4
Cadmium vapour	Blue	—	0·5— 1
Tungsten-filament lamp ..	White	143	10 —20

The ordinary tungsten-filament lamp has been included for comparison, and it is seen that only sodium vapour, mercury vapour, and neon have efficiencies which are in excess of that of the filament lamp, and it is only these, therefore, which are likely to be of value for general illumination purposes; of these three, neon is, of course, suitable only for advertising purposes on account of its colour. Some of the other gases in the table are also suitable for this purpose.

The application of sodium and mercury vapours is limited on account of their colours, and it may be thought that a mixture of gases, say, mercury vapour which is deficient in red light, and neon, in which red light preponderates, might be used to give a light approximating to daylight in colour. Such a procedure is not usually possible, however, since practically all the excitation will occur in the gas having the lower excitation potential, and the colour corresponding to this gas will preponderate.

Another phenomenon which prevents the practical use of certain gases is the general absorption of the gas into the cathode, a process known as cleaning up, which, limits the life of the lamp. Carbon dioxide presents this difficulty in addition to its having a low efficiency.

Stabilising Chokes.—As the discharge has a negative characteristic, i.e. the resistance falls with an increase of current, either a resistance or a reactance must be included in series with it to give stability. A reactive choke is generally employed, as it occasions little loss; it does, however, reduce the power factor to 0.5 or 0.6, and a condenser must often be added to improve it to 0.9 or unity, as shown in Fig. 127.

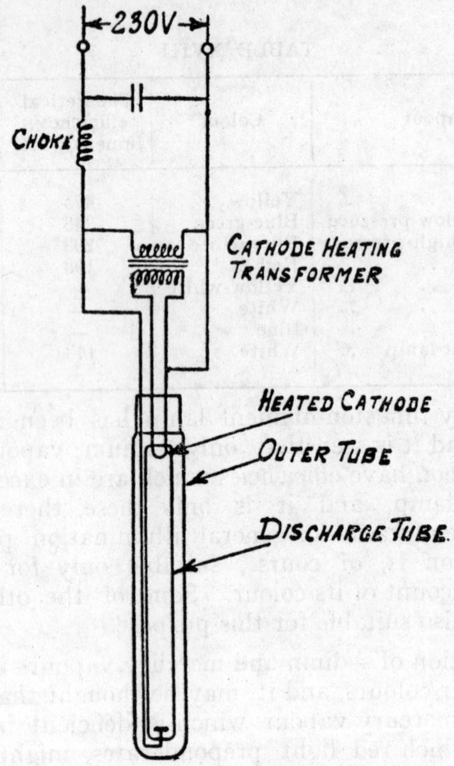

FIG. 127.—SODIUM-VAPOUR LAMP.

Hot- and Cold-cathode Lamps.—To start and maintain the discharge, electrons must be emitted from the cathode. In the cold-cathode type of lamp a high voltage is applied between the electrodes, a large proportion of which (100 to 200 V.) occurs as voltage drop at the cathode surface, and is sufficient to extract the required number of electrons from it. This high voltage drop causes a high acceleration of the positive ions in the immediate neighbourhood of the cathode, so that they bombard it with considerable force and tend to cause disintegration or sputtering. To ensure a reasonably long cathode life, the current must therefore be kept low and, on account of the negative resistance characteristic of the discharge, this results in a relatively high resistance for the luminous column and a correspondingly high voltage drop along it. For a neon lamp, which is the most common example of a cold-cathode lamp, a voltage drop of 984 to 1312 per metre is usual, so that several thousand volts may be required for long tubular lamps such as are used for advertising purposes. For starting the discharge a voltage of 1.5 or 2 times the normal operating value is required, and the supply is generally given through a transformer having a high leakage reactance.

To eliminate the use of a high voltage and allow of the construction of lamps suitable for operation direct from ordinary 230-V. circuits, hot cathodes are employed, which emit electrons with a drop of only a few volts. Considerably heavier currents may be carried, since there is less danger of cathode disintegration, and the drop in the luminous column is therefore also very much reduced. The cathode may consist of a heated filament, similar to that in the ordinary radio valve, or it may be maintained in the incandescent state by ionic bombardment. The heated filament is used in certain low-voltage neon lamps, and also in the sodium-vapour lamp, while in the mercury lamp the heavy positive ions can produce sufficient heat by bombardment.

The Sodium-vapour Lamp.—It has already been seen that of the various gases and vapours available, sodium vapour possesses the highest theoretical efficiency, and the sodium-vapour lamp was the first of the modern discharge lamps to be developed on a practical scale. The two electrodes are mounted in a glass tube or bulb, the glass of which is of special composition in order to resist the action of the hot vapour. Best operating conditions and efficiency are obtained when the tube is at a temperature of about 300°C., and in order to maintain this temperature and reduce loss of heat the discharge tube itself is placed in an evacuated outer tube, as shown in Fig. 127. A small transformer is included in the circuit for heating the cathode and a choke for stabilising the discharge. When the lamp is cold the amount of sodium vapour present is negligible, and in order that the discharge shall be self-starting when the lamp is switched on, a small quantity of one of the rare gases, such as neon or argon, is introduced ; after a few minutes the heat of the discharge through this gas is sufficient to vaporise the sodium, and the lamp then commences normal operation and emits its characteristic yellow light. The relative amounts of energy emitted by the lamp in its normal operation on the various wave-lengths are shown in Fig. 126, from which it is seen that almost all the energy is radiated at a wave-length of 5,980 AU. The sensitivity of the eye at this wave-length is 0.765, so that if all the energy were radiated at this wave-length the luminous efficiency would be $621 \times 0.765 = 475$ lumens per watt. Actually, owing to energy radiated on other wave-lengths and to losses in the choke coil and heated cathode, as well as heat loss from the tube surface, the efficiency of a sodium-vapour lamp under practical conditions is between 40 and 50 lumens per watt.

The Mercury-vapour Lamp.—The mercury-vapour lamp is similar in construction to the sodium-vapour lamp in that the discharge takes place in an inner tube enclosed in an outer evacuated tube in order to maintain the correct temperature

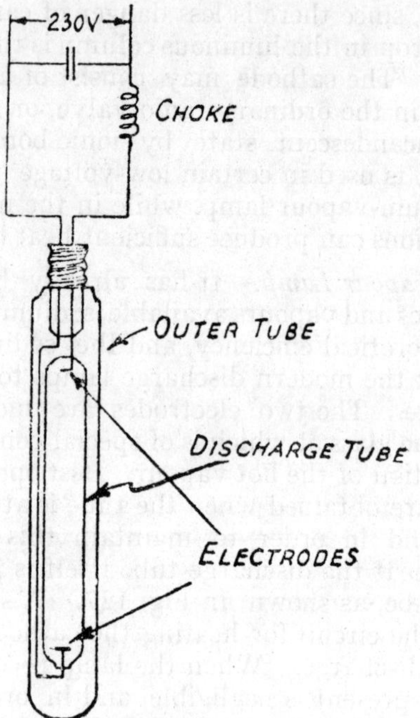

FIG. 128.—MERCURY-VAPOUR LAMP.

conditions. As previously mentioned, however, the cathode is maintained in an incandescent state by ionic bombardment, and no heating circuit is necessary. Mercury-vapour lamps have been in use for many years, but the early designs operated at a pressure of 0·01 to 0·001 mm. of mercury, and gave a blue light and a high porportion of ulra-violet rays, so that although used in a few cases for illumination purposes, they were far from satisfactory. Later developments led to the use of higher pressures (1 to 2 atmospheres), which although still giving a light with a bluish tinge, as shown by the spectral distribution curve of Fig. 126, are satisfactory for many purposes and are widely used for outdoor lighting and sometimes for industrial lighting. As with the sodium-vapour lamp, neon or argon is introduced into the tube for starting; should the lamp go out while in service it will not restart until it has cooled and the vapour pressure fallen to a value sufficiently low to allow restriking of the discharge in the neon or argon to take place. A diagram of a mercury-vapour lamp with its connections is shown in Fig. 128; such lamps are made in sizes of 250 watts and upwards and have a luminous efficiency of 30 to 40 lumens per watt.

To improve the colour of the lamp a dual arrangement is employed by one manufacturer, in which an ordinary filament lamp is contained in the same bulb as the discharge lamp. The filament is connected in series with the discharge lamp and takes the place of the stabilising choke mentioned previously.

Fluorescent Lamps

The low-pressure mercury discharge emits a considerable amount of radiation at about 2,500 AU., while the high-pressure discharge emits a considerable amount at about 3,650 AU., both of these emissions being in the ultra-violet part of the spectrum and therefore of no direct use as a source of light. Such radiations can, however, be used to excite certain materials, the important feature of these materials being that when the excited molecules return to normal they emit a radiation at a frequency different from that which caused the excitation—the radiation emitted by the materials may, in fact, be within the visible spectrum so that the ultra-violet radiations are converted to light. Materials which possess this property are said to be *fluorescent*; if the radiation from the material persists for some time after the removal of the exciting radiation, the material is said to be *phosphorescent*.

A lamp embodying this principle consists, therefore, of a tube in which takes place a mercury discharge as in the discharge lamp already described; the tube is, however, coated on the inside with a fluorescent material in the form of a powder which is excited by the ultra-violet radiation of the discharge and emits light. Various different fluorescent powders are available and give light of different colours, while by mixing the powders light of any desired colour, including daylight, can be obtained. Some of the commonly used powders are shown in Table XIX. All are excited by radiations having wave-lengths between 2,200 and 3,600 AU.

TABLE XIX

FLUORESCENT POWDERS

powder	Wavelength of maximum emitted radiation. (AU)	Colour.
Calcium tungstate ..	4,400	Blue
Magnesium tungstate ..	4,800	Blue-white
Zinc silicate ..	5,250	Green
Zine beryllium silicate ..	5,950	Yellow-white
Cadmium silicate ..	5,950	Yellow-pink
Cadmium borate ..	6,150	Pink

The first fluorescent lamps to be introduced employed the high-pressure discharge, and were similar in construction to the ordinary discharge lamp, except that the fluorescent powder was coated on the inside of the outer tube and this tube was made larger in order to keep it cool. In these lamps (made in 400-, 250-, and 80-watt sizes), the light from the fluorescent powder supplemented that produced by the main discharge.

In the more recent and more common type of fluorescent lamp a low-pressure discharge is used, and the lamps are made in the form of tubes 25·0 mm to 38·0 mm diameter and 60 to 150 cm. long, with an electrode at each end. The powder is coated on the inside of the tube, and as the operating temperature is only about 50° C. no outer envelope is necessary as with the other types of discharge lamp. The electrodes consist of coiled filaments coated with an electron-emitting material.

As with other types of discharge lamp, a stabilising choke must be used in series with it, and a capacitor is desirable to counteract the lagging power factor caused by this choke. A small capacitor (0·05μF) to suppress radio interference is connected in parallel with the lamp, as shown in the connection diagram of Fig. 129.

At starting, a switch short-circuits the lamp and allows current to flow through the two electrodes and the choke in series; after about two seconds the switch automatically opens, causing a voltage surge large enough to strike the arc between the electrodes, the arc being then maintained by the normal lamp voltage. Bombardment of the electrode surfaces by the positive mercury ions maintains their temperature so that they continue to emit electrons. The automatic switch may consist

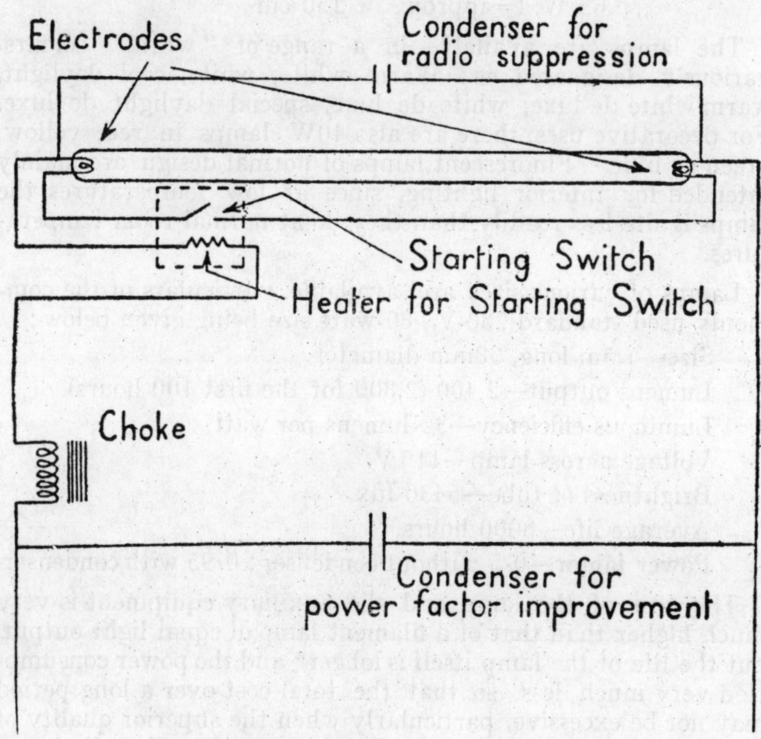

FIG. 129.—FLUORESCENT LAMP CIRCUIT.

of a bimetallic strip heated by a small heating element, as shown in Fig. 129, or it may be a glow-starter switch consisting of two bimetallic electrodes in a helium-filled bulb; a glow discharge takes place between the electrodes, which heats them and causes them to deflect and close two contacts in the starter circuit; closing the contacts extinguishes the glow and the contacts open again, causing the voltage surge to start the lamp discharge.

Fluorescent Lamps of Normal Design :

The most frequently used fluorescent lamps are straight, tubular lamps with a diameter of 38 mm. The length is dependent on the wattage:

for	20 W, l=approx.	60 cm
,,	40 W, l=approx.	120 cm
,,	65 W, l=approx.	150 cm

The lamps are available in a range of "white" colours, variously designated as: Warm white, white, cool daylight, warm white de luxe, white de luxe, special daylight de luxe. For decorative uses, there are also 40W lamps in red, yellow, green or blue. Fluorescent lamps of normal design are mainly intended for interior lighting, since at low temperatures the lamps ignite less readily than they do at normal room temperatures.

Lamps of various sizes are available, particulars of the commonly used standard 230-V., 80-watt size being given below:

Size—1.5m long, 38mm diameter.

Lumens output—2,400 (2,800 for the first 100 hours).

Luminous efficiency—30 lumens per watt.

Voltage across lamp—115 V.

Brightness of tube—5430 lux.

Average life—5000 hours.

Power factor—0·5 without condenser; 0·95 with condenser.

The cost of the lamp and the auxiliary equipment is very much higher than that of a filament lamp of equal light output, but the life of the lamp itself is longer* and the power consumption very much less, so that the total cost over a long period may not be excessive, particularly when the superior quality of the light is taken into account. In common with other discharge lamps, the fluorescent lamp takes a non-sinusoidal current from the supply on account of the characteristics of the discharge; the harmonic content of the current is 5 to 10 per cent.

A summary of the most important gas-discharge lamps is given at the end of this chapter.

Ultra-violet Lamps

The ultra-violet radiations of the mercury arc have themselves a number of uses, such as for destroying bacteria

* about 5000 burning hours compared to 1000 for an incandescent lamp.

(radiations below 2,800 AU.), for producing artificial sunlight (2,400-3,000 AU.), and for various industrial purposes. Special types of discharge lamp are in use for these purposes, and also for producing "black light" for activating fluorescent or phosphorescent paints for decorative purposes.

The Arc Lamp

If the discharge is allowed to take place in the atmosphere instead of in the controlled conditions of the discharge tube, ionisation takes place with the production of a very intense light and a considerable amount of ultra-violet radiation. For the production of ultr-violet radiation the arc lamp has been superseded by the ultra-violet lamps mentioned above, but where a high-intensity light source is required, as for search-lights and cinema projectors, it is still the most suitable source available.

Carbon electrodes are employed, and nearly all the light emanates from the tip of the positive carbon (the positive crater), which reaches a temperature of 3,500 to 4,000°C. and a brightness of 100 to 200 candles per sq. mm. With special electrodes brightnesses up to 2,000 candles per sq. mm. can be obtained.

Direct current gives a more stable arc than alternating current, and also a more concentrated light source, since there is then only one positive crater. A resistance must be used for stabilising the arc, and this leads to a low overall luminous efficiency. Except in small lamps, an automatic device must be provided for feeding the carbons into the arc as they burn away.

Filament Lamps

The filament lamp employs a fine carbon or metal filament maintained at white heat by the passage of a current and, as previously explained, emits a continuous spectrum. Such lamps are in common daily use, and their construction is therefore quite familiar.

Black-body Radiation.—It has been proved by Kirchhoff that a black body is the most efficient radiator available, since it will emit energy at every wave-length. If such a body is heated to 6,250°C. it will have a spectral distribution curve as shown in Fig. 130, and it can be seen that it emits its maximum energy within the visible spectrum; if it is heated to any other temperature, either higher or lower, the peak of the curve will be moved towards the left or right, and it would be less efficient as a light source. In practice it is not possible to realise a perfect black body, but the materials used for lamp filaments approach it very closely. With no substance, however, is it possible to approach the temperature of 6,250°C., and the gradual improvements which have been made in filament lamps since their invention by Swan in this country and Edison in America in 1879 have been due to a gradual raising of the temperature at which the filament could

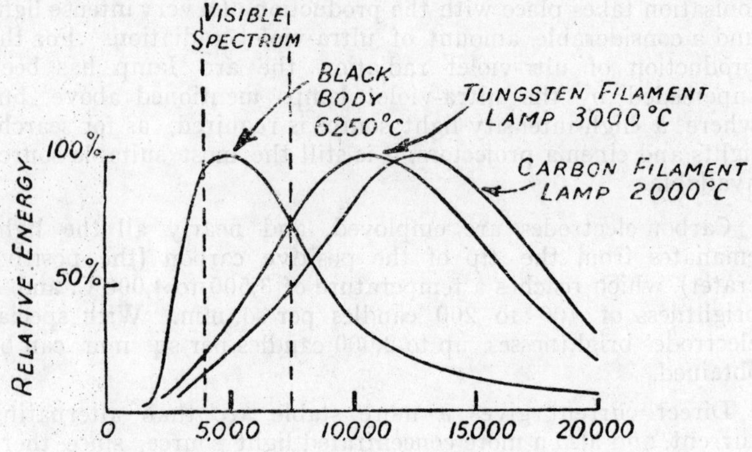

FIG. 130—SPECTRAL-DISTRIBUTION CURVES

be operated without causing it to deteriorate. The early carbon-filament lamps operated at a temperature of about 2,000°C. and gave a spectral distribution curve as shown in Fig. 130; their luminous efficiency was only 2 or 3 lumens per watt. By using a metal filament running in a vacuum, the operating temperature could be raised to about 2,500°C. and 8 to 10 lumens per watt obtained.

The Tungsten-filament Lamp.—The next step was the use of tungsten as a filament material, and the introduction of an inert gas at about atmospheric pressure into the bulb. Tungsten has a high melting-point (3,500°C.) and a low rate of evaporation, so that in modern types of lamp it can be run at a temperature within 200° or 300°C. of its melting-point. Since the introduction of the gas-filled tungsten lamp slight improvements have been made in the design of the filament, such as the use of a coiled or helical filament instead of a straight wire, and finally a coiled-coil filament, in which the single helix is coiled again on itself, as shown in Fig. 131. The luminous efficiencies obtainable from modern lamps are shown in Table XX.

FIG. 131.—COILED-COIL FILAMENT

TABLE XX

LUMINOUS EFFICIENCIES OF 230-V FILAMENT LAMPS

Rating (watts)	40*	60*	100*	200	300	500	1,000	1,500
Total lumens	415	700	1,340	2,880	4,650	8,410	18,900	30,100
Lumens per watt	10·3	11·7	13·4	14·4	15·5	16·8	18·9	20

*Coiled-coil.

N.B.—The efficiencies of 100-V. lamps are 10 to 20 per cent. higher than the above.

Polar Curves

None of the practical types of lamp emits its light uniformly in all directions on account of its unsymmetrical shape, and in

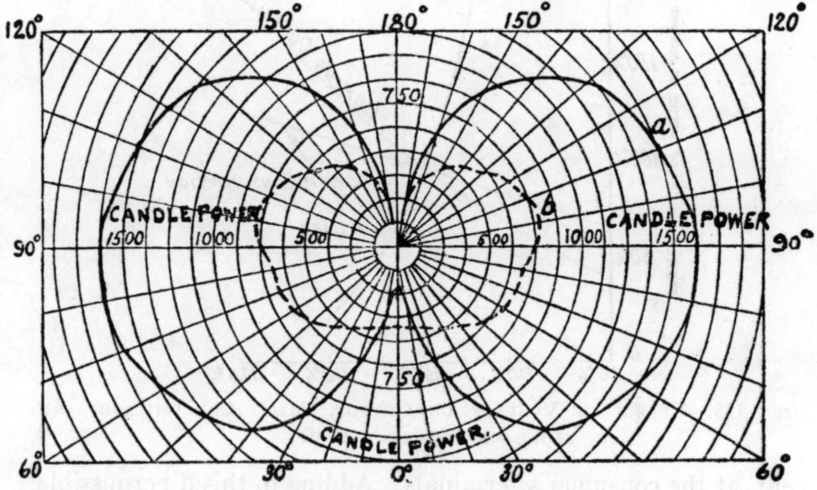

FIG. 132.—TYPICAL POLAR CURVES.
(*a*) 400-watt mercury-vapour lamp. (*b*) 500-watt tungsten-filament lamp.

designing any lighting installation it is essential to know exactly how the light is distributed. This information is usually given in the form of polar curves, as shown in Fig. 132. A radial ordinate pointing in any particular direction on such a diagram represents the candle-power of the lamp when viewed from that particular direction. The curves are usually drawn to represent the light distribution in a vertical or horizontal plane through the lamp. If a horizontal plane through the filament is considered and the average value of all the candle-power ordinates found, a figure known as the *mean horizontal candle-power* (m.h.c.p) is obtained. The average value of all the ordinates, taken in all directions, is known as the *mean spherical candle-power*. The ratio $\frac{\text{m.s.c.p.}}{\text{m.h.c.p.}}$ is known as the *spherical reduction factor*.

Effect of Voltage Variation

Although supply voltages are nominally constant, the Electricity Commissioners Regulations permit a variation of ± 6 per

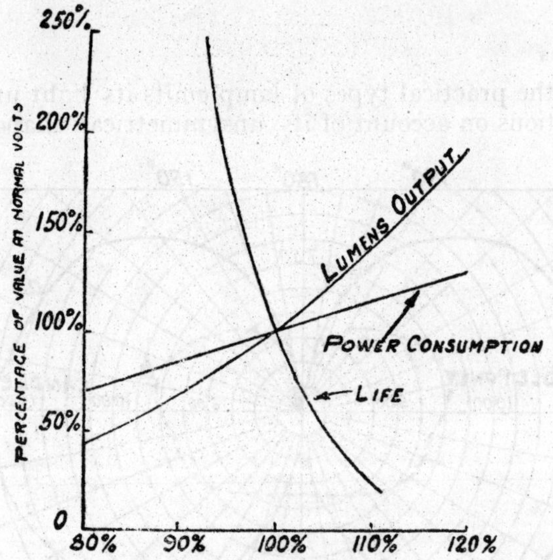

FIG—133.—EFFECT OF VOLTAGE ON OUTPUT, POWER CONSUMPTION, AND LIFE OF FILAMENT LAMPS.

cent. at the consumer's terminals. Adding to this a permissible drop of $2\frac{1}{2}$ per cent. in the consumer's wiring, a voltage variation of between + 6 per cent. and $-8\frac{1}{2}$ per cent. may occur. On a 230-V. circuit this amounts to a variation of between 212 and 244V. The effect of a voltage variation on the output and life of a typical 100-watt filament lamp is shown in Fig. 133. The life of a discharge lamp is not appreciably affected by voltage, but the output varies only slightly less than that of a filament lamp. If however, the voltage drops to 20 or 25V. below normal, there may be difficulty in starting the lamp, or if already alight it may be extinguished.

3. DISTRIBUTION AND CONTROL OF LIGHT

With most light sources it is desirable to use some additional equipment to direct the whole of the light output on to the surface to be illuminated, to diffuse the light in order to prevent glare or to change its colour.

Four general methods of light control are available:

Reflection.—For changing the direction of light through a large angle.

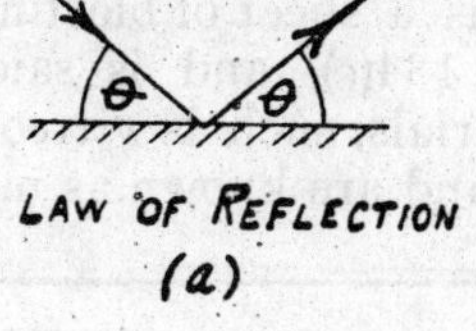

FIG. 134.—REFLECTION.

Refraction.—For changing the direction of light through a small angle.

Diffusion.—For scattering the rays in order to prevent glare.

Absorption.—For absorbing rays of certain wave-lengths in order to change the colour of light.

In many cases the fittings employed combine two or more of the above functions.

Reflection

When a ray of light impinges on a surface it is reflected from the surface at an angle equal to the angle of incidence, as shown in Fig. 134 (*a*). A certain proportion of the incident light will be absorbed by the surface, and the ratio $\frac{\text{reflected light}}{\text{incident light}}$

is known as the reflection factor, typical values of which are shown in Table XXI for various common surfaces.

TABLE XXI
REFLECTION FACTORS

	Per cent.
Silvered glass	80—85
Stainless steel	55—60
Chromium plate	55—60
Vitreous enamel	60—70

Specular and Diffuse Reflection.—If the reflecting surface is smooth like a mirror, all the light will be reflected at an angle equal to that at which it approaches, as shown in Fig. 134(*b*), and such reflection is known as specular reflection; a rough or matt surface, however, such as a sheet of blotting paper, will reflect light as shown in Fig. 134(*c*), and is said to exhibit diffuse reflection. Certain materials, such as vitreous enamel, exhibit both forms of reflection and are known as mixed reflectors.

FIG. 135.—PARABOLIC REFLECTOR.

Materials.—Of the various reflecting media available and listed in Table XXI, silvered glass gives the highest reflection factor, and nearly all the light is reflected specularly; such reflectors are therefore desirable when very accurate control of light is required, but they are expensive and fragile. For ordinary commercial use one of the other materials, usually vitreous enamel or even a cheaper ordinary enamel, is generally employed.

Reflector Contours.—The parabolic reflector shown in Fig. 135, which produces a parallel beam, is an interesting example of the principles of accurate light control by reflection. Such reflectors are used for searchlights and also for some forms of floodlight projectors and spotlights. For ordinary industrial lighting, reflectors having shapes similar to those of Fig. 136 are generally used (see also Figs. 146, 147, and 148). The angle of cut-off, or the maximum angle from the vertical at which light is directed, varies between about 40° and 60°; of the two types illustrated, that of Fig. 136(*a*) is generally preferable, as it gives a reflector of smaller dimensions and also conceals the lamp to a greater extent.

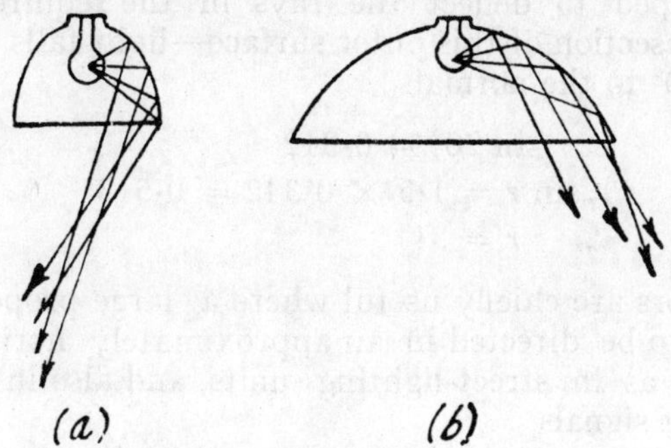

FIG. 136.—TYPICAL REFLECTOR CONTOURS.

Refraction

When a beam of light is passed through a boundary between two transparent substances having different densities, its direction is changed, as shown in Fig. 137. This phenomenon, known as refraction, can also be made use of in the control of light, and the law governing it is expressed by stating that:

$$\mu_A \sin i = \mu_B \sin r \qquad . \quad . \quad . \quad (46)$$

where μ_A and μ_B are known as the refractive indices of the two substances respectively, and i and r are the angles of incidence and of refraction, as indicated in the diagram.

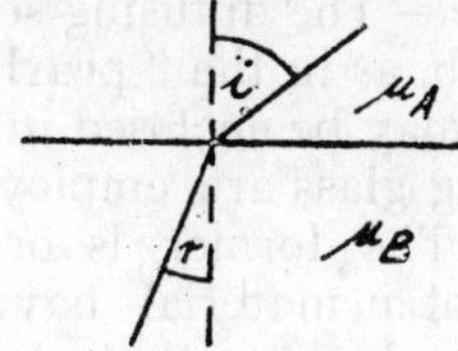

FIG. 137.—REFRACTION.

The ray will always have a smaller angle to the normal to the surface in the material of higher refractive index.

In ordinary lighting practice the materials concerned are nearly always glass and air, having refractive indices of 1·5 and 1 respectively.

A section through a typical refractor is shown in Fig. 138. It is seen that in this case the inner surface is smooth and normal to the rays of light, so that they pass into the glass without any change in direction; the outer surface, however, is accurately shaped to deflect the rays in the required direction. Consider a section of this outer surface—light falls on it at an angle of 20° to the normal.

$$\sin 20^\circ = 0{\cdot}342$$
$$\therefore \sin r = 1{\cdot}5 \times 0{\cdot}342 = 0{\cdot}513$$
$$\therefore \quad r = 31^\circ$$

Refractors are chiefly useful where a large proportion of the light has to be directed in an approximately horizontal direction, such as in street-lighting units, and also in railway and traffic-light signals.

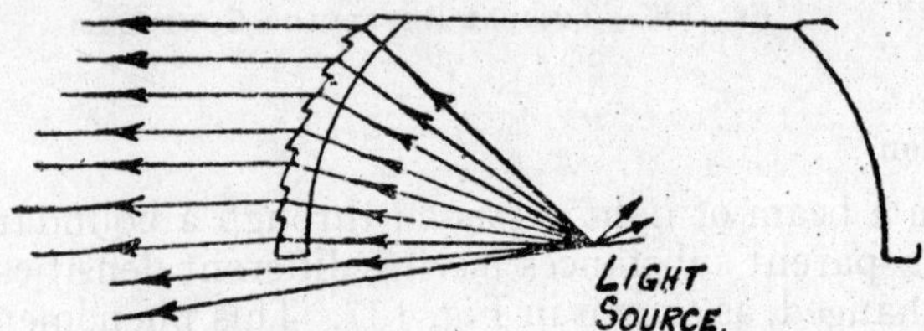

FIG. 138.—SECTION THROUGH REFRACTOR.

Diffusion

To prevent glare from a light source, a diffusing-glass screen can be introduced between the observer and the light source or the light may be reflected from a diffusing surface.

Diffusing Glassware.—The diffusing screen may be the actual glass of the lamp bulb, as in the " pearl " type of lamp, or an ordinary clear lamp may be enclosed in a diffusing-glass fitting. Two types of diffusing glass are employed, namely, opal glass and frosted glass. The former is ordinary glass containing very small particles of a material having a refractive index different from that of glass, so that there is a scattering of the rays. So-called frosted glass may be produced by coating ordinary glass with a crystalline substance, or the surface may be sand-blasted or etched to produce a similar effect. A good-quality diffusing fitting should have an approximately equal brightness over its entire surface and, of course, the filament of the enclosed lamp should be quite indistinguishable. The efficiency of such a fitting will be between 70 per cent. and 80 per cent. Frosted glass, although cheaper than opal glass, suffers from the disadvantage that it readily collects dirt and is difficult to clean.

Applications of Directionally Controlled Lighting

Lighting schemes may be classified as direct, indirect, or semi-indirect, according as to whether the light from the lamps is all directed downwards on to the working plane, whether it is all reflected on to it from the walls and ceiling, or whether a combination of both methods is used.

Direct lighting is the most efficient, but unless the lamps are mounted at a considerable height or are enclosed in deep reflectors there is danger of glare due to the lamps being within the range of vision of observers.

Indirect lighting, employing inverted or bowl reflectors which reflect all the light towards the ceiling, gives a very diffuse and almost shadowless light, but as it involves two or three reflections it is considerably less efficient than a direct-lighting scheme, particularly if the walls and ceiling have not a well-maintained highly reflecting surface.

Although both the above schemes are frequently employed and can easily be observed in shops and offices, there are various semi-indirect schemes which lie between the two and which employ translucent reflectors of either the ordinary or the inverted type and so give varying proportions of direct and indirect light. Such schemes are better in efficiency than indirect lighting, but are not so effective in eliminating shadows and glare.

Production of Coloured Light

Coloured light may be produced by using a light source of the required colour or by using any available light source and absorbing or subtracting from it the radiations of unwanted wave-lengths, this latter being known as the subtractive method of coloured-light production. It is also possible to produce light of any desired colour by combining or adding radiations from the red, green, and blue parts of the spectrum in the correct proportions; this method, however, has little practical application.

Use of Electric-discharge Lamps.—The ordinary filament-type of lamp can give only a reddish-white light, but as has already been seen (Tables XVIII and XIX) the electric-discharge lamp and the fluorescent lamp can give light of various colours, and such lamps are frequently used for this purpose.

Subtractive Coloured-light Production with the Filament Lamps.—A filament lamp produces a continuous spectrum, so that by absorbing the unwanted wave-lengths by means of an appropriate screen or filter between the lamp and the observer, light of any colour can be obtained ; for instance, a sheet of red glass or gelatine absorbs nearly all the blue, green, yellow, and orange radiations, allowing only the red rays to pass through, and therefore gives the effect of a red light. This is obviously an inefficient method, as it involves the wastage of a large proportion of the radiated energy. The approximate amount of light energy so absorbed and the effective lumens per watt of coloured light obtainable with various different-coloured filters are shown in Table XXII.

TABLE XXII

Colour of filter	Percentage absorption	Lumens per watt
No filter	0	15
Red	70	4·5
Light blue	70	4·5
Dark blue	90	1·5
Light green	70	4·5
Dark green	75	3·75
Yellow	30	10·5

Subtractive Coloured-light Production with Discharge Lamps.—When no discharge lamp of the required colour is available, it is possible to apply the subtractive method if the lamp emits radiations at several different wave-lengths. For instance, referring to Fig. 126, it is seen that a mercury-vapour lamp produces radiations in the blue and green parts of the spectrum (5,461 AU. and 5,770 AU, respectively). By absorbing the blue radiations a green light can be obtained with a luminous efficiency of about 12 lumens per watt.

Coloured Reflectors.—Instead of a coloured filter for the light a coloured reflector may be used and will produce exactly the same effect.

Artificial Daylight.—For certain purposes, such as colour matching in dyeworks and in other industries, an artificial light is required which approximates very closely to that of daylight.

Typical spectral distribution curves of noon sunlight, north skylight, and light from an overcast sky are shown in Fig. 139, from which it is seen that daylight is itself subject to considerable variation, and the purposes for which the light is to be used governs the actual distribution curve to be aimed at. The ordinary filament lamp has an excess of radiation at the red end of the spectrum, as shown in Fig. 130, and the problem in artificial daylight production from filament lamps is to produce a screen or reflector which will absorb precisely the correct amount of the unwanted wave-lengths without interfering with those which are to be retained. This is clearly an inefficient

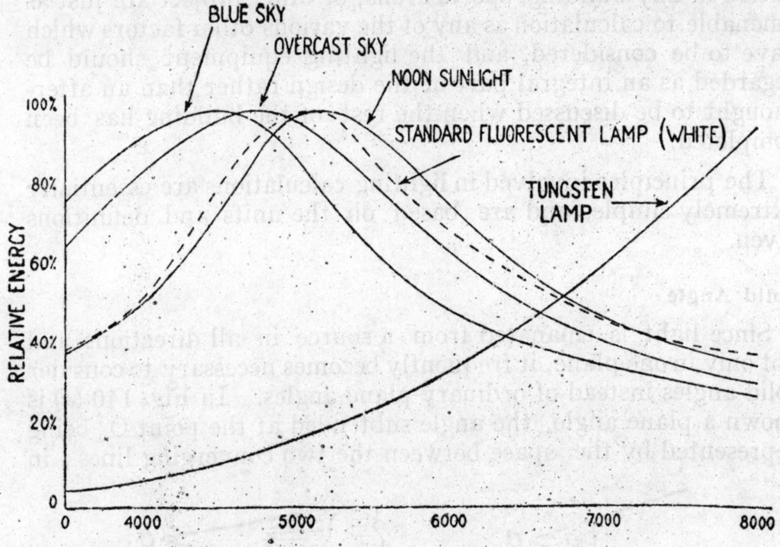

FIG. 139.—SPECIAL DISTRIBUTION CURVES FOR DAYLIGHT.

process, and to produce exact coincidence 75 per cent. of the radiant energy would have to be absorbed ; a fair approximation to daylight can, however, be obtained by absorbing 60 to 70 per cent. of the radiant light energy.

The absorption may be carried out by using a special bluish-coloured glass for the bulb of an ordinary filament lamp or by using an ordinary bulb in a fitting of this special glass. Difficulties in the manufacture of the glass prevent a very close approximation from being obtained, and a more accurate method employs a reflector with a carefully designed coloured mosaic pattern (Sheringham Daylight).

The above methods of producing artificial daylight have now been rendered almost obsolete by the advent of the fluorescent lamps which can be made to give a very close approximation to daylight. A spectral distribution curve for such a lamp is shown, together with those for daylight, in Fig. 139.

4. LIGHTING CALCULATIONS

The scientific aspects of illuminating engineering and the calculation of the light requirements for any particular purpose have only been recently brought to the fore. It may be stated now, however, that the details of the internal or external illumination of any building, sports arena, or other project are just as amenable to calculation as any of the various other factors which have to be considered, and the lighting equipment should be regarded as an integral part of the design rather than an afterthought to be discussed when the rest of the building has been completed.

The principles involved in lighting calculations are essentially extremely simple, and are based on the units and definitions given.

Solid Angle

Since light is emanated from a source in all directions and not oniy in one plane, it frequently becomes necessary to consider solid angles instead of ordinary plane angles. In Fig. 140 (*a*) is shown a plane angle, the angle subtended at the point O being represented by the space between the two converging lines ; in

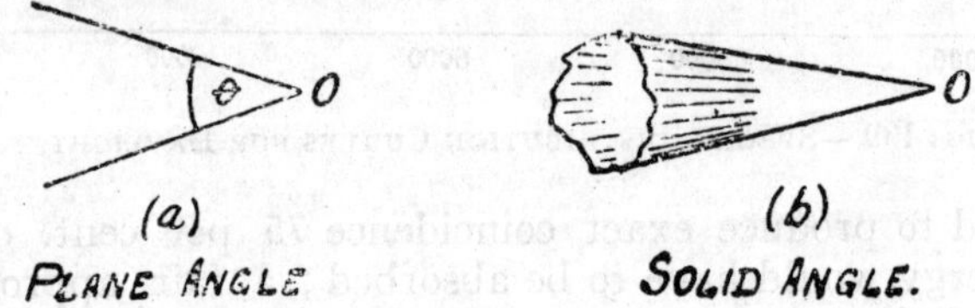

Fig. 140.—Angles.

Fig. 140 (*b*) is shown a solid angle, usually represented by the symbol ω. Here we do not have an area enclosed by two lines meeting at a point, but we have a volume enclosed by an infinite number of lines lying on a surface and meeting at a point. To define these angles more exactly : the unit of plane angle is the radian, and is defined as the angle subtended at the centre of a circle by an arc whose length is equal to the radius ; we thus have

$$\text{radians} = \frac{\text{arc}}{\text{radius}}$$

The unit of solid angle is the *steradian,* and is defined as the solid angle substended at the centre of a sphere by an area on the surface of the sphere which is numerically equal to the (radius)^2; thus we have

$$\text{steradians} = \frac{\text{area}}{(\text{radius})^2}$$

Since the area of the surface of a sphere is $4\pi r^2$, it follows that the total solid angle subtended by a point in all directions is 4π steradians.

Lumen defined in Terms of Solid Angle.—In the definition of the lumen previously given it was stated that the lamp giving 1 candle-power in all directions gave an output of 4π lumens. Since the total solid angle subtended by a point is 4π steradian, we

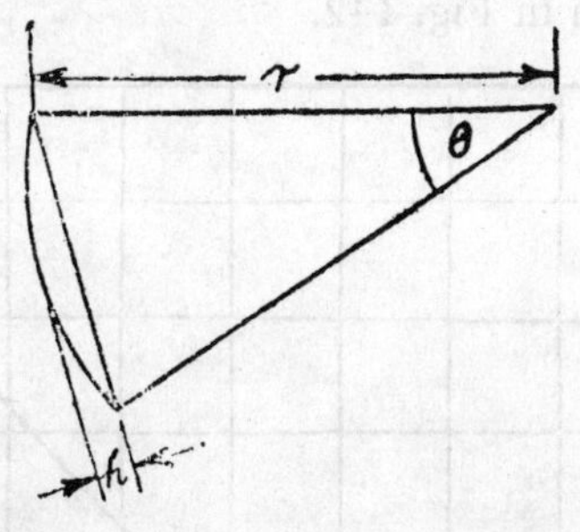

FIG. 141.—CROSS-SECTION OF SOLID ANGLE.

have a more convenient definition of the lumen as follows: *the lumen is the amount of light given out in a space represented by one unit of solid angle by a source having an intensity of 1 candle-power in all directions.*

Thus, if we know the mean spherical candle-power of a lamp we can immediately find the number of lumens it will give:

$$\text{lumen} = \text{m.s.c.p.} \times 4\pi$$

For a 32-m.s.c.p. lamp the total light output will thus be:

$$32 \times 4\pi = 402 \text{ lumens.}$$

Solid Angle in Terms of Plane Angle.—In illumination problems the solid angles which have to be considered are usually conical in shape. Such an angle is then easily represented on paper by taking a section of it, as shown in Fig. 141. The angle θ can be measured (in radians), but we must have means of converting this from the plane angle to the solid angle, of which it represents a section. Suppose the solid angle is closed by a spherical surface at a distance r from the apex. It can be shown that the area of such a surface is $2\pi rh$, so that the solid angle subtended by it is:

$$\omega = \frac{\text{area}}{r^2} = \frac{2\pi rh}{r^2}$$

Now, $$h = r - r\cos\frac{\theta}{2}$$

So that $$\omega = 2\pi\left(1 - \cos\frac{\theta}{2}\right) \quad . \quad . \quad . \quad (47)$$

Knowing θ, therefore, the corresponding solid angle, ω, can be calculated; for convenience the results can be plotted in the form of a curve, as shown in Fig. 142.

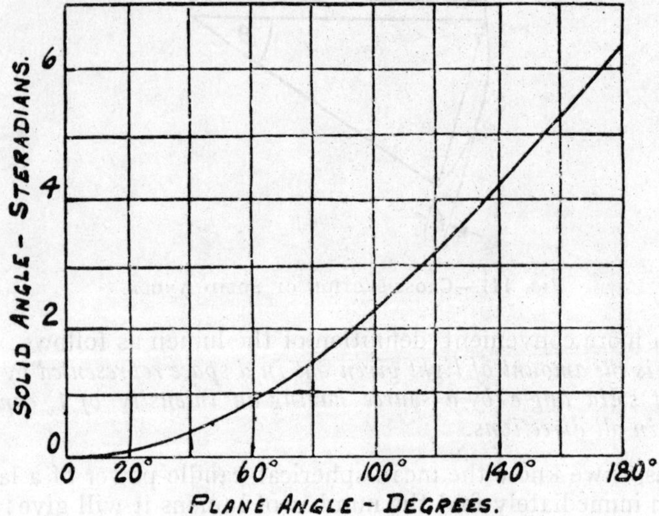

FIG. 142.—SOLID ANGLE IN TERMS OF PLANE ANGLE.

The Square Law

It has already been explained that the illumination on a surface is defined by stating the amount of light falling on it per unit area, i.e. the lumens per square foot. Suppose now that we have a source of light giving an output of F lumens within the solid angle enclosed by the four lines OA, OB, OC, and OD in Fig. 143. The whole of this light will be falling on the surface HKLM, placed at right angles to the axis of the beam and at a distance of 1m from it; the illumination on this surface is therefore $\frac{F}{\text{area HKLM}}$ lumens per square metre. If a surface PQRS at distance of 2 m from the source is now considered the area of this will, by the geometry of the figure, be 4 times that of HKLM, so that since the total number of lumens will be the same as before, the illumination on it will have decreased to $\frac{1}{4}$ of that on HKLM. Similarly, if the distance of the surface be increased to 3 m away from the source, the illumination will have decreased to $\frac{1}{9}$ of its original value. In general it can be seen that the area enclosed by the four lines increases propor-

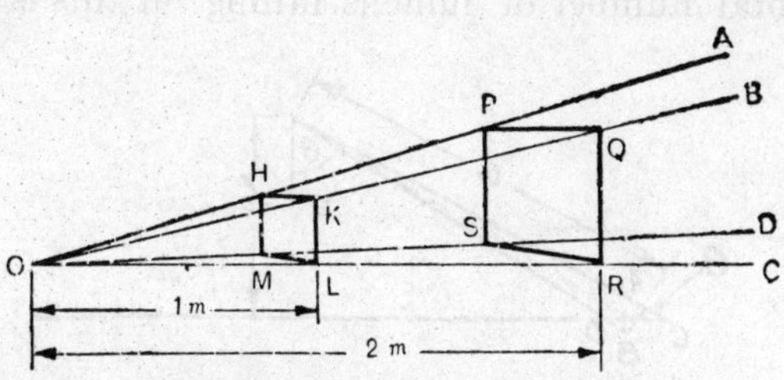

FIG. 143.—THE SQUARE LAW.

tionately to the square of the distance from the source, so that the illumination on the surface will decrease proportionally to the square of the distance, i.e. illumination $\propto \frac{1}{d^2}$.

Consider a source giving a certain candle-power (c.p.) in a particular direction and illuminating a surface at a distance d from it. If the distance is sufficiently great to be assumed spherical instead of flat, as with most practical cases, the solid angle subtended at the source of light by the area a will be a/d^2 steradians. From the definition of the lumen we have:

$$\text{lumens} = \text{candle-power} \times \text{solid angle}$$

$$= \text{c.p.} \times \frac{a}{d^2}$$

so that lumens per square metre $= \frac{\text{c.p.}}{d^2}$ . . . . . (48)

The law expressed by this equation is commonly known as the square law and is widely used in illumination problems, a typical application being shown in Example 24.

Surface Inclined at an Angle to Axis of Beam (the Cos$^3\theta$ *Law.)*—It was assumed above that the surface upon which light was falling was at right angles to the axis of the beam, but in practice this is not usually the case, and the conditions are then as shown in Fig. 144. If a small element of the beam inclined at an angle θ to the vertical is considered, the illumination on a surface such as AB at right angles to the beam axis can easily be calculated from:

$$\text{lumens per square metre} = \frac{\text{c.p.}}{d^2}$$

If, however, we consider the horizontal surface CD, it is evident that the total number of lumens falling on this is the same as

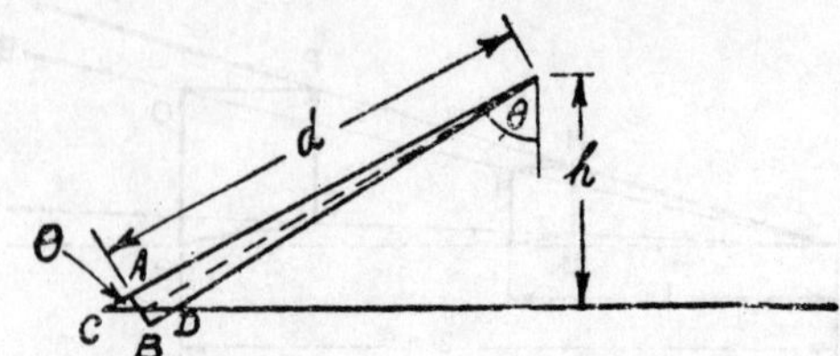

FIG. 144.—ILLUMINATION ON AN INCLINED SURFACE.

on AB; it can be seen, however, that the area of this surface will be equal to $\frac{\text{area of AB}}{\cos\theta}$. The illumination on CD will, therefore, be equal to that on AB $\times \cos\theta$, i.e.:

$$\text{illumination on CD} = \frac{\text{c.p.}}{d^2} \times \cos\theta$$

It can also be seen from the figure that h, the vertical height of the lamp above the horizontal surface, is equal to $d\cos\theta$, so that obtaining the illumination in terms of h we get:

$$\text{lumens per square metre} = \frac{\text{c.p.}}{h^2}\cos^3\theta \quad . \quad . \ (49)$$

This is also a very valuable law for illumination calculations and is known as the $\cos^3\theta$ law; by means of it the illumination at any point due to a lamp can be calculated so long as the candle-power of the lamp in that direction is known.

The metric unit of illumination is the lux (lx). This is the illumination of one lumen per square metre. (Formerly, the lumen per square foot, called the foot-candle, was used :

$$1\ \text{lm/ft}^2 = 10{\cdot}764\ \text{lm/m}^2 = 10{\cdot}764\ \text{lx}$$
$$1\ \text{lx} = 0{\cdot}093\ \text{lm/ft}^2)$$

Such a surface clearly subtends an angle of 1 steradian at the source and, since the lamp has an intensity of 1 candle-power, the amount of light falling on the surface is 1 lumen. The illumination produced is, therefore, 1 lumen per square metre. It is seen, therefore, that the lumen per square metre and the metre-candle are identical units.

Typical values of illumination met with are given in Table XXIII.

TABLE XXIII

TABLE OF ILLUMINATION LEVELS*

Survey of the recommendations of the illumination on the visual task, to serve as guidance when designing lighting installations:

Type of work	Recommended Illumination levels in lux ([1])	
1. Offices		
Drawing offices	1500	750
Office premises (normal office-work, book-keeping, typing, correspondence, reading, writing, operating office machines)	800	400
Premises where work is not carried out continuously (archives, staircase, corridor, waiting room)	150	75
2. Schools		
General classrooms	500	250
Art classrooms	800	400
Sewing classrooms	800	450
3. Industry		
Very fine (making watches and small instruments, engraving)	5000	2500([2])
Fine (fine assembly work, setting turret lathes, fine turning, fine pressing, polishing)	2000	1000([2])
Ordinary (drilling, rough turning, ordinary assembly work)	800	400
Rough (forging, rolling)	300	150
4. Shops		
Sales premises, showrooms in large cities	1000	500
In other places	500	250

TABLE XXIII (*Contd.*)

Shop Windows		
In shopping centres	2000	1000(3)
In other streets	1000	500(3)
5. Churches	150	75
6. Homes		
Living rooms		
Local lighting (visual task)	1000	500
General lighting (environmental lighting)	100	50
Kitchens		
Local lighting (working plane)	500	250
General lighting	250	125
Bedrooms, bathrooms, toilets		
Local lighting	500	250
General lighting	250	125
Corridors, Staircases, attics, cellars, store rooms, garages.		
Local lighting (e.g. for hobby corner)	500	250
General lighting	100	50

(1) 1 lux = 0·0929 lm/ft².
(2) General lighting, if necessary with local lighting.
(3) To be supplemented with spotlights up to 10 000 lux (local lighting).
* From PHILIPS LIGHTING COURSE—Part I, Lesson 6.

Methods of Calculation

Two general methods of calculation are available, namely, the light-flux methods and the square-law method. The former is appilcable to cases where the source of illumination is such as to produce an approximately uniform illumination over the working plane or where only an average value is required, while the square-law method is applicable where the illumination at a point due to one or more sources of light is required, the candle-powers of the sources in the particular direction under considera-tion being known.

The Ligh-flux Method.—From the size of the lamp or lamps employed the total lumen output is determined. Of this total output only a certain portion actually reaches the surface to be illuminated, and the ratio of the light usefully employed to the total amount of light emitted is known as the *coefficient of utilisa-tion*. Suppose, for instance, that it is desired to illuminate the surface of a table in a room ; this may be done by means of a single bare lamp suspended above the table. Some of the light emitted by such a lamp would fall on the table and a further portion of it would be reflected on to it from the walls and ceiling, but the remainder would be absorbed by the wall, ceiling, and floor surfaces; the coefficient of utilisation for such a lighting scheme would, therefore, be low, especially if the walls and ceiling were of dark-coloured or dirty material, which does not readily reflect light. Alternatively the lamp may be fitted with a reflector so designed that the whole of the available light output is directed downwards on to the table surface. The only loss in this case would be that due to the absorption of the reflector, and the coefficient of utilisation would be 0·8 or 0·9.

The estimation of the coefficient is a matter of practical experience, since it depends not only on the lighting fitting itself but also on the nature of the surrounding surfaces and the position of the light relative to these surfaces and to the surface to be illuminated; its value may lie anywhere between about 0·1 for a somewhat dirty lighting fitting in dull surroundings to about 0·9 for a well-designed and clean fitting in a room with highly reflecting walls and ceiling.

It is desirable to select the number of lamps so that a fairly even illumination over the working plane is obtained. A large number of small lamps will give a very even illumination, but will be expensive in fittings and wiring, so that a compromise must generally be made. The ratio of the spacing beetween adjacent lamps to their height above the working plane (*spacing/height ratio*) is important in this connection and a sufficiently even illumination is normally obtained if the value of this ratio does not exceed the figures given in Table XXIV.

TABLE XXIV

MAXIMUM PERMISSIBLE VALUES OF SPACING/HEIGHT RATIO

Ordinary industrial fittings	1·5
Concentrating fittings (Fig. 146)	1·0
Indirect fittings (ratio = spacing/ceiling height) ..	1·5
Standard fluorescent lamps	1·5

The method of calculation is illustrated in Example 22.

Example 22 : A room, 12 m. long, 7.5 m wide and 4.5 m high, having light-coloured walls and ceiling is to be illuminated by indirect lighting employing several inverted bowl fittings. An average illumination of 80 lumens per square metre is to be provided on a horizontal plane parallel to the floor and 0·75 m above it.

Estimate a suitable number and size of lamps.

Solution :

Total area $= 12 \times 7{\cdot}5 = 90\ \text{m}^2$

Total lumens required $= 90 \times 80 = 7200$ lumens

The coefficient of utilisation may be taken as 0·3 for a room of this sort. This allows for light lost in the bowl reflector and also in reflection from the walls and ceiling.

$$\text{Lamp lumens required} = \frac{7200}{0{\cdot}3} = 24\ 000 \text{ lumens}$$

suppose 100-watt lamps are used. These have (Table XX), an output of 1 340 lumens, so that :

$$\text{Number of lamps required} = \frac{24\ 000}{1\ 340} = 18$$

Suppose these are arranged in 6 rows of 3—the maximum spacing will be (12/6) = 2 m. The height of the ceiling above the working plane is 3·75 m, so that the spacing/height ratios is 2/3·75 = 0·535. This is very much below the minimum allowable value so that a cheaper and still satisfactory installation could be obtained with a smaller number of lamps, e.g. 200-watt lamps having an output 2,880 lumens.

$$\text{Number of lamps required} = \frac{24\ 000}{2\ 880} = 8{\cdot}4, \text{ say 3 rows of 3}$$

or, to be on the safe side, 3 rows of 4. The maximum spacing would then be (12/4) = 3 m, and the spacing/height ratio would be 3/3·75 = 0·8, which is still well within the allowable limit.

As an alternative to indirect lighting, fluorescent lamps could be used as these do not produce glare. Consider the standard 80-watt fluorescent lamp having a light output of 2,400 lumens.

$$\text{Number required} = \frac{24\ 000}{2\ 400} = 10, \text{ say 3 rows of 4.}$$

The mounting height above the working-plane would be about 3·25 m., so that the spacing/height ratio would be 3/3·25 = 0·925, which is within the allowable limit.

The total energy consumption with the fluorescent lamps would only be: 12 × 80 = 960 W, as compared to 12 × 200 = 2,400 W with the filament lamps, so that the extra initial cost of the former would be partially counterbalanced.

The Square-law, or Point-to-point Method.—If a polar curve of a lamp and its reflector is available from which the candle-power of the lamp in any particular direction can be obtained, the illumination at any point within range of the lamp can be calculated from the square law. If two or more lamps illuminate the same working plane, the illumination due to each can be added. This method is illustrated in Example 24.

Measurement of Illumination.—In order to check the accuracy of lighting calculations by actual observation and obtain data for future use, it is necessary to be able to measure values of illumination (lumens per square metre) falling on any given surface. For this purpose a portable *photometer* is used, two general types of which are available.

In the first of these types a standard lamp in contained in the apparatus, the light from which is controllable and made to fall on to a test screen. A pointer attached to the control device moves over a scale calibrated to read illumination on the test screen, so that by adjusting the latter until it is equal to the illumination on the surface to be measured, the value of this illuminiation can be ascertained by observing the position of the pointer on the scale.

The other and more modern type employs a photo-electric cell, the e.m.f. of which is dependent on the amount of light falling on it. The instrument therefore includes a millivoltmeter to indicate the e.m.f. generated by the cell, and by calibrating this in terms of illumination a direct-reading photometer is obtained.

5. FACTORY LIGHTING

Adequate lighting of factories is of importance, since, in addition to providing improved amenities for the employee, it has a definite economic value in reducing accidents, with their consequent lost time and compensation payments, and also in increasing production. Investigations have been carried out in several industries to determine the influence of lighting on production; results obtained in typesetting indicate that with an illumination of about 200 lumens per square metre a production equal to that obtainable in good daylight can be maintained, while the lower values of illumination the output falls off in accordance with the curve shown in Fig. 145. In addition to the lower output resulting from poor illumination there was also an increase in the errors.

General requirements and Types of Installation

In addition to providing an adequate illumination on the working plane, a factory-lighting installation, in common with other indoor equipments, should give a good distribution of light, employ simple and easily cleaned fittings, and avoid glare. It is necessary not only to avoid glare from the lamp itself but also reflected glare from any polished surfaces which may be within the line of vision.

General Lighting.—The usual scheme in factories and workshops is to mount a number of lamps at a height sufficient to ensure a uniform distribution of light over the working plane. In large machine shops the height is governed by the necessity

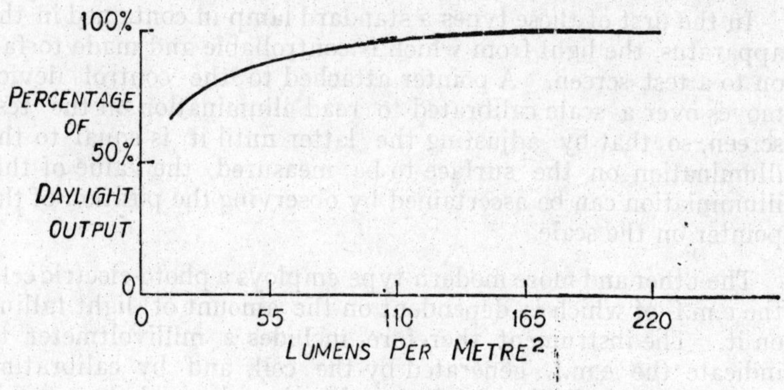

FIG. 145.—EFFECT OF ILLUMINATION ON PRODUCTION (TYPESETTING).

for keeping the lamps above the travelling crane, and in such cases it is often desirable to supplement the main lighting by side lighting, giving additional illumination on a vertical plane. Light-coloured walls and ceiling add to the effectiveness of an installation, and the value of the increased illumination obtainable from a given scheme is usually more than sufficient to pay for the necessary whitewashing or painting.

Local Lighting.—Where fairly intense illumination is required, at one or more particular points, local lighting can be provided by means of adjustable fittings attached to the machine or bench in question, or mounted on portable floor standards—such lamps should be mounted in deep reflectors to avoid glare. For maintenance work and emergency lighting portable hand lamps are used, attached to wall plugs by means of a trailing lead. With any form of local lighting which is within reach of the operator of a machine there is a danger of shock, and the use of a low voltage of not more than 50 is recommended by the Home Office; this has the further advantage that low-voltage lamps have thicker filaments, and are therefore more robust than those for normal voltage. The supply for such lamps can be obtained from a special low-voltage distribution system running throughout the factory or by means of a small transformer for each individual lamp.

It must be stressed that local lighting should never be employed alone; good general lighting is essential in order to avoid

Fig. 146.—Dispersive Reflector.
(*Philips India Ltd.*)

dark spaces between the local lighting units, which would lead to fatigue of the eye due to its continually having to adjust itself to new conditions.

LIGHT SOURCES AND THEIR APPLICATION IN INDUSTRIAL LIGHTING*

The progress in the development of the electric lamps during the past thirty three years has been spectacular; though benefits of all such developments are not felt in our country, where the range of different types of lamps manufactured is limited compared to other countries and certain categories of lamps have to be imported. We shall consider those that are generally used for industrial and commercial lighting and in particular what are indigenously made.

1. *Tungsten Filament Lamps :* In spite of the introduction of more efficient discharge lamps, the tungsten filament lamps have continued to be the most widely used lamps because of their simplicity, low initial cost, and wide range of wattages available. The efficiency varies from 10 to 20 lumens per watt for the different wattages and the average life is 1000 hours. Since a large amount of heat is produced by the lamp, installations using filament lamps should provide for proper dissipation of this heat so as to prevent unconfortable working conditions. The high brightness of the naked filament also necessitates proper screening of the lamp to prevent glare. In large industrial and office interiors-where lighting is required for long periods during the year, the filament lamp has more and more been passed over in favour of more efficient and longer life sources like fluorescent lamps, though the filament lamps have their own application in many locations. Inside-coated lamps are also manufactured, since they have lower surface brightness resulting in lesser glare which is necessary for certain applications.

2. *Tubular Fluorescent Lamps* : It can be said that the introduction of fluorescent lamps have revolutionised lighting in industries and offices. Levels of illumination, which were considered uneconomical are made possible even in our own country. During the past seventeen years this has been evident in the attempts made in many industries and office buildings to provide much better illumination than in the past. The outstanding merits of the fluorescent lamps which make it the ideal choice for solving almost all the lighting problems generally encountered in industrial and commercial interiors are :—

(1) Its high luminous efficiency—it gives 50 to 70 lumens per watt consumed.

(2) Its long life—it has an average expected life of 5000 burning hours. The above two factors make it economical in the long run.

(3) Its low surface brightness—even bare lamps when viewed direct do not give rise to uncomfortable glare as in the case of filament lamps. This together with the more uniform lighting provided by fluorescent lamps create the proper visual environment conducive to comfortable working.

(4) Heat radiation is less compared to incandescent lamps. This is of importance especially in office interiors where air conditioning has to take care of the heat load due to lighting.

(5) It is made in different colours in the white range. The proper colour is chosen to suit the particular requirement.

3. *Mercury Vapour Lamps*: These are high pressure gas discharge lamps and have high luminous efficiencies of the order of 35 to 50 lumens watt for the different wattage ratings. The wattages made are 80, 125, 250, 400, 700, 1000 and 2000 watts, but not all of them are available indigenously. While these lamps are not usually considered for office lighting since with the low ceilings in offices glare due to these higher brightness sources is not acceptable, the higher wattage mercury vapour lamps are extensively used for high-bay lighting installations in industries. Due to the high output of each lamp, the total number of points to provide a certain illumination can be kept to a minimum resulting in lesser maintenance costs. The lamp life is also high—average 5000 burning hours.

The normal mercury vapour lamps give a predominantly bluish green light which has poor colour rendering properties. Where better colour rendering was considered necessary, a combination of M. V. lamps and normal incandescent lamps was used to improve the colour quality of the light. This resulted in bringing about the desired effect, but the electric load tended to be high. The fluorescent coated mercury vapour Lamp gives crisp white light in view of supplementation of red radiations to the spectrum.

Having selected the light source, it will be necessary to decide upon the type of fitting to be used. In industrial installations, reflector type fittings for direct lighting are most suitable. In certain places fittings with slots in the reflector will be used in order to provide some light on the ceiling, presenting excessive contracts between fittings and background. In high factory halls, high bay fittings for mercury vapour lamps are used. For special applications where atmospheric conditions warrant the same, specially designed fittings such as watertight, dust proof, explosion proof and corrosion resistant fittings have to be used.

The approach to artificial lighting has been more or less based on the belief that it must fulfil minimum requirements in order to make the work in the factory more effective, easier and safer. These requirements mainly concern the quantity of light, the lighting level. Nowadays the artificial lighting is increasingly judged by its effect on the people who have to spend part of their time in that light. We speak of agreeable lighting and of lighting for comfort, making the artificial lighting instrumental in creating a more pleasant working environment. This means that we must consider quality aspects, such as distribution of the light brightness patterns and colour.

Type of Source	Characteristics	Application
Incandescent Lamps	Low initial outlay. Rather high running costs, owing to the limited luminous efficiency and relatively short life of these sources.	For lighting areas or rooms of restricted extent or where traffic or occupation density is low or where hours of burning is limited.
Discharge Lamps:	High luminous efficiency	(a) All factory premises with high ceilings.
(a) Mercury vapour	Low running costs	(b) All premises with a smoky or dust-laden atmosphere.
(b) Sodium vapour	Long life	
Fluorescent Lamps	High luminous efficiency (for the same power consumption, these types can give as much as 5 times more light than incandescent lamps)	All Factory and office premises.
	Long Life	
	Low running costs, which soon compensate the higher initial outlay. These types yield pleasant diffuse light which casts no shadows, good colour rendition.	In circumstances where colour appraisal is important.

ILLUMINATION LEVELS :

The illumination in lux (or lumen per square metre)—the amount of light actually reaching the working plane—must be in accordance with the work to be done.

In terms of visual perception the eye-tasks are graded according to their degree of fineness. The less critical the task, the lower the demands as to level and quality that need be made on the lighting. Conversely, the finer the work, the higher must be the level and the better the distribution of the light. Too low a level will call for constant visual effort, which will soon lead to physiological and psychological difficulties.

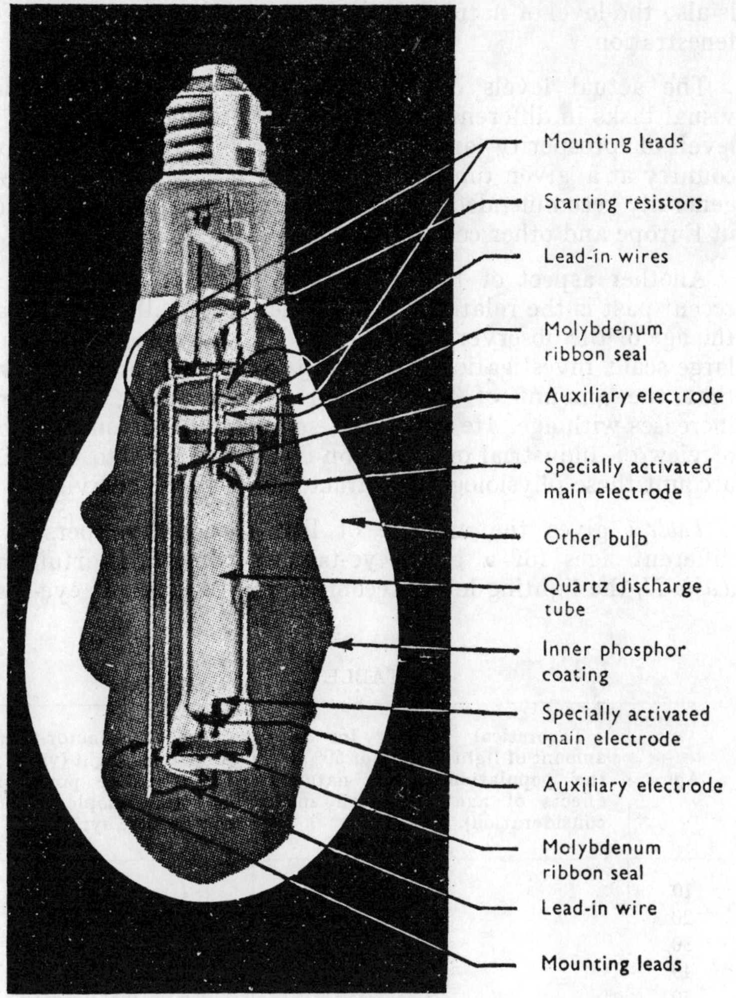

HPL FLUORESCENT MERCURY VAPOUR LAMP
(*Philips India Ltd.*)

The theoretical ground of our lighting levels in recent years has been investigated by Weston (Great Britain), Blackwell (U.S.A.), Balder (Netherlands) and Bodmann (Germany). It is interesting to see that these investigations all lead to the result that the ideal lighting level for interiors such as offices, factories and schools seems to be of the order of 1000 to 2000 lux. This is also the level of natural daylight in an interior with sufficient fenestration.

The actual levels of illumination recommended for various visual tasks in different countries are ultimately decided by the level of prosperity and total economic climate in a given country at a given time. That is why we find that the levels generally recommended in USA are higher than those provided in Europe and other countries.

Another aspect of lighting that has come to the fore in the recent past is the relation between the level of illumination and the age of the observer. It was Dr. J. C. Fortuin who, through large scale investigation involving 10,000 test persons, showed that the amount of light required for reading good print increases with age. He, therefore, suggested that from the point of view of industrial organisation it was desirable to take into account these physiological characteristics of the individual.

Table I gives the amount of light needed by persons of different ages for a given eye-task (according to Fortuin) and *Table II*, the lighting levels recommended per class of eye-tasks.

TABLE I

Age	Theoretical Factor* for the amount of light (valid for 50% of the population when natural effects of age are taken into consideration).	Practical Factor for the amount of light (valid for 90% of the population including people with defects of the eye).
10	$\frac{1}{3}$	1 (41 years)
20	$\frac{1}{2}$	1·5 (50 years)
30	$\frac{2}{3}$	2 (50 years)
40	1	4 (57 years)
50	2	6 (65 years)
60	5	—

*As an average age of employee, 40 years is taken to be 1.

TABLE II

ILLUMINATION LEVEL PER CLASS OF EYE-TASKS

Minimum for work spaces (amenity lighting)		150 lux
Class 1	Varying and Simple Tasks	500 to 250 lux
Class 2	Continuous observation medium-fine details	1000 to 500 lux
Class 3	Continuous and precise eye-tasks (such as drawing)	2000 to 1000 lux
Class 4	Very fine work (such as repairing watches)	Over 2000 lux
(Above 1000 lux, the illumination in many cases, only be increased by local lighting)		

Industrial Lighting Fittings

Reflectors for industrial purposes must be simple in design and easily cleaned, and the requirements of the majority of installations can be met by one of the following types of fitting:

Standard Reflector.—A vitreous enamelled unit has been standardised. These reflectors are made to accommodate lamps of from 40 to 1,500 watts, and the design is such that adequate and uniform illumination is obtained if they are mounted at a spacing equal to about $1\frac{1}{2}$ times their mounting height above the working plane. The size of lamp required can be determined by the light-flux method of calculation, as in Example 22. It will usually be found that about 11 watts per m^2. of floor surface will be required to give an illumination of 65 lumens per square metre.

Diffusing Fitting.—Where a more diffuse light is required than is given by the standard reflector, a diffusing glass screen can be fixed across the front of a standard type of reflector. Such units are useful where highly polished articles are being dealt with.

Concentrating Reflector.—When the fittings have to be mounted at a considerable height above the working plane, as in large machine shops and foundries, the ordinary reflector would have too wide an angle of divergence and would waste a great deal of light on the walls. A reflector, as shown in Fig. 146, with a concentrated beam is suitable for such situations.

Enclosed Diffusing Fittings.—For offices and other situations where light-coloured walls and ceiling are available, an opal globe completely enclosing the lamp gives a very even and well-diffused light. Such a unit is shown in Fig. 147.

Angle Reflector.—For providing illumination in a vertical plane where concentrating-type reflectors are used, an angle reflector, as shown in Fig. 148, can be mounted on suitable stanchions or on the walls.

Maintenance.—Conditions in the majority of factories are inevitably dusty, and regular cleaning of lighting fittings is

FIG. 147.—ENCLOSED DIFFUSING FITTING.
(*Philips Lamps, Ltd.*)

essential if they are to be maintained in a condition of reasonable efficiency. Numerous tests have been made, which show that the efficiency may be reduced by 30 to 40 per cent. in a few weeks if cleaning is neglected. The frequency of cleaning depends, of course, on the conditions in the particular factory under consideration, and varies from once or twice a week for very dusty situations to every four or six weeks under the best conditions.

6. FLOODLIGHTING

Another application of illuminating engineering to which a considerable amount of attention has recently been directed is the "flooding" with light of large surfaces, usually in the open air. This may be carried out for several purposes.

AEsthetic Floodlighting.—For enhancing the beauty of a building by night, e.g. floodlighting of churches, ancient buildings, and monuments.

Advertising.—Floodlighting of advertisement hoardings and commercial buildings.

Industrial and Commercial Floodlighting.—Illumination of railway yards, quarries, sports arenas, etc.

FIG. 148.—UNIVERSAL SHORTLIGHT FITTING
(*Philips India Ltd.*)

The Projector

For floodlighting purposes it is necessary to concentrate the light from the lamp into a relatively narrow beam, and the particular type of reflector and housing which is employed for this purpose is known as a floodlight projector. As it is usually installed out of doors and frequently in inaccessible positions, robustness and a weatherproof construction are essential.

The Reflecting Surface.—The most important part of the projector is the reflecting surface, and this may be of silvered glass, stainless steel, or chromium plate; the efficiency of silvered glass is 85 to 90 per cent., while that of polished metal is only about 70 per cent., but the latter is more robust and is therefore preferable in some circumstances. Vitreous enamel is also used.

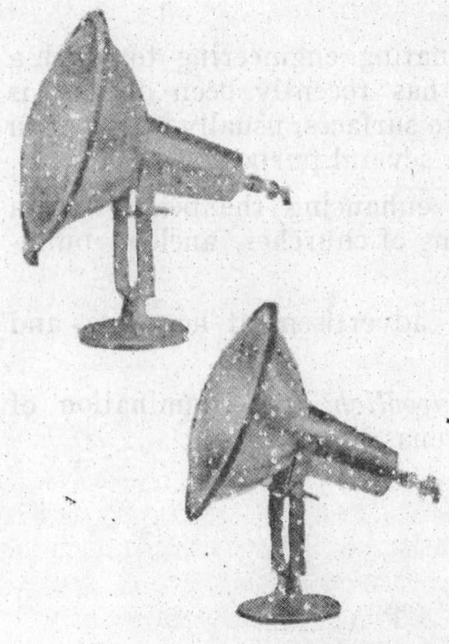

FLOODLIGHT FITTINGS (N.V.C.)
(*Philips India Ltd.*)

An approximately parallel beam is generally required for situations such as that shown in Fig. 149(*a*), while in cases where the projector has to be located near the base of the building to be illuminated an asymmetric reflector, which directs a more intense light towards the top of the building, must be used as shown in Fig. 149 (*b*).

Beam Spread.—As no commercial type of projector has a sharp cut-off, the term " beam spread " is employed to indicate the amount of divergence of the beam, and is definedas the angle within which the minimum illumination on a surface normal to the axis of the beam is one-tenth of the maximum.

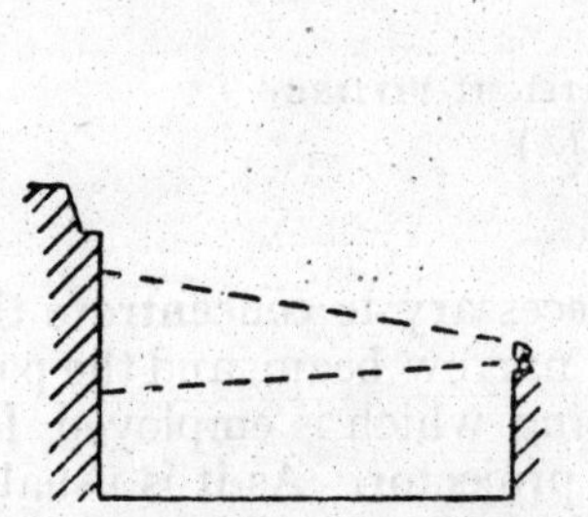

FIG. 149.—FLOODLIGHT INSTALLATIONS

The Casing.—The casing and its mounting must be arranged so that the inclination of the beam can be varied in both a vertical and a horizontal direction, since, however carefully an installation is laid out in the design office, some adjustment on site will certainly be necessary. For permanent installations cast-metal cases are used to give robustness and protection against the weather; for temporary installations or those in sheltered situations, sheet-metal casings suffice.

In some instances, when 500- or 1,000-W lamps are to be used, provision has to be made for ventilation. It is preferable, however, to secure adequate cooling by providing sufficient radiating surface, since ventilation allows the ingress of dust and dirt, which impair the efficiency of the reflector. The front of the projector is usually of clear glass, often bowed outwards to keep it as far away from the heat of the lamp as possible; diffusing glass is occasionally used where a diffuse beam is required.

It is important that the lamp should be entirely shielded from the view of passers-by, and glare or spill shields are fitted for this purpose where necessary.

Projector Lamps.—Standard 250-, 500-, or 1,000-wt. gasfilled tungsten-filament lamps are normally employed for floodlight projectors, although for narrow-angle beams, which require accurate location of the light source at the focal point of the reflector, special lamps having bunched filaments and known as projector lamps are generally employed.

Location and Mounting of Projectors

The success or otherwise of a floodlighting scheme depends very largely on the choice of suitable sites for the projectors. The source of light must, of course, be invisible to the observer, and if possible the projector itself should be invisible during the day-time.

Attention must be paid to the shadows cast by projections or abutments on the illuminated building; until recently buildings were designed on the assumption that light would always fall on them from above, and when floodlit from the side or below they may take on a totally different appearance. If floodlit from immediately in front, so that no shadows are visible to the observer, the effect is to remove all depth, giving the appearance of a piece of badly painted stage scenery.

Mounting.—The equipment may be arranged as a long-range installation with the projectors mounted on adjacent buildings or at ground level about 15 to 30 m. away; in some cases special ornamental standards may be used to house the projectors. When neither of these arrangments is possible a short-range installation must be designed with the projectors mounted in a basement area or on brackets attached to the building.

Examples of all these arrangements, as well as other special arrangements, can be seen by observing the various floodlit buildings and monuments which are becoming a common feature of our towns and cities.

Design of Floodlighting Installations

Having decided on suitable sites for the projectors, the number and size of projectors must next be determined. The light-flux method of calculation is usually employed, as described on page 312.

Illumination Requirements.—The illumination (lumens per square metre) required on the surface of a building or other area to be floodlit depends on the material of the surface, its cleanliness, and the brightness of the surroundings. Typical figures are shown in Table XXV. Reflection factors from various building surfaces is given in Table XXV (*a*).

TABLE XXV

VALUES OF ILLUMINATION—LUMENS PER SQUARE METRE (OR LUX)

Floodlit buildings	clear	dirty	Outdoor area	
Portland stone ..	30	110	Railway, shunting yards, docks, etc.	2·2—4·4
Concrete ..	55	165	Aerodrome Landing grounds	1·1—2·2
Red brick ..	100	300	Greyhound race-tracks	220—330
Buff paint ..	55	165	Boxing rings	2200—3300

TABLE XXV (*a*)

REFLECTION FACTORS

Material	State	Reflection Factor
White marble	Fairly clean	0·60—0·65
Granite	Fairly clean	0·10—0·15
Light concrete or stone	Fairly clean	0·40—0·50
Dark concrete/or stone	Fairly clean/	0·25
	Very dirty	0·05—0·10
Imitation concrete paint	Clean	0·50
White brick	Clean	0·80
Yellow brick	New	0·35
Red brick	New	0·25
Brick	Dirty	0·05

If the general brightness in the neighbourhood of a floodlit building is high, due to good street lighting or the proximity of other floodlit buildings, the values given in the above table may have to be doubled.

Having chosen a suitable value for the lumens per square metre to be provided, this may be multiplied by the area to be illuminated and the total number of lumens which must fall on the area thereby obtained. This gives the theoretical output which the lamps must have, but in practice allowance must be made for various losses which inevitably occur.

Waste-light Factor.—When several projectors are illuminating a surface there is bound to be a certain amount of overlap, and also some of the light will fall beyond the edge of the area to be illuminated. These two effects are taken into account by multiplying the theoretical lumens by a waste-light factor which has a value between about 1·2 for a rectangular area and about 1·5 when floodlighting an irregular object, such as a statue or monument.

Depreciation Factor.—Dirt and dust seriously reduce the effectiveness of a projector, and 50 to 100 per cent. more light must be provided than is theoretically required so that the illumination shall be adequate at the end of the interval between the cleaning periods.

Coefficient of Utilisation.—The lumens output required from the projector can now be determined by applying the two factors mentioned above, but the projector itself occasions some loss due to loss in the reflecting surface, absorption by the front glass, and light which is radiated directly from the bulb in a direction not along the beam. These losses are taken into account by employing a coefficient of utilisation or "beam factor" for the projector defined as $\frac{\text{beam lumens}}{\text{lamp lumens}}$ and having a value of between 0·3 and 0·5. The higher value arises with deep reflectors having a good reflecting surface, such as silvered glass.

The total number of lumens output required from the lamps can now be found from:

$$\text{lumens required} = \frac{\text{area} \times \text{lumens/m}^2 \times \text{waste-light factor} \times \text{depreciation factor}}{\text{coefficient of utilisation}}$$

A preliminary estimate of the number of projectors and their size and type can now be made by laying out scale drawings of the installation as described in Example 23, or, in simple cases, by calculation. The lumens output from various standard sizes lamp can be found from Table XX, page 297.

Example 23: It is desired to floodlight the front of a townhall in an industrial area. The dimensions are shown in Fig. 150, and the front of the building is of portland stone. The projectors can be located at ground level 15 m away. Estimate the number and size of projectors required.

Solution:

Area to be illuminated = (15 × 45) = 675 m².

Being in an industrial area, the surface will quickly become dirty, but it may be assumed that the general surrounding brightness will be low. An illumination of 80 lumens per square metre (lx) should, therefore, suffice.

Total lumens required on surface = (675 × 80)
= 54 000 lumens (lm)

Waste light factor = 1·2 (for a rectangular building).

Depreciation factor :—the atmosphere will be dirty but the projectors are easily accessible for cleaning, and a value of 1·5 may be assumed.

Lumens output from the projector = (54 000 × 1·2 × 1·5)
= 97 200 lumens (lm)

An ordinary medium-angle projector with a beam spread of about 25° will probably be found to be suitable and a coefficient of utilisation of 0·4 may be assumed.

$$\text{Total lamp lumens} = \frac{97\ 200}{0{\cdot}4} = 243\ 000 \text{ lumens.}$$

suppose that 1000 watt lamps are chosen. From Table XX, page 297, the lumens output of each = 18·9 lumens per watt (lm/W).

Total lumens output = (1 000 × 18·9) = 18 900 per lamp

$$\text{Number of lamps} = \frac{243\ 000}{18\ 900}\ 12{\cdot}9 \text{ say 15 or 16 lamps.}$$

This is a reasonable number, and it is necessary to see whether they can be arranged to cover the entire building. Choose a standard, medium-angle reflector, having a beam-spread of

25°. By drawing a diagram of the building to scale, as shown in Fig. 150, it can be seen that, if the 16 projectors are arranged in eight groups of two, the building will be fairly evenly covered ; as the upper part of the building is at a greater distance from the projector than the lower part, illumination here will be somewhat less than the average figure of 80 lumens per square metre, while on the lower part it will be greater ; the upper part will however, be viewed against the dark background of the sky and the difference will therefore not be noticeable.

In practice, several different types and arrangements of projectors would probably have to be tried before a satisfactory arrangement was decided upon, and even then the final adjustment would, of course, have to be made on site.

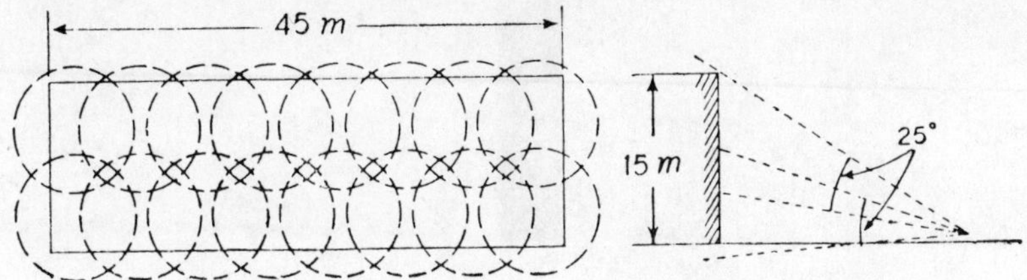

Fig. 150.—Layout of Town Hall Floodlighting (Example 23.)

7. STREET LIGHTING

Street lighting, apart from that required for promenades, shopping centres, etc., is primarily necessary in order that drivers of vehicles may see obstructions in the roadway ; if sufficient light is provided for this purpose the requirements for the convenience of pedestrians, police supervision, and other purposes will usually be adequately met.

The features in which street lighting differs from lighting for other purposes are firstly that the value of illumination is, for economic reasons, very low and the question of colour rendering is therefore of minor importance, and secondly that objects in the roadway are rendered visible by being silhouetted against a relatively bright background instead of being themselves illuminated. Furthermore, owing to the low illumination, the eye is in its most sensitive state and glare must be carefully avoided.

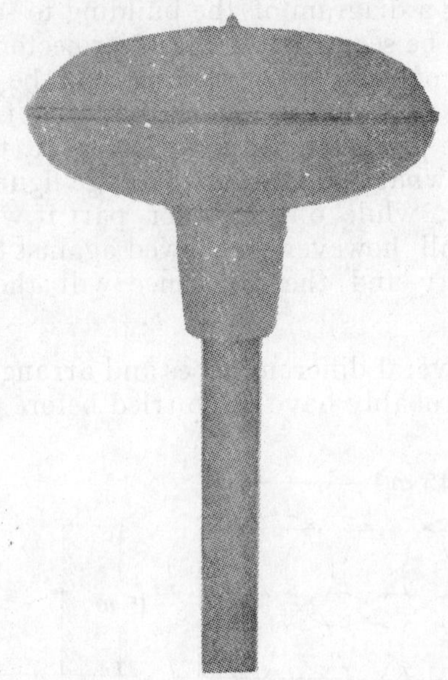

POST TOP LANTERNS (*Philips India Ltd.*)

FIG. 150 A.—(1) HRC 40: New type of fitting for lighting of streets in residential areas, parks, squares and entrances to the houses—fitting of a decarative nature. Suitable for 80 W and 125 W colour-corrected fluorescent mercury vapour lamps. This fitting combines superb appearance with brilliant illumination at minimum operational cost.

STREET LIGHTING FITTINGS (*Philips India Ltd.*)

FIG. 150 B (2) HRC 12: Street lighting fitting for any road. It carries adjustable reflectors which can be positioned to suit individual road requirements.

Two general principles are employed in the design of street-lighting installations, namely, the diffusion principle, in which light is directed downwards from the lamps with the intention of producing a more or less even illumination on the road surface, and the specular-reflection principle, in which the light is directed on to and reflected from the surface with a very large angle of incidence.*

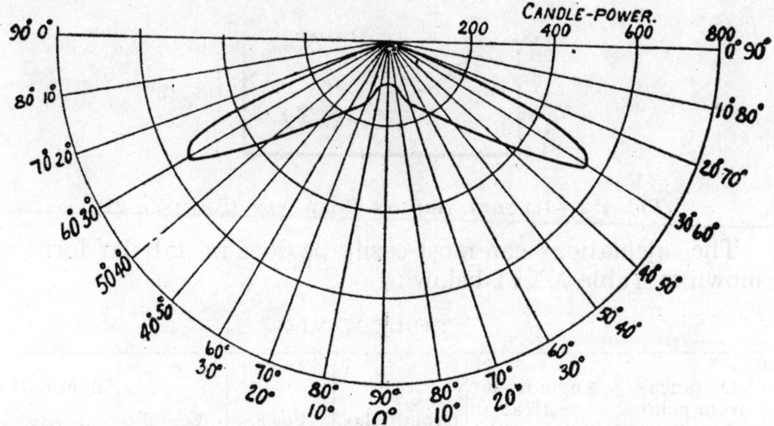

FIG. 151.—POLAR CURVE OF STREET-LIGHTING REFLECTOR. (EXAMPLE 24.)

The Diffusion Principle

Light is directed downwards from the lamp by suitably designed reflectors. These reflectors are designed to give as even an illumination over the road surface as possible, and have a cut-off of between about 30° and 45° so that the filament of the lamp is not visible except from almost beneath it, thus eliminating glare. The diffusing nature of the road surface causes the reflection of a certain proportion of the incident light in the direcion of the observer, and therefore makes the road surface appear bright. The polar curve of a typical reflector is shown in Fig. 151, and by applying the square-law method of calculation described on page 309, the illumination at any point on the road surface can be calculated, as in the following example.

Example 24: A roadway is to be illuminated by means of lamps suspended above its centre line at intervals of 35 m. and at a height of 10 m. Each lamp is fitted with a reflector having a

**Angle of incidence* is the angle between the incident light and the *normal* to the surface.

polar curve as showing in Fig. 151. Draw a curve showing the illumination at various points along the centre of the roadway.

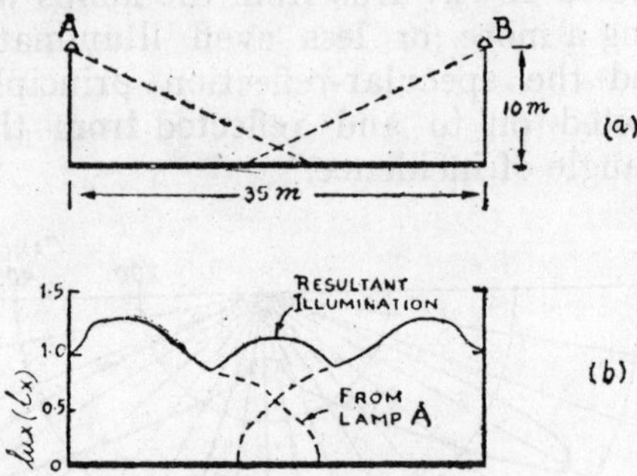

FIG. 152.—ILLUMINATION ON ROAD WAY (EXAMPLE 24).

The calculations can most easily be done in tabular form, as shown in Table XXVI below :

TABLE XXVI

Distance from point under lamp $d = m$	Angle from vertical $\theta = \tan^{-1} \frac{d}{10}$	C.P. (from polar curve)	Cos θ	Cos^3 θ	Illumination $= \frac{\text{C.P Cos}^3 \theta}{100}$
0	0	100	1·0	1·0	1·0
3	16·7	150	0·9578	0·88	1·32
6	31·0	200	0·8572	0·630	1·26
9	42·0	275	0·7431	0·41	1·125
12	50·2	390	0·6401	0·26	1·015
15	56·3	510	0·5548	0·170	0·865
18	61·0	550	0·4848	0·1200	0·66
21	64·5	510	0·4305	0·079	0·402

The illumination at various points distant 'd' from a point immediately under the lamp is calculated by means of the square law and the polar curve. These are plotted as shown in Fig. 152(b) for two adjacent lamps. Over a certain portion of the distance it can be seen that light from two lamps illuminates the surface, and the illumination is the sum of the two, giving the total illumination curve as shown by the full-line.

The Specular-reflection Principle

While a pedestrian requires the illumination of his immediate surroundings, a motorist requires to see objects about 30 metres ahead, and this latter fact has led to the specular-reflection method of street lighting. It is found that even a matt surface exhibits specular reflection if the light falls on it at an angle of only a few degrees. Referring to Fig. 153, consider an observer at Y viewing an obstruction in the roadway at X; the light from lamp A will be falling on the roadway at a fairly small angle of incidence, and will not be reflected in the direction of the observer to any large extent; light from lamps B and C, however, will fall on the roadway immediately behind the obstruction at a large angle of incidence, and will therefore be reflected towards the observer with a fairly high efficiency, and will cause the obstruction to show up quite clearly by contrast. It is the lamps at B and C, therefore, which are instrumental in showing up the obstruction, and the design of the reflector should be such as to direct most of the light on to

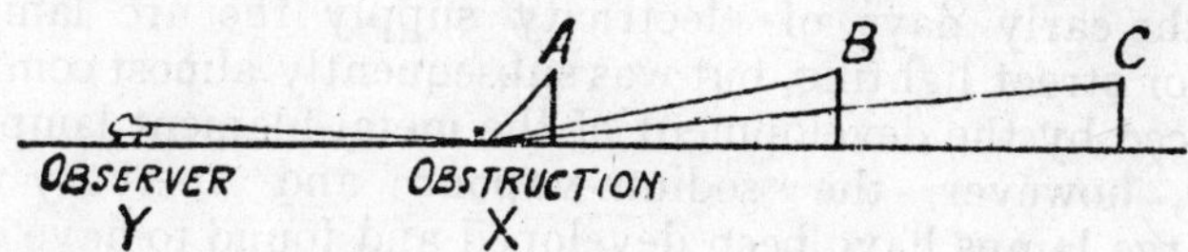

FIG. 153.—SPECULAR-REFLECTION PRINCIPLE OF STREET LIGHTING.

the road surface at a very small angle. Some light must, of course, be directed downwards to assist the pedestrian, who wishes to see objects in his immediate neighbourhood. This method of lighting is suitable only for straight sections of road, and also has the disadvantage that there is some glare, due to the light source being within the range of vision of the observer; the effect of the latter is, however, minimised by the relatively high brightness of the road surface. It is claimed that by this method objects on the roadway can be rendered visible by a smaller expenditure of power than by the diffusion method of lighting, and it is useful, therefore, in dealing with stretches of main and arterial roads.

Power Requirements for Street Lighting

The minimum values of illumination required by various classes of road are laid down in the relevant specifications and range from 2 lumens per square metre for a class A installation to 0·1 lumen per square metre for a class H installation. Class A installations are found only in important shopping centres and road junctions, and are exceptional while class H installations represent the conditions in a poorly lighted suburban street. An average well-lighted street will lie between a class C installation with 5·5 lumen per square metre and a class D installation with 2·2 lumen per square metre. The number of lamp lumens required to provide this illumination varies from 10 to 30 lumens per 0·3 m length of road for a class D installation to 2 to 3 lumens per 0·3 m length for a class H installation, so that the wattage of the lamps can easily be determined for the particular type of lamp to be used. The actual value of the illumination produced by any given installation depends, of course, very largely on the nature of the road surface, and also upon its condition, e.g. wet or dry.

A normal spacing for the lamp standards is 45 m. with a mounting height of 7·6 m.

Type of Lamp

In the early days of electricity supply the arc lamp was used for street lighting, but was subsequently almost completely displaced by the development of the metal-filament lamp. Recently, however, the sodium-vapour and mercury-vapour discharge lamps have been developed and found to have certain particular advantages for street-lighting purposes; the most important of these is the lower power consumption for a given amount of light, which, in spite of the higher cost of the lamp, makes the overall cost of an installation with discharge lamps less than one employing filament lamps. The colour and monochromatic nature of the light produced by such lamps are no disadvantage in street-lighting schemes, since correct colour rendering is, in any case, of minor importance.

Of the two types of lamp, the mercury-vapour type has been developed and used chiefly in this country, while the sodium-vapour type has been developed on the Continent and in America.

———

'IN DEFENCE OF ANGSTROM'

(*From Nature, Vol. 219, 27th July 1968, p. 318*)

This article reports the views of a group of leading spectroscopists of the Inter-Union Commission for Spectroscopy, who consider the proposal to abandon the two well-known units: (i) Angstrom and ii cm^{-1}, in the SI system, as most unwise. These two units have been used from the beginning of spectroscopy and all the immense literature in this field employs these units. Most members of the Commission further recommend indefinite retention of these units in spectroscopy since both of them are metric and very convenient for use.

Photometric Definitions & Formulæ

1. *Defn.* *Radiant Flux* is the power emitted, transformed or received in the form of radiation.

   Symbol: P. Unit: *watt* (W)

2. *Defn.* *Luminous Flux* is that quantity characteristic of radiant flux which expresses its capacity to produce luminous sensation.

   Symbol: F. Unit *Lumen* (lm) = *cd sr*.

3. *Defn.* If a flux of F lumens falls on a surface of area A, then the *Illumination* of that surface is:

   $$E = \frac{F}{A} \text{ lumens/metre}^2 \text{ or } Lux \text{ (lx)} = lm\ m^{-2}$$

4. *Defn.* If a flux of F lumens is emitted by a source in a solid angle ω then the *Luminous Intensity* (candle power) of the source in that direction is:

   $$I = \frac{F}{\omega} \text{ lumens/steradian or } Candela\ (cd)$$

5. *Defn.* If a surface of area A has an effective luminous intensity (candle power) of I candelas in a direction θ to the normal, then the *Luminance* (brightness) of that surface is:

   $$L = \frac{I}{A \cos \theta} \text{ Candela/metre}^2\ (nits).$$

6. If light from a point source of I candelas falls on a surface at distance '*d*' away with an angle of incidence θ, then the Illumination of that surface is:

   $$E = \frac{I \cos \theta}{d^2} \text{ lux } (Lambert's\ cosine\ law).$$

7. If a perfectly diffuse surface with reflection coefficient R is illuminated by E lux, then the Luminance (*brightness*) of that surface is:

22

$$L = \frac{RE}{\pi} \text{ candela/metre}^2$$

$$1 \text{ "foot-candle"} = 1 \text{ candle/foot}^2$$
$$10{\cdot}764 \text{ lux. or}$$
$$1 \text{ lux} = 0{\cdot}093 \text{ lm/ft}^2$$
$$\simeq 0{\cdot}1 \text{ lm/ft}^2$$

N.B.: (1) The *lumen* is the fundamental unit for photometry. Its basic definition is:

The lumen is of such magnitude that the luminance of a full radiator (black body) at the temperature of melting platinum is 6×10^5 candela/metre².

(2) The candela (cd) is the unit of illumination or luminous intensity or luminance in the SI.

SURVEY OF THE MOST IMPORTANT GAS-DISCHARGE LAMPS

(i) Sodium Lamps:

These are available in wattages from 45 to 200W. Since the sodium lamp radiates at a wavelength of 5890-5896 A, the light is monochromatic (of one colour). The wavelength almost coincides with that to which the human eye is most sensitive (5550 A), so that the sodium lamp has a high luminous efficiency of as much as 150 lm/W.

Sodium lamps are used for applications where strong contrasts are important and where colour rendering is a secondary consideration. They are particularly suitable for the lighting of motorways, quays, storage yards, marshalling yards, etc. and for the flood-lighting of buildings.

(ii) High-Pressure Sodium Lamps:

This lamp, the latest in the development of the gas-discharge types, has a continuous spectrum resulting in an attractive "golden" white light and a luminous efficiency of more than 100 lm/W. The new high-pressure sodium lamp, available in a 400 W version, provides the solution wherever lack of colour rendering or inefficiency make existing light sources inadequate. Among the numerous applications can be mentioned: lighting of streets, flyovers, underpasses, shopping and residential areas, squares, railway stations, aerodromes, etc; floodlighting of stadiums, sports grounds, buildings, statues, etc; indoor lighting of factories, hangars, warehouses, exhibition halls, churches, swimming pools, etc.

(iii) Mercury Lamps:

Available in wattages of 50-80-125-250-400-700-1000 and 2000W. The mercury reflecter lamp is suitable for use in places where marked soiling occurs as well as for application in high halls. This lamp is a variation of the normal mercury lamp and has a specially shaped outer bulb with an internal reflector, so that soiling of the upper part has no influence on the luminous flux, which is thus directed downwards.

Mercury reflector lamps are available in wattages of 125-250-400-700 and 1000 W; mercury blended-light lamps in wattages of 160W, 250W and 500W.

(iv) Mercury Iodide Lamps

New developments led to the introduction of the mercury iodide lamps available in a 400W version with a nominal luminous flux of 30 000 lm, and a 2 000 W version with a luminous flux of 190 000 lm.

These lamps combine high efficiency at 75 lm/W with extremely good colour rendering.

Mercury iodide lamps are used for public lighting, industrial lighting and floodlighting.

Summary of Data regarding Electric Lamps:

1. *Incandescent Lamps.* Average life: 1000 burning hours
   Common wattages: 25, 40, 60, 100, 150, 200, 300, 500, 1000
2. *Tubular Fluorescent Lamps.* Average life: 5000 burning hours.

   Common Wattages: 20, 40, 65, 80
3. *Mercury Vapour Lamps:* Average life: 5000 burning hours.
   Common wattages: 80, 125, 250, 400, 1000 and 2000.

CHAPTER V
QUESTIONS

1. The spectral-distribution curve of a lamp is given by the following figures. Using the eye-sensitivity curve of Fig. 112, estimate the theoretical luminous efficiency of the lamp in lumens per watt.

Wavelength (A°)	2 500	5 000	7 500	10 000	15 000	20 000	25 000
Energy radiated (%)	5	15	70	100	75	25	5

2. A light source having an intensity of 1000 CP in all directions is fitted with a reflector so that it directs 65% of its light along a beam having a divergence of 20°. What is the total light flux emitted along the beam and what will be the illumination produced on a surface 30m away from the source. Calculate also the candle-power of the lamp and reflector as viewed from the illuminated surface.

3. A small area 7.5m. in diameter is to be illuminated by lamps suspended at a height of 4.5m. The illumination must be not less than approximately 130 lux at any point. Estimate the power consumption of the lamps required if :

(a) a large number of small lamps are to be used, each having an efficiency of 10 lumens/watt, these being uniformly spaced over the area to be illuminated.

(b) a single lamp suspended over the centre of the area is to be used, the lamp having an efficiency of 20 lumens/watt and being fitted with a reflector which directs the light output only over the surface to be illuminated, giving a uniform candle-power over this angle.

Assume the coefficient of utilisation to be 0.4 in each case.

4. Two lamps suspended at heights of 4.5m and 6.0m respectively, and at a horizontal distance apart of 9.0m are used to light a maidan. Both lamps emit 500 candle-power in all directions. Draw "Contour" lines showing the points at which the illumination at ground level is 0.2, 0.4, 0.6, 0.8 and 1.0 lux.

5. Lamps having reflectors giving a polar curve as shown by the figures below are used in a street-lighting scheme, the lamps being suspended 60m apart above the centre line of the roadway at a height of 10m. Plot a curve showing the horizontal illumination along the centre of the roadway.

Angle to horizontal	10°	20°	30°	40°	50°	70°	90°
Candle-power	300	500	630	550	350	250	240

6. It is desired to illuminate a circular space 15m in diameter by means of a single lamp suspended at a height of 7.5m above its centre. Draw the polar curve which the lamp

and reflector must have in order that there be a uniform illumination of 100 lumens/m^2 over the whole area.

7. A machine shop 30m long by 15m wide, is to have a general illumination of 150 lux on the working plane provided by lamps mounted 5m above it. Assuming a coefficient of utilisation of 0.55, design a suitable installation :

(a) using filament lamps ;

(b) using standard 80-W fluorescent lamps.

8. Estimate the number and disposition of 1000-W floodlight projectors required to illuminate the upper 75m of one face of a clock tower, using the following data :

Height of tower = 100m
Width of tower = 15m
Approximate illumination required 85 lux.

The projectors are to be mounted at ground level 50m from the base of the tower.

Beam divergence of projectors = 10°
Coefficient of utilisation = 0·15
Efficiency of lamps = 18 lm/W.

CHAPTER VI

ECONOMIC ASPECTS OF UTILISING ELECTRICAL ENERGY

THE choice of electrical or any alternative form of equipment for performing a given service or the choice between alternative types of electrical equipment is usually dependent on the relative costs of the possible schemes, and a study of the economics of utilising electrical energy is, therefore, of particular importance. Electrical installations are particularly favoured in this respect, since it is a simple matter to insert instruments and meters to determine the actual energy consumption of any particular piece of apparatus; furthermore, as a result of data so obtained it is usually possible to make accurate preliminary estimates of energy consumptions, and therefore of costs, before any equipment is actually purchased and installed.

Distribution of Costs

The cost of owning and operating any piece of equipment, whether it be a 100-watt lamp or a 750kW. motor, can be split into two parts, which must be considered separately. These are:

(i) *Capital Costs, or Fixed Charges,* which depend only on the size or rating of the equipment in question and are independent of the amount of use to which it is put.

(ii) *Running Charges,* which depend on the hours for which the equipment is in service and the output which it delivers.

The various items coming under these two headings are summarised below:

Fixed Charges	*Running Charges*
Interest on capital.	Energy or fuel cost.
Sinking fund or depreciation.	Maintenance costs.
Rates and taxes.	Wages of operating staff.
Insurance.	
Salaries of management and clerical staff.	

In selecting equipment for any given purpose, the choice must fall upon that which makes the sum of the fixed charges and the running charges, i.e, the total operating cost, a minimum. It is usually found that a reduction in running costs can be obtained only by incurring increased fixed costs and vice versa; for instance, an electric motor of a particular type and size, and, say, 85 per cent. efficiency, will usually be less expensive than a similar motor of 87 per cent. efficiency, although the latter will have a lower running cost on account of its lower loss and may, therefore, have a lower total operating cost.

1. FIXED CHARGES

Of the various fixed charges listed above, the most important are the interest on capital cost, sinking fund, and the salaries of the management and clerical staff; a detailed consideration of the latter, as well as of insurance, rates and taxes, is, however, beyond the scope of this book, as they are not normally within the control of the engineer.

Interest Charges

It is usual to borrow money to purchase any equipment, and the rate of interest charged depends on the state of the money market, the credit of the borrower, and various other factors over which the engineer has no control; he can only influence this charge by exercising wisdom in choosing the time at which he elects to borrow. Even if equipment is purchased out of reserve cash, the normal rate of interest must still be allowed for, since the money might otherwise be earning this interest. Rates of interest vary, in normal circumstances, 5 to 6 per cent. being an average.

Sinking Fund

The useful life of any plant may be fixed by the time taken for it to wear out and become unfit for further use, or it may be fixed by its becoming obsolete due to new technical improvements. In either case money must be set aside, so that at the end of the useful life of the plant there will be a sufficient sum available to purchase new plant to carry on the business or to repay the loan which was raised to purchase the plant initially. The usual method of ensuring that this money is available is to pay annual instalments into a sinking fund.

Typical figures for the useful life of various types of equipment are shown below:

Buildings, 30-50 years.
Transmission lines, 20-25 years.
Motors and generators, 15-20 years.
Instrument and meters, 10-12 years.
Lamps, 1,000-3,000 burning hours.

Suppose we have to provide a sum of Rs. X at the end of N years. If the money were set aside at the end of each year and put into a safe, the annual deposit would obviously have to be Rs. X/N. In practice such a procedure would not be adopted; the money, as it is set aside, would be invested in some dividend-earning concern, and allowed to earn interest so that the annual deposit would be less than the above amount. It is usual to arrange to make sinking-fund payments by means of equal annual deposits, and the method of calculating the value of this deposit is as follows:

Suppose Rs. A is the annual deposit and p is the annual interest earned by this money when it is invested.

At the end of 1st year Rs. A is deposited;
after N — 1 years this will be worth Rs. $A(1+p)^{N-1}$

At the end of 2nd year Rs. A is deposited;
after N — 2 years this will be worth Rs. $A(1+p)^{N-2}$

At the end of 3rd year Rs. A is deposited;
after N — 3 years this will be worth Rs. $A(1+p)^{N-3}$

At the end of (N — 1)th year Rs. A is deposited;
after 1 year this will be worth ... Rs. $A(1+p)$

At the end of Nth year Rs. A is deposited;
this will be worth ... Rs. A

At the end of N years, therefore, the value of all the sums deposited will be:

Rs. $A(1+p)^{N-1}+A(1+p)^{N-2}+A(1+p)^{N-3}+ \dots + A(1+p)+A$

This is a geometrical progression with a common ratio of:

$$r = \frac{1}{1+p}$$

The sum is therefore:

$$\text{Rs. } \frac{rA - A(1+p)^{N-1}}{r+1} = \text{Rs. } A\frac{(1+p)^{N}-1}{p} \quad . \quad . \quad (50)$$

This sum must, of course, equal the amount Rs. X, which the sinking fund has to provide, hence the annual deposit which has to be made can be found from :

$$\text{Rs. A} = \text{Rs}\ \frac{p\,X}{(1+p)^N - 1} \quad . \quad . \quad (51)$$

If the interest be compounded more frequently than at the end of each year, or if the deposits are made at other than yearly intervals, then a modified formula can be developed in a similar way. If at the end of its useful life the plant can be sold as scrap, then the estimated salvage value may be subtracted from the amount Rs. X to be provided by the sinking fund. In some cases, however, the salvage value may be negative, i.e. it may cost money to remove the plant.

It has been assumed above that equal annual deposits are to be paid into the sinking fund. Although this is the usual procedure, it may sometimes be desirable to make the deposits correspond with the earning capacity of the plant. With an electric power system, for instance, during the first few years, when only a relatively few consumers will be connected, it will be earning little revenue, and it may be desirable to reduce or even eliminate the deposits during this period and increase them correspondingly during the later years.

The application of the above formulæ, as well as alternative methods of determining the value of a plant at any time, are illustrated by Example 25.

Example 25 :—An industrial plant has a value at the beginning of its life Rs. 240 000 and a salvage value of Rs. 24 000 at the end of 20 years. Determine the value of the plant at the end of 10 years, using the following methods of assessing the depreciation.

(*i*) *Straight-line depreciation (depreciation proportional to time)*;

(*ii*) *Reducing-balance depreciation (depreciation in any year is a fixed proportion of the value at the beginning of that year)*;

(*iii*) *Sinking-fund depreciation at 8% compounded annually (the depreciation is equal to the value of the sinking fund, this fund being obtained by equal annual deposits arranged to cover the whole of the depreciation at the end of the useful life)*.

Solution :

(i) Total depreciation = Rs. 240 000 − Rs. 24 000
= Rs. 216 000.

After 10 years, the plant will have depreciated by half this amount, i.e. by Rs. 108 000. Its value at the end of 10 years will, therefore, be :

$$\text{Rs. } 240\ 000 - \text{Rs. } 108\ 000 = \textbf{Rs. 132 000.}$$

(ii) Let yearly depreciation be F% of the value at the beginning of the year. At the end of 1st year :

$$\text{Value} = \text{Rs.}\left(240\ 000 - \frac{F}{100} \times 240\ 000\right)$$

$$= 240\ 000\left(1 - \frac{F}{100}\right)$$

At the end of the 2nd year :

$$\text{Value} = \text{Rs. } 240\ 000\left(1 - \frac{F}{100}\right) - 240\ 000\left(1 - \frac{F}{100}\right) \cdot \frac{F}{100}$$

$$= \text{Rs. } 240\ 000\left(1 - \frac{F}{100}\right)^2$$

At the end of 20th year :

$$\text{Value} = \text{Rs. } 240\ 000\left(1 - \frac{F}{100}\right)^{20}$$

The value after 20 years is, however, Rs. 24 000.

$$\text{Therefore } 24\ 000 = 240\ 000\left(1 - \frac{F}{100}\right)^{20}$$

$$\therefore \ \text{Log}_{10}\ 24\ 000 = \text{Log}_{10}\ 240\ 000 + 20\ \text{Log}_{10}\left(1 = \frac{F}{100}\right)$$

$$\therefore \ 4{\cdot}38 = 5{\cdot}38 + 20\ \text{Log}_{10}\left(1 - \frac{F}{100}\right)$$

$$\therefore \ \text{Log}\left(1 - \frac{F}{100}\right) = -0{\cdot}05$$

$$\therefore \ \left(1 - \frac{F}{100}\right) = 0{\cdot}891.$$

At the end of 10 years :

$$\text{Value} = \text{Rs. } 240\ 000\left(1 - \frac{F}{100}\right)^{10}$$

$$= \text{Rs. } 240\ 000 \times 0{\cdot}891^{10}$$

$$= \textbf{Rs. 75 840.}$$

(iii) Total value of sinking fund at the end of 20 years

= Rs. 216 000.

∴ From Equation (51).

$$\text{Annual deposit, } A = \text{Rs. } \frac{0 \cdot 08 \times 216\ 000}{(1 \cdot 08)^{20} - 1}$$

$$= \text{Rs. } \frac{0 \cdot 08 \times 216\ 000}{3 \cdot 66}$$

At the end of 10 years, the value of the sums deposited will be, from equation (50) :

$$\text{Rs. } \frac{4\ 728\ (1 \cdot 08)^{10} - 1}{0 \cdot 08} = \text{Rs. } 68\ 640.$$

This is the depreciation, so that the value of the plant will be Rs. (240 000 − 68 640) = 171 360.

2. ENERGY COSTS—PUBLIC SUPPLY

Of the running charges listed at the beginning of this chapter, the energy costs are usually the most important and must be given detailed consideration by any user of electric power.

Engergy may be purchased from a public supply company or obtained from a private generating plant, and in the past there has been a considerable amount of controversy regarding the relative merits of the two schemes. Except in special cases, however, the modern tendency is to use the public supply whenever this is available for the following reasons :

(i) The management is relieved of the responsibility of generation and can concentrate entirely on its manufacturing processes.

(ii) Ample overload capacity is available and extensions to the plant can be carried out at short notice.

(iii) There is less probability of complete and prolonged shutdown due to faults or accidents in the power-supply equipment.

(iv) The low rate at which electrical energy can be purchased in most areas makes the use of a public supply definitely more economical than the use of a private plant in the majority of cases.

There are, however, certain special circumstances where private generation is preferable and these are discussed on page 359.

The Two-part Tariff

Precisely the same considerations govern the finances of an electricity supply undertaking as any other concern, i.e. they have to meet both fixed charges corresponding to the interest, sinking fund, etc., on the generation and distribution plant which they have had to install and also running charges corresponding to the fuel costs and distribution losses. These costs are passed on to the consumer in the form of a tariff for energy, and for large consumers, as well as for a large proportion of the domestic consumers, this is a "two-part" tariff, one part of which is a fixed charge designed to cover an appropriate proportion of the fixed charges to be met by the supply undertaking, and the other part of which is a running charge dependent on the amount of energy used.

The fixed charge made to any consumer must, of course, bear some relation to the amount of plant which the supply company has to install to supply that consumer, and this is usually regarded as being proportional to his maximum load or maximum demand, the value of which is recorded by a special maximum-demand meter. This part of the tariff is, therefore, generally expressed as a certain price per kW. of maximum demand. The running cost depends on the amount of energy consumed, and is charged for at a certain price per unit. A typical tariff is thus Rs. 81 per kW.+Rs. 0.075 per unit, and a consumer can easily work out the cost of his energy as shown in Example 26.

Example 26 : Estimate the annual energy cost for an industrial consumer with a factory which take a load of 200 kW for 1 hour per day, 150 kW for 7 hours per day, 50 kW for 8 hours per day. The tariff in force is Rs. 108 per kW + 10 paise per unit.

Solution :

Maximum demand = 200 kW

Maximum demand charge = 200 × Rs. 108 = Rs. 21 600

Annual units consumed, assuming a 6-day week :

200 × 1 × 6 × 52 = 62 400 kWh

150 × 7 × 6 × 52 = 327 600 kWh

50 × 8 × 6 × 52 = 124 800 kWh

Total : = 514 800 kWh

Annual cost = 5 148 000 paise = Rs. 51 480

Total annual cost = Rs. 73 080.

Average cost per unit, including the maximum demand charge:

$$\frac{73\ 080 \times 100}{514\ 800} = \mathbf{14{\cdot}2\ p.}$$

Effect of Power Factor

The size of cable which has to be installed, and, to a lesser extent, the size of generating and transforming equipment, depend on the current with which they have to deal; a load of 1,000 kW. at, say, 0.8 lagging power factor will take a 25 per cent. greater current than 1,000 kW. at unity power factor. With a tariff as indicated above, a consumer taking his power at a low power factor pays exactly the same as a consumer having unity power factor, although he is using a larger proportion of the genereting and distribution equipment and also, of course, causing larger copper losses. Such a state of affairs is obviously inequitable, and it is usual to modify the simple tariff outlined above in order to penalise consumers who have a low power factor.

Power-factor Tariffs.—There are two methods of modifying the ordinary two-part tariff in order to increase the charge to low power-factor consumers:

(i) *Maximum kVA. Demand.*—Instead of charging a certain sum per kW. of maximum demand, a fixed charge per kVA. can be employed. This penalises for bad power factor only at the time of the consumer's peak load, but as it is at this period that a low power factor is important this is an advantage.

(ii) *Power Factor Penalty Clause.*—A certain sum may be added to the ordinary kW. maximum-demand charge for every 0.1 by which the power factor falls below some stated value, say 0.8 or 0.85.

Other Factors

With large power contracts it is common practice to insert other clauses to cover eventualities over which the supply undertaking has no control; for instance, a clause may be inserted allowing the undertaking to increase or decrease the running cost by a certain fraction of a penny for every increase or decrease of, say, 1s. per ton in the price of coal. Variations in rates and taxes payable by the supply undertaking may be covered in a similar manner.

Measurements

For costing purposes the measurements which have to be made are of total energy consumed, maximum demand, and power factor at the time of maximum demand. Measurement of energy presents no difficulty, and is done by one of the numerous makes of energy meter on the market.

Measurement of Maximum Demand.—For large consumers the day is divided up into short periods, usually of half an hour each, and the total number of units supplied during each of these periods is measured. Dividing this by the length of the period gives the average kW. over that period, and the highest of these values in a given time, i.e. a month, quarter, or year, is called the maximum demand in that time. By choosing a period of one-quarter to half an hour, an excessive value due to a momentary heavy overload caused by a fault or other unexpected occurrence is avoided. The meter which is installed for determining the maximum demand frequently records the values of the average kW. in each of the half-hour periods in addition to giving a direct indication of the maximum of these values.

For small consumers a simpler thermal type of maximum demand indicator can be used.

Measurement of Power Factor.—When one of the power-factor tariffs is in operation a reactive kVAh. meter must be installed, together with an auxiliary device which records the kVArh.* in each of the half-hour periods. The power factor in any one of the half-hour periods is then equal to cos φ,

$$\text{where } \varphi = \tan^{-1} \frac{\text{kVA Rh.}}{\text{kWh.}}$$

If the first form of power-factor tariff is in operation, the total kVA. must be determined from the above for each of the half-hour periods ; if the second form of tariff is used, then only the power factor in the maximum kW. demand period need be found. It is possible, when a maximum kVA. demand tariff is in force, to use a meter which records kVA. direct, but such meters are some-what complicated and not very widely used.

The Grid Tariff

In the U. K. practically all generation and primary transmission is in the hands of the Central Electricity Board. The

*kVArh. = Reactive kilovolt-ampere-hours

energy is fed into a network, or grid, of transmission lines operating at 132 kV. or 33 kV., which covers almost the entire country, and the various supply undertakings purchase their energy in bulk from this system. In India, the price at which the Electricity Board of each state sells energy, therefore, must form the basis of any tariff which can be used for selling energy to the consumers; this tariff covers the fixed charges and running cost of its own distribution system.

Fixed Charge

(*a*) *kW. Charge.*—Rs. 96 per year per kW. of maximum demand for the first 2,000 kW., dropping in steps to Rs 91—20 p. per kW. for demands over 8,000 kW.

The maximum demand is, for costing purposes, taken as the average of the maximum demands in the first three months of the year and in the last three months of the year. The use of energy during the summer, when the system is lightly loaded, is thus encouraged.

(*b*) *Power-factor Clause.*—If the power factor falls below 0·85 at the time of the maximum demand, the kW. charge is increased by Rs. 6-30Pfor every 0·1 by which it is below 0·85.

(*c*) *Rates Clause.*—If the rates amount to more or less than Rs. 5·10p per kW., the kW. charge shall be increased or decreased by Rs. 1·90p for each Rs. 1·20p. by which the actual value is above or below Rs. 5·10p.

(*d*) *Service Charge.*—An additional charge, depending on the circumstances, shall be made if the undertaking be connected to the grid at more than one point.

Running Charge

(*a*) *Unit Charge.*—4·4p per kWh.

(*b*) *Coal Price Clause.*—If the cost of coal, reduced to a standard calorific value of 25·586 MJ/kg, is more or less than Rs. 45·60p per tonne, the running cost shall be increased or decreased by 0·007p for each paise by which the actual cost is above or below Rs. 45·60p.

Various special charges or arrangements can also be made to suit consumers with special or unusual requirements.

3. REDUCTION OF ENERGY COSTS

Any consumer will obviously wish to arrange matters so that his annual energy costs are a minimum and, if charged on one of the common tariffs mentioned in Section 1 of this chapter, he may help matters by paying attention to the following points:

Improvement of power factor.

Improvement of load factor.

Use of off-peak energy.

Power-factor Improvement

It has already been explained that a consumer has frequently to pay more for his energy if he takes it at a low power factor, and it may therefore pay him to spend money, thereby incurring additional capital costs, in purchasing equipment for improving his power factor, in order that his energy costs may be reduced. In addition to an actual saving in total annual costs, an improvement in power factor results in reduced voltage drops in cables, and therefore leads to better operation generally.

Amongst the chief causes of bad power factor may be mentioned induction motors, particularly in small sizes and when running partially loaded, arc and induction furnaces, and electric-discharge lamps. The power factors of different types of loads are shown in Table XXVII below:

TABLE XXVII

Nature of load	Working pwoer	Power factor (lagging)
Incandescent lamp	5 W — 1 kW	1·00 (unity)
Fluorescent lamp	10 W — 200 W	0·6 — 0·8
Arc lamp	1 — 3 kW	0·3 — 0·7
Neon lamp	30 — 150 W	0·4 — 0·5
Fan	40 — 150 W	0·5 — 0·75
Resistor	100 W	0·95
Resistance heater	20 W — 100 kW	1·00 (unity)
Induction heater	1 — 100 kW	0·85
Resistance furnace	100 — 10 000 kW	0·6 — 0·9
Arc furnace	100 — 10 000 kW	0·85
Induction furnace	50 — 500 kW	0·6 — 0·8
A. C. arc welder	5 — 20 kW	0·3 — 0·4
A. C. resistance welder	1 — 50 kW	0·65

The following methods are open to a consumer who wishes to take his energy at a high power factor:

Use of high-power factor motors.

Use of induction motors with phase advancers.

Use of static capacitors for power-factor improvement.

Use of synchronous capacitors for power-factor improvement.

High-power-factor Motors.—Reference to Table I shows that there are several types of motor which operate at a power factor of approximately unity, notably the synchronous motor, the compensated induction motor, and the Schrage motor ; it can be seen also that such motors are more expensive and have a higher maintenance cost than the plain induction motor, so that in choosing such motors these additional costs must be balanced against the savings in energy cost due to their higher power factor. Of the above types the synchronous motor is particularly useful, as it can very easily be designed to operate at a leading power factor and therefore compensate for the lagging power factor of other machines.

Induction Motors with Phase Advancers.—The low power factor of an induction motor is largely due to its having to draw its exciting current (which lags behind the voltage by 90°) from the a.c. supply, and it may be improved by equipping the set with an a.c. exciter or phase advancer, which supplies this exciting current to the rotor circuit at slip frequency ; such an exciter may be mounted on the same shaft as the main motor or may be suitably driven from it, and it can easily be fitted to an existing motor. Their use is not generally economical in connection with motors below about 150kW but above this size, in cases where the use of a synchronous motor is inadmissible, they are frequently employed.

Shunt and series types of phase advancers are available according to whether the exciting winding of the advancer is connected in parallel or in series with the rotor winding of the induction motor.

Static Capacitors.—A capacitor takes a current which leads the voltage by practically 90°, and if connected in parallel with apparatus taking a lagging current it can therefore improve the power factor. Capacitors for this purpose may be connected in parallel with each individual motor, or larger units connected in parallel with the main incoming supply may be employed.

Synchronous Capacitors.—A synchronous motor running light takes, neglecting losses, a purely reactive current which is leading or lagging according as to whether the excitation is above or below normal (see Fig. 5). Such a machine, if connected in parallel with the supply, can therefore be used to give power-factor improvement in the same way as a static capacitor, and possesses the advantage that the power factor can very easily be controlled by variation of the field excitation. Except in sizes above about 500 kVA., however, the cost is greater than that of static capacitors of the same rating.

Calculation of Leading kVA, required.—Consider an installation having a lagging current at, say, 0·7 power factor, as shown by the full vectors in Fig. 154. By multiplying the current by the

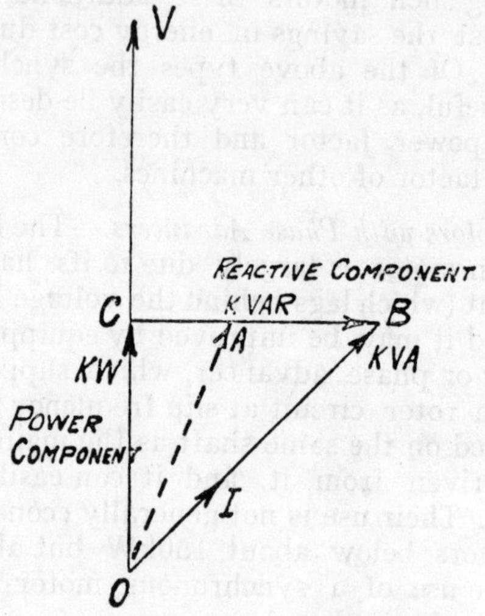

FIG. 154.—POWER-FACTOR IMPROVEMENT.

voltage (or $\sqrt{3} \times$ voltage for a 3-phase circuit), it can be made to represent, to a certain scale, the total kVA. taken by the installation; the power and reactive components of this are the kW. and lagging kVAr. respectively. If it is desired to improve the power factor to, say, 0·9, the new value of total kVA. will be as shown by the dotted vector OA. The new value of lagging kVAr. will be CA and the difference between this and the original value CB must be balanced by leading kVAr; the leading kVAr. which will therefore have to be supplied by the equipment for power-factor improvement equipment is AB.

If the amount of leading kVAr. which has to be supplied to improve the power factor from 0·7 to various values up to unity is plotted, the curve shown in Fig. 155 is obtained. It can be seen that to improve the power factor above 0·9 or 0·95 requires a large amount of leading kVAr., and the cost of the equipment to improve it to such high values may well outweigh any savings in energy costs.

The most economical value to which to improve the power factor can be determined by working out the total cost with the power factor improved to different values and tabulating or plotting a curve of the results to find at which value the cost becomes a minimum. This procedure is illustrated in the first part of Example 27.

A quicker method is to solve the problem analytically—consider a consumer taking a load of PkW. at a power factor of $\cos \varphi$ and charged at a tariff of Rs A, per year per kVA. of maximum demand plus d paise per kWh. The cost of apparatus to improve the power factor (e.g. static condensers or phase advancer) is Rs B, and the rate of interest and depreciation is p per cent. per year.

Suppose the power factor is to be improved to $\cos \varphi'$; the new kVA. will be $\frac{P}{\cos \varphi'}$, and the new maximum demand charge will be $\frac{P}{\cos \varphi'} A$ per year. The kVA. of the phase advancing apparatus to improve the power factor from $\cos \varphi$ to $\cos \varphi'$ will be $P \tan \varphi - P \tan \varphi'$ and the yearly cost of this will be:

$$\frac{Bp}{100}(P \tan \varphi - P \tan \varphi')$$

$$= B' P (\tan \varphi - \tan \varphi')$$

where B′ is the yearly cost of the phase-advancing apparatus.

The total yearly cost is thus:

$$C = \frac{P}{\cos \varphi'} A + B' P (\tan \varphi - \tan \varphi')$$

To find the value of φ' which will make this a minimum it must be differentiated and equated to zero, i.e.:

$$\frac{dC}{d\varphi'} = - PA \sec \varphi' \tan \varphi' + B'P \sec \varphi' = 0$$

$$\therefore \sin \varphi' = \frac{B'}{A}$$

$$\therefore \cos \varphi' = \sqrt{1 - \left(\frac{B'}{A}\right)^2} \quad . \quad . \quad . \quad (52)$$

It may be noted that the original power factor, which occurs only in the middle term of the expression for cost, disappears in the differentiation and so has no influence on the most economical value. If the losses in the phase-advancing apparatus or any other items have to be taken into account, this can be done by including a further term in the expression for cost.

Example 27: A factory which has a maximum demand of 175 kW at a power factor of 0·75, is charged on a tariff of Rs. 72 per kVA per year + 10 paise per unit. Investigate the economic possibilities of improving the power factor, if phase-advancing equipment can be purchased for Rs. 120 per kVA; interest, depreciation, maintenance, and cost of losses = 20% of capital cost per year.

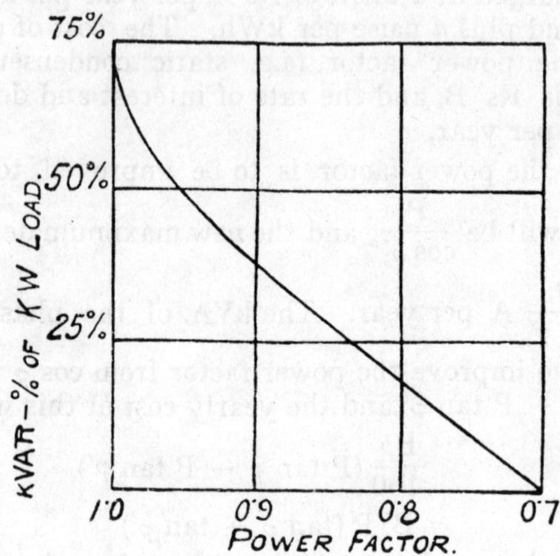

FIG. 155. REACTIVE kVA. REQUIRED TO IMPROVE POWER FACTOR FROM 0.7 TO VARIOUS OTHER VALUES.

Solution:

Before installation of capacitors:

$$\text{kVA demand} = \frac{175}{0 \cdot 75} = 234 \text{ kVA}$$

Maximum demand charge = 72×234 = Rs. 16 848 per year.

We can now choose various values of capacitor kVA. Calculate the new power factor and maximum demand charges and compare the savings with the yearly cost of capacitors. This is done in tabular form in Table XXVIII.

TABLE XXVIII

kVA of phase advancing equipment	New total kVA	New power factor	New m.d. charge (Rs. per year	Saving in m.d. charge (Rs. per year)	Cost of equipment Rs.	Yearly cost of equipment Rs.	Net yearly saving Rs.
150	175	1·0	12 600	4 248	18 000	3 600	648
125	177	0·99	12 744	4 104	15 000	3 000	1 104
100	183	0·958	13 176	3 672	12 000	2 400	1 272
75	192	0·914	13 824	3 024	9 000	1 800	1 224
50	203	0·863	14 516	2 232	6 000	1 200	1 032
25	217	0·808	15 624	1 224	3 000	600	624
0	234	0·750	16 848	0	0	0	0

It can be seen that the saving is a maximum, when the power factor is improved to *about* 0·94, and with the price of energy and equipment at the figures stated it would *not* be economical to improve it to any higher value.

Using the analytical method (Equation (52))

$$\cos \varphi' = \sqrt{1 - \left(\frac{120 \times 20}{72 \times 100}\right)^2}$$
$$= 0{\cdot}943$$

Improvement of Load Factor

The load factor is defined as the ratio $\frac{\text{average load}}{\text{maximum load}}$ and therefore depends on the shape of the daily or yearly load curve, a typical example of which is shown in Fig. 156. The maximum-demand charge depends on the maximum value of this curve, so that if this can be reduced without reducing the total number of units consumed a saving in the yearly energy costs will be effected.

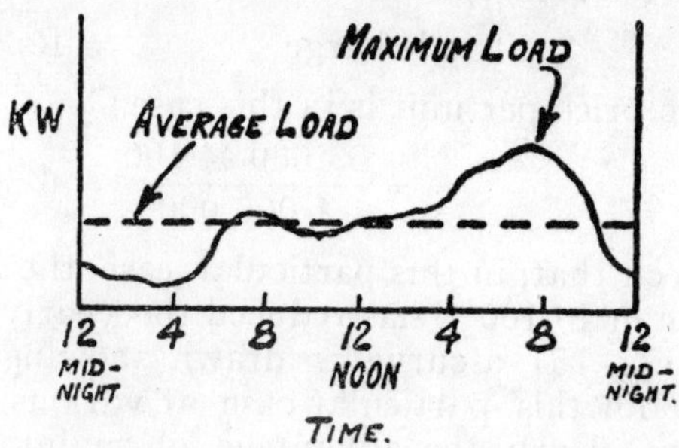

FIG. 156.—TYPICAL DAILY LOAD CURVE.

Industrial concerns can frequently effect such a reduction by arranging their production schedules so that several processes requiring large demands of energy are not carried out at the same time. The savings effected by an improvement of load factor are illustrated by the following example :

Example 28 : A consumer requires 1 000 000 units per year and his yearly load factor is 30%. The tariff in force is Rs. 120 per kW per year + 5 paise per unit. Estimate the saving in his energy costs, which would result if he improved his load factor to 100%.

Solution :

$$\text{Average load} = \frac{1\,000\,000}{8\,760} = 114 \text{ kW}$$

$$\text{Maximum load} = 114 \times \frac{100}{30} = 380 \text{ kW}$$

$$\text{Maximum demand charge} = 380 \times 120 = \text{Rs. } 45\,600$$

$$\text{Unit charge} = \frac{1\,000\,000 \times 5}{100} = \text{Rs. } 50{,}000$$

$$\text{Total charge} = \text{Rs. } 95\,600$$

$$\text{Average price per unit} = \frac{95\,600 \times 100}{1\,000\,000} = 9.56 \text{ p.}$$

If, by rearranging his production schedule, the consumer could take his energy at a load factor of 100%, the costs would be :

$$\text{Maximum load} = \text{average load} = 114 \text{ kW}$$

$$\text{Maximum demand charge} = 114 \times 120 = \text{Rs. } 13\,680$$

$$\text{Unit charge (as before)} = \text{Rs. } 50\,000$$

$$\text{Total charge} = \text{Rs. } 63\,680$$

The average price per unit is in this case :

$$= \frac{63\,680 \times 100}{1\,000\,000} = 6{\cdot}368\ p$$

It is thus seen that, in this particular case the improvement in the load factor to 100% has reduced the yearly energy costs by 50%. In Fig. 157 a curve is drawn showing the average cost of energy for this particular case at various load factors, and this shows clearly the advantage of maintaining as high a load factor as possible.

Off-peak Loads

Just as it is to the advantage of consumers to improve their load factor, so also is it to the advantage of the supply undertakings, since an improvement of the load factor of their entire distribution system means that they can sell a greater number of units without adding to their capital costs. The load on a typical supply undertaking system usually has pronounced peak loads in the morning and early evening and a very low load during the night, as shown in Fig. 156. During the night, therefore, and any other off-peak period which may occur, a large proportion of the generating and distribution equipment will be lying idle, and if the undertaking can induce consumers to take energy during this period it can be supplied

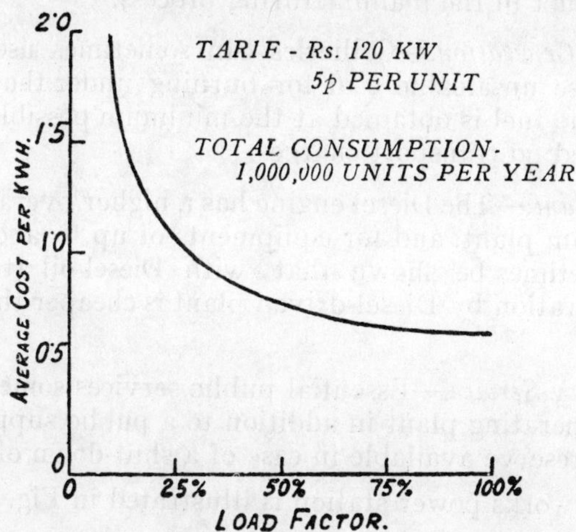

FIG. 157.—EFFECT OF LOAD FACTOR ON OVERALL ENERGY COST.

without incurring any additional capital costs and should therefore prove very profitable.

In order to encourage the use of energy during these periods many undertakings offer special off-peak tariffs with energy at a price considerably lower than that normally in force—figures of 2p to 2·5p. per unit are quoted in some cases. Any consumer should therefore inquire if such tariffs are available and, if so, should endeavour to carry out certain processes during the night or other periods when such tariffs can be obtained. Amongst such processes may be classed building- or water-heating by thermal storage, pumping, refrigeration, and various industrial processes where energy costs form a large proportion of the total.

4. USE OF PRIVATE GENERATING PLANT

There are certain cases where private generation may be more economical than the use of a public supply for reasons which usually fall under one of the following headings:

Use of Exhaust Steam.—Some industrial processes require considerable quantities of steam at a fairly low temperature and pressure and the exhaust steam from generating plant can be employed for this purpose.

Waste-heat Stations.—It may be possible to use as fuel some waste product in the manufacturing process.

Pit-head Generation.—Collieries can sometimes use low-grade or otherwise unsaleable coal for burning under the boilers—in any case the fuel is obtained at the minimum possible cost, as it has incurred no transport charges.

Diesel Plant.—The Diesel engine has a higher overall efficiency than a steam plant, and for equipments of up to about 500kW. it can sometimes be shown that, with Diesel oil at its present price, generation by Diesel-driven plant is cheaper than a public supply.

Emergency Service.—Essential public services sometimes use a private generating plant in addition to a public supply in order to have a reserve available in case of a shut-down of the latter.

A small works power station is illustrated in Fig. 158.

Use of Exhaust Steam

Amongst the industries requiring quantities of steam in their manufacturing processes are paper making, sugar manufactories, textile mills, laundries, chemical works, and dyeworks. By making use of the exhaust steam from reciprocating engines or steam turbines for these purposes the efficiency of the generating plant can be increased to 50 or 60 per cent. The major difficulty in securing this economy in practice is that of making the power load and the steam requirements balance at all times; if the power load is such as to produce more exhaust steam than is required this will have to be wasted (unless further expense and complication are introduced in providing steam-storage cylinders), while if the power load does not provide sufficient exhaust steam, then high-pressure steam will have to be throttled down to the required pressure. There are, however, numerous installations where the use of exhaust steam in this way is found to be economical, a notable example being the Imperial Chemical Industries plant at Billingham in the U.K.

Waste-heat Stations

Many industries have a certain amount of waste heat or waste products which can be used as fuel, thereby almost eliminating the fuel cost from the cost of generation.

FIG. 158.—WORKS POWER STATION WITH INTERNAL-COMBUSTION ENGINES AND D.C. GENERATORS.
(*Crompton Parkinson*)

Waste-gas Stations.—Coke ovens produce waste gas having a calorific value of about 18·63 MJ/m^3, and blast furnaces produce a gas having a calorific value of about 3·7 MJ/m^3. Gas from both these sources can be used in gas engines to drive generators, and this represents the most efficient type of waste-heat station; as an alternative the gas may be burnt under boilers to provide steam for turbines.

Waste Product as Fuel.—In some industries, such as wood-working, there is a large amount of combustible waste, and this may be burnt under boilers to produce steam. General town refuse has also been used successfully in some cases as a fuel.

Pit-head Generation

Collieries have, in the past, frequently found it economical to generate their own power, partly because coal is easily and cheaply available and also because a steam supply was almost invariably required in any case for operating the steam winding engines. With the advent of the electric winder, however, the latter reason is tending to disappear and the increasing use of electric coal-cutting, haulage, and other equipment is leading to much larger power requirements, so that the modern tendency is to purchase power from a public supply. A point to be noted in connection with pit-head generation is that there is not usually a supply of cooling water available for the condensers, so that cooling towers, with their slightly lower efficiency, must be employed.

Diesel Plant

The present low price of Diesel oil may make the operation of a Diesel-engine-driven plant an economic proposition where the power requirements are small.

Typical costs of Diesel plant in sizes of up to about 500 kW. are as follows :

Capital cost, Rs. 240 to Rs. 480 per kW.

Running costs (fuel and oil), 5 *p* to 6 *p* per unit.

In addition the wages of one or more operating and maintenance engineers must be considered.

An example illustrating the method of making a comparison between the cost of a Diesel plant and a public supply is given below :

Example 29 : A supply has to be provided for a factory having a maximum load of 250 kW and an annual load factor of 40%. Compare the costs of providing this from (a) public supply at 11 kV having a tariff of Rs. 120 per kW + 4 paise per unit and (b) a Diesel plant costing Rs. 360 per kW and having a running cost for fuel and oil of 6 paise per unit generated. Rate of interest and depreciation on :

Transformers, 8%
Diesel plant, 12%
Cost of transformers Rs. 18 per kVA.

Solution:

Total number of units per year:

$$250 \times \frac{40}{100} \times 8760 = 876\ 000 \text{ kWh}$$

(a) *Public Supply*

Cost of transformers—to ensure adequate reserve and small allowance for future extensions, assume that three 150 kVA units are chosen.

$$\text{Capital cost} = \text{Rs. } 3 \times 150 \times 18 = \text{Rs. } 8\ 100$$

$$\text{Yearly cost} = \text{Rs. } 8\ 100 \times \frac{8}{100} = \text{Rs. } 648$$

$$\text{Maximum demand charge} = \text{Rs. } 120 \times 250 = \text{Rs. } 30\ 000$$

$$\text{Unit cost} = \left(\frac{876\ 000 \times 4}{100}\right) = \text{Rs. } 35\ 040$$

$$\text{Total yearly cost} = \text{Rs. } 65\ 688$$

(b) *Diesel Plant*

Again, to provide adequate reserve, assume that three 150 kW sets are installed.

$$\text{Cost} = 3 \times 150 \times 360 = \text{Rs. } 162\ 000$$

$$\text{Yearly cost} = 162\ 000 \times \frac{12}{100} = \text{Rs. } 19\ 440$$

$$\text{Operating staff yearly wage} = \text{Rs. } 4\ 800$$

$$\text{Unit cost} = \frac{876\ 000 \times 6}{100} = \text{Rs. } 52\ 560$$

$$\text{Total yearly cost} = \text{Rs. } 76\ 800$$

It is thus seen that, with this particular load factor and tariff for the public supply, the diesel plant is about 16% more expensive than the public supply, and this is, therefore, a case where the latter is preferable. At smaller load factors, however, the balance would tend to become in favour of the diesel plant.

General Comparison of Private Plant and Public Supply

The various factors discussed in connection with public supply costs, namely improvement of power factor and load factor, are also of importance in connection with a private supply, since they influence the amount of plant which has to be installed. In addition to capital and running costs of a private plant allowance should also be made in most cases for the space occupied by it, since this will be considerably greater than that required for the transformer and switchgear usually necessary with a public supply. The question of reliability and spare plant must also be carefully considered, since any serious failure of the private plant may necessitate a total shut-down for several days, whereas in the rare cases when a failure of a public supply occurs it is not usually for more than an hour. Even when private plant is used, it is generally found desirable in addition to have a connection to the public supply to provide a reserve and also to supply power at times of very light load, when it is not worth while running one of the private generating sets, e.g. at night and week-ends; for such a connection a charge must obviously be made even though energy is not normally taken from it, and the usual procedure is to make the consumer agree to take a certain minimum number of units per year.

5. ECONOMIC CHOICE OF EQUIPMENT

It usually happens when some equipment is to be purchased that several alternatives are available, each of which possesses one or more special features, and it is necessary to be able to estimate the value of these in order to make the most economical choice.

No definite rules can be laid down to govern the choice in such cases, but several typical problems are worked out in the following paragraphs.

Initial Cost and Efficiency

It frequently happens that two pieces of equipment having quite different initial costs are available for performing a given duty. In many of these cases, however, it will be found that the more expensive of the two pieces has a lower running cost and may, therefore, be less expensive in total yearly cost.

Example 30 : A 37 kW motor is required to drive a pump which has to be in operation on full-load for 3 000 hours per year. Two motors of similar reliability and maintenance requirements are available, viz.:

Motor A :—Cost Rs. 1440 ; efficiency 88%
Motor B :—Cost Rs. 1920 ; efficiency 89%

The unit cost of energy is 6 paise per kWh and interest and depreciation may be taken as 10% per year. Which motor will give the lower yearly cost ?

Solution :

Let η be the efficiency

$$\text{Loss} = (1-\eta) \times \text{Input} = \left(\frac{1-\eta}{\eta}\right) \times \text{output}$$

$$= \left(\frac{1}{\eta} - 1\right) \times \text{Output}$$

Output = 37 kW.

Motor A

$$\text{Capital charges} = \text{Rs. } 1440 \times \frac{10}{100} = \text{Rs. } 144 \text{ per year}$$

$$\text{Loss} = \left[\left(\frac{1}{0{\cdot}88}\right) - 1\right] \times \text{output} = 0{\cdot}135 \times 37 = 5 \text{ kW}$$

$$\text{Yearly cost of loss} = \frac{5 \times 3\,000 \times 6}{100} = \text{Rs. } 900.$$

Motor B

$$\text{Capital charges} = \text{Rs. } 1920 \times \frac{10}{100} = \text{Rs. } 192 \text{ per year}$$

$$\text{Loss} = \left[\left(\frac{1}{0{\cdot}89}\right) - 1\right] \times 37 = 0{\cdot}122 \times 37 = 4{\cdot}51 \text{ kW}$$

$$\text{Yearly cost of loss} = \frac{4{\cdot}51 \times 3\,000 \times 6}{100} = \text{Rs. } 811{\cdot}8.$$

It is thus seen that although Motor B is more expensive in first cost, there is a saving of Rs. 88·2 in the cost of the losses, which more than outweighs the increased yearly capital charge. In addition, there would also be a saving in the maximum demand charge if such a tariff were in operation and if the motor were in use at the time of the maximum demand.

Capitalisation of Losses

An alternative method of solving a problem in which the cost of losses has to be balanced against an increased capital cost is to "capitalise the losses," i.e. to determine how much extra capital cost could economically be paid for a machine of higher efficiency.

Consider two motors A and B; A has a yearly cost of loss of Rs. L_A and B has a yearly cost of loss of Rs. L_B. The rate of interest is p per cent. The saving in yearly running cost resulting from the selection of motor B is Rs. $(L_A - L_B)$. At p per cent. per year a capital cost involving a yearly expenditure in interest equal to this would be $\dfrac{\text{Rs. } (L_A - L_B)\, 100}{p}$

If, therefore, the capital cost of motor B exceeded that of A by this amount, the saving in running cost resulting from the use of B would be just balanced by the extra capital charges. The above amount is known as the capitalised value of the saving in cost of losses, and if the cost of the more efficient motor exceeds that of the alternative motor by less than this amount, then there will be an overall saving by using the more expensive and more efficient motor.

Example 31 : A 75-kW motor is required to operate at full load for 1 000 hours per year, at half load for 2 000 hours per year and to be shut down for the remainder of the time. Two motors are available : Motor A—Efficiency at full load = 89% ; at half load = 88%. Motor B—efficiency at full load = 90% ; at half load = 89%.

The unit cost of energy is 7.5 paise per kW and interest and depreciation may be taken as 12% per year. If motor A cost Rs. 3 120, what is the minimum price which could economically be paid for motor B?

Solution :

Full load output = 75 kW

half load output = 37·5 kW

Yearly cost of Losses :

Motor A :—

$$\text{Full-load loss} = 75\left[\left(\frac{1}{0{\cdot}89} - 1\right)\right] = 9{\cdot}37 \text{ kW}$$

$$\text{Yearly loss} = 9{\cdot}37 \times 1\,000 = 9\,370 \text{ kWh.}$$

$$\text{Half-load loss} = 37{\cdot}5\left[\left(\frac{1}{0{\cdot}88} - 1\right)\right] = 5{\cdot}06 \text{ kW}$$

$$\text{Yearly loss} = 5{\cdot}06 \times 2\,000 = 10\,120 \text{ kWh}$$

$$\text{Total yearly loss} = 19\,490 \text{ kWh.}$$

$$\text{Yearly cost of loss} = \text{Rs. } \frac{19\,490 \times 7{\cdot}5}{100} = \text{Rs. } 1\,461{\cdot}75$$

Motor B :—

Full-load loss $= 75\left(\frac{1}{0\cdot 9} - 1\right) = 8\cdot 25$ kW

Yearly loss $= 8\cdot 25 \times 1000 = 8250$ kWh

Half-load loss $= 37\cdot 5\,[\,(1/0\cdot 89) - 1\,] = 4\cdot 69$ kW

Yearly loss $= 4\cdot 69 \times 2\,000 = 9\,380$ kWh

Total yearly loss $= 17\,630$ kWh

Yearly cost of loss $=$ Rs. $\frac{17\,630 \times 7\cdot 5}{100} =$ Rs. 1 322.

Yearly saving in loss = Rs. 1 460 — 1 322 = Rs. 138.

Capitalised value of this = Rs. $138 \times \frac{100}{12} =$ Rs. 1 150.

If motor B cost less than (Rs. 3 120 + Rs. 1 150) = Rs. 4 270, it would be cheaper in total yearly cost than A, and this is, therefore, the maximum price which could economically be paid for the more efficient motor.

Choice of Voltage

In cases where energy is supplied at a high voltage such as 3·3 kV. or 6·6 kV., it may be necessary to decide whether to employ for a particular drive a high-voltage motor or a less expensive low voltage motor and a transformer.

Example 32 : A machine requiring 75 kW for 4 000 hours per year is to be driven by an electric motor. The following equipment is available: 75 kW low voltage induction motor, cost Rs. 3 600, efficiency 91%, power factor 0·89. Transformer, cost Rs. 18 per kVA, efficiency 98% (neglect magnetising kVA).

Interest and depreciation on above 8% per year. 75 kW high voltage induction motor, cost Rs. 6 000, efficiency 91%, power factor 0·89.

Interest and depreciation on high voltage motor 12%.

Tariff for energy = Rs. 108 per kVA + 4 paise per unit. Determine the most economic arrangement,

Solution :

Output = 75 kW | Low—Voltage motor |

kVA input $= 75/(0\cdot 89 \times 0\cdot 91) = 92\cdot 5$ kVA

A 100 KVA transformer would have to be used since the choice of one of a standard size is necessary for cheapness.

cost of transformer $= 100 \times 18$ = Rs. 1 800

total capital cost $= 3\ 600 + 1800$ = Rs. 5 400

annual charge $= 5\ 400 \times (8/100) =$ Rs. 432

overall efficiency $= 0{\cdot}91 \times 0{\cdot}98 = 0{\cdot}892$

Loss (see previous example) $= [\ 1/(0{\cdot}892) - 1\ ]\ 75 = 9{\cdot}37$ kW

$$\text{Yearly cost of loss} = \left(\frac{9{\cdot}37 \times 4000 \times 4}{100}\right) = \text{Rs. } 1499{\cdot}2$$

Maximum demand $= 75/(0{\cdot}91 \times 0{\cdot}98 \times 0{\cdot}89) = 94{\cdot}5$ kVA

Maximum demand charge $= 94{\cdot}5 \times 108 =$ Rs. 10 200

Adding these costs gives: Rs. $432 + 1\ 499{\cdot}2 + 10\ 200$

$=$ Rs. 12 131·2

High—Voltage motor

Yearly capital charge $= 6000 \times (12/100) =$ Rs. 720

loss $= [\ (1/0{\cdot}91) - 1\ ] \times 75 = 7{\cdot}5$ kW

Yearly cost of loss $= (7{\cdot}5 \times 4000 \times 4)/100 =$ Rs. 1 200

Maximum demand charge $= 92{\cdot}5 \times 108 =$ Rs. 10 000

Adding these costs gives Rs. $720 + 1200 + 10\ 000 =$ Rs. 11 920.

There is thus a yearly saving of Rs. 12 131·2 — 11 920 = Rs. 211·2 in favour of the High-voltage motor.

Cost of Renewals

In some instances, the life of the equipment and, therefore, the cost of renewals can be widely influenced by the mode of operation. An example of this nature is afforded by the metal-filament lamp, curves of life and output for which are given in Fig. 133. The life of a lamp at its rated voltage is quoted by the mannfacturers to be about 1,000 hours, and in most cases it is desirable to operate lamps at their rated voltage; the following example shows, however, that it may, in certain cases, pay to purchase lamps rated for a voltage different from that of the supply.

Example 33 : Compare the cost of providing 1 000 000 lumen-hours of light with 100-W, 230-V lamps and with 100-W, 210-V lamps, when both are connected to a 210-V circuit. Cost of lamp Rs. 3·0. Life of lamp 1 000 hours at rated voltage. Energy cost 5 paise per unit. Lumens output of lamp 1 160 at rated voltage.

Solution :

(*A*) *210-volt lamps*

No. of hours burning $= 1\ 000\ 000/1\ 160 = 860$ hours

cost of lamps $= (860/1\ 000) \times 3 =$ Rs. 2·58

cost of energy $= \left(\frac{860}{1000}\right) \times 100 \times (5/100) =$ Rs. 4·30

Total cost = **Rs. 6·88**

(*B*) *230-V lamps operating at 210 V*

From curve of Fig. 133.

Output reduced to 70% of normal = 180 lumens

Life increased to 275% of normal = 2750 hours.

Energy consumption reduced to 87·5% of normal = 87·5 W

Number of hours burning $= 1\ 000\ 000/810 = 1\ 235$ h

cost of lamps $= (1\ 235/2\ 750) \times 3 =$ Rs. 1·35

cost of energy $= \frac{1235 \times 87{\cdot}5}{1000} \times \frac{5}{100} =$ Rs. 5·40

Total cost = **Rs. 6·75.**

It is thus seen to be 2% cheaper to purchase 230-V lamps for use on a 210-V circuit, if the energy cost is as low as 5 paise per unit. A lower energy cost would result in a greater saving, while if the energy cost is very high it may even pay to operate lamps at a voltage higher than their rated value.

[The foregoing three examples are illustrative of the methods of attacking economic problems connected with the choice of equipment ; other problems will no doubt present themselves to the reader, but the same general principles may be applied for their solution.]

CHAPTER VI
QUESTIONS

1. The cost of a small power station built to supply an industrial plant is Rs. 2 400 000 and the money for this can be borrowed at 5% interest. A sinking fund, also with interest at 5% is to be provided to repay the whole of the loan at the end of 15 years, the salvage value of the plant at the end of this time being estimated at Rs. 72 000. The management charges for this station are Rs. 24 000 per year, and the running cost is 3 paise per kWh. Determine the yearly sum which

will have to be paid into the sinking fund and the total yearly fixed charges on the station.

2. A consumer takes 4 GWh per year with a maximum demand of 1 MW at 0·8 power factor. What is his load factor?

Calculate the annual cost of the energy according to the following tariffs:

(a) Rs. 120 per kW of maximum demand, plus 5 p. kWh, with an addition of Rs. 6 per kW for every 0·1 by which the power factor falls below 0·85.

(b) Rs. 132 per kVA of maximum demand, plus 5 p. per kWh.

(c) Rs. 120 per kW of maximum demand, plus 5 p. per kWh, plus 2·5 p. per kVARh (assuming that the power factor is 0·8 at all times).

(d) a sliding scale of:

20 p. per kWh for the first 75 000 kWh
15 p. per kWh for the next 250 000 kWh
10 p. per kWh for the next 500 000 kWh
5 p. per kWh for the remainder.

3. An industrial concern requires 450 000 kWh per month with a maximum demand of 1 000 kW. Estimate the annual cost of energy:

(a) If supplied in bulk from the power company at Rs. 108 per kW of maximum demand plus 3 paise per unit;

(b) if obtained from a private generating plant (with suitable spare equipment) costing Rs. 600 per kW and having a running cost of 5 paise per unit.

Interest and depreciation = 15%.

What would be the overall cost per unit in each case.

4. A colliery pump, which has to deliver 45 m³ of water per min. against a head of 23 m, is to be driven by an electric motor. Other motors in the colliery take a total of 300 kW at 0·8 lagging power factor. If a synchronous induction motor is to be used for the pump, at what power factor should it operate to improve the power factor of the whole installation to 0·95 lagging? The efficiency of the pump may be taken as 80% and of the motor 88%. If the tariff in force is Rs. 108 per kVA of maximum demand plus 5 paise per kWh, what will be the

yearly saving in the total energy cost obtained by installing the synchronous induction motor, rather than an ordinary induction motor, with a lagging power factor of 0·8 and an efficiency of 90% ? Assume the pump to be operating continuously throughout the year.

5. A small factory is charged for its energy at Rs. 96 per kW plus 4 paise per kWh with an addition of Rs. 6 per kW of maximum demand for every 0·1 by which the power factor falls below 0·85. The maximum demand of the factory is 1 200 kW at a power factor of 0·6 lagging and a load factor of 50%. What is the maximum amount per kVA which could be economically spent on static capacitors to improve the power factor to 0·85 ? Take interest and depreciation as 10% per year.

6. A consumer is charged on a tariff of Rs. 108 per kVA plus 5 paise per kWh and has to drive, for 3 000 hours per year, a fan requiring 75 kW ; an induction motor, having a power factor of 0·8 and an efficiency of 90% when giving the above output, is employed for the purpose. A phase advancer for improving the power factor is available at a cost of Rs. 96 per kVA and has a loss of 200W/kVA. Assuming that the consumer takes no other load, to what value should he improve his power factor in order that his total operating cost, including interest and depreciation on the advancer at 10% per year, shall be a minimum :

(a) neglecting losses in phase advancer, and

(b) allowing for losses ?

7. A steam-power station supplying a maximum demand of 70 000 kW costs Rs. 31 92 000 and has a running cost of 1·5 paise per kWh generated. Interest and depreciation charges may be taken as 15% per year. Draw a curve showing the relation between the overall generating costs per unit and the load factor for values of the latter between 10% and 100%.

8. The estimated costs of a private oil-engine generator plant capable of supplying a factory with a maximum demand of 800 kW are as follows :

(a) cost of plant Rs. 600 000 ;

(b) cost of fuel Rs. 100 per tonne ;

(c) fuel consumption 0·295 kg per unit generated ;

(d) cost of lubricating oil, water and stores 0·35 p. per kWh generated ;

(e) cost of wages 1·1 paise per kWh generated;

(f) cost of repairs and maintenance 0·3 paise per kWh generated.

The load factor of the factory is 28%. Compare the cost of energy obtained from a public supply at a tariff of Rs. 96 per kW plus 3·5 p. per unit. Interest and depreciation at 12% per year.

9. A 375-kW, 3-phase, 750 rev/min induction motor, driving a reciprocating air compressor (torque independent of speed) has to have its speed reduced to 600 rev/min, during week-ends. Estimate the yearly cost of the losses incurred in doing this if it runs at the lower speed for 40 hours per week and the reduction is carried out by resistance inserted in the rotor circuit. Energy costs 5 paise per kWh.

What would be the yearly cost of providing an a.c. exciter to carry out the reduction if such an exciter costs Rs. 192 per kW and has an efficiency of 90%? Interest and depreciation at 15% per year. The loss in the exciter is 0·1 kW, per kW output.

10. A factory employs 80 machines running continuously at a constant speed and requiring the following maximum inputs:

(i) 10 require 15 kW each;
(ii) 20 require 6 kW each;
(iii) 50 require 3 kW each.

The average input required is 75% of the maximum. Using the curve of Fig. 58 and making any necessary assumptions, estimate the capital cost of the motors required, if the machines are driven by:

(a) Group drive, employing a single motor for the whole factory, the diversity of the loads being such that the maximum is 80% of the sum of the individual maxima. The shafting loss is 10% of the power transmitted.

(b) Group drive, with 5 machines in each group, the maximum power of each group being 85% of the sum of the individual maxima and the shafting loss being 5% of the power transmitted.

(c) Individual drive.

Enumerate the savings, which may outweigh the higher cost of motors in cases (b) and (c).

11. To illuminate a factory 100 000 lumens are required and all lamps are alight for 3 000 hours per year. Compare the yearly cost of energy and lamp renewal using:

(a) 500-W filament lamps having a life of 1 000 burning hours, giving 7 500 lumens, and costing Rs. 12·50p

(b) 80-W fluorescent lamps each having a life of 3 000 burning hours, giving 24 000 lumens, and costing Rs. 28·80 p.

Tariff for energy is Rs. 120 per kW + 7·5 paise per kWh.

If the rate of interest and depreciation for the fittings and wiring is 8% per year, how much more could economically be paid for these items in the case of the fluorescent lamps than in the case of the filament lamps?

APPENDIX

REGULATIONS AND SPECIFICATIONS

In order to assist factory owners, transport concerns, and other users of power, various authorities have laid down regulations, in some cases backed by law, which set up definite standards of safety, quality, and dimensions. Those which are of particular importance to users of electrical energy are given below :

(1) Regulations for Factories and Workshops : Given in the 'Factories Act', published by each State in India.

(2) Regulations for Mines : published by the Government of India (Home Ministry) ; The Director General of Mines Safety, Dhanbad (Bihar).

(3) Regulations for Tramways and Light Railways : Published by the Indian Electricity Act, Ministry of Railways and the Indian Standards Institution.

(4) Wiring Rules : Given in the Indian Electricity Act.

(5) Regulations for the Electrical Equipment of Ships : Published by the Indian Navy.

(6) Indian Standards Institution (IS) No. 9, Bahadur Shah Zafar Marg, New Delhi (Headquarters) and with Branch Offices at Bombay, Calcutta, Kanpur, Madras and Hyderabad. The object of this institution is to publish standard specifications for various products and materials. These standard specifications (Is) which are given below, are designed to assist the user by setting a definite standard for the behaviour, rating, dimensions, or quality of the equipment.

The only two publications of ISI so far specifically on SI Units, are given as item 1 & 2 in the BIBLIOGRAPHY. Below are listed the IS specifications in general, touching the different chapters of our Book.

INDIAN STANDARDS

A. GENERAL

Nomenclature and Symbols

1.	Electrotechnical vocabulary : Part I Fundamental definitions	1885 (Part I)-1961
2.	Electrotechnical vocabulary : Part II Machines and transformers	1885 (Part II)-1961
3.	Electrotechnical vocabulary : Part XI Electrical measurements	1885 (Part XI)-1966
4.	Graphical symbols used in electrotechnology : Part I Classification and definitions of diagrams and charts	2032 (Part I)-1962
5.	Graphical symbols used in electrotechnology : Part II Kind of current distribution systems and methods of connection	2032 (Part II)-1962
6.	Graphical symbols used in electrotechnology : Part III Circuit elements and variability	2032 (Part III)-1962
7.	Graphical symbols used in electrotechnology : Part IV Rotating machines and transformers	2032 (Part IV)-1964
8.	Graphical symbols used in electrotechnology : Part V Generating stations and substations	2032 (Part V)-1965
9.	Graphical symbols used in electrotechnology : Part VI Motor starters	2032 (Part VI)-1965
10.	Letter Symbols and signs used in electrical technology	3722—1966

B. CODES OF PRACTICE

1.	Climate proofing of electrical equipment	3202—1965
2.	Design of electrical street lighting installations	1944—1961
3.	Earthing, code of practice for	3043—1966
4.	Electrical wiring installations (system voltage exceeding 650 volts)	2274—1963
5.	Electrical wiring installations (system voltage not exceeding 650 volts) (*revised*)	732—1963
6.	Electric passenger and goods lifts, installation, operation and maintenance of	1860—1961

7.	Guide for electrical layout in residential-buildings	4648—1968
8.	Hospital lighting	4347—1967
9.	Installation and maintenance of electrical equipment in mines	4051—1967
10.	Installation and maintenance of induction motors (*revised*)	900—1965
11.	Installation and maintenance of paper-insulated power cables (up to and including 33kV) (*first revision*)	1255—1967
12.	Installation and maintenance of switchgear: Part I Switchgear (system voltage not exceeding 1 000 V)	3072 (Part I)-1965
13.	Installation and maintenance of transformers (*first revision*)	1886—1967
14.	Installation and maintenance of escalators	4591—1968
15.	Selection of ac induction motor starters (voltage not exceeding 1 000 volts)	3914—1967

C. MOTORS AND GENERATORS

1.	Degrees of protection provided by enclosures for rotating electrical machinery	4691—1968
2.	Flameproof alternating current motors for use in mines	3682—1966
3.	Flange mounted ac induction motors, dimensions of	2223—1962
4.	Induction motors, installation and maintenance, code of practice for (*revised*)	900—1965
5.	Induction motors, three-phase (*second revision*)	325—1961
6.	Induction motors, three-phase foot-mounted, dimensions of (*second revision*)	1231—1967
7.	Induction motors, three-phase, guide for testing	4029—1967
8.	Rotating electrical machines, efficiency of methods of determination of	4889—1968
9.	Rotating Electrical machines	4722—1968
10.	Rotating electrical machines, vibration of, measurement and evaluation of	4729—1968
11.	Single-phase small ac and universal electric motors (*revised*)	996—1964

12. Slide rails for electric motors, dimensions of 2968—1964
13. Terminal Marking for rotating electrical machines 4728—1968
14. Textile motors : Part I Loom motors 2972 (Part I)-1964
15. Textile motors : Part II Card motors 2972 (Part II)-1964
16. Textile motors: Part III Spinning frame motors 2972 (Part III)-1965
17. Types of construction and mounting of motors 2253—1964

D. FLAMEPROOF ELECTRICAL EQUIPMENT

1. Cable glands and Cable sealing boxes for use in mines 4821—1968
2. Flameproof enclosures of electrical apparatus 2148—1962

E. CONDUCTORS AND CABLES

1. Aluminium and steel cored aluminium conductors for overhead power lines, fittings for 2121—1962
2. Aluminium conductors for insulated cables (*first revision*) 1753—1967
3. Cadmium copper conductors for overhead railway traction 3402—1965
4. Copper conductors in insulated cables and cords 2982—1965
5. Drums for trolley and contact wire 2889—1964
6. Electrical cables and conductors, glossary of terms for 1591—1960
7. Flexible cables for miners' cap-lamps 2593—1964
8. Flexible trailing cables for use in coal mines, rubberinsulated 691—1966
9. Flexible trailing cables for use in quarries and metalliferous mines 1026—1966
10. Hard-drawn copper conductors for overhead power transmission (*revised*) 282—1963
11. Hard-drawn stranded aluminium and steel-cored aluminium conductors for overhead power transmission purposes (*revised*) 398—1961
12. Lift cables 4289—1967

13.	Mild steel wires, strips and tapes for armouring cables	3975—1967
14.	Paper insulated lead-sheathed cables for electricity supply (*revised*)	692—1965
	Paper insulated cables for mines	1027—1968
15.	Polythene insulated and PVC sheathed cables	1596—1962
16.	Polyvinyl chloride sleeving for electrical purposes	1951—1961
17.	Recommended current ratings for cables: Part I Paper insulated lead-sheathed cables	3961 (Part I)-1967
18.	Recommended current ratings for cables: Part III Rubber insulated cables	3961 (Part III)-1968
19.	Recommended current ratings for cables: Part IV Polyethylene insulated cables	3961 (Part IV)-1968
20.	Recommended current ratings for cables: Part V PVC insulated light duty cables	3961 (Part V)-1968
21.	Reels and drums for bare wire	1778—1961
22.	Rubber insulated cables Part I With copper conductors (*revised*)	434 (Part I)-1964
23.	Rubber-insulated cables: Part II With aluminium conductors (*revised*)	434 (Part II)-1964
24.	Thermoplastic insulated weather-proof cables: Part I PVC insulated and PVC sheathed	3035 (Part I)-1965
25.	Thermoplastic insulated weather-proof cables: Part II Polyethylene insulated, taped, or untaped braided and compounded	3035 (Part II)-1965
26.	Thermoplastic insulated weather-proof cables: Part III Polyethylene insulated and polyethylene sheathed	3035 (Part III)-1967
27.	Trolley and contact wire for electric traction	3476—1967
28.	Varnished cambric insulated cables (*revised*)	693—1965
29.	Rubber insulated cables for mines	4817—1968

F. ELECTRIC WELDING EQUIPMENT

1.	Arc welding transformers, single operator type (*first revision*)	1851—1966
2.	dc electric welding generators (*revised*)	2635—1966
3.	Electrical welding accessories	2641—1964
4.	Resistance welding equipment: Part I Single-phase transformers	4804 (Part I)-1968

5.	Resistance welding equipment: Part II Single-phase rocker-arm spot welding machines	4804 (Part II)-1968
6.	Single operator rectifier type dc arc welder	4559—1968

G. ILLUMINATION ENGINEERING

1.	Design of electrical street lighting installations, code of practice for	1944—1961
2.	Dust-proof electric lighting fittings	4012—1967
3.	Dust-tight electric lighting fittings	4013—1967
4.	Electric light fittings, general and safety requirements for	1913—1969
5.	Flameproof electric lighting fittings: Part I Well-glass and bulkhead types	2206 (Part I)-1962
6.	Flood-lights	1947—1961
7.	Industrial lighting fittings with metal reflectors	1777—1961
8.	Industrial lighting fittings with plastic reflectors	3287—1965
9.	Interior illumination: Part I Principles of good lighting and aspects of design, code of practice for	3646 (Part I)-1966
10.	Interior illumination: Part II Schedule for values of illumination and glare index, code of paractice for	3646 (Part II)-1966
11.	Interior illumination: Part III calculation of Coefficients of utilisation, BZ method, code of practice for	3646 (Part III)-1968
12.	Library lighting, code of practice for	2672—1966
13.	Luminaires for streetlighting	2149—1962
14.	Waterproof electric lighting fittings	3528—1966
15.	Watertight electric lighting fittings	3553—1966
16.	Well-glass lighting fittings for use underground in mines (non-flame proof type)	2493—1963

H. POWER CAPACITORS

1.	Motor capacitors	2933—1964
2.	Shunt capacitor for power systems	2834—1964

I. ELECTRICAL INSTRUMENTS

1.	Indicating instruments, electrical	1248—1968

2. Indicating instruments, electrical dimensions of 2419—1963
   Portable multipurpose electrical indicating instruments 3107—1965
3. Thermocouple pyrometers 2053—1962

INTERGRATING METERS

4. ac electricity meters : Part I General requirements (*revised*) 722 (Part I)-1962
5. ac electricity meters : Part II Single-phase 2-wire wholecurrent watt-hour meters (*revised*) 722 (Part II)-1962
6. ac electricity meters : Part II Single-phase 2-wire whole-current watt-hour meters. section 2 meters with current rantings 722 (Part II)-Sec 2 1969
7. ac electricity meters:: Part III Three-phase whole-current and transformer-operated meters, and single-phase two-wire transformer-operated meters (*first revision*) 722 (Part III)-1966
8. ac electricity meters : Part IV Three-phase watt-hour meters with maximum demand indicator (*first revision*) 722 (Part IV)-1966
9. ac electricity meters : Part V Volt ampere hour meters for restricted power factor range 722 (Part V)-1965
10. ac electricity meters : Part VI Var-hour meters 722 (Part VI)-1968
11. Time switches 1766—1961
12. ac electricity meters : Part VII Volt ampere hour meters for full power factor range 722 (Part VII) 1969

BIBLIOGRAPHY

1. On 'S.I' Units only

A. Indian

1. IS : 3616—1966 *Indian Standard Recommendation on the International System (SI) Units.* The Indian Standards Institution, New Delhi.
2. IS : SP5 : 1969 *Guide to the use of SI Units (Ibid)*
3. Rao, (VVL) *SI—A Rational Metric System of Units,* ISI Bulletin, 20, 10 (1968), pp. 399—403.
4. Act No. 89, 1956—*Weights and Measures Act,* India Publications Division, New Delhi.

B. Foreign

5. Blakman (Deane R) : *SI Units in Engineering,* Macmillan & Co. of Australia, Melbourne, Australia (1969)
6. Martin (SL) & Connor (AK) : *Basic Physics, Vol 2* (Whitcombe & Tombs Pty Ltd., Sydney, Australia (1969)
7. McGlashan (MC) : Units, Particularly SI Units—*Physics Education* (The Institute of Physics and the Physical Society), Vol. 4, 1969 (pp. 1—11)
8. Leo Young : *Systems of units in Electricity and Magnetism,* (Electronics and Electrical Engineering Texts : 1) Oliver and Boyd, Edinburgh (1969).
9. Kellaway (FW) : *Metrication* (Penguin Education X26), Penguin Books, London (1968)
10. Symbols, signs and Abbreviations recommended for scientific publications, 1969, The Royal Society, London, S.W. 1
11. Metrication in Scientific journals, The Royal Society Conference of Editors, The Royal Society, London (1968).
12. Systeme *International d' Unite's (SI)* : BSI News, October, 1968, (pp. 6—8 & 10). The British Standards Institution, London-1
13. Pera Conference (Organised by the Production Engineering Research Association of Great Britain)—'*The Practical Application of SI Units*'—(International Conference held at Brussels in June 1969)—See sec. 8 : *Energy Units and the consumer*

2. General - on Electrical Engineering Technology, etc.

1. *Electrical Technology* : H. COTTON (Seventh Edition RMKS Edition) (Pitman, London, 1960)
2. *Electric Power Utilization* : N. N. HANCOCK (Pitman, London) Price 80 s.
3. *Generation, Transmission and Utilisation of Electric Power* : A. T. STARR (Pitman, London) Price 32s 6d
4. *Noise and Man* : WILLIAM BURNS (JOHN MURRAY, London, 1968) Price 50s
5. *The Decibel Notation* : V. V. L. RAO (Second Edition) Asia Publishing House, Bombay, 1966) Price Rs. 20
6. *A Guide to the Metric System* : V. V. L. RAO (Asia Publishing House, Bombay) Price Rs. 6/-
7. *Electric Traction* : A. T. DOVER (Pitman, London) Price 60s.
8. *Solution of Problems in Electric Power* : U. G. MALLIK (Pitman London, 1968) Price 45 s.

3. Illumination

9. *Illumination Engineering Course* : H. ZIJL, Philips Technical Library, Cleaver Hume Press Ltd., London.
10. *Fluorescent Lamps and Lighting* : W. ELENBAAS (Editor) (1962)
11. *High pressure Mercury Vapour lamps and their applications* (1965)
12. *Public Lighting* : J. B. DE BOER (Editor) Philips Technical Library, (1967), N. V. Philips Gloclampen Fabrieken, Eindhoven, Holland.
13. *A Guide to Lighting in Commercial Premises* (1968)
14. *Philips Lighting Equipment*, Phillips India Limited.
15. *Philips Lighting Course* (9 lessons)
16. *Philips Planned Maintenance* (for better returns on your lighting investment).
17. *Light calculations and Measurements* : H. A. E. KEITZ.
18. *Lighting Practice* Vols. I, II & III : J. JANSEN
19. *Fluorescent Lighting* : Prof. C. ZWIKKER
20. *Gas discharge Lamps* : J. Funke and P. J. Orange
21. *Physical Aspects of Colour* : P. J. Bouma

All the above Publications (9—21) belong to the Philips Technical Library.

ANSWERS TO QUESTIONS

CHAPTER I. ELECTRIC DRIVE

		Starting torque	Starting current
1.	(a) Direct switching	262 N. m	177 A
	(b) Auto-transformer	127·5 N. m	86·8 A
	(c) Star-delta	87 N. m	59 A
	(d) Series-parallel	65·5 N. m	44·5 A

2. (a) Auto-transformer. Current 66 A, tapping 73%
   (b) Series resistance. Current 91 A, resistance 1·3Ω/phase.
3. (a) Resistance 0·845Ω· Loss 1·1 kW
   (b) Resistance 0·58 Ω. Loss 1·45 kW
4. Voltage 346 V; speed 432 rev/min. With saturated magnets voltage will be higher and speed lower.
5. 22·7 A; 22·7%
6. Speeds, 1500 rev/min and 750 rev/min.
   (a) 120 kW (b) 30 kW
7. 3000 rev/min, 1000 rev/min, 750 rev/min, and 428 rev/min.
8. Starting resistance, 4·15 Ω
9. Resistance for plugging, 3·36 Ω
   Initial braking torque, 600 N.m.
   Braking torque at half-speed, 456 N.m
9. Current, 24·8 A. Resistance, 52·3 Ω.
10. Resistance, 7·87 Ω
11. Initial braking torque, 81·5 N.m. Torque at standstill, 161·5 N.m
12. 24 kW
13. 52·4 kW, 26·6 kW.
14. 630 rev/min, 1885 N.m
15. 22·8 seconds.
16. Plugging 14·7 seconds; 61·5 rev.
    Rheostatic braking, seconds; 30·2 rev.
17. 879 kg. m^2

CHAPTER II. ELECTRIC TRACTION

1. 63 tonnes ; 6 axles
2. 790 kW, 975 kW, 1200 kW
3. When slip of B is 5% (a) A : 69 870 N, B : 45 830 N
   (b) A : 17 800 N, B :—4450 N
   When slip of B is 4% (a) A : 65 420 N, B : 50 280 N
   (b) A : 18 250 N, B :—4 900 N
4. Resistance, 8.65 Ω. Speed, 10·4 km/h.
5. At 300 A, speed = 55·4 km/h ; tractive effort = 10 650 N
6. At 300 A, speed = 46·5 km/h ; tractive effort = 10 800 N
7. (a) Tension 3200 N
   (b) Tension 6450 N, sag 0·18 m
   (c) Tension 9920 N, sag 0·119 m
   (d) Tennsion 10970 N, sag 0·23 m
8. Catenary tension, 6230 N ; sag 1·98 m
   Contact-wire tension, O ; sag, 0·15
9. In both cases, maximum speed = 54·5 km/h ;
   watt-hours per tonne-km = 60·3

CHAPTER III. HEATING AND WELDING

1. Length 17 m. Diameter 3·02 mm.
2. Series-delta 630° C. Series-star 411° C. Parallel-star 695°C.
   One group in delta 797° C. One group in star, 542° C.
3. Heat loss, 36·7 MJ/h. Heat to oven 600 MJ
   (a) 264 kWh (b) 99·5 kWh.
4. 120·4 kW.
5. 384 kW at 0·83 power factor.
6. Resistance, 255 × 10^{-6}Ω, current, 1780 A
7. Arc Voltage, 38·5 V ; kVA, 2150
8. (a) 2·9 kW (b) 3·5 kW (c) 3·48 kW
9. 54%
10. 0·8 kW.
11. (a) 8·95 hours. (b) 64° C.
    (c) 3·5 hours. (d) Rs. 60 = 60p.
12. 785 V ; 51·5 MHz

CHAPTER IV. ELECTRO-CHEMISTRY

1. 1930 Ah ; 63·5 hours.
2. 12200 t, 213 kWh per tonne
3. 190 kg, Rs. 852
4. Rs. 12600

CHAPTER V. ILLUMINATION ENGINEERING

1. 13 lm/W
2. 8150 lumens, 93 lm/m^2
3. (a) 1440 W, (b) 1070 W
5. Illumination midway between lamps, 0·275 lx.
7. (a) 500-W lamps in 3 rows of 5
   (b) 6 rows of 9
8. 25 projectors in 3 groups

CHAPTER VI. ECONOMICS.

1. Sinking-fund deposit, Rs. 108 000, Fixed charges Rs. 252 000.
2. Load factor, 45·7%. (a) Rs. 323 000, (b) Rs. 365 000
   (c) Rs. 405 000, (d) Rs. 261 400
3. (a) Rs. 270 000, 5 paise/kWh
   (b) With three 500-kW sets. Rs. 403 200, 7·5 paise/kWh.
4. Power factor, 0·98 leading. Saving, Rs. 8592 per year.
5. Rs. 210 = 72 p.
6. Power factor, (a) 0·996, (b) 0·93
7. At load factor of 50%, cost = 3·06 paise
8. Private plant, Rs. 161 000 ; public supply Rs. 145 440
9. Rs. 9 360, Rs. 2 928.
10. Rs. 9 600, Rs. 19 200, Rs. 48 000
11. Rs. 2 942 and Rs. 2·370 per year. Rs. 7 176.

INDEX

U

V

W

Z